Film
Review
1990-1

Film Review 1990-1

INCLUDING VIDEO RELEASES

F. Maurice Speed

AND

James Cameron-Wilson

VIRGIN

First published in Great Britain in 1990 by
VIRGIN BOOKS
26 Grand Union Centre, 338 Ladbroke Grove, London W10 5AH

Copyright © 1990 F. Maurice Speed and James Cameron-Wilson

British Library Cataloguing in Publication Data

Film Review
1. Cinema films – Serials
791.43'05

ISBN 1–85227–318–6   Hbk
ISBN 0–86369–374–1   Pbk

Designed by Fred Price

Phototypeset by Input Typesetting Ltd, London

Printed and bound in Great Britain by
Butler & Tanner Ltd, Frome and London

Contents

Introduction

F. MAURICE SPEED surveys the cinematic year

The weird and wonderful world of movie-making finance has always fascinated me. For instance, it seems remarkable that multi-million-dollar backing can be obtained for a movie which even to the layman looks a decidedly dodgy project. But then, when disaster strikes at the deserted box office, and the dollars have dropped down the drain, the odds are that the producer will pop up again a year or two later to raise another fortune for an equally dubious enterprise. It could only happen in the wacky world of Hollywood!

Sitting through some of these megabuck flops, waiting impatiently for the closing credits, I find myself asking for the umpteenth time, how on earth did this celluloid turkey ever get as far as the screen? How did those involved persuade themselves (and their backers) that this wasted film stock, time and money could ever draw the public into a cinema?

It is not so unusual to read in the trade press about productions exceeding their budget by millions of dollars, and overrunning their production schedules by weeks or even months. Some are films which started out as reasonable projects, but are eventually so crippled by their production costs that they end up as pre-premiere disasters without a hope of ever recovering their money. Francis Ford Coppola's third *Godfather* film may be a case in point: apparently budgeted at $44 million, it quickly fell a month behind schedule and went $4 million over budget. In the course of production, Coppola declared himself bankrupt, with liabilities of over $29 million. Although my bet here is that the maestro will eventually emerge more or less triumphant, I do sometimes wonder if inflation was born in a film studio . . .

This past year, for instance, has seen an almost hysterical rush by producers to complete and release their films in order to earn their share of what it was hoped would be an early summer bonanza. It was a rush which drew from one of the (non-competing) Hollywood big bosses the comment: 'It's crazy. What's going on is insane. These people are making movies as if nothing else matters – they have completely lost sight of reality.'

According to the well-informed *Variety*, the panic resulted in many of the more important summer films being thrown into release without the normal fine-tuning and testing. For example, the $55-million production *Days of Thunder* was said to have been raced through its post-production stages in five weeks instead of the five months that would normally be expected.

The *Variety* figures were unofficial (though their accuracy has been impressive in the past), but the final cost of some of the major movies released during the summer of 1990 was in fact around or even above the $50 million mark, making *Godfather III* by no means exceptional. One Hollywood studio boss commented: 'Add to those totals advertising costs amounting to another thirty million dollars, a ten million dollar charge on the borrowed money, plus the usual studio rental charges – and you begin to wonder who is nuts.'

One of the more rational leaders of the industry commented: 'Sure, one or two of these megabuck productions like *Total Recall*' (said to have a final production cost of between $55 million and $60 million, plus the extras mentioned above) 'may eventually get their costs back, but if that's all they get, why is anybody on the deal at all?'

As an example of what a giant gamble major movie production is, *Rambo 3* – again according to *Variety* – had final costs of around $8.5 million, but has so far earned less than $30 million at the box office. It's the same story for several of the year's supposedly 'very successful' movies. There must be plenty of worried movie executives around.

Nevertheless, for the lucky few, making movies has been little short of a having a licence to print money. The makers of *Batman*, which took $5 billion at the box office and established itself as the biggest moneymaker in the history of the cinema, are a case in point, and *Indiana Jones and the Last Crusade*, with a 'take' of $115 million from US cinemas alone, proved no slouch either. So there's still room to make a dollar or two in the cinema!

One cost the major studios have had to absorb is the astonishing sums a few of them have paid for scripts this year – not all of them by famous authors. Shane Black pocketed $1.75 million (said to be the highest amount ever paid for a script) for the film rights to his *The Last Boy Scout*, and a number of other authors became dollar millionaires, including Warren Adler, for *Private Lives*; David Mickey Evans, for *Radio Flyer*; Brian Helgeland and Manny Cotto, for *The Ticking Man*; and Laurence Dworet and Robert Roy Poole, for *Ultimatum*.

Despite all this high-cost moviemaking, however, the occasional little gem still comes alone, building on inspiration and artistry rather than money, and restoring one's faith in the strength of film. (But one has to remember that big money doesn't necessarily mean bad movies – *The Last Emperor* stands out as one shining example to the contrary.)

Looking at the industry world-wide, film production

seems to be on a downward trend: certainly this is the case in both the US and in Britain (where it has become almost negligible). In the US, the number of films completed in 1989, although still pretty hefty at 446, was down by 13 per cent on 1988's total. Many of these films went straight to video without ever getting a cinema screening – and maybe it's superfluous to add that even this was more than some of them deserved.

In Britain, the situation was very much worse. The British Film and Television Producers' Association was despondent as it considered the future of the industry. The association estimated that in comparison with the 50 films made in the UK during 1988 at a total cost of about £126 million, 1989's total was down to 27 films at a cost of £64 million. Television features were also down in both number and level of investment (although there was something of a minor boom in TV series production). Looking through a list of planned 'British' films is disheartening when you realise that so many of them are to be made abroad, in the US, in Canada and elsewhere.

By way of contrast, 1989 and at least the first half of 1990 was a lucrative time for film exhibitors. The 1989 upswing continued, and unofficially it was reckoned that admissions were up on the 1988 total by 8–10 per cent, making the fifth year in succession that the total had risen. Already there are confident predictions that a likely total of admissions by the end of 1990 will be near the 100 million mark.

This growing audience is being catered for by an increasing number of cinemas, mostly of the multi-screen variety. In 1984, there were 1233 screens operating in Britain, a

Michael Keaton, as Batman, and Kim Basinger, as Vickie Vale, face Gotham City's forces of evil in Tim Burton's blockbuster Batman, *from Warner.*

figure which had risen to 1403 by the end of 1989. The projected total for the end of 1991 is 1750. Britain's first multiplex cinema was opened four years ago at Milton Keynes, but only now has London also acquired a multiplex, with UCS's eight-screen cinema in Queensway, opened on 28 November 1989 in the old but beautifully refurbished premises of Whiteley's (formerly a famous department store).

Pathé-Cannon's long-announced plan to open a fifteen- to eighteen-screen multiplex cinema in Piccadilly can now safely be assumed to be defunct: it has been succeeded by a promise that in 1991 they will be opening a rather more modest four-screen house in Piccadilly Circus. The Odeon circuit also kept in the news by announcing plans to add a further 50 screens to their total of 256 during 1990.

Now for some more on the Goldcrest saga. The initial success and subsequent failure of this British film production company filled a few columns in the national newspapers, several pages in the trade press, and quite a bit of space in my own *Film Review* introductions a few years back. The initial success of this British 'flagship' company was sensational, setting new production standards with the prestigious international success of *The Killing Fields*, *Gandhi* and *Chariots of Fire*. It seemed to herald a new dawn for the British film industry . . . but then came three financial (and in two cases artistic) flops: the dire *Revolution*, the musical *Absolute Beginners*, and *The Mission*, which, despite its commercial failure, at least pleased the critics.

The rise and fall of Goldcrest was a long and tangled story. The company's crash dismayed the entire industry, and the consequences are still reflected today in the widespread reluctance to finance British films. Goldcrest has admittedly survived, but only as a part of the Brent Walker empire, and it bears little or no resemblance to the original company.

The full, fascinating and complicated story of Goldcrest has now been told in a book by Jake Eberts, entitled *My Indecision Is Final*. It *should* be authentic: Eberts, a former chemical engineer and ex-banker, fronted Goldcrest for eight of its ten years. Here is an illuminating story, from the horse's mouth, of what happens on the other side of the screen; the wheeling, dealing, confusion and political and personal intrigues that seem inevitable in the world of major moviemaking. Essential reading for those who love movies but have little idea of what goes on before a film reaches the screen. (Eberts, incidentally, made the recent artistic and commercial success *Driving Miss Daisy*.)

The British Government has never given much support to the struggling British film industry, but it has at least agreed to extend its present limited investment in the British Screen Finance Company for a further three years from the end of 1990. This will provide £2 million annually, with the hope that by 1994 the company will be self-sufficient. British Screen Finance has an honourable record: in the past four years it has helped substantially with the production of 44 films. In an attempt to reverse the current slump in British production, chief executive Simon Relph hopes to add to his government grant with cash from the new satellite TV companies and even from Hollywood. Everyone in the industry will be crossing their fingers for him.

The great controversy over the colourisation of old black-and-white films continues, though with less heat at the moment than in the past. In France, the appeal court ruled that a TV company could transmit the coloured version of John Huston's *The Asphalt Jungle* (against the wishes of the entire Huston family), but in the US, the Supreme Court came out against the showing of a coloured version of *The Haunting* (though the company that produced the film won't let the matter rest there, saying they still hope to get it shown at some point in the future). So this particular debate seems set to run for a while longer.

Technical advances have been few this year. The most interesting experiment was the opening of an all-round-screen cinema in West Berlin at the end of 1989 (more than a year later than scheduled). Called the Panorama Berlin, this brainchild of Swiss inventor Ernst Heiniger calls for only one camera and one projector. (The camera uses a 360-degree super fish-eye lens and 65mm film, which is projected on to a 360-degree screen, 19 yards in diameter and 6 yards tall.) At the moment, there is only one film available for projection (a documentary about the city of Berlin), and although the system is an interesting novelty, it may never become anything more.

By contrast, a recent development that will come into general use in 1990 (and which is already operating in Disneyland) is CD Sound, hailed as an audio milestone, and providing a remarkable new audio experience for movie-goers. Though it will be introduced into 70mm cinemas this year, it is not expected to reach 35mm cinemas until the summer of 1991.

A different kind of technical achievement was the completion and screening in New York, in October 1989, of a reconstructed, 209-minute version of the D. W. Griffith classic *Intolerance*, originally shown in 1916. With the original score by Joseph Carl Breil played by the Brooklyn Philharmonic Orchestra and Chorus, the film, which took eight years and $120,000 to make, got a five-minute standing ovation when it was reshown.

This year also saw the celebration of the 50-year partnership of animation masters Hanna and Barbera, creators of some three hundred TV series and 'specials', including of course the wonderful Tom and Jerry shorts. That half-century has brought the team no fewer than seven Oscars and eight Emmies, and at the ages of 77 (Hanna) and 78 (Barbera), the duo shows no sign of letting up. Among their more immediate plans is a new series of half-hour Tom and Jerry cartoons for the small screen.

There was more animation news from ex-Disney company maestro Don Bluth, whose company (with some other ex-Disney experts in it) has already produced the charming *An American Tail*, as well as *The Land Before Time* and this year's release, *All Dogs Go to Heaven*. Bluth's other plans embrace the autumn 1990 release of *Rock-a-Doodle* and the 1991 release of *Ice Whales*.

Acquisitions continue, and one of the year's major stories was the purchase of Columbia Pictures by the giant Japanese company, Sony. The deal has still to be finalised as I write, but the transfer has certainly been signed. And the final curtain now seems to have come down, after various turbulent alarums and excursions, on the acquisition of Metro-Goldwyn-Mayer/United Artists by the mercurial Italian, Giancarlo Paretti, who trumpeted his production plans at the 1990 Cannes Film Festival. With Pathé already under his belt, Paretti intends, he says, to spend $210 million on fourteen films, the first of which he intends to put into production soon. There's only one possible snag, which is that Paretti has still, at the time of writing, to make the final payment on his $1.25 billion deal. Once the payment is made, it is green lights all the way for the incredible Italian.

Money, money, money . . . But cash had nothing to do with the end of the Robert Taylor building in Hollywood. That is, the *building* still stands, but the star's name has been removed, and the edifice is now called the George Cukor building. So why the change? A group of producers petitioned for the switch, claiming that Taylor had testified in 1950 before McCarthy's infamous House Un-American Activities Committee, allegedly supporting the compilation of the notorious blacklist which prevented so many famous directors from working in America. Time has its revenge, and Taylor now finds himself blacklisted in his turn.

So that's it for another year. In my own case, sadly, illness and bereavement have meant my seeing fewer films in the cinema than for many years past, but there seems to be no lack of wonderful material out there – even if it does sometimes take some hunting out! There's no doubt that movies may all too often be mad or downright bad but the marvellous ones make it all worthwhile – and this year's crop is no exception.

Top Ten Box-Office Stars

1. Harrison Ford

2. Pauline Collins

3. Robin Williams

4. Mel Gibson

5. Jack Nicholson

6. Rick Moranis

7. Michael J. Fox

8. Bill Murray

9. Tom Hanks

10. Tom Cruise

This UK list was calculated on the strength of box-office returns in Great Britain. It does, however, take into account the alternative attractions of such films as *Batman* and *Back to the Future Part II*. Obviously those films were hugely successful not simply because of their stars, but because they were both 'pre-sold' entities. (However, they would not have been as successful as they were without Jack Nicholson and Michael J. Fox.) Although *Batman* made more money than, say, *Dead Poets Society*, it would be unfair to credit the former's success entirely to Nicholson, whereas the popularity of the latter can be more directly ascribed to Robin Williams. And although Pauline Collins is a newcomer to film, it would be hard to imagine the success of *Shirley Valentine* without her. (For the record, both Robin Williams and Tom Cruise were also in last year's list.)

Releases of the Year

In this section you will find details of all the films released in Great Britain from 1 July 1989 to the end of June 1990 – the period covered by all the reference features in the book. The precise dating of some of these releases is a little tricky in view of the lack of any rigidity in the release pattern, but the date given generally refers to the film's London release, unless otherwise stated.

In the case of films sent out on a 'floating' release the date of the film's first London showing has been added because usually this is also the first British showing.

The normal abbreviations operate as follows: Dir – for Director; Pro – for Producer; Assoc Pro – for Associate Producer; Ex Pro – for Executive Producer; Pro Ex – for Production Executive; Pro Sup – for Production Supervisor; Co-Pro – for Co-Producer; Pro Co-Ord – for Production Co-Ordinator; Ph – for Photographer; Ed – for Editor; Art – for Art Director; Pro Des – for Production Designer; M – for Music; and a few others which will obvious.

Abbreviations for the names of film companies are also pretty obvious when used, such as Fox for 20th Century-Fox, Rank for Rank Film Distributors, and UIP for Universal International Pictures. Where known, the actual production company is given first, the releasing company last.

When it comes to nationality of the film, you will find that this is noted wherever possible – those films without any mention of country of origin can usually be taken as being American – but in these days of increasing international co-productions between two, three or even four countries it is sometimes a little difficult to sort out where the premier credit is due.

Finally, unless otherwise specified (i.e. in black-and-white), it can safely be taken that the film is made in Technicolor or some similar colour process.

Censorship certificates: *U* represents films suitable for persons of any age: *PG* (Parental Guidance) represents films which some parents might consider unsuitable for their children; *12* or *15* means no persons under that age will be admitted; and films certified with an *18* (approximately the old 'X' certificate) means that nobody under that age will be admitted to the cinema while that film is showing. 'No cert' means that no certificate has been issued by the *initial showing of the film* but this does not mean that one will not subsequently be issued.

Films are reviewed by F. Maurice Speed and James Cameron-Wilson, with Charles Bacon, Mansel Stimpson and Barbie Wilde. Each review is followed by its writer's initials.

Abel. Winner of the Critics' Award at the Venice Film Festival, this off-beat, anarchic Dutch farce is full of vim and spite but loses its footing after the first hour. Director-writer-star Alex van Warmerdam plays a 31-year-old spoilt brat who still lives at home – much to his psychiatrist's despair. Despised by his father, cosseted by his mother, Abel is nothing but cause for embarrassment. All this malicious fun shows much potential but is too heavy-handed to enter the giddy realms of Orton. It could have been blacker, too. [CB]

Also with: Olga Zuiderhoek (Dove), Henri Garcin (Victor), Annet Mul (Sis), Loos Luca (Christine). Dir and Screenplay: Alex van Warmerdam. Pro: Dick Maas and Laurens Geels. Ph: Marc Felperlaan. Ed: Hans van Dongen. Art: Harry Ammerlaan. M: Vinc-

ent van Warmerdam. Sound: Georges Bossaers. (First Floor Features–Metro.) Rel: floating; first shown London (Metro) 23 March 1990. 98 mins. Cert 15.

The Abyss. Not so much a waterlogged *Heaven's Gate* as an underwater *Close Encounters*. A nuclear sub is 'shipwrecked' on the floor of the Caribbean, at the edge of the Cayman Trough, a two-and-a-half-mile deep abyss. A team of civilian divers is press-ganged by the US Navy to rescue the sub, and undergoes an adventure of unprecedented intensity and wonder. To add to the drama, the rig foreman, Virgil 'Bud' Brigman (Ed Harris), is in the process of divorcing Lindsey Brigman (Mary Elizabeth Mastrantonio), the rig designer, and the two are thrown

together in a leaking rescue vehicle. There's also Lt Coffey (Michael Biehn), a Navy Seal who's losing his grip on reality if not the grip on his gun. Harris, Mastrantonio and Biehn are all great, the sets are sensational and the pace never lets up – some scenes will take your breath away, others will leave you numb. The much-maligned ending admittedly is not for all tastes, but is pleasantly optimistic and euphoric if taken in the right spirit. And, to set the record straight, although the film cost between \$35 and \$40 million to make, it did gross \$55 million in the United States alone. [JC-W]

Also with: Leo Burmester (Catfish De Vries), Todd Graff (Alan 'Hippy' Carnes), John Bedford Lloyd (Jammer Willis), J. C. Quinn ('Sonny' Dawson), Kimberly Scott

Mary Elizabeth Mastrantonio and Ed Harris as estranged husband and wife in the stranger-than-fact The Abyss, *from Fox.*

(Lisa 'One Night' Standing), Capt. Kidd Brewer Jr, George Robert Klek, Christopher Murphy, Adam Nelson, J. Kenneth Campbell. Dir and Screenplay: James Cameron. Pro: Gale Anne Hurd. Ph: Mikael Salomon. Ed: Joel Goodman. Pro Des: Leslie Dilley. M: Alan Silvestri; 'Willing' sung by Linda Ronstadt. Costumes: Deborah Everton. Sound: Lee Orloff. (Fox.) Rel: 13 October 1989. 140 mins. Cert 12.

All Dogs Go to Heaven. This cartoon feature tells the story of a little orphan girl blessed (?) with the Dolittlian ability to talk to animals. Thanks to this talent, little Anne-Marie is held captive by a grotesque pitbull called Carface – until Burt Reynolds comes to the rescue. Burt Reyonolds? Yep, old Burt is now lending his distinctive, largely unintelligible voice to cartoons, and is well cast as Charlie, a rangy, dubious, but ultimately good-hearted Alsatian who risks his tail to rescue Anne-Marie. But Charlie is not above

exploiting Anne-Marie's ability to get the racing low-down straight from the horse's mouth, so to speak, and makes a killing at the bookies off her – before he realises he must return her to a world of human comforts. *All Dogs* is chock-a-block with action (sometimes confusingly so) and lacks the charm and

magic of the old Disney classics (so what else is new?), but has a verve and good-natured panache that is irresist-

All Dogs Go to Heaven (Rank): Charlie, the canine hustler, and Anne-Marie, the sweet orphan, in Don Bluth's inventive re-tread of some old cartoon clichés.

Love means never having to say you're dead: Holly Hunter and Richard Dreyfuss in Steven Spielberg's Always, *from UIP.*

ible. There are also seven numbers to sing along to, four composed by no less than Charles Strousse (*Applause, Annie*). [JC-W]

Voices include: Judith Barsi (Anne-Marie), Dom DeLuise (Itchy), Vic Tayback (Carface), Charles Nelson Reilly (Killer), Melba Moore (whippet angel), Loni Anderson (Flo), Candy Devine, Rob Fuller, Anna Manahan, Nigel Pegram, and Ken Page as King Gator. Dir: Don Bluth, Dan Kuenster and Gary Goldman. Pro: Bluth, Goldman and John Pomeroy. Ex Pro: George A. Walker and Morris F. Sullivan. Screenplay: David N. Weiss; from a story by Bluth, Goldman, Pomeroy, Weiss, etc. Ed: John K. Carr. Pro Des: Bluth and Larry Leker. M: Ralph Burns; songs by Charles Strousse and T. J. Kuenster. Sound: Kevin Brazier and Joe Gallagher. (Goldcrest–Rank.) Rel: 6 April 1990. 84 mins. Cert U.

Always is almost a magical movie. Like *It's a Wonderful Life* and *Heaven Can Wait*, it has very human angels and, as directed by Steven Spielberg, oozes sentimentality from every sprocket-hole. Unfortunately, its realistic depiction of oil-stained firefighters risking their lives in Montana sits oddly with the twee portrayal of the afterlife. Richard Dreyfuss stars as Pete Sandich (the role originally created by Spencer Tracy in the 1943 *A Guy Named Joe*), a daredevil pilot caught between his love of dousing forest fires and of dating Holly Hunter. Inevitable death doesn't exactly alter Dreyfuss and Hunter's love for each other, but considerably changes the circumstances! This is an unusual, romantic, self-indulgent wade into whimsy, but is seldom less than engaging and boasts several memorable scenes. The footage of burning woodland is the genuine article, filmed during the 1988 fires that devastated Yellowstone National Park. Selected as the Royal Film Performance of 1990. [JC-W]

Also with: Holly Hunter (Dorinda Durston), John Goodman (Al Yackey), Brad Johnson (Ted Baker), Audrey Hepburn (Hap), Roberts Blossom, Keith David, Ed Van Nuys, Dale Dye. Dir: Steven Spielberg. Pro: Spielberg, Frank Marshall and Kathleen Kennedy. Screenplay: Jerry Belson; based on the Dalton Trumbo screenplay for *A Guy Named Joe*. Ph: Mikael Salomon. Ed: Michael Kahn. Pro Des: James Bissell. M: John Williams; songs performed by Jimmy Buffett, The Platters, Bonnie Raitt, The Coasters, Van Morrison, etc. Costumes: Ellen Mirojnick. Sound: Ben Burtt. (Universal–UIP.) Royal Premiere: 19 March 1990. Rel: 23 March 1990. 123 mins. Cert PG.

American Stories – Histoires d'Amerique is an odd little film which appears to have been tailored for the small rather than the large screen. An assemblage of bits and pieces of stories and anecdotes, ranging from the sadly tragic to the wryly funny, related in many cases directly to the camera by a cast of brilliant Jewish players from New York, it adds up to unusual cinema of limited appeal. Despite the English-speaking soundtrack it is in fact a Belgian-French co-production. The large cast is splendid, unidentified and unknown – at any rate to me. [FMS]

Dir and Screenplay: Chantal Akerman. Ex Pro: Bertrand van Effenterre and Marilyn Watelet. Ph: Luc Ben Hamou. Ed: Patrick

Mimouni. M: Sonia Wieder Atherton. Pro Des & Costumes: Marily Watelet. (Mallia Films, Paris/Paradine Films Brussels with La Sept in co-op. with the French and Belgian Ministries of Culture–Metro.) Rel: floating; first shown London (Metro and Phoenix) 12 January 1990. 95 mins. Cert PG.

The American Way. Belated (and dated; the film was initially unveiled at the 1986 Cannes Film Festival), all-British made, wild, woolly and occasionally biting farce about a crew of Vietnam veterans who operate a flying pirate TV station which cruises around the American skies searching the airwaves for signs of a revival in high places of the Vietnam war mentality. The cinema film direction debut of video graduate Maurice Phillips, which probably accounts for the intrusive rock music soundtrack. [FMS]

Cast: Dennis Hopper (Capt.), Michael J. Pollard (Doc), Eugene Lipinski (Ace), James Aubrey (Claude), Al Matthews (Ben), William Armstrong, Nigel Pegram. Dir: Maurice Phillips. Pro: Laurie Keller and Paul Cowan. Ex Pro: Maqbool Hameed and Jean Ubaud. Sup Ex Pro: Keith Cavele. Screenplay: Scott Roberts. Ph: John Metcalfe. Ed: Tony Lawson. Pro Des: Evan Hercules. M: Brian Bennett. (Paul Cowan.) Rel: floating; first shown London (Scala) 15 September 1989. 104 mins. No cert.

Amsterdamned. Slick Dutch thriller, a cross between *Puppet on a Chain* and *Creature from the Black Lagoon*. A brutal (and imaginative) serial killer stalks the canals of Holland's principal city, furiously pursued by police inspector and divorcé Eric Visser (Huub Stapel), who also pursues the attractive Laura (Monique Van De Ven) in his spare time. Thanks to some pacy editing, inventive touches and a dark canal-side humour, *Amsterdamned* holds the interest in spite of its length. Also, there are some wonderful shots of Amsterdam. [JC-W]

Also with: Serge-Henri Valcke (Vermeer), Lou Landré (Chief), Tatum Dagelet (Anneke), Tanneke Hartzuiker, Wim Zomer, Hidde Maas, Edwin Bakker, Barbara Martijn, Lettie Oosthoek, Jaab Stobbe. Dir: Dick Maas. Pro: Laurens Geels and Dick Maas. Screenplay: Maas. Ph: Marc Felperlaan. Ed: Hans van Dongen. Pro Des: Dick Schillemans. M: Maas. (First Floor–Vestron.) Rel: 14 July 1989. 105 mins. Cert 18.

Another Woman. Sparse, beautifully written and acted drama about a woman in her fifties (Gena Rowlands) realising that her comfortable, successful life is not all she thought it was. Writer-director Woody Allen, again in serious mood, never sounds a false note as he explores the neuroses and platitudes of his New York characters, and elicits exemplary peformances from an ensemble cast. A delicious vignette for cultured, thinking adults. [JC-W]

Cast includes: Gena Rowlands (Marion), Mia Farrow (Hope), Ian Holm (Ken), Blythe Danner (Lydia), Sandy Dennis (Claire), Gene Hackman (Larry), John Houseman (Marion's father), Martha Plimpton (Laura), Harris Yulin (Paul), Philip Bosco (Sam), Betty Buckley (Kathy), David Ogden Stiers (young Marion's father), Frances Conroy, Fred Melamed, Kenneth Welsh, Bruce Jay Friedman, Dana Ivey, Kathryn Grody. Dir and Screenplay: Woody Allen. Pro: Robert Greenhut. Ex Pro: Jack Rollins and Charles H. Joffe. Ph: Sven Nykvist. Ed: Susan E. Morse. Pro Des: Santo Loquasto. M: Classical excerpts. Costumes: Jeffrey Kurland. Sound: James Sabat. (Orion–Rank.) Rel: 28 July 1989. 81 mins. Cert PG.

Apartment Zero is one of those films you either love or hate – or maybe both! Certainly there's no lack of impressive talent on view here, both in the direction (an extremely promising debut by Martin Donovan) and performances (Colin Firth and Hart Bochner both brilliant in the leading roles). It's a dark

Gena Rowlands at the centre of Woody Allen's all-star cast in Another Woman, *an intelligent observation of marriage and middle age, from Rank.*

and ominous tale of an impeccably English Argentinian who takes a mysterious young American lodger and becomes increasingly if ambiguously sexually involved with him. As the mystery builds to a climax, murder and bloody violence come to the fore. Lightening the psychological and political menace, there are quite extraordinary interpolations of TV-sitcom comedy, shared by deliciously dizzy Dora Bryan and Liz Smith as spinster flat-owning sisters. Tense, atmospheric, fascinating

Nosy neighbours Liz Smith and Dora Bryan stir the mystery pot in Mainline's Apartment Zero.

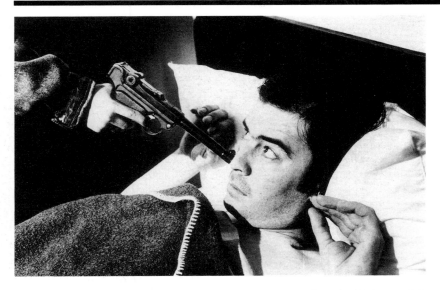

Turo Pajala wakes up to a nasty surprise in Aki Kaurismaki's unusual, bleak, but always fascinating Ariel *(Electric/Contemporary).*

Ashik Kerib (released in the UK by the ICA), the third of Russian director Sergei Paradjanou's static, stylised and poetic films.

and sometimes flawed, this is certainly no masterpiece, but is head and shoulders above most of today's thriller output. [FMS]

Cast: Hart Bochner (Jack Carney, the lodger), Colin Firth (his host, Adrian LeDuc), Dora Bryan, Liz Smith, Fabrizio Bentifoglio (Carlos Sanchez-Verne), James Telfer ('Vanessa'), Mirella D'Angelo (Laura Werpachowsky), Juan Vitali (Alberto Werpachowsky), Cipe Lincovsky (Mrs Treniev), Francesca D'Aloja, Miguel Ligero, Elvia Andreoli, Marikena Monti, Luis Romero. Dir, Story and (with David Koepp) Pro and Screenplay: Martin Donovan. Co-Pro: Brian Allman. Assoc Pro: Ezequiel Donovan and Brian Reynolds. Ex Pro: Stephen J. Cole. Ph: Miguel Rodriguez. Ed: Conrad M. Gonzalez. Pro Des: Miguel Angel Lumaldo. M: Elia Cmiral. Costumes: Angelia Fuentes. (Summit–Mainline Pictures.) Rel: floating; first shown London (Cannon, Piccadilly) 15 September 1989. 120 mins. Cert 15.

Ariel. Fairly compelling drama set in Finland, about a Lapp miner who falls on hard times. Turo Pajala, a Scandinavian Tommy Lee Jones, wanders from redundancy to being mugged to vagrancy to a life of crime before life begins remotely to look up. However, his wretched journey is a fascinating one and is the central chapter of a darkly comic trilogy, following on from *Shadows in Paradise* and preceding *The Match Factory Girl*. A bleak film illuminating a desolate landscape, *Ariel* nevertheless has its humorous moments. [JC-W]

Cast includes: Turo Pajala (Taisto Kasurinen), Susanna Haavisto (Irmeli), Matti Pellonpaa (Mikkonen), Eetu Hilkamo (Riku), Erkki Pajala, Matti Jaaranen, Kauko Laalo, Jyrki Olsonen, Marja Packalen. Dir, Pro and Screenplay: Aki Kaurismaki. Ph: Timo Salminen. Ed: Raija Talvio. Pro Des: Risto Karhula. Costumes: Tuula Hilkamo. Sound: Jouko Lumme. (Villealfa Filmproductions – Electric / Contemporary.) Rel: floating; first shown London (Metro) 6 October 1989. 74 mins. Cert 15.

Ashik Kerib. Armenian director Sergei Paradjanov's films are unique in the cinema. The director of *The Colour of Pomegranates* and *The Legend of the Suram Fortress* uses an almost hypnotic mixture of lush colour, stylised tableaux and poetry to create a fairy tale world of legend which delights some and bores others. Certainly this third film of his is more fluid and, for the most part, easier to understand. Here he tells a story about a wondrous musician (the *saaz*, a Turkish kind of balalaika, is his instrument) who, when rejected by his loved one's father, goes off on a seven-year hike through the Caucasian countryside to make his fortune and so win father's acceptance as the fair's lady's suitor. A marvellous, magical and unusual movie. [FMS]

Cast: Yri Goyan, Veronique Metonidze, Levan Natroshvili, Sofico Chaureli, etc. Dir: Sergei Paradjanov, with David Abashidze. Screenplay: Georgi Badridze; from Mikhail Lermontov's story. Ph: Albert Yavuryan. Art: Shota Gogolashvili, Georgi Meschishvili and Nikolai Zandukeli. M: Djavanshir Kuliev. (Gruzia Film Pro–ICA.) Rel: floating; first shown London (ICA) 22 September 1989. 78 mins. No cert.

Asterix and the Big Fight. There is panic in Gaul when Getafix loses his marbles and cannot remember the formula for the Magic Potion that enables the villagers to fend off the Roman army. This is the sixth of the Asterix films and should appeal to undemanding children, if to nobody else. However, the animation is of a very high order, the result of the most ambitious undertaking in this field in Europe, utilising three hundred artists and technicians for two years. [JC-W]

With the voices of: Bill Oddie (Asterix), Bernard Bresslaw (Obelix), Ron Moody (Prolix), Sheila Hancock (Impedimenta), Peter Jones (Getafix), Brian Blessed (Caous), Michael Elphick (Crysus), Andrew Sachs (Ardeco), Tim Brooke-Taylor (Cacofonix), Sean Barret, Kathryn Hurlbutt, Geoffrey Mathews, Elizabeth Proud, Kerry Shale, Ian Thompson. Production Dir: Nicolas Pesques. Dir: Philippe Grimond. Director of animation: Keith Ingham. Ex Pro: Yannik Piel. Screenplay: Yannik Voight and Adolf Kabatek; English adaptation: George Roubicek. M: Michel Colombier. (Extrafilm Prod/Gaumont Paris–Palace.) Rel: 13 October 1989. 80 mins. Cert U.

Getafix off his rocker in the Palace release, Asterix and the Big Fight.

Doc Brown (Christopher Lloyd) illustrates an alternative route to the present in UIP's Back to the Future – Part II. And Michael J. Fox, as Marty McFly (right), finds the future a mixed blessing.

Asya's Happiness. Another Russian museum piece, made twenty years ago and only now getting an official blessing for release. A quiet, black-and-white movie with a negligible story about a pretty, lame Russian peasant girl who loved somewhat unwisely but refused the marriage offers. With long monologues and little action, it still remains fascinating, mostly for the portrait it paints of the harsh life, but with enduring qualities of humour and humanity, which was the peasant's lot in the Russia of that time. [FMS]

Cast: Iya Savvina (Asya), Lyubov Sokolova, Alexander Surin, Gennady Yegorychev, Ivan Petrov. Dir: Andrei Mikhalkov-Konchalovsky. Screenplay: Yury Klepikov. Ph: Georgy Rerberg. Ed: L. Pokrovsky. Art: Mikhail Romadin. Sound: Raissa Margacheva. (Artificial Eye.) Rel: floating; first shown 10 November 1989. 98 mins. Cert PG.

Back to the Future – Part II. Marty McFly's family is in trouble again, this time in the year 2015. In order to save his future son from imprisonment, Marty is spirited forward in time, courtesy of Dr Emmet Brown's DeLorean time machine. There, Marty confronts his own future and the evil machinations of his nemesis, big Biff Tannen. Directed at breakneck speed and swarming with futuristic in-jokes (the abolition of lawyers, redundant CDs, *Jaws 19*), *Future II* is a bright, sly and thoroughly escapist success story. Crispin Glover's absence as Marty's father is a shame, but Elisabeth Shue is suitably engaging in the role of Marty's girl-friend Jennifer (played previously by Claudia Wells). [JC-W]

Also with: Michael J. Fox (Marty McFly/Marty McFly Jr/Marlene McFly), Christopher Lloyd (Doctor Emmet Brown), Lea Thompson (Lorraine), Thomas F. Wilson (Biff Tannen/Griff), James Tolkan (Strick-

An unfriendly alien with a score to settle in Peter Jackson's gross, amusing, low-budget Bad Taste, *from Blue Dolphin.*

land), E. Casanova Evans (Michael Jackson), Jay Koch (Ronald Reagan), Charles Gherardi (Ayatollah Khomeini), Harry Waters Jr, Joe Flaherty, Flea, Jeffrey Weissman, Casey Siemaszko, Billy Zane, J. J. Cohen, Judy Ovitz, James Ishida. Dir: Robert Zemeckis. Pro: Bob Gale and Neil Canton. Ex Pro: Steven Spielberg, Frank Marshall and Kathleen Kennedy. Screenplay: Gale; from a story by Zemeckis and

Gale. Ph: Dean Cundey. Ed: Arthur Schmidt and Harry Keramidas. Pro Des: Rick Carter. M: Alan Silvestri; songs from Michael Jackson, Sammy Hagar, Perry Como and The Four Aces. Costumes: Joanna Johnston. Sound: Charles L. Campbell and Louis L. Edemann. (Universal/Amblin–UIP.) Rel: 24 November 1989. 107 mins. Cert PG.

Bad Taste. Arguably the most disgusting film ever be to be shown uncut in British cinema. Having said that, *Bad Taste* is a remarkable achievement for Peter Jackson, a sick New Zealand filmmaker who spent over four years making this comedy-thriller gross-out. Jackson wrote, produced, directed, photographed, edited and starred in the film so that – initially, at least – he could try out his new 16mm Bolex. The result is rough and ready, but the special effects are truly extraordinary. Witness a man stuffing brains back into his own damaged cranium, a chainsaw cleaving a head in two, an exploding sheep, a man inspecting his own entrails, and so on. Story? A gang of nasty aliens invades a sleepy New Zealand town to spirit the occupants back

to space as *homo sapiens* fast food. Tasteless, cheap and sometimes amusing 'entertainment' – for the mentally disturbed. [JC-W]

Cast includes: Peter Jackson (Derek), Mike Minett (Frank), Terry Potter (Barry), Pete O'Herne, Craig Smith, Doug Wren. Dir, Pro, Screenplay, Ph and Ed: Peter Jackson. Consultant Pro: Tony Hiles. Additional Screenplay: Tony Hiles and Ken Hammon. M: Michelle Scullion. Sound: Brent Burge. (Wingnut Films/New Zealand Film Commission–Blue Dolphin.) Rel: floating; first shown London (Prince Charles) 15 September 1989. 93 mins. Cert 18.

Batman. The mysterious Caped Crusdader and the malevolent Joker pit their wits against each other in a grimy, timeless Gotham City. Warner Brothers' epic film (costing more than $40 million) attempts to inject some reality into the high camp of the DC Comics hero, and comes up with a dark, brooding, cartoon nightmare thin on laughs. 'We wanted to dig beneath the surface

Jack Nicholson, the real star of the mega-hit Batman *(Warner), in his outrageous portrayal of the Joker.*

and find out *why* Bruce Wayne feels the need to be Batman,' explains director Tim Burton. The photography is wondrous and the sets are awe-inspiring, but this *Batman* lacks the artistic integrity of *Blade Runner* and the thrilling wish-fulfilment of *Superman*, collapsing between two stools. Michael Keaton is brave casting in the title role, but is wasted in a performance anybody else could have done better – if you're going to cast Keaton, *use* him. However, Jack Nicholson's Joker is chillingly eccentric. [JC-W]

Also with: Kim Basinger (Vicki Vale), Robert Wuhl (Alexander Knox), Pat Hingle (Commissioner Gordon), Billy Dee Williams (Harvey Dent), Michael Gough (Alfred), Jack Palance (Grissom), Jack Nicholson (Jack Napier), Jerry Hall (Alicia), William Hootkins (Eckhardt), Tracey Walter (Bob the Goon), Lee Wallace (Mayor), Richard Strange, Carl Chase, Phil Tan, Vincent Wong, John Dair, Christopher Fairbank, George Roth, Kate Harper, Bruce McGuire, Richard Durden, Hugo E. Block, David Baxt, Sharon Holm, Dennis Lill. Dir: Tim Burton. Pro: Jon Peters and Peter Guber. Co-Pro: Chris Kenny. Ex Pro: Benjamin Melniker and Michael Uslan. Screenplay: Sam Hamm and Warren Skaaren, from a story by Hamm, based on characters created by Bob Kane. Ph: Roger Pratt. Ed: Ray Lovejoy. Pro Des: Anton Furst. M: Danny Elfman; songs by Prince, Percy Faith/Max Steiner, Hill Bowen & his Orchestra. Costumes: Bob Ringwood. Sound: Don Sharpe. (Warner.) Rel: 11 August 1989. 126 mins. Cert 12.

The Bear – L'Ours. Delightful French (English-speaking) animal biographical film reminiscent in many ways of the old Disney 'True Life' series. The main characters are a baby bear (La Douce, a marvellous ham actor and a certain winner of hearts, whose mother is killed in a rock slide), his fearsome elders and the hunters he turns into bear protectors – and it all adds up to a good 'green' message. Produced by Claude Berri (the director of the magnificent 'Manon' duo of movies) and filmed against the spectacular scenic background of the high Dolomites (standing in for the Rockies). A pleasing lack of sentimentality, an almost wordless script and only one real fault; the inclusion of the needless, off-key baby bear dream sequence. Great heartwarming stuff for all the family. [FMS]

Cast: La Douce (bear cub), Tcheky Karyo and Jack Wallace (hunters), Andre Lacombe

La Douce, the baby bear who was the winning star of the Columbia Tri-Star French release The Bear – L'Ours.

(dog handler), Bart (big bear). Dir: Jean-Jacques Annaud. Pro: Claude Berri. Assoc Pro: Pierre Grunstein. Screenplay: Gerard Brach; based on the James Oliver Curwood novel *The Grizzly King*. Ph: Philippe Rousselot. Ed: Noelle Boisson. Pro Des: Tony Ludi. M: Philippe Sarde. Sound Des: Laurent Quaglio. (Price Entertainment–Columbia Tri-Star.) Rel: 22 September 1989. 94 mins. Cert PG.

Bert Rigby, You're a Fool. A delightfully dated musical comedy with buckets of charm and cliché, put across with such zest and expertise that it glides effortlessly over the rough patches. TV and stage phenomenon Robert Lindsay (*Citizen Smith* and *Me and My Girl*) is Bert Rigby, a striking coal miner from

Anne Bancroft and Robert Lindsay in love with showbusiness in Rob Reiner's affectionate, screwball Bert Rigby, You're a Fool, *from Warner.*

Michael Douglas, a racist cop in Osaka, in Ridley Scott's picturesque Black Rain *(UIP).*

the north of England who goes to Hollywood to make his fortune as a Gene Kelly dancealike. Corny and irresistible, the film should work wonders if you're in the right mood. [JC-W]

Also with: Robbie Coltrane (Sid Trample), Cathryn Bradshaw (Laurel Pennington), Jackie Gayle (I. I. Perlestein), Bruno Kirby (Kyle DeForest), Corbin Bernsen (Jim Shirley), Anne Bancroft (Meredith Perlestein), Liz Smith (Mrs Rigby), Lila Kaye, Fanny Carby, Carmen Du Sautoy, Mike Grady, Liberty Mounten, George Malpas, Robert Hines, Dominique Barnes, Ian Hawks, Arsenio (Sonny) Trinidad. Dir and Screenplay: Carl Reiner. Pro: George Shapiro. Ph: Jan De Bont. Ed: Bud Molin. Pro Des: Terence Marsh. M: Ralph Burns; songs include 'The Continental', 'Isn't It Romantic?', 'Puttin' On the Ritz', 'Dream a Little Dream Of Me' and others of that ilk. Costumes: Ruth Myers. Sound: Joe Kenworthy. (Lorimar–Warner.) Rel: 10 November 1989. 94 mins. Cert 15.

Bill and Ted's Excellent Adventure. Yet another comedy leapfrogging

through time and back, with the addition of some celebrity participants: Socrates, Abraham Lincoln, Sigmund Freud, Genghis Khan and distinguished company. Two high-school numbskulls, Bill and Ted (Alex Winter and Keanu Reeves), find they're about to flunk their history exam when they describe Napoleon as 'a short, dead dude' and Joan of Arc as Noah's wife. Enter the avuncular Rufus (George Carlin – out of a phone booth) to spirit them back in time, letting the boys experience history for themselves and bring back a few legends to help boost their end-of-term presentation. An appalling comedy, this was a surprising success at the American box office, aided by Winter's and Reeves's endearing performances and some original, inventive dialogue. A 'most triumphant' mess, as they might say. [JC-W]

Also with: Terry Camilleri (Napoleon), Dan Shor (Billy the Kid), Tony Steedman (Socrates), Rod Loomis (Freud), Al Leong (Genghis Khan), Jane Wiedlin (Joan of Arc), Robert V. Barron (Abraham Lincoln), Clifford David (Beethoven), Hal Landon Jr (Capt. Logan), Bernie Casey (Mr Ryan), Amy Stock-Poynton (Missy/Mom), J. Patrick McNamara (Mr Preston), Frazier

Bain, Diane Franklin, Kimberley LaBelle, Martha Davis. Dir: Stephen Herek. Pro: Scott Kroopf, Michael S. Murphey and Joel Soisson. Ex Pro: Ted Field and Robert W. Cort. Screenplay: Chris Matheson and Ed Solomon. Ph: Timothy Suhrstedt. Ed: Larry Bock and Patrick Rand. Pro Des: Roy Forge Smith. M: David Newman; rock songs performed by Big Pig, Range War, Shark Island, etc. Costumes: Jill Ohanneson. (De Laurentiis Entertainment–Premier Releasing.) Rel: 13 April 1990. 89 mins. Cert PG.

Black Rain. Hard-hitting, intensely atmospheric cops 'n' robbers thriller set in Osaka. Michael Douglas and Andy Garcia star as a pair of New York cops who witness a murder in a restaurant and apprehend the killer, Sato, a Japanese mob leader. However, when they are requested to escort him to Osaka, Sato escapes immediately on arrival, leaving Douglas and Garcia at sea in a violent, alien culture. Douglas – a maverick cop, of course – is determined to find his man, even against insurmountable odds. As directed by Ridley Scott this is no ordinary police thriller, but a pictorial odyssey of con-

Paul Newman as governor and lover in Warner's Blaze, *defending his politics, and with Lolita Davidovich as Blaze Starr.*

temporary Japan. Scott creates a futuristic, twilight zone of blinking neon and belching mist, and although he never succeeds in engaging the emotions, your senses will be pummelled. [JC-W]

Cast includes: Michael Douglas (Nick), Andy Garcia (Charlie), Ken Takakura (Masahiro), Kate Capshaw (Joyce), Yusaka Matsuda (Sato), Shigeru Koyama, John Spencer, Guts Ishimatsu, Tomisaburo Wakayama, Stephen Root. Dir: Ridley Scott. Pro: Stanley R. Jaffe and Sherry Lansing. Ex Pro: Craig Bolotin and Julie Kirkham. Screenplay: Bolotin and Warren Lewis. Ph: Jan De Bont. Ed: Tom Rolf. Pro Des: Norris Spencer. M: Hans Zimmer; songs performed by Greg Allman, Iggy Pop, Soul II Soul, Bobby Darin, Ryuichi Sakamoto, UB40, etc. Costumes: Ellen Mirojnick. (Paramount–UIP.) Rel: 26 January 1990. 125 mins. Cert 18.

Black Rain (Japanese version). See **Shohei Imamura's Black Rain**.

Blaze. A spectacular performance from Paul Newman, spicy dialogue by Ron Shelton and some sharp lighting from Haskell Wexler enliven this fascinating

(true) story. However, this is not so much the history of Blaze Starr, 'exotic dancer', as a summary of her relationship with Earl K. Long, self-proclaimed 'fine governor of the great state of Louisiana'. Newman, made up to look older than he is, storms to the centre of the film affecting a Lee Marvin growl and a geriatric stagger. The truth is, Earl Long was a colourful political figure who fought for the negro cause and pooh-poohed the moral severity of his time. It is Newman's film and is, in effect, little more than a celluloid-framed performance. (Incidentally, the real Blaze Starr takes a cameo – as Lily.) [JC-W]

Also with: Lolita Davidovich (Blaze Starr/Fannie Belle Fleming), Jerry Hardin (Thibodeaux), Jeffrey DeMunn (Tuck), Robert Wuhl (Red Snyder), Louanne Stephens (Lora Fleming), Gailard Sartain, Garland Bunting, Richard Jenkins, Brandon Smith, Jay Chevalier, Blaze Starr, Gilbert Lewis. Dir and Screenplay: Ron Shelton; from the book *Blaze Starr: My Life As Told*

To Huey Perry, by Blaze Starr and Huey Perry. Pro: Gil Friesen and Dale Pollock. Ex Pro: David Lester and Don Miller. Ph: Haskell Wexler. Ed: Robert Leighton. Pro Des: Armin Ganz. M: Bennie Wallace; songs performed by Fats Domino, Hank Williams Sr, King Cotton and His Swamp Coolers, etc. Costumes: Ruth Myers. Sound: Kirk Francis. (Touchstone–Warner.) Rel: 23 February 1990. 120 mins. Cert 15.

Born on the Fourth of July. Touted as the 1989 Oscar favourite, Oliver Stone's long-awaited companion to *Platoon* nabbed eight nominations but only

19

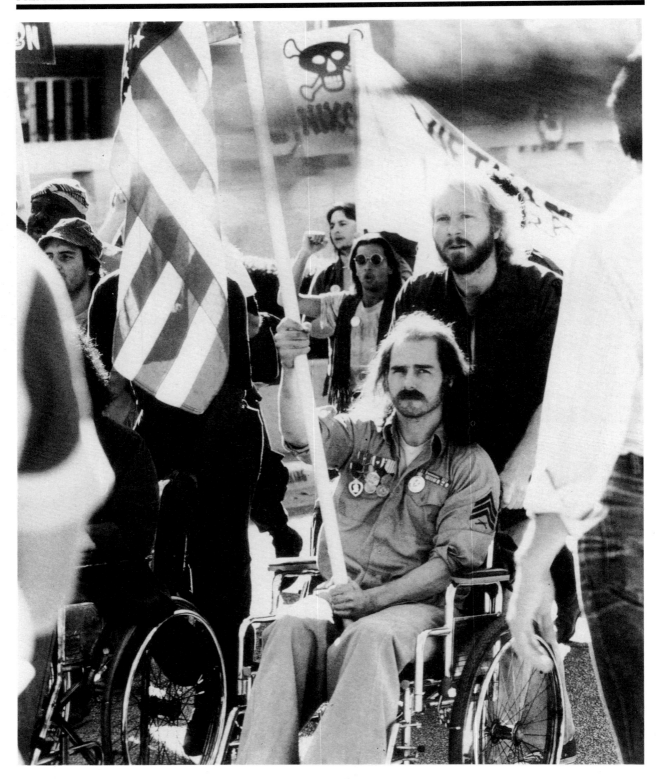

Tom Cruise in UIP's Born on the Fourth of July, *as the victim of glory.*

won two awards – for best director and editing. Perhaps Hollywood is showing signs of disenchantment with the Vietnam epic, already having saluted *Platoon* and *The Deer Hunter*. Nevertheless, *Born on the Fourth of July* is a stunning piece of bravura film-making and a gut-wrenching, moving human story. Tom Cruise (in the role vacated by Al Pacino) comes of age as the embittered Ron Kovic, the war hero who is disowned by his country after being shot in the back and losing the use of his lower body. The film opens with Kovic playing war games as a child, following him through to high school and a recruitment lecture that stirs the jingoistic fibre of every boy listening. The honour of America must be upheld, and Kovic signs up to join in the glory of heroism – only to find himself plunged into a waking nightmare. Stone leaves nothing to the imagination, showing the mutilation of Vietnamese children, the humiliation of Kovic in a rat-infested hospital and the moral decay of a man who thought he was giving his life to an honourable cause. This is strong meat and thought-provoking cinema, executed with the aplomb of a director who knows his art from his elbow. A masterpiece. [JC-W]

Also with: Kyra Sedgwick (Donna), Raymond J. Barry (Mr Kovic), Jerry Levine (Steve Boyer), Frank Whaley (Timmy), Willem Dafoe (Charlie), Bryan Larkin (young Ron), Caroline Kava (Mrs Kovic), Josh Evans (Tommy Kovic), Tom Berenger (recruiting sergeant), Lili Taylor (Jamie Wilson), Seth Allen, Jamie Talisman, Sean Stone, Anne Bobby, Richard Panebianco, Rob Camilletti, Stephen Baldwin, Richard Grusin, Ed Lauter, Oliver Stone (news reporter), Dale Dye, John Getz, David Warshofsky, Jason Gedrick, William Baldwin, James LeGros, R. D. Call, David Herman, Bruce MacVittie, Bob Gunton, Mark Moses, Abbie Hoffman (strike organiser), Reg. E. Cathey, Holly Marie Combs, Mike Starr, Beau Starr, Gale Mayron, Lisa Barnes, Michael Wincott, Cordelia Gonzalez, Edith Diaz, Tony Frank, Jayne Haynes, Jodi Long, John C. McGinley, Lucinda Jenney, Annie McEnroe, Daniel Baldwin. Dir: Oliver Stone. Pro: A. Kitman Ho and Oliver Stone. Screenplay: Stone and Ron Kovic; based on the latter's autobiography. Ph: Robert Richardson. Ed: David Brenner and Joe Hutshing. Pro Des: Bruno Rubeo. M: John Williams; songs performed by The Temptations, Van Morrison, Don McLean, The Fifth Dimension, Trini Lopez, etc. Costumes: Judy Ruskin. Sound: Tod A. Maitland. (Universal–UIP.) Rel: 2 March 1990. 144 mins. Cert 18.

Bull Durham. This is a familiar story, about a fallen first league baseball star, coming to terms with playing in the minor league, and in the end succeeding in planing the chip off his shoulder. It's difficult to understand the baseball lingo (apart from the plethora of foul words), but there's enough mild comedy and good acting in this sporting comedy-romance to give you value for money – as long as you don't worry about the loose moral tone! Full credit to the trio of leading players: Kevin

Love among the baseball bats: Susan Sarandon, as Annie, flirts with the once major-league star Cras (Kevin Costner) in Bull Durham *(Rank).*

Costner (as the ex-star Crash Davis); Tim Robbins (as Nuke Laloosh); and Susan Sarandon (as Annie, who gives her favours annually to the most promising player of the season, until love comes along in the person of Crash). [FMS]

Also with Trey Wilson, Robert Wuhl, William O'Leary, David Neidorf, Danny Gans, Tony Silardi, Lloyd Williams, Rick Marzan, George Buck, Jenny Robertson, Greg Avelone, Carey 'Garland' Bunting, Robert Dickman, Timothy Kirk, Don Davis, Stephen Ware, Tobi Eshelman, C. K. Bibby, Henry G. Sanders. Dir and Screenplay: Ron Shelton. Pro: Thom Mount and Mark Burg. Ex Pro: David V. Lester. Ph: Bobby Byrne. Ed: Robert Leighton and Adam Weiss. Pro Des: Armin Ganz. M: Michael Convertino. (Orion Pictures/Mount Co. Pro.–Rank.) Rel: floating; first shown London (Prince Charles) 25 August 1989. 108 mins. Cert 15.

The 'Burbs. Deep in the heart of American suburbia the inhabitants of a cul-de-sac plot to unveil the mystery of the new people at No. 669. The Klopeks have been in residence for a month but only come out at night and they *still* haven't mown their lawn. The suspicious neighbours unite to put the

mind of suburbia at rest. Surprisingly, Tom Hanks merely strolls through his role as an ordinary family man at odds with the unconventional, while his co-stars overact to the point of distraction. There *are* some funny moments (and a welter of in-jokes), but Dana Olsen's script seldom offers grist for grinning. [JC-W]

Cast includes: Tom Hanks (Ray Peterson), Bruce Dern (Mark Rumsfield), Carrie Fisher (Carol Peterson), Rick Ducommun (Art Weingartner), Corey Feldman (Ricky Butler), Wendy Schaal (Bonnie Rumsfield), Henry Gibson (Dr Werner Klopek), Brother Theodore, Courtney Gains, Gale Gordon, Dick Miller, Robert Picardo, Franklyn Ajaye, Heather Haase, Dana Olsen. Dir: Joe Dante. Pro: Michael Finnell and Larry Brezner. Co-Pro and Screenplay: Dana Olsen. Ph: Robert Stevens. Ed: Marshall Harvey. Pro Des: James Spencer. M: Jerry Goldsmith. Costumes: Rosanna Norton. Sound: George Simpson. (Universal–UIP.) Rel: 28 July 1989. 102 mins. Cert PG.

Camp Thiaroye – Camp de Thiaroye. Though extremely professionally made, this lean and impressive Senegalese/Tunisian/Algerian co-production is not likely to get much – if any – showing in France (it was turned down by the Cannes Festival) in view of its consistently anti-French story and attitude. It's the story – almost certainly virtually unknown outside France and Africa – of a horrifying atrocity during the last

21

A tough time for Johnno (Damien Walters) and his Italian fisherman friend Tony (Joe Petruzzi), in the Australian film for children Captain Johnno *(BFI).*

war: after four years in the army (during which any lingering illusions of white supremacy were finally dispelled), a company of French colonial troops was installed in a transit camp prior to demobilisation. An argument developed when they were given only half the back pay due to them, leading to open rebellion. The French general in charge surrounded the camp by night with a ring of tanks and proceeded to blow it and all within to bits. Though made in a documentary style,

War is hell: Michael J. Fox, Don Harvey and Sean Penn in Brian De Palma's Casualties of War, *from Columbia Tri-Star.*

I am nonetheless told that many of the details diverge from historical facts, wilfully so in some cases, it seems . . . But the film certainly carries a powerful punch and one can't help feeling that where there's smoke there *must* be fire. [FMS]

Cast: Ibrahima Sane (Diatta), Sijiri Bakaba (Pays), Jean-Daniel Simon (Capt. Raymond), Gustave Sorgho, Camara Dansogho Mohamed, Gabriel Zahon, Casimir Zoba, Mohamad Cahara, Pierre Orma. Dir and Screenplay: Ousmane Sembene and Thierno Faty. Ph: Ismail Lakhdar Hamina. Ed: Kahena Atia and Riveill. M: Ismaila Lo. (Sidek (Dakar) Instituto Luce (Italy)-SNPC (Dakar)/Satpec, Tunis/Enaproc Algiers–Metro.) Rel: floating; first shown London (Metro) 25 August 1989. 140 mins. No cert.

Candy Mountain. Rambling road movie about a hustling drifter on the

trail of an elusive, legendary guitar-maker. Julius (Kevin J. O'Connor) is a surly, uncharismatic individual, but the characters he meets along the road (from New York to Nova Scotia) are, for the most part, colourful diversions in this slow-moving dirge for humanity. Those excelling themselves in an all non-star cast include Harris Yulin, Bulle Ogier, Roberts Blossom and 'Dr John'. [JC-W]

Also with: Harris Yulin (Elmore), Tom Waits (Al Silk), Bulle Ogier (Cornelia), Roberts Blossom (Archie), Leon Redbone (Huey), 'Dr John' (Henry), Rita MacNeil (Winnie), Joe Strummer (Mario), Laurie Metcalf (Alice), Jayne Eastwood (Lucille), Kazuko Oshima (Koko), Eric Mitchell, Mary Joy, Bob Joy, David Johansen, David Margulies, Rockets Redglare, Nancy Fish, Harry Fox, Wayne Robson, Tantoo Cardinal, Jo-Ann Rolls. Dir: Robert Frank and Rudy Wurlitzer. Pro: Ruth Waldburger. Assoc Pro: Tom Rothman. Ex Pro: Gerald Dearing. Screenplay: Wurlitzer. Ph: Pio Corradi. Ed: Jennifer Auge. Art: Brad Ricker and Keith Currie. M: Max Rebennack, 'Dr John', David Johansen, Leon Redbone, Rita MacNeil and Tom Waits. Sound: David Joliat. (Xanadu/Films Plain Chant/Films Vision 4 Inc./Films A2–Recorded Releasing.) Rel: floating; first shown London (ICA) 29 December 1989. 91 mins. Cert 15.

Captain Johnno. An interesting novelty, made by the Australian Children's Television Foundation, with the intention of not merely entertaining the youngsters, but also treating issues not usually introduced into children's films; in this instance the tragedy of deafness. Johnno is a sea-loving 12-year-old who has to come to terms with his disability. [FMS]

Cast: Damian Walters (Johnno), John Waters (Frank), Joe Petruzzi (Tony), Michele Fawdon (Kathleen), Rebecca Sykes (Julie). Dir: Mario Andreacchio. Pro: Jane Ballantyne. Ex Pro: Patricia Edgar. Screenplay: Rob George. Ph: Roger Dowling. Ed: Andrew Ellis. Pro Des: Vicki Niehus. M: Stephen Matters. Costumes: Jenny Miles. (Australian Children's Television Foundation–BFI.) Rel: floating; first shown London (ICA) 7 April 1990. 100 mins. Cert U. (With subtitles for the deaf.)

Casualties of War. True story about an American private who brings his unit to court martial for the abduction, rape and murder of a Vietnamese farm girl. In the wake of such harrowing 'Nam dramas as *The Deer Hunter, Platoon* and even John Irvin's *Hamburger Hill*, Brian De Palma's treatment of war as hell is surprisingly mild given the subject matter. Ennio Morricone's operatic score and Stephen H. Burum's lush photography also help to distance the viewer from the full force of the real-life horrors. Besides, Sean Penn's brutal sergeant and Michael J. Fox's goody-two-shoes private are far too black-and-white to be credibly truthful. [JC-W]

Cast includes: Michael J. Fox (Eriksson), Sean Penn (Meserve), Don Harvey (Clark), John C. Reilly (Hatcher), John Leguizamo (Diaz), Thuy Thu Le (Oahn), Erik King, Jack Gwaltney, Ving Rhames, Dan Martin, Dale Dye, Al Shannon, Sam Robards, Darren E. Burrows, J.J. Dir: Brian De Palma. Pro: Art Linson. Screenplay: David Rabe; based on the book by Daniel Lang. Ph: Stephen H. Burum. Ed: Bill Pankow. Pro Des: Wolf Kroeger. M: Ennio Morricone; songs performed by The Doors, Steppenwolf, etc. Costumes: Richard Bruno. Sound: Gary Wilkins. (Columbia Tri-Star.) Rel: 26 January 1990. 114 mins. Cert 18.

Cat Chaser. Straightforward, virtually motionless, sub-*film noir* melodrama set in Miami Beach. What story there is concerns the money-grabbing, adulterous affair of a lonely motel owner (Peter Weller) with the wife (Kelly McGillis) of a wealthy, cruel Dominican ex-patriate. A subplot about the Dominican revolution of 1961 buzzes around like a wasp in pain and then disappears. Worse still, there's an embarrassing B-movie voice-over that is a pain in the ears. Kelly McGillis, a wonderful actress, does little but smoulder behind dark glasses and take her clothes off. Why? Oh, *why?* [JC-W]

Cast includes: Peter Weller (Moran), Kelly McGillis (Mary), Charles Durning (Jiggs), Frederic Forrest (Nolan), Tomas Milian (De Boya), Juan Fernandez (Rafi), Phil Leeds, Tony Bolana, Adrianne Sachs, Alexis Arguelleo, Michael Weller. Dir: Abel Ferrara. Pro: Peter Davis and William Panzer. Ex Pro: Guy Collins. Screenplay: Elmore Leonard, Jim Borrelli and Alan Sharp; based on Leonard's cult novel. Ph: Anthony Richmond. Ed: Kim Kennedy. Pro Des: Dan Leigh. M: Chick Corea. Costumes: Michael Kaplan. Sound: Henry Lopez. (Vestron–Entertainment.) Rel: 8 December 1989. 93 mins. Cert. 18.

Celia. Melbourne, 1957. A remarkable debut from 28-year-old Australian writer-director Ann Turner who manages

The remarkable Rebecca Smart as Celia, *in Ann Turner's powerful debut film from Australia (Electric/Contemporary).*

to slip into the mind of this 9-year-old (Celia) as if she were a fellow girlfriend. Few films exploring the mental complications, paranoia and flights of fantasy of childhood have come this close. Having said that, the film loses momentum towards the end and rather overdoes the analogy between a plague of rabbits and the Communist scare of '59. But these are petty worries when the film has so much to offer: not least 12-year-old Rebecca Smart's totally involving, bright and perceptive central performance. Rites of passage were never so right. [CB]

Also with: Nicholas Eadie (Celia's father, Ray), Maryanne Fahey (Celia's mother, Pat), Victoria Longley (Alice), William Zappa (John Burke, the policeman). Dir and Screenplay: Ann Turner. Pro: Timothy White and Gordon Glenn. Ex Pro: Bruce Menzies. Ph: Geoffrey Simpson. Ed: Ken Sallows. Pro Des: Peta Lawson. M: Chris Neal. (Seon Films–Electric/Contemporary.) Rel: 16 March 1990. 103 mins. Cert 15.

Checking Out. In the tradition of *The Loved One* and *The End*, this desperate farce makes light of dying, but is more a grey area than a black comedy. Jeff Daniels is Ray Macklin, an executive for Bon-Aire ('The airline with no crash record'), who becomes obsessed with mortality when his best friend dies in the middle of telling a joke ('He didn't even get to the punchline'). Unfortunately, Daniels is neither convincing nor charismatic enough to hold this movie together, while the film itself could have tried exhibiting a darker edge. If you're making a comedy about death, poor taste *is* allowed, you know. [JC-W]

Also with: Melanie Mayron (Jenny Macklin), Michael Tucker (Harry Lardner), Kathleen York (Diana), Ann Magnuson (Connie Hagen), Allan Harvey (Pat Hagen), Jo Harvey Allen (Barbara), Ian Wolfe, Billy Beck, Trudi Dochtermann, John Durbin, Adelle Lutz, Felton Perry, Stephen Tobolowsky, Matthew Hurley, Courtney Sonne, Ruth Manning, David Byrne (bartender). Dir: David Leland. Pro: Ben Myron. Co-Pro: Garth Thomas. Ex Pro: George Harrison and Denis O'Brien. Screenplay: Joe Eszterhas. Ph: Ian Wilson. Ed: Lee Percy. Pro Des: Barbara Ling. M:

Emily Lloyd and Kiefer Sutherland, however hard they tried, just weren't the stuff of Bonnie and Clyde in Palace's Chicago Joe and the Showgirl.

Carter Burwell. Sound: Mark Ulano. (HandMade–Virgin Vision.) Rel: 29 September 1989. 98 mins. Cert 15.

Chicago Joe and the Showgirl. Hammersmith, London, 1944. Emily Lloyd, forever stretching herself as an actress, plays a would-be gangster's moll in this muddled true-life drama. Screenwriter David Yallop (*Minder*) unwisely attempts to enter the confused mind of low-life stripper Betty Jones by crowding the narrative with fantasy sequences. Betty (*alias* Georgina Grayson) is a war-time bride (separated) who glosses over the drudgery of her life by imagining herself a movie star. Enter American hustler Ricky Allen (Kiefer Sutherland – dull) who falls under her spell and succumbs to her fantasy urges. Only in the film's last third does it reach anywhere near its potential, showing the chilling side effects of a war that, to some, has made death a

glamorous sideshow. Hans Zimmer's 'here-comes-the-cavalry' score only makes things worse. [JC-W]

Also with: Patsy Kensit (Joyce Cook), Keith Allen (Lenny Bexley), Liz Fraser (Mrs Evans), Alexandra Pigg (Violet), John Junkin (George Heath), Ralph Nossek, Colin Bruce, Roger Ashton-Griffiths, Harry Fowler, Janet Dale, John Surman, Hugh Millais, Stephen Hancock, Gerard Horan, Angela Morant, Malcolm Terris. Dir: Bernard Rose. Pro: Tim Bevan. Screenplay: David Yallop. Ph: Mike Southon. Ed: Dan Rae. Pro Des: Gemma Jackson. M: Hans Zimmer and Shirley Walker. Costumes: Bob Ringwood. Sound: Peter Glossop. (Polygram/Working Title/BSB–Palace.) Rel: 6 April 1990. 103 mins. Cert 18.

A Chorus of Disapproval. Michael Winner, after years of directing Charles Bronson, returns to his preferred arena of comedy and/or farce. With his persuasive powers as producer, Winner convinced playwright Alan Ayckbourn to submit his work for celluloid immortality for the first time, and probably for the last. A stage hit in London, the story follows the rise and fall of one

Guy Jones (Jeremy Irons), employee of an electronics firm, who cuts a swathe through the hearts of an ensemble of amateur actresses appearing in a seaside production of *The Beggar's Opera*. Winner directs with the subtlety of a prizefighter, selecting odd camera angles and meaningless close-ups to butcher any laughs there might have been. An extraordinarily talented all-star cast struggles pathetically for survival, while Anthony Hopkins gives probably the worst performance of his career. [JC-W]

Also with: Prunella Scales (Hannah Ap Llewellyn), Richard Briers (Ted Washbrook), Barbara Ferris (Enid Washbrook), Gareth Hunt (Ian Hubbard), Lionel Jeffries (Jarvis Huntley-Pike), Patsy Kensit (Linda Washbrook), Alexandra Pigg (Bridget Baines), Jenny Seagrove (Fay Hubbard), Sylvia Syms (Rebecca Huntley-Pike), Pete Lee-Wilson (Crispin Usher). Dir, Pro and (with Alan Ayckbourn) Screenplay: Michael Winner; from the play by Ayckbourn. Assoc Pro: Ron Purdie. Ph: Alan Jones. Ed: Arnold Crust (*alias* Winner). Art: Peter Young. M: John Du Prez. Sound: Bob Taylor. (Andre Blay/Elliot Kastner–HoBo Films.) Rel: 3 November 1989. 100 mins. Cert PG.

Cinema Paradiso. Magical Italian masterpiece about a middle-aged man's journey into his past – to Giancaldo, Sicily, where he grew up, befriended the town's cinema projectionist and took over the post himself. A love letter to the movies, *Cinema Paradiso* is over-long, self-indulgent and over-sentimental, but it contains a gallery of memorable images and is stuffed full of supreme craftsmanship. One suspects that the film is largely autobiographical (it was filmed in the director's hometown of Bagheria), and does include scenes that are painfully true to life. Winner of the Special Jury Prize at the 1989 Cannes Film Festival and the Oscar for Best Foreign Film. [JC-W]

Cast includes: Philippe Noiret (Alfredo), Jacques Perrin (Salvatore), Salvatore Cascio (Salvatore as a child), Mario Leonardi (Salvatore as an adolescent), Agnese Nano (Elena), Leopoldo Trieste (Father Adelfio), Antonella Attili, Isa Danielli, Pupella Maggio (of *Amarcord* fame). Dir and Screenplay: Giuseppe Tornatore. Assoc Pro: Riccardo Caneva and Alexandre Mnouchkine. Ex Pro: Mino Barbera. Ph: Blasco Giurato. Ed: Mario Mora. Pro Des: Andrea Crisanti. M: Ennio Morricone; 'Love Theme' by Andrea Morricone. Costumes: Beatrice Bordone. (Sovereign Pictures/Les Films Ariane (Paris)/Cristaldifilm (Rome)–Palace.) Rel: floating; first shown London (Curzon, Mayfair) 23 February 1990. 124 mins. Cert PG.

The Citadel – El Kalaa. Bitterly satirical observation of small-town Algerian society, that at once celebrates the detail of village life and its meticulous ceremonies, and opens Western eyes to a barbaric world of Muslim tradition. Kaddour is a village simpleton frustrated by his attempts to find a bride. At last his eye falls on his neighbour's wife, provoking a disastrous turn of events. His adoptive father, who is wooing a fourth bride, steps in to lend a hand – leading to a humiliating, wrenching finale. Starting out as rural comedy, *The Citadel* gradually reveals a satirical cutting edge and ends as admonitory nightmare. [CB]

Cast includes: Khaled Barkat (Kaddour), Djillali Ain-Tedeles (Sidi), Fettouma Ousliha (Helima), Momo (Aissa), Fatima Belhadj (Nedjama), Boumedienne Sirat, Nawel Zaatar, Hamid Habati. Dir and Screenplay: Mohamed Chouikh. Pro: Mohamed Tahar Harhoura. Ph: Allel Yahiaoui. Ed: Yamina Chouikh. M: Jawad Fasla. Sound: Rachid Bouafia. (Centre Algerien pour l'Art et l'Industrie Cinematogra-

Amateur dramatics. Prunella Scales with Jeremy Irons in A Chorus of Disapproval *(HoBo).*

phiques–Metro.) Rel: floating; first shown London (Metro) 30 March 1990. 95 mins. Cert PG.

A City of Sadness – Beiqing Chengshi. Slow-moving, detailed account of the lives of the Lin family, following their spiritual deterioration over a period of years following World War II. Through their eyes, director Hou Hsiao-hsien examines the entire history of post-war

Taiwan – explained through endless scenes over food and drink. Demanding cinema, and rewarding if you're into Taiwan, but this'll probably bore the socks off most people. Winner of the Golden Lion at the 1989 Venice Film Festival. [CB]

Cast includes: Tony Leung (Lin Wen-ching, fourth son), Hsin Shu-fen (Hinomi), Chen Sown-yung (Lin Wen-heung, first son), Kao Jai (Lin Wen-leung, third son), Li Tien-lu (Lin Ah-lu, father), Wu Yi-fang, Nakamura Ikuyo, Kenny Cheung, Chen Shu-fang, Lin Yang, H. T. Jan. Dir: Hou Hsiao-hsien. Pro: Chiu Fu-Sheng. Ex Pro: H. T. Jan and Michael Yang. Screenplay: Wu Nien-jen

Michael Keaton as you've never seen him before, in Warner's compulsive Clean and Sober.

and Chu Tien-wen. Ph: Chen Hwai-en. Ed: Liau Ching-sown. Art: Liu Chih-Hwa and Lin Tsun-wen. M: Naoki Tachikawa. Costumes: Chu Jin-wen. (3-H Films/Era International–Artificial Eye.) Rel: floating; first shown London (Renoir) 23 March 1990. 158 mins. Cert 15.

Clean and Sober. Michael Keaton turns straight actor to play Daryl Poynter, a Philadelphia real-estate hustler massively addicted to drugs, alcohol and cigarettes. Poynter is also in deep dung with the police and hides out at a 'chemical dependency centre' to keep low for a while. The irony is that he thinks all his problems are financial, not drug-orientated. With intelligence and restraint, *Clean and Sober* examines the rehabilitation of a man on the verge of a nervous breakdown, and manages to avoid the easy path to melodrama. Keaton is convincing in a difficult role, and often reminds one of Jack Nicholson in his late thirties. The supporting cast is excellent,

particularly Morgan Freeman, M. Emmet Walsh and, as a fellow patient, Kathy Baker. Hower, the film is not the wrenching experience that perhaps it should have been. We should leave the cinema traumatised, not merely feeling glum. [JC-W]

Also with: Kathy Baker (Charlie Standers), Morgan Freeman (Craig), Tate Donovan (Donald Towle), Henry Judd Baker (Xavier), Claudia Christian (Iris), M. Emmet Walsh (Richard Dirks), Dakin Matthews, Pat Quinn, Nick Savage, Pamela Dunlap, Harley Kozak. Dir: Glenn Gordon Caron. Pro: Tony Ganz and Deborah Blum. Ex Pro: Ron Howard. Screenplay: Tod Carroll. Ph: Jan Kiesser. Ed: Richard Chew. Pro Des: Joel Schiller. M: Gabriel Yared; 'Domino' performed by Van Morrison. Costumes: Robert Turturice. Sound: Lon E. Bender. (Imagine–Warner.) Rel: 8 June 1990. 124 mins. Cert 18.

Cold Feet. Goofball western comedy with Keith Carradine as a ne'er-do-well trickster, Sally Kirkland as his gluttonous 'fiancée' and Tom Waits as a psychotic troublemaker. In Mexico the unlikely trio sew a cache of emeralds into the gut of a champion horse and so smuggle the precious stones into the US. There, the double-crossing starts. Off-beat farce from the Rumanian director of *Echo Park* occasionally hits the funny bone but more often misses it. A rocky ride. Look out for Jeff Bridges' cameo as a gun-toting barman. [JC-W]

Cast includes: Keith Carradine (Monte), Sally Kirkland (Maureen), Tom Waits (Kenny), Bill Pullman (Buck), Rip Torn (sheriff), Kathleen York (Laura), Macon McCalman, Bob Mendelsohn, Vincent Schiavelli, Marc Phelan, Tom McGuane. Dir: Robert Dornhelm. Pro: Cassian Elwes. Co Pro: Mary McLaglen. Ex Pro: Cary Brokaw. Screenplay: Tom McGuane and Jim Harrison. Ph: Brian Duggan. Ed: David Rawlins.

Sally Kirkland and Keith Carradine get Cold Feet *over some hot emeralds in Virgin's mildly diverting comedy-Western.*

Pro Des: Bernt Capra. M: Tom Bahler. Costumes: Carol Wood. Sound: Robert J. Anderson. (Avenue–Virgin.) Rel: floating; first shown London (ICA) 27 April 1990. 94 mins. Cert 15.

Comic Book Confidential. A Canadian comedy review of some 40 years of the often controversial American comic books like *Marvel, Mad, Raw* and the 'underground' *Zap* comics – most of which at one time or another were circulated in Britain – and the men who wrote and drew them. An informative and funny coverage of the subject. [FMS]

Featuring: Lynda Barry, Charles Burns, Sue Coe, Robert Crumb, Will Eisner, Al Feldstein, Shary Flenniken, W. M. Gaines, Bill Griffith, Jaime Hernandez, Jack Kirby, Harvey Kurtzman, Stan Lee, Paul Mavrides, Frank Miller, Victory Moscoso, Francoise Mouly, Dan O'Neill, Harvey Pekar, Gilbert Shelton and Art Spiegelman. Dir: Ron Mann. (ICA). Rel: floating; first shown London (ICA) 8 December 1989. 90 mins. No cert.

Conquest of the South Pole. Off-the-wall, visually striking independent Scottish film about five out-of-work Edinburgh men who decide to re-create Roald Amundsen's expedition to the South Pole. Unfortunately, confined as they are to the port of Leith, they are forced to supply unlimited amounts of imagination, although the penguins and huskies they acquire do help. Low on

Imagination triumphs over poverty in the BFI's surprising and original Conquest of the South Pole.

Blood and cuisine: Helen Mirren and Michael Gambon as the gangster and his missus in Peter Greenaway's extraordinary The Cook, the Thief, His Wife & Her Lover *(Palace).*

budget, high on humour and originality. Filmed on location in the rotting docklands of Leith, Edinburgh. [CB]

Cast includes: Stevan Rimkus (Sloopianek), Laura Girling (Louise), Leonard O'Malley (Butcher), Gordon Cameron (Brown), Ewen Bremner (Penguin), Alastair Galbraith (Frankieboy), John Michie (Roddy), Julie-Kate Olivier (Rosie). Dir: Gillies MacKinnon. Pro: Gareth Wardell. Ex Pro: John Kelleher. Screenplay: Wardell; based on the stage play by Manfred Karge. Ph: Sean Van Hales. Art: Andrew Harris. M: Guy Woolfenden. (Jam Jar Films/Film Four International–BFI.) Rel: floating; first shown London (Electric, Notting Hill) 16 March 1990. 90 mins. Cert 12.

The Cook, the Thief, His Wife & Her Lover. A challenging, astounding and outstanding piece of cinema, a kind of twentieth-century Jacobean tragedy. A monstrous *nouveau riche* rogue owns a fashionable restaurant, The Hollandais, where he dines every night surrounded by his sickly yes-men. There, the Thief expounds on the virtues of good food and *la dolce vita* while insulting everyone and everything around him. His Wife falls in love with a fellow diner, a civilised bibliophile, and seduces him regularly between courses – in the loo, the kitchen, the pantry, and so on. The Cook – a Frenchman, *naturellement* – becomes host to the deceit, protecting the couple from the wandering eye of

Crooks and cookies: Peter Falk and Emily Lloyd pose for the policeman's camera in the Warner release, Cookie, *directed by Susan Seidelman.*

Her Husband. After exploring the alphabet in *A Zed and Two Noughts*, and numerals in *Drowning by Numbers*, director Peter Greenaway vents his creative juices on the corporeal, examining a world made up of food and drink, waste matter and urine, carnality, flatulence, vomit, nudity, blood and decomposition – you name it. A stylish and eloquent, certainly repellent, but unforgettable and magnificent attack on all our sacred cows. Witness it at your peril – you may never be the same again. [JC-W]

Cast includes: Richard Bohringer (Richard, the Cook), Michael Gambon (Albert, the Thief), Helen Mirren (Georgina, his Wife), Alan Howard (Michael, her Lover), Tim Roth (Mitchel), Liz Smith (Grace), Ciaran Hinds, Gary Olsen, Ewan Stewart, Roger Ashton Griffiths, Ron Cook, Emer Gillespie, Janet Henfrey, Ian Sears, Ian Dury, Diane Langton, Roger Lloyd Pack. Dir and Screenplay: Peter Greenaway. Pro: Kees Kasander. Co-Pro: Pascal Dauman and Daniel Toscan du Plantier. Ph: Sacha Vierny. Ed: John Wilson. Pro Des: Ben Van Os and Jan Roelfs. M: Michael Nyman. Costumes: Jean-Paul Gaultier. Sound: Garth Marshall. (Allarts Cook/Erato Films/Films Inc.–Palace.) Rel: 13 October 1989. 120 mins. Cert 18.

Cookie. Amiable Mafia comedy from Susan Seidelman, who seems to have a thing about wacky, zany female characters. First it was Madonna in *Desperately Seeking Susan*, then Ann Magnuson in *Making Mr Right*. Here, our very own Emily Lloyd (complete with a passable Brooklyn accent) plays the wacky, zany (of course) daughter of a New York mobster (Peter Falk), becoming his chauffeuress and then his consultant in the ways of gang warfare ethics. Ms Lloyd is a delight and Falk is alright, but Dianne Wiest, as Cookie's mother, is disastrously over-the-top-and-out-of-the-skylight. [JC-W]

Cast includes: Peter Falk (Dino), Dianne Wiest (Lenore), Emily Lloyd (Carmela Maria Angelina Theresa Voltecki, *alias* Cookie), Michael V. Gazzo, Brenda Vaccaro, Adrian Pasdar, Jerry Lewis, Lionel Stander, Bob Gunton, Ben Rayson, Ricki Lake, Joe Mantello, Thomas Quinn, David Wohl, Joy Behar, Frank Gio, Rockets Redglare, Crystal Field. Dir: Susan Seidelman. Pro: Laurence Mark. Co-Pro: Jennifer Ogden. Ex Pro: Seidelman, Nora Ephron and Alice Arlen. Screenplay: Ephron and Arlen. Ph: Oliver Stapleton. Ed: Andrew Mondshein. Pro Des: Michael Haller. M: Thomas Newman; songs performed by The Four Aces, Barry White, Transvision Vamp, The Primitives, Jimmy Dorsey & His Orchestra, Kylie Minogue, etc. Costumes: Albert Wolsky. Sound: Tod Maitland. (Lorimar–Warner.) Rel: 6 October 1989. 93 mins. Cert 15.

Courage Mountain. Charlie Sheen and Leslie Caron together at last – in a *Heidi* update! Actually, this international co-production is not as bad as it sounds, although Sheen as a pipe-playing goatherd has to be seen to be believed. In this story by Fred and Mark Brogger – based on the characters created by Johanna Spyri in 1831 – Heidi is 14 and comes into a large inheritance. She decides to spend her money on a 'smart' education in Northern Italy, but because of the war (WWI) ends up in a Dickensian orphanage instead. It is up to Sheen, the lonely goatherd, to rescue her. Engaging family entertainment, *Courage Mountain* (what does *that* mean?) is beautifully shot, aided by lush music and a winning performance from Juliette Caton (the angel in Scorsese's *The Last Temptation of Christ*) as Heidi. Young children should love it. [JC-W]

Also with: Charlie Sheen (Peter), Leslie Caron (Jane Hillary), Jan Rubes (grandfather), Yorgo Voyagis (Bonelli), Laura Betti (Signora Bonelli), Joanna Clarke (Ursula), Nicola Stapleton, Kathryn Ludlow, Jade Magri. Dir: Christopher Leitch. Pro: Stephen Ujlaki. Ex Pro: Joel A. Douglas. Screenplay: Weaver Webb; from a story by Fred and Mark Brogger. Ph: Jacques Steyn. Ed: Martin Walsh. Pro Des: Robb Wilson King. M: Sylvester Levay. Sound: Bernard Bats. (Epic Prods/Stone Group/France–Entertainment). Rel: 6 April 1990. 98 mins. Cert U.

Cousins. Those who didn't have the considerable pleasure of seeing the original French film *Cousin, Cousine* (released in Britain in late 1975 and noted in the 1977–8 *Film Review* as 'Delightful . . . something of a throwback to the vintage years of the French cinema') will undoubtedly find the Americanised remake charming and amusing enough, retaining at least the original premise that love can become a powerful enough force to override all family and moral obligations. The film also retains some of the wit and some of the ironic tone of the original, though too often subtlety has been replaced by vulgarity. Performances, as with the original, are faultless. Forgetting, or missing, *Cousin, Cousine*, you'll find this a pleasing and old-fashionedly amusing comedy. [FMS]

Cast: Ted Danson (very good as Larry), Isabella Rossellini (charming as Maria), Sean Young (Tish), William Petersen (Tom), Lloyd Bridges (Uncle Vince), Norma Aleandro (Edie), Keith Coogan (Mitch), Gina DeAngelis (Aunt Sofia), George Coe (Phil), Katie Murray, Alex Bruhanski, Stephen E. Miller, Gerry Bean, Gordon Currie, Saffron Henderson, Michelle Goodger, Andrea Mann, Mark Frank, Leroy Schultz, Gloria Harris, John Civitarese, Kate Danson, David and John Hurwitz. Dir: Joel Schumacher. Pro: William Allyn. Ex Pro: George Goodman. Screenplay: Stephen Metcalfe; based on the French film written and directed by Jean-Charles Tacchella. Ph: Ralf Bode. Ed: Robert Brown. Pro Des: Mark S. Freeborn. M: Angelo Badalamenti. (Paramount–UIP.) Rel: 8 September 1989. 113 mins. Cert 15.

Creator. California, 1985. Rather touching, eager-to-please romantic comedy set in the world of science. Peter O'Toole plays Harry Wolper, an eccentric, cigar-chewing biologist who is still in love with his wife 30 years after her death. He is working on a clandestine project to reproduce her through the culture of her living cells – but real life keeps getting in his way. Although he had been awarded the Nobel Prize for his work, it is Harry's passion for living that is his greatest gift. Filmed in '85. [JC-W]

Also with: Mariel Hemingway (Meli), Vincent Spano (Boris), Virginia Madsen (Barbara), David Ogden Stiers (Sid), John Dehner (Paul), Karen Kopins, Kenneth Tigar, Elsa Raven, Lee Kessler, Rance Howard, Ellen Geer, Anthony Peck, Jeff Corey. Dir: Ivan Passer. Pro: Stephen Friedman. Screenplay: Jeremy Leven; based on his novel of the same name. Ph: Robbie Greenberg. Ed: Richard Chew. Art: Josan F. Russo. M: Sylvester Levay. Costumes:

Julie Weiss. Sound: Jeff Wexler. (Kings Road–Entertainment.) Rel: floating; first shown London (The Mezzanine) 8 June 1990. 108 mins. Cert 15.

Crusoe. This screen version of the Defoe classic tale has undergone some startling changes. It is still about a man

Cousins Larry and Maria (Ted Danson and Isabella Rossellini) just can't help what they feel for each other, despite both being married, in UIP's Cousins, *a remake of the French comedy* Cousin, Cousine.

Love and eternity among the test-tubes for Mariel Hemingway and Peter O'Toole in Ivan Passer's warm-hearted Creator, *from Entertainment.*

Ted Danson and Jack Lemmon wring our heartstrings in UIP's Dad.

shipwrecked and alone on a desert island who has to adapt to his new circumstances, but now he's a slave trader and his Man Friday, when he arrives, is anything but the compliant servant that Defoe made him. The story has also acquired a greater racial and psychological complexity, and there's more action, too. So forget Defoe, and enjoy this well-directed actioner shot against idyllic desert island backgrounds. For the record, previous versions I can recall include Buñuel's Mexican film in 1952, *Robinson Crusoe of Mystery Island* in 1936 and even *Robinson Crusoe on Mars* in 1964. [FMS]

Cast: Aidan Quinn (Crusoe), Ade Sapara (warrior), Elvis Payne (runaway slave), Richard Sharp (Colcol), Colin Bruce (clerk), William Hootkins (auctioneer), Shane Rimmer (Mr Mather). Dir: Caleb Deschanel. Pro: Andrew Braunsberg. Screenplay: Walon Green. Ph: Tom Pinter. Pro Des: Velco Despotovic. Art: Nemanja Petrovic. M: Michael Kamen. Assoc Pro: Peter Sobajic. (Island Pictures–Virgin Vision.) Rel: floating; first shown London (Cannon,

Tottenham Ct Rd) 11 August 1989. 95 mins. Cert 15.

Dad. Jake Tremont (Jack Lemmon) is a retired 78-year-old man who has succumbed to old age. He has become totally reliant on his wife and depends on her for the simplest actions of day-to-day life. However, when Mrs Tremont goes into hospital after suffering a heart attack, he is left to the ministrations of his son John, a successful business executive. Ted Danson, as the son, can also claim the title role as a father in his own right, a good provider, but a man who has lost contact with the meaning of family. No surprises here, but if you like old-fashioned tales of family commitment and domestic friction, this is as polished and heartfelt as it gets. Not quite *Ordinary People*, but you'll probably need a Kleenex or two. Written and directed by Gary David Goldberg, creator of TV's *Family Ties*. [JC-W]

Also with: Olympia Dukakis (Bette Tremont), Kathy Baker (Annie), Kevin Spacey (Mario), Ethan Hawke (Billy), Zakes Mokae (Dr Chad), J. T. Walsh, Peter Michael

Goetz, John Apicella, Art Frankel, Chris Lemmon, Gina Raymond, Lewis Arquette (voice only). Dir and Screenplay: Gary David Goldberg; based on the novel by William Wharton. Pro: Joseph Stern and Gary David Goldberg. Ex Pro: Steven Spielberg, Frank Marshall and Kathleen Kennedy. Ph: Jan Kiesser. Ed: Eric Sears. Pro Des: Jack DeGovia. M: James Horner. Costumes:

Claire Hackett as an independent Liverpudlian struggling to escape the shackles of her upbringing in Willy Russell's triumphant Dancin' Thru the Dark *(Palace).*

Samuel Irons, son of Jeremy, in Portobello Productions' enchanting Danny The Champion of the World, *from the story by Roald Dahl.*

Molly Maginnis. Sound: Ron Judkins. (Amblin/Universal–UIP.) Rel: 23 February 1990. 118 mins. Cert PG.

Dancin' Thru the Dark. With this, his third screenplay, Willy Russell once again examines the depressed working-class heroine stuggling to escape the shackles of her environment (Liverpool). On the night before her wedding, Linda and her wisecracking girl-friends go to Bransky's (fictitious) nightclub to drink and dance the night away. Unfortunately, drunken fiancé Dave and the boys turn up, not to mention Linda's former boy-friend, now a London-based, chart-bound rock singer. Linda, dancing in the dark, is forced to decide between the inevitable drudgery of tomorrow or the prospect of a new life with a glamorous defector. Again, Willy Russell pits humour against the battlements of moral dilemma and comes up laughing. It is ironic, then, that Russell himself remains firmly rooted in Liverpool, achieving the impossible by exploiting his landscape rather than deserting it. If only London could boast a cinematic force so vibrant and loyal. [JC-W]

Cast includes: Claire Hackett (Linda), Con O'Neill (Peter), Simon O'Brien (Kav), Angela Clarke (Maureen), Julia Deakin (Bernadette), Mark Womack (Eddie), Conrad Nelson (Dave), Louise Duprey (Frances), Andrew Naylor (Billy), Sandy Hendrickse (Carol), Peter Watts (Robbie), Colin Welland (Bransky's manager), Peter Beckett, Julian Littman, Ben Murphy, Willy Russell (drunk in pub). Dir: Mike Ockrent. Pro: Andree Molyneux and Annie Russell. Ex Pro: Richard Broke, Chris Brown, Charles Negus-Fancey, Nik Powell and Steve Woolley. Prod Ex: Christopher Cameron. Screenplay: Willy Russell; from his play *Stags and Hens*. Ph: Philip Bonham-Carter. Ed: John Stothart. Pro Des: Paul Joel. M: Willy Russell; songs performed by Ruby Turner, Con O'Neill, Billy Ocean, The She Rockers, etc. Costumes: Laura Ergis. Sound: Peter Edwards (Palace/British Screen/BBC/Formost Films–Palace.) Rel: 2 March 1990. 95 mins. Cert 15.

Danny The Champion of the World. Charmingly unpretentious Roald Dahl story set 'somewhere in England' in 1955. William Smith (Jeremy Irons) leads a peaceful existence working at his garage and living in a caravan with his 9-year-old son Danny (Samuel Irons). But this peaceful idyll is shattered when the vulgar, stinking rich and terribly fat landowner Victor Hazell (Robbie Coltrane) attempts to buy him out. With the help of Danny, William holds his ground and plays Hazell at his own game. A gentle, enjoyable British comedy that should please all ages. [JC-W]

Also with: Cyril Cusack (Doc Spencer), Lionel Jeffries (Mr Snoddy), Ronald Pickup (Captain Lancaster), Jean Marsh (Miss Hunter), Jimmy Nail, William Armstrong, Michael Hordern, John Woodvine, Andrew Maclachlan, Jonathan Adams, James Walker, John Grillo. Dir: Gavin Millar. Pro: Eric Abraham. Co-Pro: Robin Douet. Screenplay: John Goldsmith; from the book by Roald Dahl. Ph: Oliver Stapleton. Ed: Peter Tanner and Angus Newton. Pro Des: Don Homfray. M: Stanley Myers. Costumes: Anne Sinclair. Sound: Tony Jackson. (Portobello Pro. in assoc. with Thames Television, British Screen, etc. – Portobello Pro.) Rel: 28 July 1989. 98 mins. Cert U.

In deep water: Nicole Kidman in Phillip Noyce's excellent nautical thriller, Dead Calm *(Warner).*

Dead Calm. Stylish, heart-stopping and virtually wordless Australian thriller set in the middle of the Pacific – *where there's no one to help*. Nicole Kidman, a young Australian Sigourney Weaver, confronts the charms and mercuriality of Billy Zane, a young Brando, aboard an eighty-foot ketch. Meanwhile, Kidman's husband – Sam Neill – is trapped below the deck of a sinking ship full of dead bodies. Thrillers of this calibre are few and far between. [JC-W]

Cast includes: Sam Neill (John Ingram), Nicole Kidman (Rae Ingram), Billy Zane (Hughie Warriner), Rod Mullinar, Joshua Tilden, George Shevtsov, Michael Long, Benji U. D. A. D. (the dog). Dir: Phillip Noyce. Pro: Terry Hayes, Doug Mitchell and George Miller. Screenplay: Terry Hayes; based on the novel by Charles Williams. Ph: Dean Semler. Ed: Richard Fran-cis-Bruce. Pro Des: Graham 'Grace' Walker. M: Graeme Revell; songs performed by Tim O'Connor, The Tokens, SPK. Costumes: Norma Moriceau. Sound: Ben Osmo, Lee Smith. (Kennedy-Miller–Warner.) Rel: 3 November 1989. 95 mins. Cert 15.

Dead Poets Society. A life-enhancing, cliché-devoid drama starring Robin Williams as an English professor at a Vermont high school. An unorthodox teacher of poetry, John Keating (Williams) instils a zest for verse and living in his strait-laced students, ultimately leading to tragedy. Williams has never been better, whether caricaturing John Wayne as Macbeth or handling the film's quieter, more dramatic moments. Amazingly a Disney production, this masterpiece defies Hollywood convention and is all the better for it. The acting is top-drawer across the board (introducing a roster of promising faces), matched by superb lighting and bravura direction. [JC-W]

Also with: Robert Sean Leonard (Neil Parry), Ethan Hawke (Todd Anderson), Josh Charles (Knox Overstreet), Gale Hansen (Charlie Dalton), Dylan Kussman (Richard Cameron), Allelon Ruggiero (Steven Meeks), James Waterston (Gerard Pitts), Norman Lloyd, Kurtwood Smith, Carla Belver, Leon Pownall, George Martin, John Cunningham, Debra Mooney, James Donnell Quinn. Dir: Peter Weir. Pro: Steven Haft, Paul Junger Witt and Tony Thomas. Assoc Pro: Duncan Henderson. Screenplay: Tom Schulman. Ph: John Seale. Ed: William Anderson. Pro Des: Wendy Stites. M: Maurice Jarre; Handel, Beethoven, etc. Sound: Charles Wilborn. (Touchstone/Silver Screen Partners–Touchstone/Warner.) Rel: 22 September 1989. 129 mins. Cert PG.

Dealers. A superficial, unconvincing but fairly engrossing drama set in the cut-throat, cut-glass world of high finance and stock market trading. A sort of English *Wall Street*, the film stars Paul McGann as a ruthless trader who teams up with a beautiful American (Rebecca DeMornay), to help turn around their bank's £100 million deficit. Italian cars, Soho restaurants and easy women swarm across the plot to jazz up this upmarket TV soap opera. If only the stock market was this predictable. [JC-W]

Cast includes: Paul McGann (Daniel Pascoe), Rebecca DeMornay (Anna Schuman), Derrick O'Connor (Robby Barrell), John Castle (Frank Mallory), Paul Guilfoyle (Lee Peters), Rosalind Bennett (Bonnie), Adrian Dunbar, Nicholas Hewetson, Sara Sugarman, Dikran Tulaine, Annabel Brooks, Paul Stacey, Beverley Hills. Dir: Colin Bucksey. Pro: William P. Cartlidge. Ex Pro: Andrew Brown and John Hambley. Screenplay: Andrew MacLear. Ph: Peter Sinclair. Ed: Jon Costelloe. Pro Des: Peter J. Hampton. M: Richard Hartley. Costumes: Dizzy Downs. Sound: Richard Dunford. (Euston Films–Rank). Rel: 22 September 1989. 91 mins. Cert 15.

The Decline of Western Civilisation: Part 2, The Metal Years. A documentary *strictly* for fans of Heavy Metal! *Variety* put it in a nutshell: 'Documentarian director Penelope Spheeris takes a hard-edged look at heavy metal rock and stuff like that. To her credit, she tries to tackle a mindless subject with intelligence and stuff like that.' Sadly, intelligence isn't enough with material like this. [FMS]

With Joe Perry and Steven Tyler (of Aerosmith), Gene Simmons and Paul Stanley (of Kiss), Alice Cooper, Lemmy (of Motorhead), Ozzy Osbourne, C. C. Deville, Bobby Dall, Bret Michaels and Rikki Rockett (of Poison), Bill Gazzarri, Chris Holmes, Tawn Mastrey, Darlyne Pettinicchio, Lizzy Borden, and other groups like Faster Pussycat, Seduce, Odin, London and Megadeth. Dir: Penelope Spheeris. Pro: Jonathan Dayton and Valerie Faris. Assoc Pro: Guy Louthan. Ex Pro: Miles Copeland III and Paul Colichman. Ex in charge of Pro: Daniel Raskov. Ph: Jeff Zimmerman. Ed: Earl Ghaffari. M Sup: Seth Kaplan for OSS. (New Line Cinema/IRS World Media Pro--Palace Pictures.) Rel: floating; first shown London (ICA) 11 August 1989. 90 mins. Cert 15.

Deep Star Six. Underwater no one can hear you scream . . . Deep Star Six is a secret undersea laboratory six miles beneath the ocean's surface. There, eleven men and women fight for their lives as an unknown creature attacks

their base. Crossing Jules Verne with *Alien*, the film is a complex, suspenseful thriller that successfully exploits man's fascination with the deep. The scene in which Snyder (Miguel Ferrer, son of Jose) dies from decompression should

Robin Williams as John Keating, the English teacher with a difference in Peter Weir's superb Dead Poets Society *(Warner).*

Paul McGann and Rebecca DeMornay shake up the stock market in Rank's glitzy, shallow Dealers.

Marius Weyers and Miguel Ferrer hunt for the unknown in Guild's Deep Star Six.

stick in your wildest nightmares. (And compare *The Abyss*.) [JC-W]

Also with: Nancy Everhard (Joyce Collins), Greg Evigan (McBride), Nia Peeples (Scarpelli), Matt McCoy (Richardson), Cindy Pickett (Diane Norris), Marius Weyers (Van Gelder), Taurean Blacque, Elya Baskin, Thom Bray, Ronn Carroll. Dir and (with Patrick Markey) Pro: Sean S. Cunningham. Screenplay: Lewis Abernathy and Geoff Miller; from a story by Abernathy. Ph: Mac Ahlberg. Ed: David Handman. Pro Des: John Reinhart. M: Harry Manfredini. Sound: Hans Roland. (Carolco–Guild.) Rel: 1 December 1989. 99 mins. Cert 15.

The Delinquents. It's not often that a really famous actress makes her film debut in a starring role, and Kylie Minogue doesn't disappoint her fans in a meaty part tailor-made for the adolescent market. A ten-handkerchief tearjerker, *The Delinquents* (based on a

Kylie Minogue and Charlie Schlatter share a rare moment of tranquillity in Kylie's big film debut, The Delinquents *(Warner).*

novel by Pat Cash's aunt) is a classy Mills & Boon romance set in Australia, 1957. Minogue and American Charlie Schlatter play the star-crossed lovers in a world hostile to ideal romance, a society forever separating the couple for bureaucratic and pig-headed reasons. Kylie shows she has talent to burn, Schlatter is likeable in an underwritten part, and the period detail is never forced. We've seen it all before, but the tale is an engaging and credible one, albeit aimed squarely at the proverbial lump in the throat. [JC-W]

Cast includes: Kylie Minogue (Lola), Charlie Schlatter (Brownie), Angela Punch McGregor (Mrs Lovell), Bruno Lawrence (Bosun), Todd Boyce (Lyle), Desireé Smith (Mavis), Melissa Jaffer (Aunt Westbury), Lynette Curran, Lyn Treadgold, Duncan Wass, Rosemary Harris, Yvonne Hopper, Christine Long. Dir: Chris Thomson. Pro: Alex Cutler and Mike Wilcox. Ex Pro: Graham Burke, Greg Coote and John Tarnoff. Screenplay: Clayton Frohman and Mac Gudgeon; based on the novel by Criena Rohan. Ph: Andrew Lesnie. Ed: John Scott. Pro Des: Laurence Eastwood. M: Miles Goodman; songs performed by Gene Vincent, Eddie Cochran, Jerry Lee Lewis, Little Richard, Fats Domino, The Platters, Dinah Shore, Kylie Minogue, etc. Costumes: Bruce Finlayson. Sound: Paul Brincat. (Village Roadshow–Warner.) Rel: 26 December 1989. 103 mins. Cert 12.

Diamond Skulls. Lifeless thriller about a brooding aristocrat guilty of running down a pedestrian and not reporting the accident. His tight circle of protective, loyal retainers close in to shield his name, unaware that m'lord has other things on his mind. A notable cast struggle with their empty characters in this ill-judged attack on the upper classes. [JC-W]

Cast includes: Gabriel Byrne (Lord Hugo Buckton), Amanda Donohoe (Lady 'Ginny' Buckton), Michael Hordern (Lord Crewne), Judy Parfitt (Lady Crewne), Struan Rodger (Peter), Douglas Hodge (Jamie), Matthew Marsh (Raul), Sadie Frost (Rebecca), Peter Sands, Ralph Brown, Ian Carmichael, William Hoyland, Emma Boulting, Peter Allen. Dir: Nick Broomfield. Pro: Tim Bevan. Screenplay: Tim Rose Price. Ph: Michael Coulter. Ed: Rodney Holland. Pro Des: Jocelyn James. M: Hans Zimmer. Sound: John Midgley. (Film Four/British Screen/Working Title–Virgin Vision.) Rel: 8 June 1990. 87 mins. Cert 18.

Dick Tracy is arguably the most proficient translation to screen of a comic

The clean-cut superstar as infallible comic strip hero: Warren Beatty as Dick Tracy *lectures The Kid (Charlie Korsmo) – or is he just directing the 38th take? And Al Pacino as Big Boy Caprice.*

strip yet, complete with animated backdrops and grotesquely made-up villains. Warren Beatty stars (and directs) as the square-jawed dick battling crime lord Big Boy Caprice (an unrecognisable, over-the-top and tiresome Al Pacino). Glenne Headley (replacing Sean Young at the last minute) co-stars as Dick's dame Tess Trueheart, but Madonna as Breathless Mahoney hots up the action with lashings of sexual innuendo and revealing costumes. There's plenty to go round, with the added attraction of cameos from Dustin Hoffman, James Caan and Dick Van Dyke, but somehow Dick Tracy suffers from its own overkill. The characters are caricatures, the plot is familiar and the slam-bang action ultimately numbing. Enjoy the trailer. [JC-W]

Also with: Charlie Korsmo (The Kid/Dick Tracy Jr), Dustin Hoffman (Mumbles/Robert Evans), William Forsythe (Flattop),

Charles Durning (Chief Brandon), Mandy Patinkin (88 Keys), Paul Sorvino (Lips Manlis), Dick Van Dyke (DA Fletcher), R. G. Armstrong (Pruneface), Stig Eldred, Ed O'Ross, Seymour Cassel, Allen Garfield, John Schuck, Charles Fleischer, Jack Kehoe, Marshall Bell, Tom Signorelli, James Tolkan, Kathy Bates, Hamilton Camp, Catherine O'Hara, Henry Silva, James Caan, Bert Remsen, Frank Campanella, Bing Russell, Michael J. Pollard, Estelle Parsons, Ian Wolfe, Mary Woronov, Henry Jones. Dir and Pro: Warren Beatty. Ex Pro: Barrie M. Osborne, Art Linson and Floyd Mutrux. Screenplay: Jim Cash and Jack Epps Jr; based on characters created

35

by Chester Gould. Ph: Vittorio Storaro. Ed: Richard Marks. Pro Des: Richard Sylbert. M: Danny Elfman; original songs by Stephen Sondheim. Costumes: Milena Canonero. Sound: Dennis Drummond. Special character make-up: John Caglione Jr and Doug Drexler. (Touchstone/Silver Screen Partners–Warner.) Rel: 6 July 1990. 103 mins. Cert PG.

Directed by Andrei Tarkovsky. An outstanding documentary made by Michael Leszczylowski (Tarkovsky's co-editor on *The Sacrifice*), for which the assistant cameraman shot some 50 hours of video. Extracts from TV interviews, readings from Tarkovsky's book *Sculpting in Time* and his notebooks, plus an interview with his widow, add up to a searching portrait of the director and his ideas about both film and life. An important record for posterity of Tarkovsky's methods of working and his philosophy, this documentary is far more enthralling than many feature films. [FMS]

Michael Keaton, Stephen Furst, Christopher Lloyd and Peter Boyle as an odd quartet, dreaming on in Howard Zieff's feisty The Dream Team *(UIP).*

Reading voice: Erland Josephson. Narrator: Brian Cox. Dir and Screenplay: Michal Leszczylowski. Pro: Lisbet Gabrielson. Ph: Arne Carlsson. Ed: Leszczylowski and Lasse Summanen. (SFI Pro/Swedish Film Institute–Artificial Eye.) Rel: floating; first shown London (Renoir) 14 July 1989. 101 mins. Cert 15.

The Dream Team. Four mental patients are stranded in New York City when their therapist disappears after becoming the sole witness to a murder (carried out by a pair of cops). His patients ('the veggies') hate each others' guts but strive to pull themselves together to rescue the good doctor and to save the day. Along the way – through a world far crazier than they are – they come to recognise a new sanity in themselves. As is to be expected from Ron Howard's Imagine Entertainment, *The Dream Team* has a lot of heart and a ballparkful of good intentions, plus a decent story to hang it all on. Michael Keaton is back to his engaging self as a likeable but violent loony, with a stronger grip on reality than on sanity (think about it), while the other patients – Christopher Lloyd,

Peter Boyle, Stephen Furst – are all given their star turns. The supporting cast is likewise top-notch, with Lorraine Bracco particularly effective as Keaton's girl-friend of yore. [JC-W]

Cast includes: Michael Keaton (Billy Caulfield), Christopher Lloyd (Henry Sikorsky), Peter Boyle (Jack McDermott), Stephen Furst (Albert Ianuzzi), Lorraine Bracco (Riley), Dennis Boutsikaris (Dr Weitzman), Milo O'Shea (Dr Newald), Philip Bosco (O'Malley), James Remar (Gianelli), Lizbeth MacKay (Henry's wife), Jack Gilpin, Macintyre Dixon, Michael Lembeck, Brad Sullivan, Larry Pine, Harold Surratt, Robert Weil, Janet Feindel, James O'Regan, Shelley Goldstein. Dir: Howard Zieff. Pro: Christopher W. Knight. Ex Pro: Joseph M. Caracciolo. Screenplay: Jon Connolly and David Loucka. Ph: Adam Holender. Ed: C. Timothy O'Meara. Pro Des: Todd Hallowell. M: David McHugh; songs performed by Buster Poindexter, Was Not Was, UB40, Ray Charles, The Frierson Family Singers. Costumes: Ruth Morley. Sound: Fred J. Brown. (Imagine/Universal –UIP.) Rel: 15 December 1989. 113 mins. Cert 15.

Dreams. Everything Steven Spielberg touches does not turn to gold, and his

production of Akira Kurosawa's octet of short vignettes is both uneven and overlong. However, there is plenty of magic to be found in the 81-year-old director's 28th film, not least a surreal wedding march of foxes. Unfortunately, some of the episodes are drenched in apocalyptic doom, clouding the visual mastery of the whole film. Special effects were supplied by George Lucas's Industrial Light & Magic. [CB]

Cast includes: Akira Terao (I), Mitsunori Isaki (I as a boy), Martin Scorsese (Van Gogh), Chishu Ryu (old man), Mieko Harada (Snow Fairy), Mitsuko Baisho (Mother), Chosuke Ikariya, Hisahi Igawa, Toshihiko Nakano. Dir and Screenplay: Akira Kurosawa. Pro: Hisao Kurosawa. Ex Pro: Steven Spielberg. Ph: Takao Saito. Ed: Tome Minami. Art: Yoshiro Muraki and Akira Sakuragi. M: Shinichiro Ikebe. Costumes: Emi Wada. Sound: Kenichi Benitani. (Warner.) Selected release: 25 May 1990. 120 mins. Cert PG.

Driving Me Crazy. Documentary about the efforts of a film crew to put on record a rehearsal of a new black music stage show due to be staged in Germany. Everything goes wrong as the whole thing sinks into chaos. Amusing in places, but not quite as funny as was intended. [FMS]

Those concerned: singers; Clent Bowers, Carol Dennis, Barbara Mills, Claire Bathe: dancers include; Gerard Alexander, Lathaniel Cooper, Randy Davis, Charles Epps, etc: band; Linda Twine, Eddie Alex, Steve Furtado, Tommy McKenzie. Dir: Nicholas Broomfield. Pro: Andrew Braunsberg. Ph: Robert Levi. Ed: John Mister. Co-Pro: Steve Menkin. Lighting Des: Michael Lesser. (Virgin/VCL Communications in assoc. with Telemunchen.) Rel: floating; first shown London (ICA) 13 October 1989. 87 mins. Cert 15.

Driving Miss Daisy. Atlanta, Georgia; 1948–73. Enchanting, sensitive screen adaptation of Alfred Uhry's celebrated Pulitzer Prize-winning play loosely based on the relationship between the playwright's grandmother and her black chauffeur. Jessica Tandy and Morgan Freeman prove perfect casting as the crotchety Jewish eccentric and her dignified yet humble companion, and never – not for an instant – do they succumb to caricature. The film, shot on a relatively modest budget, was a huge financial success, proving that audiences are prepared to fork out for

Jessica Tandy, with Morgan Freeman as her trusty chauffeur and companion, in Bruce Beresford's Driving Miss Daisy *(Warner).*

a production without special effects and violence – if the material is good enough. A sheer joy from beginning to end. Winner of four Oscars, for Best Picture, Best Actress, Screenplay Adaptation and Make-up. [JC-W]

Cast includes: Morgan Freeman (Hoke Colburn), Jessica Tandy (Daisy Werthan), Dan Aykroyd (Boolie Werthan), Patti Lupone (Florine Werthan), Esther Rolle (Idella), Joann Havrilla, William Hall Jr, Alvin M. Sugarman, Crystal R. Fox, Bob Hannah. Dir: Bruce Beresford. Pro: Richard D. Zanuck and Lili Fini Zanuck. Ex Pro: David Brown. Co-Ex Pro: Jake Eberts. Screenplay: Alfred Uhry; from his own play. Ph: Peter James. Ed: Mark Warner. Pro Des: Bruno Rubeo. M: Hans Zimmer; songs performed by Ella Fitzgerald, Louis Armstrong, Eartha Kitt, etc. Costumes: Elizabeth McBride. Sound: Hank Garfield. Make-up: Manlio Rocchetti, Lynn Barber and Kevin Haney. (Warner.) Rel: 23 February 1990. 99 mins. Cert U.

Drugstore Cowboy. Portland, Oregon, 1971. Idiosyncratic, darkly humorous drama about a crew of 'pharmacy busters' – four dope fiends who prey on drugstores to feed their habit and to make a fast buck. 'But don't get the idea that it was easy,' Matt Dillon explains in his voice-over narrative; 'being a dope fiend was hard work.' Some nice glimpses of period detail (not

Drugged on crime: Matt Dillon and Kelly Lynch cruise in the fast lane in Virgin Vision's notable Drugstore Cowboy.

too forced) and laid-back performances take the hard edge off the more realistic drug-taking sequences. And the scene in which Dillon has to extricate a corpse from his hotel during a sheriffs' convention is almost hilarious. [JC-W]

Cast includes: Matt Dillon (Bob), Kelly Lynch (Dianne), James Le Gros (Rick), Heather Graham (Nadine), Max Perlich (David), James Remar (Gentry), Beah Richards (drug counsellor), William S. Burroughs (Tom the priest), Grace Zabriskie, Janet Baumhover, Neal Thomas, Stephen Rutledge, Ray Monge. Dir and (with Daniel Yost) Screenplay: Gus Van Sant Jr. Pro: Nick Wechsler and Karen Murphy. Ex Pro: Cary Brokaw. From the novel by James Fogle. Ph: Robert Yeoman. Ed: Curtiss Clayton. Pro Des: David Brisbin. M: Elliot Goldenthal. Costumes: Beatrix Aruna Pasztor. Sound: Ron Judkins. (Avenue–Virgin.) Rel: 8 December 1989. 100 mins. Cert 18.

A Dry White Season. Well-written, truthfully played adaptation of Andre Brink's banned book about a white man's involvement in South African racism. Donald Sutherland, in a thankfully restrained performance, stars as Ben du Toit, a wealthy Afrikaner schoolteacher whose Shangri-la comes tumbling down when he investigates the suspicious suicide of his gardener (Winston Ntshona). Marlon Brando shanghais the acting honours as an enormous, eccentric lawyer who warns du Toit that 'justice and law are distant cousins, not on speaking terms at all' – a performance of extraordinary self-indulgence in an otherwise straight-faced political tract. Colin Welland's majestic screenplay stings in all the right places, while Euzhan Palcy's direction is for the most part unclut-tered by Hollywood melodrama. Only the last few minutes descend into a genre at odds with the film's spirit. [JC-W]

Also with: Janet Suzman (Susan du Toit), Zakes Mokae (Stanley), Jurgen Prochnow (Captain Stolz), Susan Sarandon (Melanie), Winston Ntshona (Gordon), Marlon Brando (McKenzie), Thoko Ntshinga, Gerard Thoolen, Susannah Harker, Rowen Elmes, David DeKeyser, John Kani, Richard Wilson, Michael Gambon, Ronald Pickup, Paul Brook, Rosemary Martin. Dir (and with Colin Welland) Screenplay: Euzhan Palcy. Pro: Paula Weinstein. Ex Pro: Tim Hampton. Based on the novel by Andre Brink. Ph: Kelvin Pike and Pierre-William Glenn. Ed: Sam O'Steen and Glenn Cun-ningham. Pro Des: John Fenner. M: Dave Grusin; songs performed by Ladysmith Black Mambazo and the cast of *Sarafina*; featured score performance by Hugh Mase-kela. Sound: Roy Charman. (Star Partners II/MGM–UIP.) Rel: 19 January 1990. 107 mins. Cert 15.

Dust in the Wind – Lianlian Fengchen. Fast on the heels of *A City of Sadness* comes *Dust in the Wind*, yet another leisurely observation of Taiwan life from the celebrated director Hou Hsiao-hsien (*The Time to Live, the Time to Die*, and *Daughter of the Nile*). This study was actually filmed in 1986 and follows the path of two young lovers who leave home to find work in Taipei, the capital of Taiwan. There, the young man takes a job as a messenger boy until he is called up for military service. Not so much a story, but a quasi-auto-biographical examination of the world Hsiao-hsien lives in. Assured cinema, but not to everybody's taste. [CB]

Zakes Mokae and Donald Sutherland struggle with powerful issues in Euzhan Palcy's lucid A Dry White Season (*UIP*).

Cast includes: Hsin Shu-fen, Wang Ching-wen, Lee Tien-lu. Dir: Hou Hsiao-hsien. Pro: Hsu Kuo-hang. Screenplay: Wu Nien-jen and Chu Tien-wen. Ph: Li Ping-pin. (Central Motion Pictures–ICA.) Rel: floating; first shown London (ICA) 30 March 1990. 107 mins. Cert 15.

Earth Girls Are Easy. Very, very silly comedy-fantasy about a triumvirate of cool aliens who invade the hearts and libidos of California's Valley Girl set. Valerie Dale (Geena Davis), a manicurist who thinks Finland is the capital of Norway, is in the middle of a bust-up with her fiancé when the aliens land in her swimming pool. As if she didn't have enough on her plate . . . Geena Davis displays signs of comic potential and great legs, but her real-life husband, Jeff Goldblum, is wasted as a six-foot-four extraterrestrial who doesn't say much. As glitzy, energetic trash, some of this works, but a lot of it doesn't. [JC-W]

Also with: Jeff Goldblum (Mac), Julie Brown (Candy Pink), Jim Carrey (Wiploc), Damon Wayans (Zeebo), Michael McKean (Woody), Charles Rocket (Ted), Larry Linville, Rick Overton, Diane Stilwell, Richard Hurst, Leslie Morris, Stacey Travis, Nicole Kramer. Dir: Julien Temple. Pro: Tony Garnett. Assoc Pro: Terrence E. McNally. Screenplay: Julie Brown, Charlie Coffey and Terrence E. McNally. Ph: Oliver Stapleton. Ed: Richard Halsey. Pro Des: Dennis

Cora Miao and Russell Wong in Eat a Bowl of Tea *(Artificial Eye), another charming comedy from Wayne Wang (director of the US/Chinese gem,* Dim Sum*).*

Gassner. M: Nile Rodgers; songs performed by Hall and Oates, B–52s, Depeche Mode, Julie Brown, etc. Costumes: Linda Bass. Sound: Kirk Schuler. (Kestrel Films/Braveworld–Fox.) Rel: 22 December 1989. 100 mins. Cert PG.

Eat a Bowl of Tea. Wayne Wang, director of the small but perfect Chinese/American celluloid gem *Dim Sum,* comes up with another gentle, observant and lightly humorous comedy, set in New York's Chinatown (but very largely made in Hong Kong). A warm romance, it is essentially about the groom's inability, largely because of overwork, to produce the offspring which his bride and their fathers are increasingly anxiously demanding: this against a strongly critical background of the infamous Exclusion Law which kept down to a negligible trickle Chinese entry to America and eventually almost left New York's Chinatown without any population. [FMS]

Cast: Victor Wong (Wah Gay), Russell Wong (Ben Loy), Cora Miao (Mei Oi), Eric Tsang Chi Wai (Ah Song), Lau Siu Ming (Lee Gong), Wu Ming Yu, Hui Fun, Law Fan, Lee Sau Kee, Yuen Yat Fai, Wong Wai, Philip Chan. Dir: Wayne Wang. Pro: Tom Sternberg. Assoc Pro: Patricia Chong. Ex Pro: Lindsay Law and John K. Chan. Screenplay: Judith Rascoe; based on the book by Louis Chu. Ph: Amir Mokri. Ed: Richard Candib. Pro Des: Bob Ziembicki. M: Mark Adler. Costumes: Marit Allen. (An American Playhouse Theatrical Film-Tom Sternberg/Wayne Wang Pro.–Artificial Eye.) Rel: floating; first shown London (Camden Plaza and Metro) 8 December 1989. 104 mins. Cert 12.

Eight Men Out. Exquisitely photographed, impeccably researched

Let's lunch: Geena Davis, Jeff Goldblum, Jim Carrey and Damon Wayans prove that Earth Girls Are Easy *(Fox).*

D. B. Sweeney ('Shoeless' Joe Jackson), Jace Alexander (Dickie Kerr), Gordon Clapp (Ray Schalk), Perry Lang (Fred McMullin), John Mahoney (Kid Gleason), James Read (Lefty Williams), John Sayles (Ring Lardner), Studs Terkel (Hugh Fullerton), Maggie Renzi (Rose Cicotte), Nancy Travis (Lyria Williams), Don Harvey, Bill Irwin, Michael Rooker, Richard Edson, Michael Mantell, Kevin Tighe, Tay Strathairn, Jesse Vincent, David Carpenter, Richard Lynch, Ken Berry, Leigh Harris, John Anderson, Dick Cusack. Dir and Screenplay: John Sayles. Pro: Sarah Pillsbury and Midge Sanford. Co-Pro: Peggy Rajski. Ex Pro: Barbara Boyle and Jerry Offsay. Ph: Robert Richardson. Ed: John Tintori. Pro Des: Nora Chavooshian. M: Mason Daring. Costumes: Cynthia Flynt. Sound: David Brownlow. (Orion–-Rank.) Rel: 21 July 1989. 120 mins. Cert PG.

Charlie Sheen co-stars as the disgraced Oscar 'Hap' Felsch in Rank's heavy-going baseball history, Eight Men Out.

dramatisation of one of the most shameful seasons in American baseball history. Set in 1919–20 (the period of director John Sayles's last film, the brilliant *Matewan*), *Eight Men Out* examines the disgrace and guilt surrounding the Chicago White Sox for accepting bribes to lose the World Series. A sincere and very boring film. [JC-W]

Cast includes: John Cusack (Buck Weaver), Clifton James (Charles Comiskey), Michael Lerner (Arnold Rothstein), Christopher Lloyd (Bill Burns), Charlie Sheen ('Hap' Felsch), David Strathairn (Eddie Cicotte),

El Dorado. This long (though now cut by almost 30 minutes since it was first shown in Madrid in April 1988), lavish (claimed, at $8 million, to be the most

A golden homage to the gods in Carlos Saura's long, slow but meticulously accurate El Dorado *(Palace Pictures), the story of the ill-fated expedition led up the Amazon by Aguirre in the 1560s.*

expensive Spanish production ever), slow and spectacular Spanish/French film covers the ill-fated Conquistadors' expedition up the Amazon in 1560 in search of the fabled country of El Dorado – the same ground as Herzog's *Aguirre, the Wrath of God*. In spite of the cost, this version is somewhat less successful. Often very beautiful to look at (though sometimes better to look away from), Carlos Saura's epic scale movie alternates between violent action and lengthy exposition as it meticulously chronicles the way in which the expedition gradually disintegrated as it toppled into mutiny and Aguirre's increasing madness and assassination. Some fine sequences, but too thinly spaced out. [FMS]

Cast: Omero Antunutti (Aguirre), Lambert Wilson (Pedro de Ursua), Eusebio Poncela (Guzman), Gabriela Roe (Ines), Ines Sastra (Elvira), Jose Sancho (La Bandera), Patxi Bisquert (Pedrarias), Francisco Algora (Llamoso), Feodor Atkine (Monoya), Abel Viton, Paco Merino, Mariona Gonzalez, Gladys Catania, David Gonzalez, Alfred Catania. Dir and Screenplay: Carlos Saura. Pro: Andres Vincente Gomez. Ph: Teo Escamilla. Ed: Pedro del Rey. Art: Terry Pritchard. M Dir: Alejandro Masso. (Iberoamericana de TV co-pro. with Chrysalide Films, Canal Plus and FR3 Films with collaboration of Quinto Centenario and participation of TVE and RAI Sacis–Palace Pictures.) Rel: floating; first shown London (Cannon, Shaftesbury Ave) 4 August 1989. 124 mins. Cert 15.

Encounter at Raven's Gate. Quirky, low-budget and refreshingly original sci-fi thriller about the strange goings-on in a drought-ridden Outback community. Birds fall from the sky, wells dry up overnight and electricity supplies mysteriously short-circuit. The chilling alien presence is only felt and never seen, but the deadly repercussions turn man against man and dog against its owner. Special effects are kept to a minimum, the power of the film relying on blinding lights and manic acting. Director Rolf De Heer is no Peter Weir or Russell Mulcahy, but he can skirt round the clichés with the best of them. [JC-W]

Cast includes: Steven Vidler (Eddie Cleary), Celine Griffin (Rachel Cleary), Ritchie Singer (Richard Cleary), Vince Gil (Skinner), Saturday Rosenberg (Annie), Max Cullen (Taylor), Terry Camilleri (Hemmings), Kevin Thiele, Sylvia Thiele, Peter Douglas, Paul Philpott, Ernie Ellison, Max

Lorenzin. Dir: Rolf De Heer. Pro: De Heer and Marc Rosenberg. Ex Pro: Antony I. Ginnane. Screenplay: Rosenberg and De Heer; adapted from an original screenplay by James Michael Vernon. Ph: Richard Michalak. Ed: Suresh Ayyar. Pro Des: Judith Russell. M: Graham Tardif and Roman Kronen. Costumes: Clarissa Patterson. (Helmdale/FGH/International Film Management–Castle Premier.) Rel: 16 March 1990. 93 mins. Cert 15.

Enemies, A Love Story. New York, 1949. Highly-praised film adaptation of Isaac Bashevis Singer's soul-tortured novel about a Jew making his way in America after escaping from Nazi Germany. Ron Silver – as dour (and unsympathetic) as ever – is Herman Broder, a ghost-writer who believes that his wife, Tamara (Anjelica Huston), died in the war. In this belief, he marries a shiksa, sets up home in

Ron Silver as Herman, a man plagued by beautiful women (Margaret Sophie Stein, Anjelica Huston and Lena Olin) in Paul Mazursky's highly-acclaimed Enemies, A Love Story *(Fox).*

Coney Island and takes a beautiful mistress. When his wife returns from the dead, Herman's life becomes a nightmare – with darkly comic undertones. Huston, Lena Olin and Margaret Sophie Stein, as the three women in Herman's life, all shine, but Ron Silver is just too glum a polygamist to win our hearts. And another complaint: why were the 'forties always so poorly lit? However, as a Jewish *Micki & Maude*, this is a believable farce, aided and abettted by superlative production values. [JC-W]

Also with: Lena Olin (Masha), Margaret Sophie Stein (Yadwiga), Alan King (Rabbi Lembeck), Judith Malina, Rita Karin, Phil Leeds, Elya Baskin, Paul Mazursky. Dir and Pro: Paul Mazursky. Co-Pro: Pato Guzman and Irby Smith. Ex Pro: James G. Robinson and Joe Roth. Screenplay: Mazursky and Roger L. Simon; from the novel by Isaac Bashevis Singer. Ph: Fred Murphy. Ed: Stuart Pappé. Pro Des: Pato Guzman. M: Maurice Jarre; clarinet soloist: Giora Feidman; songs performed by Tommy Dorsey and his orchestra, the Andrews Sisters, Billie Holiday, Juanita Hall, etc. Costumes: Albert Wolsky. Sound: Don Cohen. (Morgan Creek–Fox.) Rel: 6 April 1990. 120 mins. Cert 15.

Terry Jones as the king in the noisy, strip-cartoon comedy Erik the Viking *(UIP), which he also directed and wrote.*

An Enemy of the People – Ganashatru

After a four year absence from the studios because of illness, Satyajit Ray, the master of Indian cinema, returns to filming with an odd choice of subject, an adaptation of Henrik Ibsen's classic play. Though pertinent to one of today's major problems, this story of a doctor's generally unpopular fight against polluted water supplies is somewhat on the heavy side. It was also very clearly made entirely in the studios – though Ray was apparently ordered to do this by his doctor, who said that location filming would be too arduous. Ray retains his command over the medium but, watchable as it is, I fancy this film won't be far up his merit league. [FMS]

Cast: Soumitra Chatterji (Dr Gupta), Dhritiman Chatterji (Nishith Gupta), Ruma Gubathakurta (Maya Gupta), Mamata Shankar (Indrani Gupta), Dipankarde (Haridas), Sunhendu Chatterji (Biresh Guha), Manos Mitra, Vishwa Guhathhakurta, Satya Banerji, Rajaram Yagnik. Dir, Screenplay (based on the Ibsen play) and M: Satyajit Ray. Ph: Barun Raha. Ed: Dulal Dutt. Art: Ashoke Bose. (National Film Development Corp–Electric/Contemporary.) Rel: floating; first shown London (Renoir) 29 December 1989. 100 mins. Cert U.

Erik the Viking

Erik the Viking has the distinction of being one of the noisiest films of the year: I doubt if it will be one of the most successful. British to the core, it is an odd concoction along the lines of comic-strip stuff for kids (but obviously intended for adult kids), about a Viking who decides there must be more to life than rape and murder, the Norsemen's staple pleasures, and sets out on a pilgrimage to the edge of the world and Valhalla to prove his point. But this commendable moral content is pretty blurred, and many of the somewhat Monty Python-ish cast don't seem able to decide if they are playing in a farce or heavy drama – though writer-director Terry Jones, as an effete King Arnulf, appears to have no doubts! A real ham sandwich, made with half-baked bread. [FMS]

Cast includes: Tim Robbins (Erik), Gary Cady (blacksmith), Terry Jones (king), Eartha Kitt (Freya), Mickey Rooney (Erik's granddad), John Cleese (Halfdan the Black), Tsutomu Sekine (slavemaster), Imogen Stubbs (princess), Samantha Bond (Helga), Freddie Jones (missionary), Antony Sher, John Gordon Sinclair, Tim McInnerny, Charles McKeown, Richard Ridings, Danny Schiller. Dir and Screenplay: Terry Jones. Pro: John Goldstone. Ex Pro: Terry Glinwood. Pro: Neville C. Thompson. Ph: Ian Wilson. Ed: George Akers. Pro Des: John Beard. M: Neil Innes. Costumes: Pam Tait. (John Goldstone/Prominent Features–UIP.) Rel: 29 September 1989. 102 mins. Cert 12.

Ernest Saves Christmas

Disney's Christmas package for the holidays. With the assistance of Ernest, Santa, aged 151 and a bit tired, smooths out the snags that confront him just in time to complete his task before the holly-and-the-ivy deadline. Grand fun from first to last, and no recourse to the syrup jar. [FMS]

Cast: Jim Varney (Ernest), Douglas Seale (Santa), Oliver Clark, Noelle Parker, Robert Lesser, Gailard Sartain, Billie Bird, Bill Byrge, Buddy Duglas, Patty Maloney. Dir: John Cherry. Pro: Stacy Williams and Douglas Claybourne. Co-Pro: Justis Green and Coke Sams. Assoc Pro: Ed Turner. Ex Pro: Martin Erlichman and Joseph L. Akerman. Screenplay: B. Kline and Ed Turner; from the latter's story. Ph: Peter Stein. Ed: Sharyn Ross. Art: Ian Thomas. M: Mark Snow. Cos Des: Peter Mitchell. Sound: Rich Schirmer. (Touchstone–Warner.) Rel: 17 November 1989. 92 mins. Cert U.

The Fabulous Baker Boys

Moody, leisurely drama about two sibling lounge pianists (Beau and Jeff Bridges) who play the best hotels in and around Seattle, Washington. When Frank Baker (Beau) decides to spice up the act by bringing a singer on board, the sizzling newcomer transforms their lives – professionally and privately. Michelle Pfeiffer, as the golden spanner in the works, is sensational, both as actress and singer – this is her first singing role since *Grease 2* in 1982. Dave Grusin's score, too, is great, matched by Michael Ballhaus's atmospheric photography. Songs include 'Feelings', 'My Funny Valentine', 'Making Whoopee', 'The Look of Love', and their ilk. For her performance as Susie Diamond, Michelle was nominated for an Oscar as Best Actress and actually won the Golden Globe, the National Board of Review, the New York Film Critics' Circle, the National Society of Film Critics and the Los Angeles Film Critics awards. Phew! [JC-W]

Cast includes: Jeff Bridges (Jack Baker), Ellie Raab (Nina), Jennifer Tilly (Monica Moran), Xander Berkeley, Dakin Matthews, Gregory Itzin, Wendy Girard, David Coburn, Albert Hall. Dir and Screenplay: Steve Kloves. Pro: Paula Weinstein, Sydney

That *scene on the piano: Michelle Pfeiffer serenades Jeff Bridges in Rank's surprise hit,* The Fabulous Baker Boys.

Pollack and Mark Rosenberg. Ph: Michael Ballhaus. Ed: Bill Steinkamp. Pro Des: Jeffrey Townsend. M: Dave Grusin. Costumes: Lisa Jensen. Sound: Stephen Von Hase. (Gladden–Rank.) Rel: 9 March 1990. 113 mins. Cert 15.

Family Business. Sean Connery, Dustin Hoffman and Matthew Broderick team up as the unlikeliest criminal Scottish-Jewish-Italian family in living memory. Connery is grandfather Jessie McMullen, a lifelong crook with a flair for getting his own way; Hoffman is his son Vito ('a friggin' midget', says Connery), an ex-con turned meat-packer; and Broderick is Adam, Vito's son, with brains, a full scholarship and an unrealised passion to enter a life of crime. Reluctantly Vito agrees to participate in what looks like a fail-safe robbery, dreamed up by Adam and encouraged by Jessie. Although Connery is always watchable, *Family Business* is a disappointing dramatic comedy, never overcoming the

implausibility of its casting. Not for a minute can we believe in these characters, however much we may admire the actors involved. Strictly for fans of the stars. [JC-W]

Also with: Rosana DeSoto (Elaine), Janet Carroll (Margie), Victoria Jackson (Christine), Bill McCutcheon, Deborah Rush, Marilyn Cooper, James Tolkan, Marilyn

Sokol, Tony DiBenedetto and B. D. Wong (Jimmy Chiu). Dir: Sidney Lumet. Pro: Lawrence Gordon. Ex Pro: Jennifer Ogden and Burtt Harris. Screenplay: Vincent

Like grandfather, unlike son: Dustin Hoffman, Sean Connery and Matthew Broderick as criminal elements of the McMullen family, in Sidney Lumet's disappointing Family Business *(Palace).*

Nick Nolte (centre) stars as the Caucasian monarch in John Milius's stumbling epic Farewell to the King *(Vestron).*

Patrick; based on his own novel. Ph: Andrzej Bartowiak. Ed: Andrew Mondshein. Pro Des: Philip Rosenberg. M: Cy Coleman. Costumes: Ann Roth. Sound: Allan Byer. (Tri-Star–Palace.) Rel: 9 February 1990. 110 mins. Cert 15.

Far North. Family melodrama in which a city-wise woman, Kate (Jessica Lange), returns home to visit her father in hospital. There, she encounters the rivalry of her older sister, Rita (Tess Harper), and the stubborn intractability of her curmudgeonly father, Bertram (Charles Durning). Kate's mother is as mad as a March hare and her niece, Rita's daughter, is an uncontrollable nymphomaniac. Although set largely in the woods of Minnesota, the film reeks of theatricality and cannot escape its mannered style. It's not surprising, then, to learn that playwright Sam Shepard was behind the camera – directing a script he'd written specifically for Ms Lange. [JC-W]

Also with: Donald Moffat (Uncle Dane), Ann Wedgeworth (Amy), Patricia Arquette (Jilly), Nina Draxten (Gramma), Al Lange, Jane Lange. Dir and Screenplay: Sam Shepard. Pro: Malcolm R. Harding and Carolyn Pfeiffer. Ex Pro: Shep Gordon. Ph: Robbie Greenberg. Ed: Bill Yahraus. Pro Des: Peter Jamison. M: The Red Clay Ramblers and J. A Deane. Costumes: Rita Salazar. Sound: Richard King. (Alive

Films/Nelson/Circle JS Prod–Rank.) Rel: 2 February 1990. 89 mins. Cert 12.

Farewell to the King. Borneo, 1945. Captain Nigel Fairbourne (Nigel Havers) is assigned to penetrate the rain forest to persuade the natives to fight the Japs. There, he discovers an exotic kingdom, headed by King Learoyd (Nick Nolte), a deserter from MacArthur's army. A war movie with all the sweep and spectacle of an epic, *Farewell to the King* is manacled by a lumbering cinematic style and anodyne quality, leaving one with the disconcerting feeling of watching a sequel to *South Pacific*. [JC-W]

Also with: James Fox (Col Ferguson), Marilyn Tokuda (Yoo), Frank McRae (Sgt Tenga), Aki Aleong (Col Mitamura), Elan Oberon (Vivienne), John Bennett Perry (MacArthur), William Wise, Gerry Lopez, Marius Weyers, Choy Chan Wing. Dir and Screenplay: John Milius. Pro: Albert S. Ruddy and Andre Morgan. Ph: Dean Semler. Ed: C. Timothy O'Meara and Anne V. Coates. Pro Des: Gil Parrondo. M: Basil Poledouris. (Vestron.) Rel: 7 July 1989. 117 mins. Cert PG.

Fellow Traveller. Much-trodden territory is given a stylised flourish in this well-crafted, heavily period BFI/BBC/HBO co-production. Asa Kaufman, a member of the Screenwriters' Guild ('I'm not a writer, Flaubert was a writer'), is a Communist sympathiser and has to flee to London to escape persecution by the House Committee on Un-American Activities. In Blighty he rekindles a friendship with an old female acquaintance, dreams of halcyon days in Hollywood and exorcises a reservoir of guilt. Although literate and acted well enough, the film is a jumble of flashbacks, fantasy sequences and imagined scenes of Kaufman's work on a children's TV series, 'The Adventures of Robin Hood'. Ultimately, the production collapses from a lack of narrative direction and is far too bogged down by an arty-farty need to impress. [JC-W]

Cast includes: Ron Silver (Asa Kaufman), Hart Bochner (Clifford Byrne), Imogen Stubbs (Sarah Aitchison), Daniel J. Travanti (Jerry Leavy), Katherine Borowitz (Joan Kaufman), Alexander Hanson (Robin Hood), Julian Fellows (D'Arcy), Richard Wilson (Sir Hugo Armstrong), Doreen Mantle (landlady), Jonathan Hyde, Peter Corey, Briony McRoberts, Roger Hammond, Angus MacInnes, Nicholas Jones, Trevor Cooper, Guy Manning, Michael Stainton. Dir: Philip Saville. Pro: Michael Wearing. Screenplay: Michael Eaton. Ph: John Kenway. Ed: Greg Miller. Pro Des: Gavin Davies. M: Colin Towns. Costumes: Al Barnett. Fight Arranger: William Hobbs. (BBC/HBO–BFI.) Rel: floating; first shown London (Metro) 5 January 1990. 97 mins. Cert 15.

Field of Dreams. Baseball allied to Other World fantasy sounds like a certain double death sentence for any movie shown in British cinemas. But I hope this fate won't befall *Field of Dreams*, which in spite of its faults has a lot to offer in terms of gentle and wholesome entertainment. It's a whimsical story about a young and inexperienced Iowan farmer who starts to hear celestial voices coming out of his corn: in response to their pleas he invests his all in building a baseball pitch on the farm so that a team of dead pitchers can play their game again. A charming and innocent film which beautifully establishes a mood of mystery and magic. [FMS]

Cast: Kevin Costner (excellent as the farmer), Amy Madigan (ditto as the wife), Gaby Hoffmann (a cute kid), Ray Liotta, Timothy Busfield (Mark), James Earl Jones (Terence Mann), Burt Lancaster (Dr Graham), Frank Whaley, Dwier Brown, Fern Persons, Kelly Coffield. Dir and Screenplay (based on W. P. Kinsella's book *Shoeless Joe*): Phil Alden Robinson. Pro: Lawrence and Charles Gordon. Assoc Pro: Lloyd Levin. Ex Pro: Brian Frankish. Ph: John Lindley. Ed: Ian Crawford. Pro Des: Dennis Gassner. M: James Horner. Costumes: Linda Bass. (Gordon Co–Guild.) Rel: 5 January 1990. 106 mins. Cert PG.

The Fly II. This sequel to the re-make holds up surprisingly well within its teen *Beauty and the Beast* format. Eric Stoltz (*Mask*) stars as Martin Brundle (son of Jeff Goldblum), a lab experiment who matures at five times the speed of ordinary infants. At five years of age Martin is already inventing sophisticated gadgets and sowing his wild oats in the direction of Daphne Zuniga. But then he isn't human, is he? Later on, the (stunning) SFX get very unsavoury and are likely to cause indigestion. As sequels go, this is a superior strain. [JC-W]

Also with: Daphne Zuniga (Beth), Lee Richardson (Bartok), John Getz (Stathis),

Frank Turner (Shepard), Ann Marie Lee (Jainway), Gary Chalk (Scorby), Harley Cross (young Martin), Saffron Henderson, Matthew Moore, Rob Roy, William Taylor, Jeff Goldblum (Seth on video). Dir: Chris Walas (SFX supervisor on *The Fly*). Pro: Steven-Charles Jaffe. Ex Pro: Stuart Cornfeld. Screenplay: Mick Garris, Jim and Ken Wheat and Frank Darabont; from a

Burt Lancaster and Kevin Costner in Field of Dreams, *Guild's unlikely charmer, mixing baseball and fantasy to delightful effect.*

Anne Marie Lee, Frank C. Turner and Lee Richardson witness an extraordinary birth in Fox's chilling The Fly II.

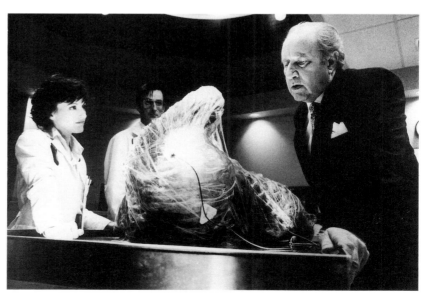

story by Mick Garris. Ph: Robin Vidgeon. Ed: Sean Barton. Pro Des: Michael S. Bolton. M: Christopher Young. Costumes: Christopher Ryan. Sound: Leslie Shatz. SFX: Chris Walas Inc. (Brooksfilms–Fox.) Rel: 8 September 1989. 105 mins. Cert 18.

Fools of Fortune. Soapy, somewhat unconvincing saga of tragedy and revenge that grips three generations of an Irish family. Spies, murder, unrequited love and an unwanted pregnancy queue up to take their turn in what ends up like a glossy mini-series squeezed into 104 minutes. As an English latecomer to the plot, Mary Elizabeth Mastrantonio is excellent, and Catherine McFadden is suitably celestial as the last twig on the family tree. Unfortunately, Iain Glen – who has the largest part – too often resembles Frank Spenser in *Some Mothers Do Have 'Em*, while Hans Zimmer's score plays like an overwrought opera. [JC-W]

Cast includes: Mary Elizabeth Mastrantonio (Marianne), Iain Glen (Willie), Julie Christie (Mrs Quinton), Michael Kitchen (Mr Quinton), Sean T. McClory (young Willie), Niamh Cusack (Josaphine), Neil Dudgeon (Sgt Rudkin), Catherine McFadden (Imelda), Ronnie Masterson, Tom Hickey, John Kavanagh, Sean McGinley, Niall Toibin. Dir: Pat O'Connor. Pro: Sarah Radclyffe. Assoc Pro: Caroline Hewitt. Ex Pro: Tim Bevan and Graham Broadstreet.

Roy Scheider under pressure in Guild's coldwar thriller, The Fourth War.

Screenplay: Michael Hirst; based on the novel by William Trevor. Ph: Jerzy Zielinski. Ed: Michael Bradsell. Pro Des: Jamie Leonard. M: Hans Zimmer. Costumes: Judy Moorcroft. Sound: Pat Hayes. (Polygram/Working Title/Film Four–Palace.) Rel: floating; first shown London (Curzon, West End) 22 June 1990. 104 mins. Cert 15.

The Fourth War. One year before the liberation of Czechoslovakia, hothead Vietnam vet Colonel Jack Knowles (Roy Scheider) is assigned to the West German-Czech border. Trained to kill, to stand up for himself, he cannot accept the pussyfooting rules of the American army, to be 'a platoon officer in a nunnery'. With malicious contempt for his superiors, Knowles starts a one-man war against the Russian border guards, at first teasing and mocking them before resorting to more outrageous tactics. But Knowles hasn't bargained for retaliation from an officer not unlike himself – a Russian veteran of Afghanistan, aching to spark off a lethal confrontation . . . John Frankenheimer, who earned his stripes as a front-ranking Cold War film-maker with *The Manchurian Candidate* (1962), toys with some neat ideas in this sly thriller, backing them up with his accustomed flair. However, in spite of some juicy character playing by Scheider, Bill Conti's singalong score and Jurgen Prochnow's blue eyes, it is the beautiful, wintry landscape that steals the show. [JC-W]

Also with: Jurgen Prochnow (Valachev), Tim Reid (Lt Col Clark), Lara Harris (Elena), Harry Dean Stanton (General Hackworth), Dale Dye (sergeant major), Bill MacDonald, Harold Hecht Jr, Alice Pesto. Dir: John Frankenheimer. Pro: Wolf Schmidt. Ex Pro: William Stuart and Sam Perlmutter. Screenplay: Stephen Peters and Kenneth Ross; from Peters's novel. Ph: Gerry Fisher. Ed: Robert F. Shugrue. Pro Des: Alen Manzer. M: Bill Conti. Costumes: Ray Summers. Sound: Ganton/Trudel. (Kodiak–Guild.) Rel: 22 June 1990. 91 mins. Cert 15.

Fresh Horses. All the soppy music in the world cannot evoke audience sympathy for a romance that just isn't there. Andrew McCarthy, a likeable actor at the worst of times, plays Matt Larkin, a wealthy, good-looking college senior engaged to an attractive, caring and wonderful rich girl. In short, his life is laid out for him on a silver salver. And then he meets 'Jewel' (Molly Ringwald), a shy, unprepossessing married teenager from the wrong side of the tracks. And now comes the hard part. He falls in love with her, quarrels with her a lot and alienates his friends and family. With the help of a surer directorial hand, this might have made for interesting drama, but here it's perplexing and trite. Still, some of the supporting performances are worth a look, particularly Molly Hagan's shrewd yuppie temptress. [JC-W]

Also with: Patti d'Arbanville (Jean), Ben Stiller (Tipton), Leon Russom (Mr Larkin), Molly Hagan (Ellen), Viggo Mortensen (Green), Doug Hutchison (Sproles), Chiara Peacock, Marita Geraghty, Rachel Jones, Welker White, Christy Budig, Kent Poole. Dir: David Anspaugh. Pro: Dick Berg. Ex Pro: Allan Marcil. Screenplay: Larry Ketron; from his play. Ph: Fred Murphy. Ed: David Rosenbloom. Pro Des: Paul Sylbert. M: David Foster and Patrick Williams. Costumes: Colleen Atwood. (Weintraub–Columbia Tri-Star.) Rel: 29 June 1990. 103 mins. Cert 15.

Full Moon in Blue Water. Oddball comedy-drama starring Gene Hackman as the owner of a run-down bar in Blue Water, in the Galveston Bay area of Texas. Part character study, part human comedy, *Full Moon* . . . is a constantly unexpected blend of old-fashioned schmaltz and low-key Tennessee Williams. Unfortunately, the film – scripted by playwright Bill Bozzone – suffers from a claustrophobic

staginess, although the performances frequently breathe real life into the proceedings. Hackman, as always, is uniformly watchable, while Elias Koteas creates a compelling characterisation as a simpleton with cars and guns on his mind, reminding one of a young De Niro. [JC-W]

Also with: Teri Garr (Louise), Burgess Meredith (the General), Kevin Cooney (Charlie O'Donnell), David Doty (Virgil), Gil Glasgow (Sheriff Baytch), Becky Gelke (Dorothy), Marietta Marich, Lexie Masterson, William Larsen, Mark Walters. Dir: Peter Masterson. Pro: Lawrence Turman, David Foster and John Turman. Ex Pro: Moshe Diamant and Eduard Sarlui. Screenplay: Bill Bozzone. Ph: Fred Murphy. Ed: Jill Savitt. M: Phil Marshall. Costumes: Rondi Davis. (Trans World–Entertainment.) Rel: 7 July 1989. 95 mins. Cert 15.

Georgette Meunier. Low-budget black comedy from Germany co-directed and written by a Swiss woman and a Frenchman. Georgette Meunier is sexually obsessed by her brother, and when he vanishes during wartime she is driven to murder. After accidentally knocking off her husband, and serving time for it, Georgette resorts to mass murder, causing panic in a small provincial town. Decadent, economical entertainment. [CB]

Cast includes: Tiziana Jelmini (Georgette), Thomas Schunke (Emile), Dina Leipzig (Esmeralda), Heinz Rathsack (prison director), Etsuko Sakamakl (fortune teller), Mathias Mayer (priest), Manfred Hulverscheidt (Richard Meunier), Miklos Koniger (Leopold Zsoldos). Dir and (with Felix Schnieder-Henninger) Screenplay: Tania Stocklin and Cyrille Rey-Coquais. Ph: Ciro Cappellari and Anka Schmid. M: Nikolaus Utermohlen. Costumes: Yasmine Ramadan and Andrea Hollmann. Sound: Margarethe Heitmuller and Chris Sugiyama. (Electric.) Rel: floating; first shown London (Everyman, Hampstead) 1 April 1990. 82 mins. Cert 18.

Getting It Right. The routine life of a 31-year-old virgin, London hairdresser Gavin Lamb (Jesse Birdsall), changes dramatically when he attends a wild party hosted by a rich, 45-year-old socialite (Lynn Redgrave). From then on Gavin's life is a series of amorous encounters with an unlikely assortment of women, from the neurotic Lady Minerva Munday (Helena Bonham-Carter) to his down-to-earth assistant, Jenny (Jane Horrocks). True love is

Burgess Meredith, Gene Hackman and Teri Garr support the bar in Full Moon in Blue Water, *from Entertainment.*

bound to prevail, but not before young Gavin has learned a few startling lessons about life. A quite charming concoction, and frequently very funny, with an extraordinary performance from John Gielgud as a *nouveau riche* millionaire with vowel trouble. [JC-W]

Also with: Peter Cook (Mr Adrian), John Gielgud (Sir Gordon Munday), Lynn Redgrave (Joan), Shirley Anne Field (Anne), Pat Heywood (excellent, as Mrs Lamb), Bryan Pringle (Mr Lamb), Nan Munro, Richard Huw, Kevin Drinkwater, Ian Redford, Judy Parfitt, Noriko Aida, Richard Strange, June Ellis, Pauline Quirke, Elizabeth Jane Howard. Dir: Randal Kleiser. Pro: Jonathan D. Krane and Randal Kleiser. Co-Pro: Gregory Hinton. Ex Pro: Rusty Lemorande. Screenplay: Elizabeth Jane Howard. Ph: Clive Tickner. Ed: Chris Kelly. Pro Des: Caroline Amies. M: Colin Towns; title song performed by Dusty Springfield; add. music: Verdi, Chopin, Mozart, etc. Costumes: Hazel Pethig. Sound: John Midgley. (Management Company Entertainment Group–Medusa.) Rel: 20 October 1989. 102 mins. Cert 15.

Helena Bonham-Carter, Bryan Pringle and Pat Heywood at a somewhat tense breakfast in Medusa's Getting It Right.

Wot, seen a ghost? Bill Murray, Dan Aykroyd and Harold Ramis return, predictably, in Ghostbusters II *(Columbia Tri-Star).*

Ghostbusters II. The Big Apple, five years later. All the hatred and evil of New York City has materialised into an underground river of lethal slime and the 'busters are back in business. Not so much a sequel to the highest grossing comedy of all time as a re-make – which is a shame, because even though there's some fun there are no surprises this time round. In its opening weekend in America, *Ghostbusters II* grossed a phenomenal $29,472,894, an all-time record – unbroken until the release of *Batman* a week later. [JC-W]

Cast includes: Bill Murray (Peter Venkman), Dan Aykroyd (Raymond Stantz), Sigourney Weaver (Dana Barrett), Harold Ramis (Egon Spengler), Rick Moranis (Louis Tully), Ernie Hudson (Winston Zeddemore), Annie Potts (Janine Melnitz), Peter MacNicol (Janosz Poha), Harris Yulin (the judge), David Margulies (Mayor of New York), Kurt Fuller, Janet Margolin, Wilhelm Von Homburg, Mary Ellen Trainor, Richard Foronjy, Christopher Neame, Judy Ovitz, Cheech Marin, John Hammil, Brian Doyle Murray, Phillip Baker Hall. Dir: Ivan Reitman. Pro: Reitman. Ex Pro: Bernie Brillstein, Joe Medjuck and Michael C. Gross. Screenplay: Harold Ramis and Dan Aykroyd. Ph: Michael Chapman. Ed: Sheldon Kahn and Donn Cambern. Pro Des: Bo Welch. M: Randy Edelman. Costumes: Gloria Gresham.

Sound: Tom C. McCarthy and Fred Judkins. (Columbia Tri-Star.) Rel: 1 December 1989. 108 mins. Cert PG.

Gleaming the Cube. Well-photographed action-thriller in which a teenage rebel sets out – on a skateboard – to find the killers of his adopted Vietnamese brother. This tarted-up teen flick set in Orange County's Little Saigon is never entirely sure whether it's *Skatetown USA* or a more serious tract on racism and corruption. However, it is well made and efficiently scripted, and is an unusual diversion that knocks the wheels off Linda Blair's *Roller Boogie*. [JC-W]

Cast includes: Christian Slater (Brian Kelly), Steven Bauer (Al Lucero), Richard Herd (Ed Lawndale), Le Tuan (Col Trac), Min Luong (Tina Trac), Art Chudabala (Vinh Kelly), Ed Lauter (Mr Kelly), Nicole Mercurio (Mrs Kelly), Peter Kwong, Charles Cyphers, Max Perlich, Tony Hawk, Tommy Guerrero, Christian Jacobs, Jack Riley, Angela Moya, J. Jay Saunders, Arsenio 'Sonny' Trinidad. Dir: Graeme Clifford. Pro: Laurence Turman and David Foster. Screenplay: Michael Tolkin. Ph: Reed Smoot. Ed: John Wright. Pro Des: John Muto. M: Jay Ferguson. Costumes: Ann Somers Major. Sound: Donald B. Summer. (Gladden Entertainment–Rank.) Rel: 20 October 1989. 105 mins. Cert PG.

Glory. Stirring, impeccably crafted drama chronicling the black man's role in the American Civil War. In 1863 Robert Gould Shaw, a 25-year-old white Bostonian, was put in charge of 1000 negro soldiers, making up the now legendary 54th Massachusetts Regiment. At first subjected to racial ridicule by their own side, the black boys in blue painstakingly earned the respect of their Union comrades, culminating in a heroic charge on a Confederate stronghold in South Carolina. Matthew Broderick, as Shaw, has never been better than here, as the obstinate, confused leader of the regiment, but is still dwarfed by a superlative ensemble of black actors in supporting roles. Standouts are Denzel Washington and Morgan Freeman as – respectively – a rebellious firebrand and his worldly-wise sergeant, both deservedly showered with acting honours, Washington walking away with an Oscar for Best Supporting Actor. In every department *Glory* is film-making at its greatest, from the photography and costumes to the music and battle choreography, but

Denzel Washington in his Oscar-winning role as 'Trip' in Edward Zwick's superb war film, Glory, *from Columbia Tri-Star.*

never does the technical know-how overshadow the power of the film's historic story. A classic, unforgettable war film with a human message that should be as extensive as the Mason-Dixon Line. [JC-W]

Also with: Denzel Washington (Trip), Cary Elwes (Cabot Forbes), Morgan Freeman (Rawlins), Jihmi Kennedy, Andre Braugher, John Finn, Donovan Leitch, John David Cullum, Alan North, Bob Gunton, Cliff DeYoung, Jay O. Sanders, Peter Michael Goetz, Ethan Phillips, Mark A Jones, Jane Alexander (Mrs Shaw). Dir: Edward Zwick. Pro: Freddie Fields. Screenplay: Kevin Jarre; based on the books *Lay This Laurel* by Lincoln Kirstein and *One Gallant Rush* by Peter Burchard, and the letters of Robert Gould Shaw. Ph: Freddie Francis. Ed: Steven Rosenblum. Pro Des: Norman Garwood. M: James Horner; featuring The Boys' Choir of Harlem. Costumes: Francine Jamison-Tanchuck. Sound: Lon E. Bender. (Columbia Tri-Star.) Rel: 2 March 1990. 122 mins. Cert 15.

The Gods Must Be Crazy 2. Not many follow-up films are as good as the orig-

inal but by common consent this is the exception: an apt successor to the original simple and delightfully entertaining comedy from Botswana. Great credit to Jamie Uys for both movies,

Bushman Xixo (N!xau) greets New York lawyer Ann Taylor (Lena Farugia) and a nervous Mateo (Eric Bowen) in the delightfully amusing The Gods Must Be Crazy 2 *(Fox).*

which are wittily concerned with the reactions of an innocent to the complexities of civilisation. A real collector's piece. [FMS]

Cast: N!xau, Lena Farugia, Hans Strydom and the local natives. Dir and Screenplay: Jamie Uys. Pro Manager: Gerda van den Broek. Ph and 2nd Unit Dir: Buster Reynolds. Ed: Renée Engelbrecht and Ivan Hall. Narrator: Paddy O'Bryne. M: Charles

Great Balls of Fire!: *Dennis Quaid assaults the ivories in Jim McBride's enjoyable biopic of rock 'n' roller Jerry Lee Lewis, from Rank.*

Fox. (Boet Troskie Pro.–Fox.) Rel: floating; first shown London (Cannon, Oxford St) 18 May 1990. 98 mins. No cert.

Great Balls of Fire! Knockabout, good-natured screen biography of rock 'n' roll legend Jerry Lee Lewis. Dennis Quaid stars as the 'Killer' in an extraordinary but entertaining interpretation, while Winona Ryder, as his child bride Myra Gale, steals the thunder from underneath him. In support, Alec Baldwin as Jimmy Swaggart, Jerry Lee's cousin, is uncanny in capturing exactly the preacher's exaggerated mannerisms. The film is thankfully modest in its intentions, covering a palatable two years in the singer's life – from 1956 to 1958, when the brash Louisiana lad shot from anonymity to superstardom and a disastrous British tour. In the words of its director and co-scripter, Jim McBride, *Great Balls* is 'loyal to the legend – a story we essen-tially invented, based on the facts we knew'. Songs on show include the cele-brated 'Great Balls of Fire!', 'Whole Lotta Shakin' Goin' On' and 'Breath-less', the last named also being the title of an earlier McBride film. [JC-W]

Also with: Trey Wilson (Sam Phillips), Joe Bob Briggs (Dewey 'Daddy-O' Phillips), Stephen Tobolowsky (John Phillips), Lisa Blount (Lois Brown), Robert Lesser (Alan Freed), Michael St Gerard (Elvis), John Doe, Steve Allen, Joshua Sheffield, Mojo Nixon, Jimmy Vaughan, David Ferguson, Lisa Jane Persky, Paula Person, Valerie Wellington, Booker T. Laury, Peter Cook, Kim Smith, David Sibley, Ruth Kettlewell, John Tordoff. Dir and (with Jack Baran) Screenplay: Jim McBride, based on the book by Myra Lewis and Murray Silver. Pro: Adam Fields. Ex Pro: Michael Grais and Mark Victor. Ph: Affonso Beato. Ed: Lisa Day, Pembroke and Bert Lovitt. Pro Des: David Nichols. Costumes: Tracy Tynan. Sound: Petur Hliddal. (Orion–Rank.) Rel: 10 November 1989. 107 mins. Cert 15.

Halloween 4 – The Return of Michael Myers. Dull and startlingly unoriginal sequel to *Halloween 2* (no. 3 having nothing to do with the moronic mass murderer Michael M. Myers). It is ten years since MMM diced and sliced a body, and since then he has been locked up in a maximum security insti-tution for the criminally insane. Now, under federal law, he is eligible for transfer to a normal state hospital; it is a dark, stormy night and Halloween is approaching . . . More trick than treat. [JC-W]

Cast includes: Donald Pleasence (Dr Loomis), Ellie Cornell (Rachel Carruthers), Danielle Harris (Jamie Lloyd), George P. Wilbur (Michael M. Myers), Michael Pataki (Dr Hoffman), Beau Starr (Sheriff Meeker), Kathleen Kinmont (Kelly), Sasha Jenson (Brady), Gene Ross, Carmen Filpi, Ray-mond O'Connor, Jeff Olson, Karen Alston, Harlow Marks. Dir: Dwight H. Little. Pro: Paul Freeman. Ex Pro: Moustapha Akkad. Screenplay: Alan B. McElroy; from a story by McElroy, Dhani Lipsius, Larry Rattner and Benjamin Ruffner. Ph: Peter Lyons Collister. Ed: Curtiss Clayton. Art: Roger S. Crandall. M: Alan Howarth; theme by John Carpenter. Costumes: Rosalie Wallace. Sound: Mark McNabb, Anthony R. Milch. (Trancas International–Fox.) Rel: 3 Nov-ember 1989. 88 mins. Cert 18.

Hamlet Goes Business. Two years before Franco Zeffirelli signed up Mel Gibson to play the Prince of Denmark, Finland's Aki Kaurismaki updated the Shakespearean tragedy and transplanted it to Scandinavia. The director himself describes his film as a 'black-and-white underground B-movie classical drama', although he fails to own up to the comedy that he has injected into it. Hamlet himself, a dour, selfish character addicted to rockabilly music and comics, is no joke, but the mixture of classical tragedy and small-town Finnish business is hilarious. This is a genuine oddity, a quirky delight, and the director's own favourite. Particularly memorable (and amusing): Ophelia's bathtub suicide and Laertes's murder-by-wireless. [JC-W]

Cast includes: Pirkka-Pekka Petelius (Hamlet), Kati Outinen (Ophelia), Elina Salo (Gertrude), Esko Salminen (Klaus), Esko Nikkari (Polonius), Turo Pajala (Rosencrantz), Aake Kaliala (Guildenstern), Kari Vaananen, Hannu Valtonen, Mari Rantasila, Peutti Auer. Dir, Pro and Screenplay: Aki Kaurismaki. Ph: Timo Salminen. Ed: Raija Talvio. Sound: Veikko Aaltonen and Jouko Lumme. (Villealfa Filmproductions–Electric.) Rel: floating; first shown London (Everyman) 23 February 1990. 86 mins. Cert 15.

Hard Road. The tenth production of the Children's Film Unit since it started to operate in 1980. Differing from the old Children's Film Foundation, which did such great work in the past, the unit is made up of adult professionals and children, ranging from 6 to 16 years old, who do their bit on both sides of the camera. This is an unusual 'road' film, about two bored 13-year-old youngsters who borrow dad's Ferrari and set off in it for the seaside. All good fun. [FMS]

Dir: Colin Finbow. (Children's Film Unit.) Rel: floating; first shown London (ICA) 2 September 1989. 90 mins. Cert U.

Hard Times – Tempo Dificeis. Something of an oddity, this black-and-white Portuguese version of Dickens's classic sticks closely to the original story, keeping the same gallery of characters and the campaigning intent. But the style is curiously stilted, and the setting is now a depressing little town known as Poco do Mondo, or World's End. For students interested in cinematic

Amateur histrionics? Kati Outinen and Pirkka-Pekka Petelius act out heroic love in Aki Kaurismaki's extraordinary Hamlet Goes Business, *from Electric Pictures.*

style and for collectors of oddball movies, *Hard Times* is fascinating but there is little here to attract anyone else – least of all the manner in which the players declaim rather than speak their lines. [FMS]

Cast: Henrique Viana (Mr Bounderby), Joaquim Mendes (Stephen Blackpool), Julia Britton (Louisa Gradgrind), Ruy Furtado (Thomas Gradgrind), Eunice Munoz, Isabel de Castro, Isabel Ruth, Lia Gama, Ines Medeiros, Luis Estrela, Pedro Cabrita Reis, Maria Pereira, Pedro Hestes, Maria Jose Oliveira, Beatriz Moreno. Dir, Pro, Ed and Screenplay: Joao Botelho; based on the Dickens novel. Ex Pro: Manuel Guanilho and Joao Pinto. Ph: Elso Roque. Art: Jasmine Matos. Set Des: Luis Monteiro. M: Antonio Pinho Vargas. (Joao Botelho, Lisbon/Artificial Eye Pro–Artificial Eye.) Rel: floating; first shown London (Camden Plaza), 2 June 1989 (unfortunately omitted from 1989–90 annual). 96 mins. Cert PG.

Hard to Kill. (Previously known as *Seven Year Storm*.) Former martial arts consultant Steven Seagal stars in his second film, which is so bad that Warner Bros refused to show it to the press in either America or the UK. Still, it broke box-office records when it opened Stateside in February ('90) and has confirmed Seagal as some watchable muscle. His real-life wife, Kelly LeBrock, co-stars as the bimbo nurse

who oversees LA cop Mason Storm (Seagal) as he struggles out of a seven-year coma. When he awakes, all Storm has on his mind is revenge – for the killers of his wife and kid. It's tough being an LA cop, particularly when you're trapped in a lumbering, ragged B-movie like this. [CB]

Also with: Bill Sadler (Vernon Trent), Frederick Coffin (Kevin O'Malley), Bonnie Burroughs (Felicia Storm), Andrew Bloch (Capt. Dan Hulland), Branscombe Richmond, Charles Boswell, Zachary Rosencrantz, Stanley Brock, Evan James, Jerry Dunphy, Jim Thompson, Catherine Quinn. Dir: Bruce Malmuth. Pro: Gary Adelson, Joel Simon and Bill Todman Jr. Ex Pro: Lee Rich and Michael Rachmil. Screenplay: Steven McKay. Ph: Matthew F. Leonetti. Ed: John F. Link. Pro Des: Robb Wilson King. M: David Michael Frank. Sound: Glenn Anderson. Martial arts choreography: Steven Seagal. (Warner.) Rel: 1 June 1990. 95 mins. Cert 18.

Harlem Nights. Harlem, 1938. When Sugar Ray's illegal nightclub does better business than its rivals, local mobster Bugsy Calhoune steps in to take over. However, the latter hadn't bargained on the intervention of Sugar Ray's adopted son, Quick Brown. An affectionate homage to the Hollywood gangster melodrama of yesteryear, *Harlem Nights* is well made and plotted, but no amount of profanity can replace the genuine belly laughs this film so badly needs. Making his debut behind

Three giants of American comedy: Eddie Murphy, Richard Pryor and Redd Foxx in UIP's disappointing Harlem Nights.

the camera, Eddie Murphy displays an assured if uninspired directorial hand. [JC-W]

Cast includes: Eddie Murphy (Quick Brown), Richard Pryor (Sugar Ray), Redd Foxx (Bennie Wilson), Danny Aiello (Phil Cantone), Michael Lerner (Bugsy Calhoune), Della Reese (Vera), Stan Shaw (Jack Jenkins, Heavyweight Champion of the World), Jasmine Guy (Dominique La Rue),

War of the Heathers: Winona Ryder, Kim Walker, Lisanne Falk and Shannen Doherty in Michael Lehmann's black, black Heathers *(Premier Releasing).*

Lela Rochon ('Sunshine'), Desi Arnez Hines II (young Quick), Berlinda Tolbert, Vic Polizos, David Marciano, Arsenio Hall, Tommy Ford, Uncle Ray, Michael Goldfinger, Joe Pecoraro, Ji-Tu Cumbuka, Nick Savage, Ricky Aiello, Mike Genovese. Dir, Ex Pro and Screenplay: Eddie Murphy. Pro: Robert D. Wachs and Mark Lipsky. Ph: Woody Omens. Ed: George Bowers. Pro Des: Lawerence G. Paull. M: Herbie Hancock; songs performed by Louis Armstrong, Duke Ellington, Eddy Duchin, Billie Holiday, The Andrew Sisters, Count Basie, etc. Costumes: Joe I. Tompkins. Sound: Gene S. Cantamessa. (Paramount–UIP.) Rel: 25 May 1990. 116 mins. Cert 15.

Heathers. Heather Duke, Heather McNamara and Heather Chandler may

be beautiful and bright, but they're the most hated bitches at Westerburgh High, Ohio. To them, high school is about getting ahead, not getting along. Veronica (Winona Ryder) is a 'Heather' too, but a reluctant member of the power-drunk peer-pressure group. Although these bitches are her best friends she sniffs mutiny in the air. Enter dark horse J.D. (Christian Slater), a guy who eats jocks for elevenses and solves schoolyard bullying with gunplay. 'Look', argues Veronica, 'my Bonnie and Clyde days are over' – but the body count has started. *Heathers* acquired cult status in the States and does boast a refreshing screenplay, creating its own etymology with terms such as 'Diet Coke-heads', 'strip-croquet' and 'the upchuck factor', while reducing whole sentences to 'Very' and 'Later'. Unfortunately, Michael Lehmann overdirects Daniel Waters's miraculous script with the misguided eagerness of a first-time film-maker. However, he cannot extinguish his cast's enthusiasm. Depending on your point of view, *Heathers* works either as a chilling thriller or as a hilarious black comedy. [JC-W]

Also with: Shannen Doherty (Heather Duke), Lisanne Falk (Heather McNamara), Kim Walker (Heather Chandler), Penelope Milford (Pauline Fleming), Glenn Shadix, Lance Fenton, Patrick Labyorteaux, Jeremy Applegate, Jon Matthews, Carrie Lynn, Phil Lewis, Renee Estevez, Jennifer Rhodes, Bill Cort, Larry Cox, Aaron Mendelsohn, Mark Bringelson, Chuck Lafont, Mark Carlton. Dir: Michael Lehmann. Pro: Denise Di Novi. Ex Pro: Christopher Webster. Screenplay: Daniel Waters. Ph: Francis Kenney. Ed: Norman Hollyn. Pro Des: Jon Hutman. M: David Newman. Costumes: Rudy Dillon. Sound: Douglas Axtell. (New World Pictures/Cinemarque Ent.–Premier Releasing.) Rel: 17 November 1989. 103 mins. Cert 18.

Henry V. Anyone unlucky enough never to have seen the late Laurence Olivier's film of Shakespeare's play will probably find this new adaptation an impressive achievement. For those who *do* remember the Olivier version, the lack of poetry, magnificent spectacle, colour, music and, of course, that magical voice, make this, for all its grittiness, merely second best. But actor-director Kenneth Branagh (working with a greatly reduced budget) still deserves praise, as do many of the cast, notably Brian Blessed, Paul Scofield,

Kenneth Branagh's vigorous production of Henry V *featured Branagh (above) as King Henry, Emma Thompson as the Princess of France, Paul Scofield as a worried King of France, and Michael Maloney as the Dauphin.*

Derek Jacobi, David Parfitt and particularly Richard Briers, giving a performance that contrasts sharply with his frequent work in TV comedy series. Olivier was a hard act to follow, but young Branagh still proves he's a star of considerable talent, both behind and in front of the camera. [FMS]

Cast includes: Derek Jacobi (Chorus), Kenneth Branagh (Henry), Brian Blessed (Exeter), Alec McCowen (Ely), Ian Holm (Fluellen), John Sessions (Macmorris), Richard Briers (Bardolph), Robert Stephens (Pistol), Robbie Coltrane (Falstaff), Judi Dench (Mistress Quickly), Paul Scofield (French King), Michael Maloney (Dauphin), Emma Thompson (Katherine), Geraldine McEwan (Alice), Simon Shepherd (Gloucester), James Larkin (Bedford), Charles Kay (Canterbury), Paul Gregory (Westmoreland), Fabian Cartwright, Stephen Simms, Jay Villiers, Edward Jewesbury, Daniel Webb, Jimmy Yuill, Shaun Prendergast, Pat Doyle, Michael Williams, Geoffrey Hutchings, Christian Bale, Harold

Innocent, Richard Clifford, Colin Hurley, Richard Easton, Christopher Ravenscroft, David Lloyd Meredith, Nicholas Ferguson, Tom Whitehouse, Nigel Greaves, Julian Gartside, Mark Inman, Chris Armstrong, Calum Yuill. Dir: Kenneth Branagh. Pro: Bruce Sharman. Ex Pro: Stephen Evans. Ph: Kenneth MacMillan. Assoc Pro: David Parfitt. Ed: Michael Bradsell. Pro Des: Tim Harvey. Costumes: Phyllis Dalton. M: Patrick Doyle. (Renaissance Films PLC in assoc. with BBC and Curzon Films Dist.) Rel: floating; first shown London (Curzon, Mayfair) 6 October 1989. 135 mins. Cert PG.

Henry . . . Portrait of a Serial Killer. The audience plays peeping tom in this devastatingly realistic documentary-style profile of a murderer. Basing his

Gary Busey spies on domestic tranquillity in Vestron's chilling, accomplished Hider in the House.

film on the stories of a real-life killer, director John McNaughton gives us a chilling account of Henry's macabre and horribly casual method of taking a life. McNaughton never takes a moral stand, however, so we never get into the mind of the killer or understand his motivation, the result being a relentless series of scenes of brutal murders, with the odd bit of bizarre humour thrown in. Hopeless, heartless and mindless, but nonetheless strangely compelling. For sickies only. [BW]

Cast includes: Michael Rooker (Henry), Tom Towles (Otis), Tracy Arnold (Becky). Dir: John McNaughton. Pro: McNaughton, Lisa Dedmond and Steven A. Jones. Ex Pro: Waleed B. Ali and Malik B. Ali. Screenplay: McNaughton and Richard Fire. Ph: Charlie Lieberman. Ed: Elena Maganini. Art: Rick Paul. M: McNaughton, Ken Hale and Steven A. Jones. (Maljack–Scala.) Rel: floating; first shown London (Scala) 8 March 1990. 83 mins. No cert.

Hider in the House. One of the year's most accomplished thrillers – in which the villain is a likeable if not entirely loveable guy. Tom Sykes (Gary Busey), victim of an abused childhood, was burned with cigarettes by his father and retaliated by setting fire to his parent's house. Twenty years later, just released from a mental hospital, Tom walls himself into the spacious attic of a large house undergoing refurbishment. Plugging himself into the house's intercom system, the unseen stranger eavesdrops on the life of the new tenants and adopts the Dryers as the family he never had. But when he takes the law into his own hands, Tom's paradise rips apart at the seams. A well-made thriller, this, with a welcome absence of tricks, aided by a round of above-average performances. At times, the suspense is unbearable. [JC-W]

Also with: Mimi Rogers (Julie Dryer), Michael McKean (Phil Dryer), Kurt Christopher Kinder (Neil Dryer), Candy Hutson (Holly Dryer), Bruce Glover, Jake Busey, Elizabeth Ruscio, Leonard Termo. Dir: Matthew Patrick. Pro: Edward Teets and Michael Taylor. Co-Pro: Stuart Cornfeld and Lem Dobbs. Screenplay: Lem Dobbs. Ph: Jeff Jur. Ed: Debra Smith. Pro Des: Vicki Paul. (Vestron.) Rel: 1 December 1989. 105 mins. Cert 18.

Homeboy. Somewhat aimless character study of a bum boxer hanging out in Asbury Park, New Jersey. Based on a story by Mickey Rourke – who used to be a boxer himself – the film dispenses with such *Rocky* clichés as winning over the odds, and shows the sport in all its brutal reality. An atmospheric, gritty showcase for Rourke, who gives another remarkable performance, *Homeboy* also highlights a marvellous turn from Christopher Walken as a narcissistic small-time crook. However, the film is fatally wounded by Eric Clapton's self-conscious score. [JC-W]

Also with: Debra Feuer (Ruby), Kevin Conway (Grazziano), Thomas Quinn (Lou), Antony Alda, Jon Polito, Ruben Blades, Willy De Ville, Iran Barkley, Larry Hazzard. Dir: Michael Seresin. Pro: Alan Marshall and Elliot Kastner. Screenplay: Eddie Cook; from a story by Mickey Rourke. Ph: Gale Tattersall. Ed: Ray Lovejoy. Pro Des: Brian Morris. M: Eric Clapton and Michael Kamen. Costumes: Richard Shissler. (Braveworld–Fox.) Rel: 14 July 1989. 115 mins. Cert 15.

Honey, I Shrunk the Kids. Promising title, goldarn awful movie. A nerdy scientist (Rick Moranis) invents a machine that miniaturises matter, and accidentally shrinks his and the neighbours' kids. Dumped at the bottom of the garden with the rubbish, the children must reach their house before nightfall. What sounds like a fun companion piece to *The Incredible Shrinking Woman* is actually a witless sci-fi adventure more in the tradition of the cod *Fantastic Voyage*. Appalling special effects, embarrassing acting and a philanthropic ant further undermine any merit this monstrosity may have promised in the first place. Having said that, this was Disney's biggest opening box-office blockbuster in the history of the studio. Next up: *Honey, I've Made the Kids Invisible* (really!). [JC-W]

Cast includes: Rick Moranis (Wayne Szalinski), Matt Frewer (Big Russ Thompson), Marcia Strassman (Diane Szalinski), Kristine Sutherland (Mae Thompson), Thomas Brown (little Russ Thompson), Jared Rushton (Ron Thompson), Amy O'Neill (Amy Szalinski), Robert Oliveri (Nick Szalinski), Carl Steven, Mark L. Taylor, Kimmy Robertson, Dir: Joe Johnston. Pro: Penney Finkelman Cox. Ex Pro: Thomas G. Smith. Screenplay: Ed Naha and Tom Schulman; from a story by Stuart Gordon, Brian Yuzna and Ed Naha. Ph: Hiro Narita. Ed: Michael A. Stevenson. Pro Des: Gregg Fonseca. M: James Horner; 'Turn It Up' sung by Nick Kamen; theme from *Amarcord* by Nino Rota. Costumes: Carol Brolaski. Sound: Wylie Stateman. (Walt Disney.) Rel: 9 February 1990. 93 mins. Cert U.

The House of Bernarda Alba. Hot on the heels of the West End stage version, comes the first screen dramatisation of Federico Garcia Lorca's celebrated play – filmed fifty years after his murder by fascists in 1936. A well-made but somewhat stagey adaptation, the film follows the lives of six women, incarcerated in their own grief after the death of the patriarch. When, after eight years of forced mourning, a man arrives in the women's midst, all emotional hell is let loose. A sextet of fine Spanish actresses do the histrionics justice. [CB]

Cast includes: Irene Gutierrez Caba (Bernarda), Ana Belen (Adela), Florinda Chico (Poncia), Enriqueta Carballeira (Augustias), Vicky Pena (Martirio), Aurora Pastor (Magdalena), Mercedes Lezcano (Amelia), Pilar Puchol (Criada). Dir: Mario Camus. Ex Pro: Jaime Borrell, Jose Miguel Juarez and Antonio Oliver. Screenplay: Marisa Ibarra; based on the adaptation by Camus and Antonio Larreta. Ph: Fernando

Mickey Rourke as the brain-damaged Johnny Walker in Braveworld-Fox's Homeboy, *from the actor's own story.*

Arribas. Ed: Jose M. Biurrun. Art: Rafael Palmero. M: Angel Alvarez. Sound: Bernardo Menz. (Paraiso S.A./TVE S.A.–Gala.) Rel: floating; first shown London (Cannon Premiere) 2 March 1990. 104 mins. Cert 15.

How to Get Ahead in Advertising. Dennis Bagley is rich, successful and married to an English cover-girl beauty. An advertising executive, he claims he can sell shampoo to a bald man, stating that 'the world is a shop – everything has a price tag'. However, the challenge of selling a pimple cream (suggested title: 'The Boil Buster') sends him off the deep end and Bagley develops a talking carbuncle above his collarbone. A wickedly funny farce,

How to Get Ahead in Advertising is one of the most stylish, original and significant British films since *A Clockwork Orange*. Bruce Robinson's script, bursting with challenging ideas and some priceless one-liners, is both hilarious and terrifying, and is well served by a bravura performance from Richard E. Grant as the manic Bagley. A highly entertaining, coherent and timely comedy that provides a scary menu of food for thought. Music, photography, production design, etc, are all top-rung, making this another film to be proud of from the director of *Withnail & I*. [JC-W]

Also with: Rachel Ward (Julia Bagley), Richard Wilson (Bristol), Jacqueline Tong (Penny Wheelstock), John Shrapnel (psychiatrist), Susan Wooldridge (Monica), Mick Ford (Richard), Jacqueline Pearce, Roddy Maude-Roxby, Pauline Melville, Rachel Fielding, Tony Slattery, Pip Tor-

Rachel Ward converses with the boil on Richard E. Grant's neck in HandMade–Virgin's hilarious and brilliant How to Get Ahead in Advertising.

rens, Gordon Gostelow, Sean Bean, Francesca Longrigg, Vivienne McKone, Kerryann White. Dir and Screenplay: Bruce Robinson. Pro: David Wimbury. Co-Pro: Ray Cooper. Ex Pro: George Harrison and Denis O'Brien. Ph: Peter Hannan. Ed: Alan Strachan. Pro Des: Michael Pickwoad. M: David Dundas and Rick Wentworth. Costumes: Andrea Galer. Sound: Clive Winter. (HandMade–Virgin.) Rel: floating; first shown London (Lumiere) 28 July 1989. 104 mins. Cert 15.

The Hunt for Red October. Sean Connery, captain of a Russian nuclear submarine (*Red October*), defects to the US and takes his entire crew and sub with him. The problem is to convince the States that his mission is a peaceful one. Of course, to American eyes a Soviet nuclear sub heading for the coast of Maine – pursued by the bulk of the Russian fleet – looks anything but pally. It is up to gung-ho CIA analyst Alec Baldwin to sort the chaff from the fleet. Based on the bestselling novel by Tom

Clancy, authenticity is the name of the game, but the straight-faced concentration on the hardware does make this look vaguely like an animated naval textbook. [JC-W]

Cast includes: Sean Connery (Capt. Marko Ramius), Alec Baldwin (Jack Ryan), Scott Glenn (Capt. Bart Mancuso), James Earl Jones (Admiral James Greer), Sam Neill (Capt. Vasily Borodin), Joss Ackland (Soviet Ambassador), Richard Jordan, Peter Firth, Tim Curry, Courtney B. Vance, Stellan Skarsgard, Jeffrey Jones, Timothy Carhart, Larry Ferguson, Fred Dalton Thompson, Daniel Davis, Anthony Peck, Tomas Arana, Sven-Ole Thorsen, Rick Ducommun, John McTiernan Sr. Dir: John McTiernan. Pro: Mace Neufeld. Ex Pro: Larry de Waay and Jerry Sherlock. Screenplay: Larry Ferguson and Donald Stewart; based on the novel by Tom Clancy. Ph: Jan De Bont. Ed: Dennis Virkler and John Wright. Pro Des: Terence Marsh. M: Basil Poledouris. Sound: Richard Bryce Goodman. (Paramount–UIP.) Rel: 18 April 1990. 135 mins. Cert PG.

I'm Gonna Git You Sucka. Sporadically amusing parody of black exploitationers, boasting an all-star cast of the genre, including Bernie Casey (*Hit Man*), Isaac Hayes (*Truck Turner*) and Jim Brown (*Slaughter* and *Black Gunn*).

Set in 'Any Ghetto USA', the film turns clichés on their head as it follows the quest of army penpusher Jack Spade to avenge the death of his brother who tragically 'O.G-ed' (death by wearing too many gold chains). Young writer-director Keenen Ivory Wayans stars as Spade, and establishes an imposing physical presence, while, as a member of the 'new wave' of black *auteur* filmmakers, showing considerable flair and some restraint in the pratfall department. Very promising. Previously known as *I'mo Git Ya Sucka*. [JC-W]

Also with: Bernie Casey (John Slade), Antonio Fargas (Flyguy), Steve James (Kung Fu Joe), Isaac Hayes (Hammer), Jim Brown (Slammer), Ja'net DuBois (Ma Bell), Dawnn Lewis (Cheryl), John Vernon (Mr Big), Clu Gulager, Clarence Williams III, David Alan Grier, Kim Wayans, Wren Brown, Nadia Wayans, Marlon Wayans, Shawn Wayans. Dir and Screenplay: Keenen Ivory Wayans. Pro: Peter McCarthy and Carl Craig. Co-Pro: Eric Barrett and Tamara Rawitt. Ex Pro: Raymond Katz and Eric L. Gold. Ph: Tom Richmond. Ed: Michael R. Miller. Pro Des: Melba Farquhar and Catherine Hardwicke. M: David Michael Frank; songs performed by The Gap Band, The Kids Next Door, Jennifer Holliday, Kim Wayans, The Four Tops &

What the hell is that? Courtney B. Vance and Scott Glenn sort the blips from the Russians in the Tom Clancy blockbuster, The Hunt for Red October *(UIP).*

Aretha Franklin, The Jackson Five, Isaac Hayes, Jermaine Jackson, Curtis Mayfield, Carl Douglas, etc. Costumes: Ruth E. Carter. Sound: Oliver L. Moss. (MGM/UA–UIP.) Rel: 10 November 1989. 89 mins. Cert 15.

Imago Meret Oppenheim. Glenda Jackson speaks the narration in this feature-length documentary about the little-known Swiss artist who was one of the leaders of the surrealist movement of the 1930s. Drawings, letters, poems and sculptures are brought together to record her exploration of dreams, the unconscious, identity, 'metamorphosis, the playful and the androgynous'. Filmed on location in Italy, Switzerland and Paris. [FMS]

Dir: Pamela Robertson-Pierce and Anselm Spoerri. (ICA.) Rel: floating: first shown London (ICA) 14 October 1989. 90 mins. No cert.

In Country. Samantha Hughes is a small-town 18-year-old. Her father died

in the Vietnam war before she was born, at her age now, and she wants to know how and why. But nobody cares. Not even Sam's mother, now remarried, nor her uncle, a Vietnam vet himself. *In Country* examines the scars left behind by Vietnam on the children, as well as the direct victims, and is terribly affecting without the bludgeon of physical violence. Emily Lloyd, as

Sam, is glowingly natural and copes commendably with her Kentuckian accent, exploring the guts of a girl who

Norman Jewison's powerful, touching In Country *(Warner) was one of the year's maturer looks at the effects of Vietnam. Sam (Emily Lloyd) and Uncle Emmett (Bruce Willis) face up to some painful truths.*

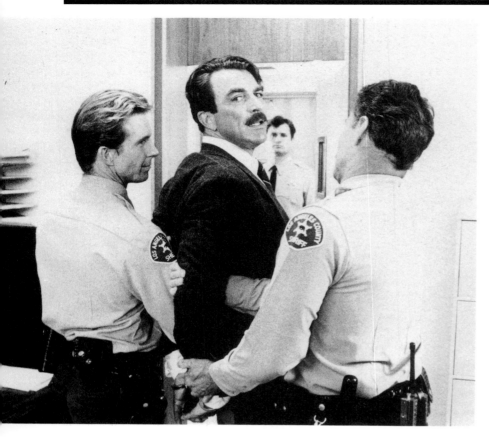

Tom Selleck, as An Innocent Man *(Warner), is framed by the cops.*

An Innocent Man. Following in the footsteps of every major star before him (McQueen, Eastwood, Redford – you name 'em), Tom Selleck goes to prison. Of course, Selleck's jailbird is innocent, an airport engineer and caring husband framed by a couple of corrupt cops. Inside, he has to adjust to a cruel world and alter his principles accordingly, but even when he's gutting an inmate with a shard of glass you know Tom's alright – just a regular guy. Anyway, in spite of the Marlboro Man's wholesome image, this is Selleck's toughest movie yet – with a pair of delicious villains to spice up our indignation. [JC-W]

Cast includes: Tom Selleck (Jimmie Rainwood), F. Murray Abraham (Virgil Cane), Laila Robins (Kate Rainwood), David Rasche (Mike Parnell), Richard Young (Danny Scalise), Badja Djola (John Fitzgerald), Todd Graff (Robby), Bruce A. Young (Jingles), J. Kenneth Campbell (Lt Freebery), J. J. Johnston (Joseph Donatelli), M. C. Gainey, Peter van Norden, James T. Morris, Terry Golden, Holly Fulger, Philip Baker Hall, Maggie Baird. Dir: Peter Yates. Pro: Ted Field and Robert W. Cort. Ex Pro: Scott Kroopf. Screenplay: Larry Brothers. Ph: William A. Fraker. Ed: Stephen A. Rotter and William S. Scharf. Pro Des: Stuart Wurtzel. M: Howard Shores; 'When the Night Comes' performed by Joe Cocker. Costumes: Rita Ryack. Sound: Dan Sable. (Touchstone/Silver Screen–Warner.) Rel: 22 June 1990. 114 mins. Cert 18.

wants to befriend the father she never knew, to know the food he liked, the music he listened to, while despairing that she can never share her love of Springsteen or *E.T.* with him. Norman Jewison directs with a flawless feel for small-town American life (where McDonald's isn't a dirty word) and is well served by an excellent script which, although profoundly tragic, never loses touch with the humour of the mundane. An intelligent, moving film. [JC-W]

Also with: Bruce Willis (Emmett Smith, Sam's uncle), Joan Allen (Irene), Kevin Anderson (Lonnie), John Terry (Tom), Peggy Rea (Mamaw), Judith Ivey (Anita), Richard Hamilton (Grampaw), Dan Jenkins, Stephen Tobolowsky, Jim Beaver, Heidi Swedberg, Ken Jenkins, Revd W. G. Harvey. Dir: Norman Jewison. Pro: Jewison and Richard Roth. Ex Pro: Charles Mulvehill. Screenplay: Frank Pierson and Cynthia Cidre; from the novel by Bobbie Ann Mason. Ph: Russell Boyd. Ed: Anthony Gibbs and Lou Lombardo. Pro Des: Jackson DeGovia. M: James Horner; songs performace by Bruce Springsteen, The Mamas and the Papas, The Four Tops, Jackie De Shannon, Martha & the Vandellas, k.d. lang, Hank Williams Jr, Hothouse Flowers, etc. Costumes: Aggie Guerard Rodgers. Sound: Scott Smith. (Warner.) Rel: 12 January 1990. 115 mins. Cert 15.

In Fading Light. Surprisingly arresting small-scale semi-documentary made by the Amber Film co-operative for £300,000. Set in the stark world of the North Shields fishing industry, the film follows the confrontation between a girl and her estranged father as they set off to sea. The fishing sequences are filmed with a raw beauty, almost making up for the film's stodgier scenes of human interaction. [CB]

Cast includes: Joanna Ripley (Karen Olsen), Dave Hill (Alfie Olsen), Sammy Johnson (Dandy Mac), Brian Hogg (Micky Molloy), Mo Caffrey (Irene), Joe Caffrey (Yopper). Dir and Pro: the Amber production team. Screenplay: Tom Hadaway. Ph: Amber. M: Alasdair Robertson and Ray Stubbs; songs performed by The Waterboys. (Amber Films/ACTT Workshop Declaration/Channel Four/Northern Arts–ICA.) Rel: floating; first shown London (ICA) 12 February 1990. 102 mins. No cert.

Internal Affairs. Tough, atmospheric thriller with Richard Gere giving a sleazy, selfless performance as a relentlessly unlikeable rogue cop. Nobody, it would seem, is safe from the clutches of Dennis Peck, who has the better part of LA in his back pocket. When Internal Affairs Investigator Raymond Avilla (Andy Garcia) locks on to his case, Peck declares psychological warfare on the man, eventually embroiling Avilla's wife to terrifying ends. Against our better instincts we pray for a glimmer of redemption in this character, but Peck is the very incarnation of evil, a silver-tongued lady's man and a cold-hearted killer who *always* gets his way. Garcia, in the less showy role, is the embodiment of rock-solid understatement, allowing us almost imperceptible glimpses of his deterioration as he cracks under Gere's powerful spell. A dark, moody thriller, *Internal Affairs* is layered with seedy menace and subtle suspense, revealing a craftsman (Eng-

Robert De Niro and Ed Harris discuss bloodier times in David Jones's superbly acted Jacknife, *from Vestron.*

lish director Mike Figgis) at the peak of his powers. Strong meat. [JC-W]

Also with: Nancy Travis (Kathleen Avilla), Laurie Metcalf (Amy Wallace), Richard Bradford (Grieb), William Baldwin (Van Stretch), Michael Beach (Dorian Fletcher), Katherine Borowitz (Tova Arrocas), Faye Grant (Penny), John Kapelos (Steven Arrocas), Annabella Sciorra (Heather), Xander Berkeley, John Capodice, Victoria Dillard, Pamella D'Pella, Susan Forristal, Allan Havey, Lew Hopson, Julio Oscar Mechoso, Harry Murphy, Billie Neal, Arlen Dean Snyder, Ron Vawter, Justin DeRosa, Mike Figgis, Frank Mancuso Jr, Jimmy Ortega, John Getz. Dir: Mike Figgis. Pro: Frank Mancuso Jr. Ex Pro.: Pierre David and René Mal. Screenplay: Henry Bean. Ph: John A. Alonzo. Ed: Robert Estrin. Pro Des: Waldemar Kalinowski. M: Mike Figgis. Costumes: Rudy Dillon. Sound: David Brownlow. (Paramount–UIP.) Rel: 4 May 1990. 115 mins. Cert 18.

The Iron Triangle. An action-crammed drama, inspired by the contents of a blood-stained diary that

belonged to an unknown Vietcong soldier. Interesting in that it shows the war from both sides, the film is nevertheless marred by some trite voice-over dialogue ('We couldn't have been more different – maybe we couldn't have been more alike') and an abundance of Vietnamese characters speaking with American accents. Still, there are some good battle scenes, a rousing score and excellent photography, helping to elevate this well-intentioned straight-faced B-movie to the level of endurable melodrama. A bad film, but nonetheless a thought-provoking and engrossing one. [JC-W]

Cast includes: Beau Bridges (Major Keene), Haing S. Ngor (Captain Tuong), Johnny Hallyday (Jacques), Liem Whatley (Ho), Iilana B'Tiste (Khan Ly), James Ishida, Ping Wu, Richard Weygint, Allan Moore, Bobby McGee, Sunny Trinidad. Dir and (with John Bushelman and Lawrence Hilbrand) Screenplay: Eric Weston. Pro: Tony Scotti and Angela P. Schapiro. Ex Pro: Ben Scotti and Fred Scotti. Ph: Irv Goodnoff. Ed: Roy Watts. Pro Des: Errol Kelly. M: Michael Lloyd, John D'Andrea and Nick Strimple. Sound: Douglas Jackson and Jeff Okun. (Scotti Brothers/Eurobrothers–Medusa.) Rel: 29 September 1989. 90 mins. Cert 18.

Jacknife. Three characters in search of themselves congregate in a sleepy Connecticut mill town. Dave Flanagan (Ed Harris), a truck driver and Vietnam veteran, and his sister Martha (Kathy Baker), a schoolteacher, live together in an atmosphere of disillusionment. He cannot exorcise the ghosts of Vietnam, she cannot come to terms with her emotional solitude. Enter Joseph Megessey (Robert De Niro), Vietnam vet and car mechanic, who drops in on his old buddy Dave. Joseph is a clown, an irrepressible man who enjoys life as if it were one long party. Over a period of a few weeks the trio expose some home truths and painful memories are exhumed. An undercurrent of impending violence pervades the film which, although slow-moving and stagey to a fault, displays three brilliant performances – which you'd expect from the likes of De Niro, Harris and Baker. [JC-W]

Also with: Sloane Shelton (Shirley), Charles Dutton (Jake), Loudon Wainwright III (Ferretti). Dir: David Jones. Pro: Robert Schaffel and Carol Baum. Screenplay: Stephen Metcalfe; based on his play *Strange Snow*. Ph: Brian West. Ed: John Bloom. Pro Des: Edward Pisoni. M: Bruce Broughton.

and interviews, all contributing to a convincing picture of what it is like 'to be born black, impoverished, gay and gifted'. [FMS]

Those appearing include (apart from Baldwin): Maya Angelou, Amiri Baraka, David Baldwin, William Styron, Ishmael Read, Bobby Short, David Leeming, Lucien Happersberger, Bernard Hasses, William Cole, Engin Cezzar, Yasha Kernel, James Briggs Murray, Frances Foster, Cynthia Packard, Alexa Birdsong. Dir and (with William Miles) Pro: Karen Thorsen. Co-Pro: Douglas K. Dempsey. Assoc. Pro: Joy Birdsong and Joe Wood. Ex Pro: Susan Lacy and Albert Maysles. Screenplay: Thorsen and Dempsey. Ph: Don Lenzer. (Nobody Knows Productions/Maysles Films/American Master–BFI.) Rel: floating; first shown London (Riverside Studios) 20 April 1990. 87 mins. Cert PG.

James Baldwin takes tea in Istanbul in 1965. From the BFI-released documentary, James Baldwin: The Price of the Ticket, *about the novelist's life and work.*

Catherine Wilkening, Lothaire Blutheau and Johanne-Marie Tremblay discover some surprising realities from the New Testament in Denys Arcand's brilliantly original Jesus of Montreal *(Artificial Eye).*

Sound: Gary Alper and Patrick Rousseau. (Kings Road–Vestron.) Rel: 8 September 1989. 98 mins. Cert 15.

James Baldwin: The Price of the Ticket. A documentary about the life and times of the late James Baldwin: a mixture of his civil rights activist speeches, archival inserts, home movies

Jesus of Montreal. The story of Christ is acted out by a quintet of actors on Montreal's Mount Royal, overlooking the city. There is no stage, and the play moves from location to location, inviting its audience to move with it. Biblical scenes are acted out in the setting that best serves them: Jesus walking on the water, the Crucifixion on the mount, the Resurrection from the tomb, etc. And the spectators, hypnotised by the simple conviction of the recreated events, are led from place to place by a uniformed guard. The rest of the film explores the relationship between the five actors in their private lives. A sub-plot involves the controversy of the play, exposing the hypocrisy of organised religion as the local priesthood takes exception to the work's unconventional and realistic approach to the New Testament. The publicity for *Jesus of Montreal* claimed that the film was about 'The Gospel according to St Mark . . . the dubbing of pornographic movies . . . and Paul Newman's salad dressing.' This was an entirely frivolous representation of a drama that is predominantly concerned with exploring our religious faith. Denys Arcand, the *enfant terrible* of French-Canadian cinema, takes sidelong swipes at everything from the cruelty of mass auditions to advertising, but his film is not *about* such lateral issues. These diversions merely enrich the texture of his complex, invigorating picture. Winner of the Grand Prix at the 1989 Cannes Film Festival and Oscar nominee for Best Foreign-Language film. [JC-W]

Cast includes: Lothaire Blutheau (Daniel), Catherine Wilkening (Mireille), Johanne-Marie Tremblay (Constance), Rémy Girard (Martin), Robert Lepage (René), Gilles Pelletier, Yves Jacques, Denys Arcand, Marie-Christine Barrault. Dir and Screenplay: Denys Arcand. Pro: Roger Frappier and Pierre Gendron. Ph: Guy Dufaux. Ed: Isabelle Dedieu. Art: François Séguin. M: Yves Laferrière. Costumes: Louise Jobin. Sound: Patrick Rousseau and Marcel Pothier. (Max Films/Gerard Mital/National Film Board of Canada, etc.–Artificial Eye.) Rel: floating; first shown London (Lumiere) 19 January 1990. 120 mins. Cert 18.

Johnny Handsome. Downbeat character study of a disfigured New Orleans crook who's given the chance to improve his life. Unfortunately, Johnny Handsome (a cruel nickname) uses the prison facilities for free plastic surgery as a sly opportunity to wreak revenge on the colleagues who put him behind bars in the first place. Walter Hill directs with great aplomb but is left at sea by the sheer vacuity of his leading character. [JC-W]

Cast includes: Mickey Rourke (John Sedley/'Johnny Handsome'), Ellen Barkin (Sunny Boyd), Elizabeth McGovern (Donna McCarty), Morgan Freeman (Lt A. Z. Drones), Forest Whitaker (Dr Steven Resher), Lance Henriksen (Rafe Garrett), Scott Wilson (Mikey Chalmette), David Schramm, Yvonne Bryceland, Peter Jason, Jeff Meek, Allan Graf, Ed Walsh. Dir: Walter Hill. Pro: Charles Roven. Ex Pro: Mario Kassar and Andrew Vajna. Screenplay: Ken Friedman; based on the novel *The Three Worlds of Johnny Handsome* by John Godey. Ph: Matthew F. Leonetti. Ed: Freeman Davies. Pro Des: Gene Rudolf. M: Ry Cooder. Sound: Richard Goodman. (Carolco–Guild.) Rel: 11 May 1990. 94 mins. Cert 15.

Judgment in Berlin. The caption 'inspired by a true story' can disguise any number of fictions, but this ineptly executed drama is so dull that it *has* to be true. An East Berliner, escaping to the West, hijacks a Polish plane and has to stand trial for risking aviation safety. Martin Sheen, as the kindly, upstanding Judge Herbert T. Stern, presides over the case on behalf of the neutral Americans and you just know – in your heart of hearts – what's going to happen. What *is* surprising is Sean Penn's courtroom cameo (filmed before Marlon Brando's in *A Dry White*

A fur cop? Jerry Lee and James Belushi as narcotics cops in Rod Daniel's K-9 *(UIP).*

Season) as a fellow German defector. Penn the Younger, as directed by Penn the Elder, almost steals the show. [JC-W]

Also with: Sam Wanamaker (Bernard Hellring), Max Gail (Judah Best), Juergen Heinrich (Uri Andreyev), Heinz Hoenig (Helmut Thiele), Carl Lumbly (Edwin Palmer), Max Volkert Martens (Hans Schuster), Cristine Rose (Marsha Stern), Sean Penn (Guenther X), Marie-Louise Sinclair, Joshua Sinclair, Jutta Speidel, Harris Yulin, Eileen Ryan, R. D. Call. Dir: Leo Penn. Pro: Joshua Sinclair and Ingrid Windisch. Ex Pro: Martin Sheen, William R. Greenblatt and Jeffrey Auerbach. Screenplay: Sinclair and Penn; based on the book by Herbert J. Stern. Ph: Gabor Pogany. Ed: Teddy Darvas. Art: Jan Schlubach and Peter Alteneder. M: Peter Goldfoot. Costumes: Ingrid Zore. (Sheen/Greenblatt–HoBo.) Rel: 23 March 1990. 95 mins. Cert PG.

K–9. Quite amusing and engaging comedy-drama about a San Diego narcotics cop and his new partner – a dog. The canine (geddit?) is an Alsatian drug-sniffer, the cop a maverick rule-breaker who failed to cry at the end of *Old Yeller*. Together, the quarrelsome duo hope to unmask a drugs baron (the always evil Kevin Tighe) and to live to wag the tail. In spite of the familiar plot ingredients there are plenty of funny moments and nice touches, while James Belushi and Jerry Lee (as himself) hold their own in amongst the stunts and firepower. Favourite scene: that in which Pruitt Taylor Vince hurls a snooker ball at Jerry Lee's face, the latter catching it in his mouth, chewing it into two and then spitting it out. Some tough dog. [JC-W]

Cast includes: James Belushi (Dooley), Mel Harris (Tracy), Kevin Tighe (Lyman), Ed O'Neill (Brannigan), Jerry Lee (himself), James Handy, Daniel Davis, Cotter Smith, John Snyder, Pruitt Taylor Vince, David Haskell, Alan Blumenfield, Bill Sadler,

Wendel Meldrum, Coleen Morris, Gary Combs. Dir: Rod Daniel. Pro: Lawrence Gordon and Charles Gordon. Co-Pro: Steven Siegel. Ex Pro: Donna Smith. Screenplay: Siegel and Scott Myers. Ph: Dean Semler. Ed: Lois Freeman-Fox. Pro Des: George Costello. M: Miles Goodman; songs performed by Amy Holland, James Brown, Yellow, Rose Royce. Costumes: Eileen Kennedy. Sound: Donald Summer. (Universal–UIP.) Rel: 6 October 1989. 102 mins. Cert 15.

The Karate Kid Part III. Danny LaRusso (Ralph Macchio) is back in fighting form, helping his mentor Miyagi (Noriyuki 'Pat' Morita) open up a bonsai shop, while winning a new girl-friend and lotsa fresh enemies. In its bid to top its box-office busting predecessors, *KKIII* offers more karate (seven fights in all), more villains and more bonsai trees. While newcomer Thomas Ian Griffith supplies some undiluted villainy, the charm and culture of the previous film is sacrificed. *KKIII* is predictable to a fault, but is

Richard E. Grant and Julie Walters in an uncomfortable embrace in Palace's thoroughly unfortunate Killing Dad.

entertaining enough within the limitations of its genre. Top honours go to Roy Nagatoshi and James Barrett, credited as the movie's bonsai plant advisers! [JC-W]

Also with: Robyn Lively (Jessica), Martin L. Kove (Kreese), Sean Kanan (Mike Barnes), Jonathan Avildsen, Christopher Paul Ford, Randee Heller, Pat E. Johnson, Frances Bay. Dir and Co-Ed: John G. Avildsen. Pro: Jerry Weintraub. Co-Pro: Karen Trudy Rosenfelt. Ex Pro: Sheldon Schrager. Screenplay: Robert Mark Kamen. Ph: Stephen Yaconelli. Co-Ed: John Carter. Pro Des: William F. Matthews. M: Bill Conti. Sound: Barry Thomas. (Columbia Tri-Star.) Rel: 28 July 1989. 111 mins. Cert PG.

Kickboxer. The title is self-explanatory. Set in Thailand, *Kickboxer* is all about . . . well, kickboxing. Plenty of blood and violence, some pretty inept acting and nice photography. I still prefer Ludo. [FMS]

Cast: Jean Claude Van Damme (Kurt), Dennis Alexio (Eric), Dennis Chan (Xian Chow), Tong Po, Haskell Anderson, Rochelle Ashana. Dir: Mark DiSalle and David Worth. Pro: Mark DiSalle. Fight Dir: Van Damme. Screenplay: Glenn Bruce; from a story by DiSalle and Van Damme. Ph: Jon

Kranhouse. Ed: Wayne Wahram. Pro Des: Shay Austin. M: Paul Hertzog. (Kings Road Entertainment–Entertainment.) Rel: 18 August 1989. 100 mins. Cert 18.

Killing Dad. There's nothing killing about this abortion, least of all its sense of humour. Richard E. Grant is miscast as Alistair Berg, a Frank Spencer-ish hair tonic salesman who is dispatched to Southend-on-Sea to find his long-lost father. The latter, a boozing, womanising Denholm Elliott, only inspires revulsion in Berg Jr, who decides to indulge in a spot of patricide. A cast of wonderful actors (Elliott, Grant, Julie Walters, Anna Massey, Ann Way) work overtime scrambling for laughs, but their lurid characters are painfully overworked. A black comedy that's not so much subversive as sub-Orton. [JC-W]

Also with: Denholm Elliott (Nathy Berg), Julie Walters (Judith), Anna Massey (Edith Berg), Laura de Sol (Luisa), Ann Way (caretaker), Jonathan Phillips, Kevin Williams, Tom Radcliffe, Emma Longfellow. Dir and Screenplay: Michael Austin. Pro: Iain Smith. Ph: Gabriel Beristain. Ed. Edward Marnier. Pro Des: Adrienne Atkinson. M: Chaz Jankel and David Storrs. Costumes: Sandy Powell. Sound: Ian Voigt. From the novel *Berg* by Ann Quinn. (Applecross/STFE/British Screen–Palace Pictures.) Rel: 1 September 1989. 93 mins. Cert PG.

The Kill-Off. Luane Devore (Loretta Gross) is a chatterbox with a nasty streak. No dark secret in the crumbling New Jersey coastal town in which she lives is unknown to her. Although ageing and bed-ridden, Luane is an integral, if isolated, cog in this society on the edge. A woman with such power can't last long, but who will pull the trigger? Maggie Greenwald's atmospheric, sparse thriller plays like an Agatha Christie with a sick sense of humour. No cosy, tea-sipping aunts here, just a ragbag of gross, pitiful characters in search of a normal life. An ensemble cast play their parts with deadpan conviction, adding a wry, gritty touch to this bloodstained *film noir*. [JC-W]

Also with: Jackson Sims (Pete), Steve Monroe (Ralph), Cathy Haase (Danny Lee), Andrew Lee Barrett (Bobbie), Jorjan Fox (Myra), William Russell (Rags). Dir and Screenplay: Maggie Greenwald; based on the novel by Jim Thompson. Pro: Lydia Dean Pilcher. Ex Pro: Alexander W. Kogan and Barry Tucker. Ph: Declan Quinn. Ed:

Joanna Pacula closes in on her distressed niece Meredith Salenger in Columbia Tri-Star's demonic thriller, The Kiss.

James Y. Kwei. Pro Des: Pamela Wood-bridge. M: Evan Lurie. Costumes: Daryl Kerrigan. (Films Around the World–Palace.) Rel: 9 February 1990. 92 mins. Cert 18.

King of the Wind. Slapdash adaptation of the Marguerite Henry novel about a mute Arab boy and his horse. Various locations and an all-star cast come and go at the speed of Red Rum, punctuating this lame rollercoaster excursion which is about as compulsive as watching grass grow. Another re-make of *National Velvet* is in order. [JC-W]

Cast includes: Frank Finlay (Edward Coke), Jenny Agutter (Hannah Coke), Nigel Hawthorne (Achmet), Navin Chowdhry (Agba), Ralph Bates (LeDuc), Neil Dickson (Earl of Godolphin), Barry Foster (Mr Williams), Jill Gascoigne (Mrs Williams), Joan Hickson (Duchess of Marlborough), Anthony Quayle (Lord Granville), Ian Richardson (Bey of Tunis), Norman Rodway (Captain 'Blueskin' Blake), Peter Vaughan (Captain), Richard Harris (King George II), Glenda

Jackson (Queen Caroline), Melvyn Hayes, Barry Stanton, Ben Aris, Paul Sarony, Mark Collingwood. Dir: Peter Duffell. Pro: Michael Guest, Paul Sarony, Peter S. Davis and William Panzer. Ex Pro: Patrick Dromgoole, Johnny Goodman and Guy Collins. Screenplay: Phillip Frey; based on the novel by Marguerite Henry. Ph: Brian Morgan. Ed: Lyndon Matthews. Pro Des: Ken Sharp. M: John Scott. Costumes: Lynnette Cummin. Sound: Mike Davey. (HTV International–Enterprise.) Rel: 25 May 1990. 102 mins. Cert U.

The Kiss. The question is, where did Aunt Felice come from? No sooner has Mummy died, than this beautiful *Vogue* model turns up and the accidents start to happen: Amy's best friend catches her beads in an escalator and is all but strangled, Jack is attacked by a special effects cat and Amy gets her monthly two weeks early – in the middle of a biology class. Of course, beautiful Aunt Felice is a witch and all she wants is to kiss young Amy on the lips – once. A quite well-plotted demonic thriller, with a promising opening and suspenseful finish – filmed in Canada. [JC-W]

Cast includes: Joanna Pacula (Aunt Felice), Meredith Salenger (Amy), Mimi Kuzyk (Brenda), Nicholas Kilbertus (Jack), Jan Rubes (Tobin), Pamela Collyer, Peter Dvorsky, Sabrina Boudot, Shawn Levy, Celine Lomez. Dir and (with John Watson) Pro: Pen Densham. Ex Pro: Richard B. Lewis. Screenplay: Stephen Volk and Tom Ropekewski; from a story by Volk. Ph: François Protat. Ed: Stan Cole. Pro Des: Roy Forge Smith. M: J. Peter Robinson. Costumes: Renee April. (Tri-Star Columbia.) Rel: 21 July 1989. 98 mins. Cert 18.

Komitas. Painterly, stylised look at the life of Armenian monk and composer Komitas (1869–1935), as well as the slaughter of two million Armenians at the hands of the Turks in 1915. A strange, almost wordless picture made by a Russian with German money in the Armenian language, filmed between 1985 and 1988. Some might call this inaccessible cinema . . . [CB]

Cast includes: Samvel Ovasapian (Komitas), Onig Saadetian (Terlemesian), Margarita Woskanian (pupil), Revd Yegishe Mangikian, Revd Gegham Khatcherian, Sybille Vogelsang, Kaweh Jaryani, Sonja Askarian. Dir and Screenplay: Don Askarian. Ph:

Ronnie Kray (Gary Kemp) torments a victim in a good old-fashioned way, in Rank's disappointing The Krays.

Jorgos Arvantis and Martin Gressmann. Ed: Rene Perraudin and Marion Regentrop. Art: Jurgen Kiebach and Michael Poladian. M: Komitas, Donizetti, Teyra and Armenian folk music. Costumes: Bernhard Muhl. Sound: Michael Bootz. (Margarita Woskanjan Filmproduction/WDR/SFB/Channel Four/RTSR, etc–ICA.) Rel: floating; first shown London (ICA) 20 April 1990. 96 mins. No cert.

The Krays. After Mick Jagger in *Performance*, Roger Daltrey as *McVicar* and Phil Collins as *Buster* come Spandau Ballet's Gary and Martin Kemp as the notorious Kray twins. Oddly, this gangland thriller chooses to concentrate on the Kray's upbringing and family life, rather than on their reign of terror over London's East End. On the plus side, Billie Whitelaw stars as the brothers' indomitable mother (who insists that all visiting gangsters check their shoes for mud), while a veteran cast fills out the remaining Kray ensemble. The dialogue creaks with cliché and the direction swells with self-importance, but the worst fault of this numbing (long-planned) disappointment is the uneven snail's pace of the narrative. Very slow, very pretentious and thank God for Billie Whitelaw. [JC-W]

Littlefoot, the young brontosaurus (on left) teams up with a young dinosaur in the Lucas/Spielberg animated feature, The Land Before Time *(UIP).*

Cast includes: Billie Whitelaw (Violet Kray), Tom Bell (Jack 'The Hat' McVitie), Gary Kemp (Ronnie Kray), Martin Kemp (Reggie Kray), Susan Fleetwood (Rose), Charlotte Cornwell (May), Jimmy Jewel (Cannonball Lee), Avis Bunnage (Helen), Kate Hardie (Frances), Alfred Lynch (Charlie Kray), Steven Berkoff (George Cornell), Gary Love, Victor Spinetti, Barbara Ferris, Julia Migenes, John McEnery, Patti Love, Michael Balfour, Murray Melvin, Norman Rossington, Vernon Dobtcheff, Michael Elphick, etc. Dir: Peter Medak. Pro: Dominic Anciano and Ray Burdis. Assoc Pro: Paul Cowan. Ex Pro: Jim Beach and Michele Kimche. Screenplay: Philip Ridley. Ph: Alex Thomson. Ed: Martin Walsh. Pro Des: Michael Pickwoad. M: Michael Kamen. Costumes: Lindy Hemming. Sound: Godfrey Kirby. Technical adviser: Charlie Kray. (Parkfield/Fugitive–Rank.) Rel: 27 April 1990. 119 mins. Cert 18.

The Land Before Time. From the team that made the delightful *An American Tail* (released July 1987) comes this less successful Spielberg-Lucas animated feature. In technical terms it's fine, but somehow dinosaurs are not as heart-winning as mice, even if the story is somewhat along the lines of *Tail*, with young Littlefoot separated from his family and having a lot of varied adventures before he rejoins them in the Great Valley. [FMS]

With the voices of: Pat Hingle (narrator/Rooter), Gabriel Damon (Littlefoot), Helen Shaver (his mum), Candice Houston (Cera), Judith Barsi (Ducky), Will Ryan (Petrie), Burke Barnes (Daddy Topps), etc. Dir: Don Bluth. Pro: Bluth, Gary Goldman and John Pomeroy. Assoc Pro: Deborah Jelin Newmyer. Ex Pro: Steven Spielberg and George Lucas. Co-Ex Pro: Frank Marshall and Kathleen Kennedy. Screenplay: Stu Krieger; based on a story by Judy Freudberg and Tony Geiss. Ed: Dan Molina and John K. Carr. Pro Des: Don Bluth. M: James Horner. (Sullivan-Bluth Studios Pro in assoc. with Amblin Entertainment–Universal-UIP.) Rel: 25 August 1989. 69 mins. Cert U.

Last Exit to Brooklyn. Ambitious, hard-hitting film version of Hubert Selby Jr's controversial 1964 novel set in Brooklyn during a 1952 metal workers' strike. A sort of poor man's *Once Upon a Time in America/Brooklyn*, the melodrama is replete with unsavoury characters just waiting for their comeuppance – a series of brutal confrontations occurring at night. Starting with an assault by Brooklyn locals on a visit-

No ordinary riot – melodrama reigns supreme in Guild's Last Exit from Brooklyn.

ing soldier and ending with an epic gang-rape, this none-too-subtle social study wears its sleaze on its sleeve, and proudly. [JC-W]

Cast includes: Stephen Lang (Harry Black), Jennifer Jason Leigh (Tralala), Burt Young (Big Joe), Peter Dobson (Vinnie), Jerry Orbach (Boyce), Alexis Arquette (Georgette), Zette (Regina), Frank Military (Steve), Christopher Murney (Paulie), Camille Saviola (Ella), Ricki Lake (Donna), John Costelloe, Steve Baldwin, Robert Weil, Rutanya Alda, Al Shannon, Christopher Curry, Hubert Selby Jr, Mike Starr, Frank Vincent. Dir: Uli Edel. Pro: Bernd Eichinger. Screenplay: Desmond Nakano; from the book by Hubert Selby Jr. Ph: Stefan Czapsky. Ed: Peter Przygodda. Pro Des: David Chapman. M: Mark Knopfler. Costumes: Carol Oditz. Sound: Danny Michael

and Milan Bor. (Neue Constantin Film/Bavaria Film/Allied Filmmakers–Guild.) Rel: 5 January 1990. 102 mins. Cert 18.

The Legend of the Holy Drinker – La Leggenda del Santo Bevitore. There's mystery and magic, allied to a deep sense of religious faith, in Ermanno Olmi's delicate translation from book to screen of Joseph Roth's parable. The drinker is a Polish immigrant in 1920s Paris, down on his luck, and sleeping under newspapers beside the Seine. Then one day an ambiguous, elderly English gentleman accosts him and presses 200 francs on him – to be repaid to the statue of Theresa of Lisieux the following Sunday. But however hard and sincerely the drinker tries, he never makes the repayment, thanks to a weak will, women and wine, from which

Rutger Hauer as the tippler in The Legend of the Holy Drinker – La Leggenda del Santo Bevitore, *directed by Ermanno Olmi, a stylish tale of magic and religious faith.*

The Leningrad cowboys discover that in the US boondocks the streets aren't paved with gold, in Aki Kaurismaki's outrageous Leningrad Cowboys Go America *(Artificial Eye).*

combination he peacefully dies. Made in English with small interludes of unsubtitled French, this is a subtle and sensitive film, and its strengths easily outweigh the disadvantages of its length and lack of pace. With a superb performance by Rutger Hauer (in spite of his irritatingly out-of-place American accent), and a small gem from Anthony Quayle (making his final appearance) as the stranger. A memorable achievement. [FMS]

Lenny Henry leaps from television to the big screen in the film of his one-man show, Lenny Live and Unleashed *(Palace).*

Rest of cast: Sandrine Dumas (Gabby), Dominique Pinon (Woitech), Sophie Segalen (Karoline), Jean Maurice Chanet (Kanjak), Cecile Paoli (shop girl), Joseph de Medina (the fat man), Franco Aldigheri (cop). Dir, Ed and (with Tullio Kezich) Screenplay: Ermanno Olmi. Pro: Roberto Cicutto and Vincenzo de Leo. Ex Pro: Marcello Siena. Ph: Dante Spinotti. Pro Des: Gianni Quaranta. Art: Jean-Jacques Caziot. M: Stravinsky. (Aura Films/Cecchi Gori Group Tiger Cinematografica/RAI-TV Channel 1–Artificial Eye.) Rel: floating; first shown London (Lumiere) 1 September 1989. 125 mins. Cert PG.

Leningrad Cowboys Go America. No, that's not a misprint, but an appropriate monicker for this bizarre comedy about a Northern European band travelling across America. The Leningrad

Cowboys, too off-the-wall to get work in their own country, fly to New York to find fame and fortune. There, they discover rock 'n' roll, poverty and hunger, and secure their first gig at a Mexican wedding. On the way they see an America not advertised in the travel brochures and manage to bewilder a country supposedly inured to outrageous acts. Aki Kaurismaki, the cult director of *Ariel* and *Hamlet Goes Business*, plays his absurdist comedy absolutely straight and creates an uneven, frequently riotous homage to Americana. Scandinavian cinema will never be the same again. [JC-W]

Cast includes: Matti Pellonpää (Vladimir the manager), Kari Väänänen (Igor the village idiot), Sakke Järvenpää, Heikki Keskinen, Pimme Korhonen, Sakari Kuosmanen, Puka Oinonen, Silu Seppälä, Mauri Sumén, Mato Valtonen and Pekka Virtanen (the Leningrad Cowboys), Nicky Tesco (lost cousin), Jim Jarmusch (New York car dealer), Olli Tuominen, Richard Boes, William W. Robertson, Frank Johnson. Dir: Aki Kaurismaki. Pro: Kaurismaki, Klas Olofsson and Katinka Farago. Screenplay: Kaurismaki; from a story by Sakke Järvenpää, Aki Kaurismaki and Mato Valtonen. Ph: Timo Salminen. Ed: Raija Talvio. M: Mauri Sumén. Sound: Jouko Lumme. (Villealfa Filmproductions/Swedish Film Institute/Finnish Film Foundation–Artificial Eye.) Rel: floating; first shown London (Renoir) 16 February 1990. 78 mins. Cert 12.

Lenny Live and Unleashed. Those – and there are many – who find Lenny Henry's style of comedy irresistible and have accordingly made him one of the most popular of small-screen comics (at least one national critic has hailed him as 'the best British comedian of his generation') will almost certainly revel in this large-screen record of his one-man show. But it may not win over those who find Henry's cocky and self-satisfied style difficult to take. [FMS]

Cast: Lenny Henry; with guest appearances by Robbie Coltrane and Jeff Beck. Dir: Andy Harries. Pro: Martyn Auty and Harries. Ex Pro: Nik Powell and Stephen Woolley. Screenplay: Henry and Kim Fuller. Add. material by Ann Caulfield and Geoff Atkinson. Ph: Peter Sinclair. Ed: Gerry Hambling. Pro Des: Christopher Hobbs. (Palace/Sleeping Partners Pro in assoc. with Telso International and British Satellite Broadcasting–Palace Pictures.) Rel: 28 July 1989. 94 mins. Cert 15.

Lethal Weapon 2 starts bang in the middle of a car chase and never lets up from there. Even the film's one love scene is terminated by a rain of bullets. This is force-fed entertainment of the Hollywood kind, bursting with excessive violence, cartoon South African villains (thanks to *glasnost* having written Russia off as the enemy) and witty one-liners. Mel Gibson and Danny Glover return as the invincible LA cops, this time on the tail of a South African drugs ring protected by diplomatic immunity. Less credible than the first film, but breakneck fun for all that. [JC-W]

Cast includes: Mel Gibson (Martin Riggs), Danny Glover (Roger Murtaugh), Joe Pesci (Leo Getz), Joss Ackland (Arjen Rudd), Derrick O'Connor (Pieter Vorstedt), Patsy Kensit (Rika Van Den Haas), Darlene Love (Trish Murtaugh), Traci Wolfe (Rianne Murtaugh), Steve Kahan, Mark Rolston, Jenette Goldstein, Damon Hines, Ebonie Smith, Patrick Cameron, Mary Ellen Trainor, Norm Wilson, Sam the Dog, Burbank the Cat. Dir: Richard Donner. Pro: Donner and Joel Silver. Co-Pro: Steve Perry and Jennie Lew Tugend. Screenplay: Jeffrey Boam; from a story by Shane Black and Warren Murphy. Ph: Stephen Goldblatt. Ed: Stuart Baird. Pro Des: J. Michael Riva. M: Michael Kamen, Eric Clapton and David Sanborn. Sound: Willie Burton. Songs performed by George Harrison ('Cheer Down'), The Beach Boys, Eighth Wonder and Patsy Kensit, etc. (Warner.) Rel: 15 September 1989. 111 mins. Cert 15.

Let's Get Lost. Moving and stylish documentary on the wayward life and music of jazz trumpeter and singer Chet Baker. A legend in his own time, Baker was a musician who wielded his trumpet in much the same way as James Dean manipulated his acting talent. Drugs and the bad times followed, and Chet threw himself from a hotel window in Amsterdam – on Friday, 13 May 1988. Bruce Weber, fashion photographer and celluloid biographer of boxer Andy Minsker (*Broken Noses*), presents a compelling portrait of a troubled genius. A harrowing, seductive chronicle. [CB]

Cast includes: Lisa Marie, Flea (of The Red Hot Chili Peppers), Chris Isaak, Cherry Vanilla, Andy Minsker, Jack Sheldon, Ruth Young, Dick Bock. Dir and Pro: Bruce Weber. Ex Pro: Nan Bush. Ph: Jeff Preiss. Ed: Angelo Corrao. Sound: Maurice Schell. (Little Bear–Mainline.) Rel: floating; first

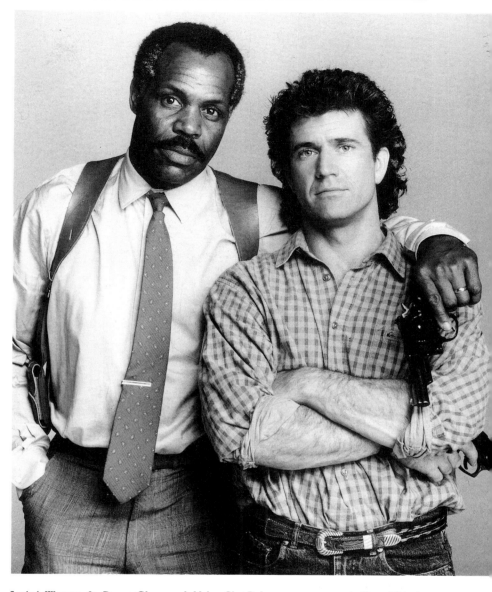

Lethal Weapon 2: *Danny Glover and Mel Gibson as the family man and his partner, a human time-bomb – from Warner.*

Chet Baker as a young man, in Bruce Weber's *compulsive, atmospheric biopic,* Let's Get Lost (Mainline).

shown London (Metro) 2 February 1990. 120 mins. Cert 15.

Leviathan. This edge-of-the-seat sequel to *Alien* (set underwater in the tradition of *The Abyss* and *Deep Star Six*) is a well-made, gripping thriller about 'something' loose on a mining station 16,000 feet beneath the surface of the Atlantic. Eight colourful characters (a negro, an Italian, a Hispanic, a couple of women, etc.) fight for their lives when they unleash an unknown force from a Russian shipwreck. 'Talk about having a bad day', mutters one

Just when she thought it was safe to go underwater: Amanda Pays in the gripping Leviathan, from Fox.

character, seconds before extinction. Good humour, state-of-the-art special effects and a spectacular soundtrack make this a ride to remember. [JC-W]

Cast includes: Peter Weller (Beck), Richard Crenna (Doc), Amanda Pays (Willie), Daniel Stern (Sixpack), Ernie Hudson (Jones), Michael Carmine (DeJesus), Lisa Eilbacher (Bowman), Hector Elizondo (Cobb), Meg Foster, Eugene Lipinsky, Larry Dolgin. Dir: George Pan Cosmatos. Pro: Luigi and Aurelio De Laurentiis. Ex Pro: Lawrence Gordon and Charles Gordon. Screenplay: David Peoples and Jeb Stuart; from a story by Peoples. Ph: Alex Thomson. Ed: Roberto Silvi and John F. Burnett. Pro Des: Ron Cobb. M: Jerry Goldsmith. Costumes: April Ferry. Creature Effects; Stan Winston. Underwater Photography: Mike Valentine. Sound: Robin Gregory. (Fox.) Rel: 11 May 1990. 96 mins. Cert 18.

Life and Nothing But – La Vie et Rien d'Autre is a movie masterpiece and nothing but, and another distinguished example of Bertrand Tavernier's complete command of the film medium. This story of dedication takes place in 1920 on the battlefield of Verdun, where two women (one a well-off Parisian wife, and the other a young local schoolteacher) are both seeking their 'missing' men among the 350,000 who died without name or number in the mud. A tired, disillusioned army major has the impossible task of providing a name and history for the recovered bodies, but is then suddenly faced with the extra demand of finding the one among the many who can be accurately described as the Unknown Soldier, to be buried with honour under the Arc de Triomphe in Paris. It's an ironic, sour story that eventually becomes a moving, hopeful and even romantic one. The trio are played superbly by Philippe Noiret (at his commanding best in his 100th role), Sabine Azema (as the searching wife) and Pascale Vignet (the teacher) and all the perfectly chosen supporting cast deserve commendation. Like Tavernier's very first film, *L'Horloger de Saint-Paul* (1974), this is a memorable movie. [FMS]

Cast: Philippe Noiret (Major Dellaplanne), Sabine Azema (Irene), Pascale Vignet (Alice), Maurice Barrier (Mercadot), François Perrot (Perrin), Jean-Pol Dubois (Andre), Daniel Russo (Lt Trevise), Michel Duchaussoy (General Villerieux), Arlette Gilbert, Louis Lyonnet, Charlotte Maury, François Caron, Thierry Gimenez, Frederique Meninger, Pierre Trabaud, Jean-Roger Milo. Dir and (with Jean Cosmos) Screenplay: Bertrand Tavernier; dialogues by Cosmos. Pro: Rene Cleitman. Ex Pro: Frederic Bourboulon and Albert Prevost. Ph: Bruno de Keyzer. Ed: Armand Psenny. Sound: Michel Desrois. Costumes: Jacqueline Moreau. M: Oswald d'Andrea. (Hachette Premiere/AB Films/Little Bear/Films A2–Artificial Eye.) Rel: floating; first shown

Philippe Noiret and Sabine Aezema in Bertrand Tavernier's Life and Nothing But – La Vie et Rien d'Autre.

London (Chelsea and Renoir) 27 October 1989. 134 mins. Cert PG.

Life Is a Long, Quiet River – La Vie Est un Long Fleuve Tranquille. After a career in advertising and promotional movies, Etienne Chatiliez moves easily into commercial feature production with this jolly French comedy about two babies – one from a bourgeois family and the other from a less fortunate background – who get switched when a nurse takes revenge on her lover. She keeps her secret for fifteen years but then, still feeling vengeful, she lets out the truth. A lot of the farcical fun comes from the contrasting lifestyles of the two families, and there are a number of good performances. [FMS]

Cast includes: Benoit Magimel (Momo), Valerie Lalande (Bernadette), Helene Vincent (Mme Le Quesnoy), Andre Wilms (M Le Quesnoy), Christine Pignet, Maurice Mons, Daniel Gelin, Catherine Hiegel, Patrick Bouchitey, Claire Prevost, Tara Romer, Jerome Floch. Dir and (with Florence Quentin) Screenplay: Etienne Chatiliez. Pro: Florence Quentin. Ex Pro: Charles

Cassot. Ph: Pascal Lebeque. Ed: Chantal Delattre. Art: Geoffrey Larcher. Costumes: Elisabeth Tavernier. M: Gerard Kawczynski. (Telemar/MK2/FR3 Films–Electric/ Contemporary.) Rel: floating; first shown London (Screen on the Hill) 27 October 1989. 90 mins. Cert 15.

Life Is Rosy – La Vie Est Belle. Rather jolly if somewhat incomprehensible little African musical comedy, a Zairean/Belgian/French co-effort, starring Zaire's singing star Papa Wamba. A thin storyline brings him from the country to the big city, where after all the routine trials and tribulations he makes good. [FMS]

Rest of cast: Krubwa Bibi (Kabibi), Landu Nzunzimbus (Mamou), Kanku Kasongo (Nvouandou), Lokina Mengi Feze, Kalimazi Lomoume, Mazaza Mukoko, Mujinga Mbuji, Bwando Ngimbi, Tumba Ayila, Pepe Kalle, Alamba Engongo, Maitre Nono. Dir: Benoit Lamy and Nganura Mweze. Co-Pro: Vera Belmont and Mweze. Screenplay: Mweze, Maryse Leon and Benoit Lamy. Ph: Michel Baudour. Ed: Martine Giordano. Art: Mutoke Wa Mputo and Barly Baruti. M: Papa Wemba. Add M: Klody, Zaiko Langa Langa and Tshala Muana. (Lamy Films, Brussels/Stephan Films, Paris/Sol'oeil Films, Kinshasa; in assoc. with Belgian and Zairean offices of radio and TV–Blue Dolphin.) Rel: floating; first shown London (ICA) 14 July 1989. 83 mins. Cert PG.

Limit Up. Daft supernatural comedy set in the whirlwind world of the Chicago Commodity Exchange. Nancy Allen – sporting chipmunk cheeks – plays Casey Falls, a 'runner' on the floor who dreams of being a trader, and sells her soul to the devil for the privilege. A Ferrari, TV fame and a *Time* magazine cover follow, but the escalating market price of the soya bean could cause world-wide starvation – and earn

Commodities trader Casey Falls (Nancy Allen) finds her life taken over by a demon in trainers, Nike (Danitra Vance), a sort of Whoopi Goldberg with cloven hooves, in Limit Up *(Medusa).*

69

Rocky *meets* Midnight Express: *Sylvester Stallone goes to prison in Guild's muscular, efficient* Lock Up.

Casey a fortune. Tag it 'Working Girl sprouts a halo and flies to Chicago'. [JC-W]

Also with: Dean Stockwell (Peter Oak), Brad Hall (Marty Callahan), Danitra Vance (Nike), Rance Howard (Chuck Feeney), Sandra Bogan (Andy Lincoln), Ray Charles, William J. Woff, Ava Fabian, Robbie Martini, Luana Anders, Richard Martini, Sally Kellerman. Dir: Richard Martini. Pro: Jonathan D. Krane. Co-Pro: Patricia Duff. Line Pro: Tikki Goldberg. Screenplay: Richard Martini and Lu Anders. Ph: Peter Lyons Collister. Ed: Sonny Baskin. Pro Des: R. Clifford Searcy. M: John Tesh. Costumes: Reve Richard. Sound: Nicholas Allen. (MCEG–Medusa.) Rel: 22 June 1990. 88 mins. Cert 12.

Lock Up. Sylvester Stallone plays a sweet innocent incarcerated in hell (maximum security prison The Gateway) for beating up some toughs who were beating up his old adopted father. Donald Sutherland is the evil warden with whom Sly embarks on a battle of

wills. Actually, there's no denying the efficiency of this escapism – it's heart-pounding stuff, and Stallone gives possibly his best performance since *Party at Kitty and Studs*. Of note: this was filmed at real-life hell-hole Rahway, the East Jersey State Prison. [JC-W]

Cast includes: Sylvester Stallone (Frank Leone), Donald Sutherland (Warden Drumgoole), John Amos (Meissner), Sonny Landham (Chink Weber), Darlanne Fluegel (Melissa), Tom Sizemore (Dallas), Frank McRae (Eclipse), William Allen Young, Larry Romano, Jordan Lund. Dir: John Flynn. Pro: Lawrence Gordon and Charles Gordon. Ex Pro: Michael S. Glick. Screenplay: Richard Smith, Jeb Stuart and Henry Rosenbaum. Ph: Donald E. Thorin. Ed: Michael K. Knue and Donald Brochu. Pro Des: Bill Kenney. M: Bill Conti. Costumes: Bernie Pollack. Sound: Charlie Wilborn. (White Eagle/Carolco–Guild.) Rel: 2 February 1990. 106 mins. Cert 18.

Lola. A genuine museum piece. Out of cirulation for more than twenty years, this 1960 French black-and-white film by Jacques Demy was one of the best things that came out of the *nouvelle*

vague, a charming musical now brought back into the cinema in a brand new print by the Electric-Everyman people. It features a memorable performance by the young Anouk Aimée as the cabaret singer of the title. [FMS]

Also with: Marc Michel (Roland), Jaques Harden (Michel), Alan Scott (Frankie), Elina Labourdette, Margo Lion, Annie Duperoux, Catherine Lutz, Corinne Marchand, Yvette Anziani, Dorothee Blank, Annik Noel, Isabelle Lunghini. Dir and Screenplay: Jacques Demy. Pro: Carlo Ponti and Georges Beauregard. Ph: Raoul Coutard. Ed: Anne-Marie Cotret. Art: Bernard Evein. M: Michel Legrand. (Electric Pictures.) Rel: floating; first shown London (Everyman) 13 October 1989. 91 mins. Cert PG.

Look Who's Talking. Charming little romantic comedy about a loveable New York taxi driver with blue eyes who turns paternal on a harried single mother. She thinks he's a klutz, ignores him and goes looking for a suitable father for her baby. Of course, this is cornball, predictable stuff, but it could have been almost perfect if it wasn't for

The young Anouk Aimée measures out a whisky for sailor Alan Scott in Jacques Demy's Lola, *brought back to the screen after twenty years by Electric Pictures.*

one over-worked gimmick: the talking baby. Bestowed with the voice of Bruce Willis (who received $10 million for his work), the infant is full of wisecracks as he observes his crazy new world. Naturally, he wants the cab driver for his daddy, and, as the latter is sweetly played by John Travolta, so do we. As mum, Kirstie Alley shapes up as a deft comedienne, while George Segal returns out of the past in a smarmy cameo. But it was the baby that captured the public's imagination and this trifle ran away with over $140 million at the US box office. [JC-W]

Cast includes: John Travolta (James), Kirstie Alley (Mollie), Olympia Dukakis (Rosie), George Segal (Albert), Abe Vigoda (Grandpa), Bruce Willis (voice of Mikey), Twink Caplan, Joy Boushel, Louis Heckerling, Neal Israel, Molly Israel. Dir and Screenplay: Amy Heckerling. Pro: Jonathan D. Krane. Ph: Thomas Del Ruth. Ed: Debra Chiate. Art: Reuben Freed. M: David Kitay; songs performed by The

Beach Boys, Talking Heads, Janis Joplin, The Bee Gees, Gene Pitney, Pete Townshend, etc. Costumes: Molly Maginnis. Sound: Ralph Parker. (Tri-Star–Columbia.) Rel: 6 April 1990. 96 mins. Cert 12.

Paul Balthazar Getty (right) *reverts to old tricks in Harry Hook's excellent adaptation of William Golding's* Lord of the Flies *(Palace).*

Lord of the Flies. Nightmarish updating of Golding's novel, about 25 US military school cadets – aged between 7 and 12 – stranded on a mountainous tropical island. Balthazar Getty (great-grandson of the oil tycoon) stars as Ralph, who attempts to take charge, introducing rules and discipline, but is overthrown by the more basic forces

The Mysterious Alien Creature ('Mac') from Guild's Mac and Me, *aimed at youngsters.*

of nature. A metaphor for society as a whole, this is a dynamic, painterly adaptation with a very cruel streak. Executive producer Lewis Allen previously produced the 1963 black-and-white version helmed by Peter Brook. This one was filmed in Jamaica by another English director, Harry Hook (*The Kitchen Toto*). [JC-W]

Also with: Chris Furrh (Jack), Danuel Pipoly (Piggy), Badgett Dale (Simon), Andrew Taft, Edward Taft, Gary Rule, Bob Peck, Michael Greene. Dir and Ed: Harry Hook. Pro: Ross Milloy. Ex Pro: Lewis Allen and Peter Newman. Screenplay: Sara Schiff; based on the 1954 novel by Sir William Golding. Ph: Martin Fuhrer. Supervising Ed: Tom Priestly. Pro Des: Jamie Leonard. M: Philippe Sarde. Costumes: Doreen Watkinson. Sound: Douglas B. Arnold. (Nelson Entertainment/Castle Rock–Palace.) Rel: 6 July 1990. 95 mins. Cert 15.

Loverboy. Once again, Patrick Dempsey is the unlikely teenage Casanova in this obvious and over-the-top farce. The appropriately named Randy Bodek (Dempsey) is a dead loss at school and a disappointment to his parents. The first of many misunderstandings occur when his father misinterprets his sexual leanings, but in fact Randy is making something of a reputation as a pizza boy who services – at a price – the frustrated, stinking-rich housewives of Beverly Hills. Randy's aim is to finance his return to school so that he can win back his own girlfriend. (Who would believe *that* story?) The film aims high and low for its laughs, but is well enough structured to hang together rather neatly. [JC-W]

Also with: Kate Jackson (Diane Bodek), Carrie Fisher (Monica Delancy), Barbara Carrera (Alex Barnett), Kirstie Alley (Dr Joyce Palmer), Robert Ginty (Joe Bodek), Nancy Valen (Jenny Gordon), Bernie Coulson (Salt), Charles Hunter Walsh, Robert Camilletti, Vic Tayback, Kim Miyori, Robert Picardo, Peter Koch, Rebecca Holden. Dir: Joan Micklin Silver. Pro: Gary Foster and Willie Hunt. Ex Pro: Leslie Dixon and Tom Ropelewski. Screenplay: Robin Schiff, Ropelewski and Dixon; from a story by Schiff. Ph: John Hora. Ed: Rick Shaine. Pro Des: Dan Leigh. M: Michel Colombier; songs performed by Brian Wilson, Tony Bennett, Fred Astaire, Jerry Lee Lewis, Giant Steps, etc. Costumes: Rosanna Norton. Sound: Jerry Ross. (Crescent–Columbia Tri-Star.) Rel: 25 May 1990. 98 mins. Cert 15.

Mac and Me. A sort of benign variation on *E.T.* which the kids should love and the less demanding adult moviegoer should find good fun. There's a spectacular climactic conflagration, and an uproarious finale when

Minor players in the Major League *(Fox): Corbin Bernsen, Charlie Sheen and Tom Berenger practise baseball in this frequently hilarious comedy.*

the Outer Space rubberoid family take the Oath of Allegiance and become good, clean (and conventionally dressed!) American citizens. [FMS]

Cast: Jade Calegory (who is a real paraplegic – Eric), Christine Ebersole (mother), Jonathan Ward (Michael, elder brother), Lauren Stanley (Debbie), Tina Caspary (Courtney), Vinnie Torrente (Mitford), Martin West, Ivan Jorge Rado, Danny Cooksey, Laura Waterbury, Ronald McDonald. Dir: Stewart Raffill. Pro: R. J. Louis. Ex Pro: Mark Damon and William B. Kerr. Screenplay: Raffill and Steven Feke. Ph: Nick McLean. Ed: Tom Walls. Pro Des: W. Stewart Campbell. M: Alan Silvestri. M Sup: Brooks Arthur. (R. J. Louis/Orion–Guild.) Rel: 21 July 1989. 100 mins. Cert U. (Not, as you might think, a Columbia film, in spite of the fact that a lot is made of the can of Coca-Cola which brings the ailing aliens back to life!)

Major League. Riotous baseball comedy, a must for diehard fans of American sport. The rich-bitch wife (Margaret Whitton) of the late owner of the Cleveland Indians decides to wreck her husband's team so that she can re-locate the game to Miami. So she selects the worst outfit of rookies and has-beens in sporting history, aiming to hit the bottom of the league. You know what's going to happen, but it's fun getting there and there are moments that generate an almost *Rocky*esque sense of wish-fulfilment. Amazingly, the story was inspired by fact, but what the *real* Cleveland Indians would make of this farce is anybody's guess. [JC-W]

Cast includes: Tom Berenger (Jake Taylor), Charlie Sheen (Ricky Vaughn), Corbin Bernsen (Roger Dorn), Margaret Whitton (Rachel Phelps), James Gammon (Lou Brown), Rene Russo (Lynn Wells), Wesley Snipes (Willie Mays Hayes), Charles Cyphers, Chelcie Ross, Dennis Haysbert, Andy Romano, Bob Uecker, Steve Yeager, Peter Vuckovich, Stacy Carroll. Dir and Screenplay: David S. Ward. Pro: Chris Chesser and Irby Smith. Ex Pro: Mark Rosenberg. Ph: Reynaldo Villalobos. Ed: Dennis M. Hill. Pro Des: Jeffrey Howard. M: James Newton Howard. Costumes: Erica Edell Phillips. Sound: Susmu Tokunow. (Braveworld–Fox.) Rel: 22 September 1989. 107 mins. Cert 15.

Max, Mon Amour. Shown originally at the 1986 Cannes Festival, this Nagisa Oshima film revolves around a British diplomat's wife who forms a romantic attachment to a chimpanzee. The producer and co-screenwriter are both ex-collaborators of Luis Buñuel, and the maestro of the absurd's influence is certainly plain. The film will be offensive to some; to others merely a good joke which rather fizzles out towards the end. It's a pity – though perhaps inevitable – that the chimp is so obviously played by a man in a monkey's skin. [FMS]

Cast: Charlotte Rampling (Margaret, the monkey lover), Anthony Higgins (husband), Bernard-Pierre Donnadieu (Archibald), Victoria Abril (Maria), Anne-Marie Besse (Suzanne), Nicole Calfan (Hélène), Pierre Etaix (detective), Bernard Haller, Sabine Haudepin, Christopher Hovik, Fabrice Luchini, Diana Quick, Pierre Guillermo, Nicolas Hawtrey, Claude Jaeger, Milena Vukotic, Laurent Spielvogel, Anne Kreis, Robin Steiger, Ailsa Berg. Dir: Nagisa Oshima. Pro: Serge Silberman. Screenplay: Oshima and Jean-Claude Carriere. Ph: Raoul Coutard. Ed: Helene Plemiannikov. Pro Des: Pierre Guffroy. M: Michael Portal. (Greenwich Film Pro., Paris/Greenwich Films, New York–Electric Pictures.) Rel: floating; first shown London (ICA) 18 May 1990. 92 mins. Cert 18.

Melancholia. Get past the title and into the ambiguous undercurrents of this

A very odd love affair . . . Charlotte Rampling and the chimp she dotes on in the French black comedy, Max, Mon Amour.

fascinating Anglo-German thriller. A burnt-out German art critic working in London is suddenly dragged back into his terrorist-supporting past by an unexpected phone call from Munich, leading him into a convoluted political plot and eventually a double killing. This bleak moral tale is all the more commendable when one knows that it is a first for the director, Andi Engel; up to now he has been content merely to bring into this country, and show at his several cinemas, some outstanding movies from Europe and elsewhere. [FMS]

Cast: Jeroen Krabbe (the art-critic killer), Susannah York (Catherine), Ulrich Wildgruber (Manfred), Jane Gurnett (Sarah), Kate Hardie (Rachel), Saul Reichlin (doctor), John Sparkes, Detlef Bertheisen, Muchette Van Helsingen, John Joyce. Dir and (with Lewis Rodia) Screenplay: Andi Engel. Pro: Colin MacCabe. Co-Pro: Helga Bahr. Assoc Pro: Katy Radford. Ex in charge of Pro: Jill Pack. Sup Ed: Helga Borsche. Ed: Christopher Roth. Ph: Denis Crossan. Pro Des: Jock Scott. M: Simon Fisher Turner. Costumes: Annie Curtis Jones. Sound: Nigel Holland. (BFI Productions in assoc. with Lichtlik Filmproduktion, Channel 4, Nordeutscher Rundfunk, Film Fonds Hamburg, Hamburger Filmburo–BFI.) Rel: floating; first shown

London (Camden Plaza and Metro) 20 October 1989. 88 mins. Cert 15.

Millennium. More meddling with the future, with Kris Kristofferson as aircrash inspector Bill Smith involved with a platinum-coiffured Cheryl Ladd from the next millenium. This is the sort of tosh that Arthur Hailey and Alan Ayckbourn might have come up with after a drunken night on the tiles together. [JC-W]

Also with: Daniel J. Travanti (Arnold Mayer), Robert Joy (Sherman), Lloyd Bochner, Brent Carver, David McIlwraith, Maury Chaykin, Al Waxman, Lawrence Dane, Thomas Hauff, Peter Dvorsky. Dir: Michael Anderson. Pro: Douglas Leiterman. Co-Pro: Robert Vince. Ex Pro: John Foreman, Freddie Fields, Louis M. Silverstein and P. Gael Mourant. Screenplay: John Varley; based on his short story 'Air Raid'. Ph: Rene Ohashi. Ed: Ron Wisman. Pro Des: Gene Rudolf. M: Eric N. Robertson. Costumes: Olga Dimitrov. Sound: Jim Hopkins. (Gladden Entertainment–Rank.) Rel: 20 October 1989. 108 mins. Cert PG.

Miss Firecracker. Beth Henley is a master at chronicling the detail and emotions of small-town America south of the Mason-Dixon Line. Here, she successfully opens out her own play centring round a local beauty/talent contest. For Carnelle Scott, winning

Holly Hunter as Carnelle Scott, a won'erful, gool ol' girl with the wrong dreams, in Beth Henley's Miss Firecracker, *from Rank.*

the contest is all she lives for, and only if she loses can she begin to see her life in the perspective it deserves. Repeating her stage role, Holly Hunter is sensational as Carnelle, cramming her performance with brilliant little touches and opening her face to all the complexities of her character. For every second, Ms Hunter is unforgettably watchable. The rest of the film wavers dramatically between the stagey and the idiosyncratic, but it's rooted in a truthful look at Southern values. [JC-W]

Also with: Scott Glenn (Mac Sam), Tim Robbins (Delmount Williams), Mary Steenburgen (Elain Rutledge), Alfre Woodard (Popeye Jackson), Christine Lahti (Clara Archer), Veanne Cox, Ann Wedgeworth, Trey Wilson, Amy Wright, Kathleen Chalfant, Robert Fieldsteel, Greg Germann, Avril Gentles, Bert Remsen, Homer Swayze, Hardy White Jr. Dir: Thomas Schlamme. Pro: Fred Berner. Ex Pro: Lewis Allen and Ross E. Milloy. Screenplay: Beth Henley; based on her play *The Miss Firecracker Contest*. Ph: Arthur Albert. Ed: Peter C. Frank. Pro Des: Kristi Zea. M: David Mansfield. Costumes: Molly Maginnis. Sound: Glen Berkovitz. (Corsair–Rank.) Rel: 15 June 1990. 103 mins. Cert PG.

Monkey Shines. A handsome college athlete (Jason Beghe) is paralysed from the neck down in an accident and discovers reservoirs of hatred he never knew he had. Only his trained capuchin monkey, Ella, can understand his frustration and translate his desires into murder. George A. Romero, creator of *The Night of the Living Dead*, hasn't lost his ability to chill – as the scene with the hypodermic needle in the face deftly illustrates. [JC-W]

Cast includes: Jason Beghe (Allan Mann), John Pankow (Geoffrey Fisher), Kate McNeil (Melanie Parker), Joyce Van Patten (Dorothy Mann), Stanley Tucci (Dr John Wiseman), Christine Forrest, Stephen Root, Janine Turner, William Newman, Tudi Wiggins, Tom Quinn, Tina Romero, Lia Savini. Dir and Screenplay: George A. Romero; based on the novel *Monkey Shines* by Michael Stewart. Pro: Charles Evans. Ex Pro: Peter Grunwald and Gerald S. Paonessa. Ph: James A. Contner. Ed: Pas-

Ella in George A. Romero's Monkey Shines, *one of the year's most original thrillers, from Rank.*

quale Buba. Pro Des: Cletus Anderson. M: David Shire. Costumes: Barbara Anderson. Make-up F/X: Tom Savini. Sound: John Sutton. (Orion–Rank.) Rel: 23 February 1990. 113 mins. Cert 18.

Monsieur Hire is a little man, one of life's social outcasts. He is also something of a blank canvas, a figure on whom other people superimpose their own opinions of him. But Monsieur Hire (who has no Christian name) is a complex enigma, a tailor who dresses like an undertaker, lives on his own and spies on his pretty young neighbour, Alice. This being an adaptation of a Georges Simenon novel, a murder has been committed and somebody is guilty – but not who you might expect. The thrust of the story is actually predictable enough, but garnished with some surprises. Michel Blanc is superb in the title role and is well matched by his supporting cast. An intimate, masterfully crafted and desperately poignant film. [JC-W]

Also with: Sandrine Bonnaire (Alice), Luc Thuillier (Emile), André Wilms (police inspector), André Baudin. Dir: Patrice Leconte. Screenplay: Leconte and Patrick Dewolf; based on the novel *Les Fiançailles de M Hire* by Georges Simenon. Pro: Philippe Carcassonne and Rene Cleitman. Ph: Denis Lenoir. Ed: Joelle Hache. Art: Ivan Maussion. M: Michael Nyman and Johannes Brahms. Costumes: Elisabeth Tavernier. Sound: Dominique Hennequin. (Carcassonne/Cleitman–Palace.) Rel: floating; first shown London (Lumiere) 20 April 1990. 80 mins. Cert 15.

Michel Blanc as Monsieur Hire *(Palace), a loser who's brighter than people think, but more vulnerable than he realises.*

Iain Glen, as John Hanning Speke, and Patrick Bergin, as Sir Richard Burton, escape from bloodthirsty tribesmen in Bob Rafelson's sprawling, exciting homage to history, Mountains of the Moon *(Guild).*

Motion and Emotion: The Films of Wim Wenders. Perceptive documentary on the work of the German filmmaker responsible for *The American Friend, Paris Texas* and *Wings of Desire*. Combining film clips with interviews, this is a balanced examination of the man and his cinema, although what some of his colleagues have to say is a mite obvious, and occasionally trite. [CB]

With: Ry Cooder, Harry Dean Stanton, Peter Falk, Sam Fuller, Patricia Highsmith, Dennis Hopper, Robby Muller, Kraft Wetzel, Wim Wenders, Hanns Zischler. Dir: Paul Joyce. Pro: Chris Rodley. Ph: Peter Dorney. Ed: Tony Lawson. Sound: Jim Corcoran and Jim Hilton. (Lucida Productions–ICA.) Rel: floating; first shown London (ICA) 2 April 1990. 92 mins. No cert.

Mountains of the Moon. Historical and epic story of the rivalry between Sir Richard Burton and John Hanning Speke, nineteenth-century adventurers exploring the source of the Nile in 'the bleak and hopeless landscapes' of East Africa. Directed by Bob Rafelson, a film-maker more associated with contemporary American subjects, the film is an accessible study of raw, exciting times crammed with pertinent but hardly superficial period detail. Patrick Bergin's charismatic performance as Burton and some exceptional photography further enhance this powerful history lesson. [JC-W]

Also with: Iain Glen (John Hanning Speke), Richard E. Grant (Oliphant), Fiona Shaw (Isabel), James Villiers (Lord Oliphant), Peter Vaughan (Lord Houghton), Delroy Lindo (Mabruki), Bernard Hill (Dr Livingstone), Doreen Mantle (Mrs Speke), Anna Massey (Mrs Arundell), Leslie Phillips (Mr Arundell), Roger Rees (Papworth), John Savident, Adrian Rawlins, Matthew Marsh, Richard Caldicot, Christopher Fulford, Garry Cooper, Roshan Seth, Jimmy Gardner, Peter Eyre, Frances Cuka, Roger Ashton-Griffiths, Leonard Juma, Philip Voss, Pip Torrens, Stewart Harwood, Ralph Nossek, George Malpas. Dir: Bob Rafelson. Pro: Daniel Melnick. Ex Pro: Mario Kassar and Andrew Vajna. Screenplay: William Harrison and Bob Rafelson; based on Harri-

Father and daughter fight for justice: Armin Mueller-Stahl and Jessica Lange in Costa-Gavras's searing, gripping Music Box *(Guild).*

son's biographical novel *Burton and Speke*, and on original journals by Richard Burton and John Hanning Speke. Ph: Roger Deakins. Ed: Thom Noble. Pro Des: Norman Reynolds. M: Michael Small. Costumes: Jenny Beavan and John Bright. Sound: Simon Kaye. (Melnick/Indieprod–Guild.) Rel: 20 April 1990. 135 mins. Cert 15.

Music Box. Intelligent, well-written and bitingly topical courtroom drama about the kindly Mike Laszlo, a Hungarian accused of war crimes after living in the USA for 40 years. His daughter, Ann Talbot (Jessica Lange), a gifted criminal attorney, is convinced of her father's innocence and knows what a good man he is – *now*. The case tears the life of the family apart, unearthing hideous memories and destroying all the good and the love that the Talbots had to give to the world. Even if Ann's father *had* been a Nazi war criminal, what is the point of opening up old wounds? (But wait till you hear the testimonies of the victims.) Great cinema, mature drama,

challenging entertainment. For her performance, Jessica Lange won a fifth Oscar nomination. [JC-W]

Also with: Armin Mueller-Stahl (Mike Laszlo), Frederic Forrest (Jack Burke), Donald Moffat (Harry Talbot), Lukas Haas (Mikey Talbot), Cheryl Lynn Bruce, Mari Torocsik, J. S. Block, Sol Frieder, Michael Rooker, Albert Hall. Dir: Constantin Costa-Gavras. Pro: Irwin Winkler. Ex Pro: Joe Eszterhas and Hal W. Polaire. Screenplay: Eszterhas. Ph: Patrick Blossier. Ed: Joele Van Effenterre. Pro Des: Jeannine Claudia Oppewall. M. Philippe Sarde. Costumes: Rita Salazar. Sound: Pierre Gamet, Gerard Lamps and William Flageollet. (Carolco–Guild.) Rel: 15 June 1990. 126 mins. Cert 15.

My First Forty Years. Sudsy, episodic saga of sex, scandal and *la dolce vita* spanning four decades in the life of an Italian beauty. 'Freely' adapted from the book *I miei primi 40 anni* by Marina Ripa di Meana, *My First Forty Years* hurls names like Aristotle and Jackie Onassis and Liz and Richard Burton around with abandon, while hiding behind a disclaimer at the film's end: any similarity to actual persons is

purely coincidental. Ha! While this sub-Sidney Sheldon epic attempts to have its cake and eat it, we barely get to nibble at the souffle. Gorgeous supermodel Carol Alt plays Marina, but can't act her way out of a brassiere. Her body double, Carmen Stowe, steals all the best curves. [JC-W]

Also with: Elliott Gould (Nino Ranuzzi), Jean Rochefort (Prince Riccio), Pierre Cosso (Massimiliano Caracciolo), Massimo Venturiello (Roberto D'Angelo), Isabel Russinova, Paola Quattrini, Riccardo Garrone, Capucine, Teo Teocoli, Sebastiano Somma. Dir: Carlo Vanzina. Pro: Mario and Vittorio Cecchi Gori. Screenplay: Carlo and Enrico Vanzina; freely based on the book by Marina Ripa di Meana. Ph: Luigi Kuveiller. Ed: Ruggero Mastroianni. Pro Des: Antonino Formica. M: Umberto Smaila; with songs from Paul Anka, Trini Lopez, Gilbert O'Sullivan, Carly Simon, Mungo Jerry, Harry Nilsson, Barry White, Al Stewart, etc. Costumes: Jost Jakob. (C.G. Silver Film/Reteitalia SPA–Columbia Tri-Star.) Rel: 8 September 1989. 107 mins. Cert 18.

My Left Foot. Dublin, 1932–59. The true story of Christy Brown, a victim of cerebral palsy who overcame the

Daniel Day Lewis, seen here with doctor Fiona Shaw, gives the performance of his life as Christy Brown in Granada-Palace's My Left Foot.

odds to become an articulate writer and a talented painter – using his left foot. Daniel Day Lewis is nothing short of sensational as Christy, bringing a surprising depth and wit to the physical excesses that the role demands. Credit, too, must go to the first-time director Jim Sheridan who unveils his story with economy and restraint, letting the power of the material work for itself. A truly moving experience. [JC-W]

Also with: Ray McAnally (Mr Brown), Brenda Fricker (Mrs Brown), Ruth McCabe (Mary), Fiona Shaw (Dr Eileen Cole), Hugh O'Conor (young Christy), Eanna McLiam, Alison Whelan, Declan Croghan, Cyril Cusack, Keith O'Conor, Adrian Dunbar, Marie Conmee. Dir and (with Shane Connaughton) Screenplay: Jim Sheridan. Pro: Noel Pearson. Ex Pro: Paul Heller and Steve Morrison. Ph: Jack Conroy. Ed: J. Patrick Duffner. Art: Austen Spriggs. M: Elmer Bernstein. Costumes: Joan Bergin. (Granada–Palace.) Rel: floating; first shown London (Curzon, Mayfair) 18 August 1989. 98 mins. Cert PG.

Mystery Train. Uniquely cinematic tapestry of three stories set in and around the Arcade Hotel in downtown Memphis, Tennessee. A collection of characters float in and out of the narrative: a young Japanese couple come to Memphis to visit the sites of Elvisdom; an Italian widow is stranded there for a night and is forced to share a bedroom with a garrulous stranger; and an English drunk has to hide out at the hotel after killing a liquor-store clerk. The only thing these stories have in common is the sound of a gunshot in

Youki Kudho and Masatoshi Nagase find comfort with the spirit of Elvis in Jim Jarmusch's wonderful Mystery Train *(Palace).*

Three women in love: Annabeth Gish, Lili Taylor and Julia Roberts in the wonderful, warm-hearted Mystic Pizza *(Virgin Vision).*

the night and an encounter with the bizarre night clerk and his bellboy. Hilarious incidental detail and fine photography contribute to make this a minor classic, a must for connoisseurs of the oddball. From the director who brought us *Stranger Than Paradise* and *Down by Law*. [JC-W]

Cast includes: Youki Kudoh (Mitzuko), Masatoshi Nagase (Jun), Nicoletta Braschi (Luisa), Elizabeth Bracco (DeeDee), Joe Strummer (Johnny), Rick Aviles (Will), Steve Buscemi (Charlie), Jodie Markell (tour guide), Sy Richardson (news-seller), Vondie Curtis-Hall (Ed), Rockets Redglare (liquor-store clerk), Screamin' Jay Hawkins (night clerk), Cinque Lee (bellboy), Rufus Thomas, Tom Noonan, Stephen Jones, Tom Waits (voice only). Dir and Screenplay: Jim Jarmusch. Pro: Jim Stark. Ex Pro: Kunijiro Hirata and Hideaki Suda. Ph: Robby Müller. Ed: Melody London. Pro Des: Dan Bishop. M: John Lurie; songs from Elvis Presley, Otis Redding, Roy Orbison, Rufus Thomas, etc. Costumes: Carol Wood. (MTI/JVC–Palace.) Rel: floating; first shown London (Lumiere) 8 December 1989. 111 mins. Cert 15.

Mystic Pizza. Three hot females work at Leona's Mystic Pizzeria (in the sleepy Connecticut town of Mystic) and find themselves involved with very different men. In their way, the girls are all looking for love but are invariably disappointed by the men they end up with. Or are they? A little mechanical in the writing, perhaps, but otherwise this is a warm, vibrant breath of cinema, ringing with some sensational performances. In fact, I'll go so far as to say that seldom has this critic been so moved by such a marvellous ensemble cast. Julia Roberts, who plays the somewhat physical Daisy Araujo, is impressive in her first starring role. [JC-W]

Also with: Annabeth Gish (Kat Araujo), Lili Taylor (Jojo Barboza), Vincent Phillip D'Onofrio (Bill Montijo), William R. Moses (Tim Travers), Adam Storke (Charles Gordon Winsor), Conchata Ferrell (Leona Valsouano), Joanna Merlin (Margaret), Porscha Radcliffe, Arthur Walsh, John Fiore, Gene Amoroso, Janet Zarish, John Cunningham. Dir: Donald Petrie. Pro: Mark Levinson and Scott Rosenfelt. Screenplay: Amy Jones, Perry Howze and Alfred Uhry; from a story by Jones. Ph: Tim Suhrstedt. Ed: Marion Rothman. Pro Des: David Chapman. M: David McHugh. Costumes:

Jennifer Von Mayrhauser. Sound: Russel Fager. (Samuel Goldwyn–Virgin Vision.) Rel: 5 January 1990. 104 mins. Cert 15.

National Lampoon's Winter Holiday (US: *NL's Christmas Vacation*). Like the other *Lampoon* films, this is a mildly amusing comedy with some very funny moments. This time Mr Griswold (Chevy Chase) staggers from one disaster to another in his attempts to give his family an old-style Dickensian Christmas; a typical sequence has him trying to get a forest-sized fir tree into his drawing room. In his element, Chase is splendidly supported by some comedy stalwarts like Randy Quaid and Mae Questel. [FMS]

Cast: Chevy Chase, Beverly d'Angelo (wife), Randy Quaid (Eddie), Diane Ladd (Nora), E. G. Marshall (Art), Doris Robert (Francis), Julia-Louis-Dreyfus (Margo Chester), Mae Questel (Aunt Betheny), William Hickey (Uncle Lewis), Brian Doyle-Murray, Juliette Lewis, Johnny Galecki, Nicholas Guest, Miriam Flynn, Ellen Hamilton Latzen. Dir: Jeremiah S. Chechik. Pro: John Hughes and Tom Jacobson. Assoc Pro: W. S. Beasley, Mauri Syd Gaton and R. E. Ward. Ex Pro: Matty Simmons. Screenplay: John Hughes. Ph: Thomas Ack-

New York Stories *(Warner):* Oedipus
Wrecks *has Mae Questel embarrassing Woody
Allen in his funniest movie for years.*

erman. Ed: Jerry Greenberg. Pro Des:
Stephen Marsh. Art: Beala B. Neel. Costume Des: Michael Kaplan. Sound: James
Alexander. M: Stephen Marsh. (Hughes
Entertainment–Warner.) Rel: floating. 97
mins. Cert PG.

New York Stories. When Woody Allen
suggested to his producer Robert
Greenhut that he produce three short
films of Woody's as an omnibus venture, Greenhut took the idea one step
further and engaged the co-operation of
Martin Scorsese and Francis Coppola
as well. The result is a genuine curate's
egg, three short films created by a trio
of great American film-makers, all set
in the Big Apple. Apparently, Greenhut handed out $7 million to each director and gave them carte blanche. Scorsese's film, *Life Lessons,* is a self-indulgent tale about a Jackson Pollockesque painter (Nick Nolte)
obsessed with his muse (Rosanna
Arquette). For some infuriating reason
Scorsese seldom stops his camera from

gliding round his actors, but his story
does throw some light on the torture of
creating art out of painting. Coppola's
self-indulgent *Life Without Zoe* is less a
film than an excuse to exploit the talents
of his daughter, costume designer Sofia
Coppola. This over-photographed story
is a trifle about the spoilt Manhattan
child of mercurial parents (Talia Shire,
Giancarlo Giannini), who discovers a
missing diamond earring. Very tedious.
Woody Allen's self-indulgent *Oedipus
Wrecks* is an amusing return to form
about a successful lawyer's obsession
with his mother. Sheldon Mills – né
Millstein – (Woody Allen) is constantly
embarrassed by his mother (Mae Questel), a four-foot-something Jewish
tyrant who tells the world all about her
son's shortcomings. Once again Allen
wrings great mirth from his paranoia
about being Jewish and going bald and
about being human. A gem. [JC-W]

Life Lessons. Cast includes: Nick Nolte
(Lionel Dobie), Rosanna Arquette (Paulette), Patrick O'Neal (Phillip Fowler),
Steve Buscemi (Gregory Stark), Peter
Gabriel, Deborah Harry, Paul Herman,
Richard Price. Dir: Martin Scorsese. Pro:
Barbara DeFina. Ex Pro: Robert Greenhut.

Screenplay: Richard Price. Ph: Nestor
Almendros. Ed: Thelma Schoonmaker. Pro
Des: Kristi Zea. M: songs performed by
Procol Harum, Cream, Ray Charles, Bob
Dylan & The Band, Transvision Vamp, etc.
Costumes: John Dunn. Sound: Frank Graziadei. **Life Without Zoe**. Cast includes: Talia
Shire (Charlotte), Giancarlo Giannini (Claudio), Heather McComb (Zoe), Don Novello
(Hector), Selim Tlili (Abu), Carole Bouquet
(Princess Soroya), Paul Herman (Clifford,
the doorman), Gia Coppola, Carmine
Coppola. Dir and (with Sofia Coppola)
Screenplay: Francis Coppola. Pro: Fred
Roos and Fred Fuchs. Ex Pro: Robert
Greenhut. Ph: Vittorio Storaro. Ed: Barry
Malkin. Pro Des: Dean Tavoularis. M: Carmine Coppola and Kid Creole & The Coconuts. Costumes: Sofia Coppola. Sound:
James Sabat, Frank Graziadei. **Oedipus
Wrecks**. Cast includes: Woody Allen (Sheldon), Mia Farrow (Lisa), Julie Kavner
(Treva), Mae Questel (mother), Marvin
Chatinover, Molly Regan, Jessie Keosian,
George Schindler, Bridgit Ryan, Paul
Herman (Detective Flynn), Mayor Edward
I. Koch (himself). Dir and Screenplay:
Woody Allen. Pro: Robert Greenhut. Ex
Pro: Jack Rollins and Charles H. Joffe. Ph:
Sven Nykvist. Ed: Susab E. Morse. Pro
Des: Santo Loquasto. M: songs performed
by Benny Goodman, Liberace, David Rose
& His Orchestra, etc. Costumes: Jeffrey

79

Bros will be bros: brothers Truman and Briar Gates (Patrick Swayze and Liam Neeson) work out a little misunderstanding about ethics and family honour in Warner's Next of Kin.

Kurland. Sound: James Sabat. (Touchstone–Warner.) Rel: 10 November 1989. 125 mins. Cert 15.

Next of Kin. By-the-numbers cop thriller dressed up to look a little better than most, but not much. Patrick Swayze plays Truman, a hillbilly cop transplanted to the concrete streets of Chicago where his younger brother, Gerald (Bill Paxton), is murdered in cold blood. Swayze knows who the killer is, but cannot find the evidence. Older brother Briar (Liam Neeson), still living in the backwoods of Kentucky (with his satellite dish), comes to Chicago to do what a cop can't do . . . A piranha-out-of-water, Briar escalates a clan war between them rednecks and a ruthless Sicilian family. [JC-W]

Also with: Adam Baldwin (Joey), Helen Hunt (Jessie), Andreas Katsulas (Isabella), Ben Stiller (Lawrence), Michael J. Pollard (Harold), Ted Levine (Willy), Del Close, Valentino Cimo, Paul Herman, Charlie Williams, Joseph P. Ryan. Dir: John Irvin. Pro: Les Alexander and Don Enright. Ex Pro: Larry De Waay. Screenplay: Michael Jenning. Ph: Steven Poster. Ed: Peter Honess. Pro Des: Jack T. Collis. M: Jack Nitzsche;

numbers performed by Patrick Swayze and Larry Gatlin, Ricky Van Shelton, Gregg Allman and Lori Yates, Rodney Crowell, Ricky Skaggs, Duane Eddy, B. B. King, Mario Lanza, etc. Costumes: Donfeld. Sound: Martin Maryska. (Lorimar–Warner.) Rel: 27 April 1990. 109 mins. Cert 15.

A Night in Havana – Dizzy Gillespie in Cuba. A showcase for Gillespie and a record of his star turn at the 5th International Festival of Havana. Reveals something of the man behind one of the most excitingly played trumpets of our jazz age. [FMS]

Dir: John Holland. (ICA.) Rel: floating; first shown London (ICA) 14 August 1989. 100 mins. No cert.

A Nightmare on Elm Street 5 – The Dream Child. Five films ago, Freddie Krueger was a genuinely terrifying, shadowy figure who murdered teenagers from within their own nightmares. The killings were imaginatively staged within realistic frameworks, while the excessive gore was defused by a throwaway, deadpan humour. This fourth sequel suffers heavily from sequeldom. Freddie is out of the closet and has to live up to his media image as the popular clown with a sick sense of humour. Sadly, *Elm Street* has become a gross parody of itself, isn't very funny and – worse still – has lost its ability to shock. Krueger insulting a nun with the word 'bitch' is about as bad as it gets. Still, there are a couple of nice set pieces: one when Alice (Lisa Wilcox again) finds herself in a perspective-defying maze; and another when Freddie breaks out of his hiding place – Alice herself! [JC-W]

Also with: Robert Englund (Freddie Krueger), Danny Hassel (Dan), Whitby Hertford (Jacob), Kelly Jo Minter (Yvonne), Erika Anderson (Greta), Nick Mele, Beatrice Boepple, Joe Seely, Valorie Armstrong, Burr DeBenning, Steven Grives. Dir: Stephen Hopkins. Pro: Robert Shaye and Rupert Harvey. Ex Pro: Sara Risher and Jon Turtle. Screenplay: Leslie Bohem; based on characters created by Wes Craven. Ph: Peter Levy. Ed: Chuck Weiss and Brent Schoenfeld. Pro Des: C. J. Strawn. M: Jay Ferguson; numbers performed by Samantha Fox, W.A.S.P., Doctor Ice, etc. Krueger make-up: David Miller. (New Line–Enterprise.) Rel: 11 May 1990. 90 mins. Cert 18.

No Holds Barred. Yes, it's a film about (American) wrestling in general and, apparently, American star grappler Hulk Hogan in particular. (Non wrestling fans please note.) The weak story is about a TV network boss trying to get the Hulk to change over from his present channel. [FMS]

Lisa Wilcox and Erika Anderson suffer a gastronomic nightmare in A Nightmare on Elm Street 5 – The Dream Child, *from Enterprise.*

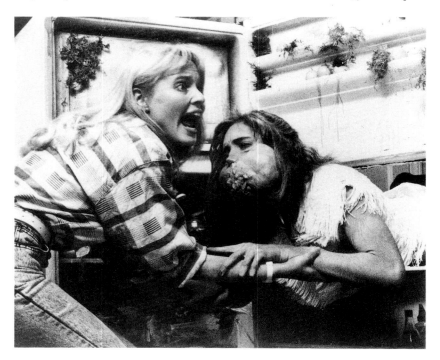

Robbie Coltrane finds it hard to conceal his interest, particularly in scenes like this – from Virgin's Nuns on the Run.

Cast: Hulk Hogan, Kurt Fuller (Brell), Joan Severance (Samantha), Tom 'Tiny' Lister, Mark Pellegrino, Bill Henderson, Charles Levin, David Palmer, Stan 'The Lariat' Hansen, Armelia McQueen, Jesse 'The Body' Ventura, Gene Okerlund, Howard Finkel. Dir: Thomas J. Wright. Pro: Michael Rachmil . Ex Pro: Vince McMahon and Hulk Hogan. Co-Ex Pro: Richard Glover. Screenplay: Dennis Hackin, Ph: Frank Beascoehea. Ed: Tom Pryor. Pro Des: James Shanahan. M: Jim Johnston. (Shane Pro–Cannon.) Rel: floating; first shown London (Cannon, Panton St) 13 October 1989. 90 mins. Cert 15.

Notebook on Cities and Clothes. Self-indulgent and humourless home movie parading as a documentary about Japanese fashion designer Yohji Yamamoto. Switching between Paris and Tokyo, German film-maker Wim Wenders ponders on 'identity versus fashion', the colour of black and the evolution of the image – from oil to digital. Unfortunately, Yamamoto is not the most engaging of interview sub-jects and Wenders doesn't help by photographing endless city streets on poor definition video. Sponsored by the Georges Pompidou Centre in Paris. [JC-W]

Dir and Screenplay: Wim Wenders. Ex Pro: Ulrich Felsberg. Ph: Robbie Muller, Wim Wenders, Masatoshi Nakajima, etc. Ed: Dominique Auvray, Lenie Savietto and Anne Schnee. M: Laurent Petitgand. Sound: Jean-Paul Mugel, Axel Arft and Reiner Lorenz. (Road Movies–Artificial Eye.) Rel: floating; first shown London (Renoir) 8 June 1990. 80 mins. Cert U.

Nuns on the Run. Give the public a catchy title and you've got yourself a hit. This energetic farce won glowing reviews in America and proved surpris-ingly popular – considering its familiar plot lines. Eric Idle and Robbie Col-trane play a pair of jolly nice bank rob-bers who decide to retire, double-cross their boss and steal a couple of million from the Triads. Botching the theft as usual, Eric and Robbie disguise them-selves as nuns and hide out in a London convent. The mob, the police and the Triads come looking for them, but our heroes are (apparently) invisible as sis-ters of God. That is, until Eric leaves the loo seat up . . . And they said the *Carry Ons* were dead. [JC-W]

Cast includes: Eric Idle (Brian Hope), Robbie Coltrane (Charlie McManus), Camille Coduri (Faith), Janet Suzman (Sister Superior), Robert Patterson ('Case' Casey), Robert Morgan (Abbott), Winston Dennis (Morley), Richard Simpson (Mr Norris), Doris Hare, Lila Kaye, Tom Hickey, Colin Campbell, Gary Tang, Nigel Fan, Tatiana Strauss, Stewart Harwood, Peter Geeves, Aran Bell. Dir and Screen-play: Jonathan Lynn. Pro: Michael White. Co-Pro: Simon Bosanquet. Ex Pro: George Harrison and Denis O'Brien. Ph: Mike Gar-fath. Ed: David Martin. Pro Des: Simon Holland. M: Yello and Hidden Faces. Cos-tumes: Sue Yelland. Sound: Tony Jackson. (HandMade–Palace.) Rel: 4 May 1990. 95 mins. Cert 12.

Old Gringo. Mexico, 1913. 'I was only trying to change my life, but they were trying to change their world', says Jane Fonda as Harriet Winslow, a 52-year-old virgin spinster plunged into the Mexican Revolution. There is only one reason for a virgin to be in a film and

Jane Fonda and Gregory Peck in the long-awaited Old Gringo, *from Columbia.*

that is so that she can lose her maidenhood. Harriet's suitors include Ambrose Bierce (a rather affecting Gregory Peck), the legendary writer disillusioned with words and looking for real life before death; and General Arroya (Jimmy Smits), a man torn between duty and more personal ghosts. *Old Gringo* was an epic undertaking which took eight years to materialise, but is a disappointing, stodgy work, with too much acting and too many painted skyscapes. However, Peck makes a welcome return to the screen after an absence of nine years (forgetting his guest role in *Silent Voice*) and is well served by Aida Bortnick and Luis Puenzo's script. [JC-W]

Also with: Patricio Contreras (Col Frutos Garcia), Jenny Gago (La Garduna), Gabriela Roel (La Luna), Sergio Calderon, Guillermo Rios, Jim Metzler, Anne Pitoniak, Pedro Armendariz Jr, Hector Rivera. Dir and (with Aida Bortnik) Screenplay: Luis Puenzo; from the novel *Gringo Viejo* by Carlos Fuentes. Pro: Lois Bonfiglio. Ex Pro: David Wisnievitz. Ph: Felix Monti. Ed:

Juan Carlos Macias, William Anderson and Glenn Farr. Pro Des: Stuart Wurtzel and Bruno Rubeo. M: Lee Holdridge. Costumes: Enrico Sabbatini. Sound: Tom C.

After being adapted for stage and screen musicals, Dickens's Oliver Twist *now provides the Disney animated feature,* Oliver and Company. *A fearsome Fagin sends the Artful Dodger into pocketpicking action.*

McCarthy. (Fonda Films–Columbia.) Rel: floating; first shown London (Cannon, Shaftesbury Ave) 20 October 1989. 119 mins. Cert 15.

Oliver and Company. It's interesting to compare this admittedly amusing and entertaining Disney animated feature with the studio's previous pro-

ductions like *Bambi* and *Dumbo*. The charm is considerably less now, the music modern and loud and less melodious, the pace fast and furious, and only a few of the characters have the old endearing Disney magic. Based – well, sort of – on the Dickens classic, it's the story of a cute stray kitten adopted by a weirdly worldwise Fagin and his company of streetwise New York dogs. It's rough and tumble stuff and brilliantly done but I wonder if today's kids will take it to their hearts as they did those classics of yesteryear? I can't. [FMS]

With the voices of: Joey Lawrence (Oliver), Billy Joel (Dodger), Cheech Marin (Tito), Richard Mulligan (Einstein), Roscoe Lee Browne (Francis), Sheryl Lee Ralph (Rita), Dom DeLuise (Fagin), Taurean Blacque (Roscoe), Carl Weintraub (Desoto), Robert Loggia (Bill Sikes), Natalie Gregory (Jenny), William Glover (Winston), Georgette (Betty Midley). Dir: George Scribner. Animation Screenplay: Jim Cox, Timothy J. Disney and James Mangold. Supervising Animators: Mike Gabriel, Glen Keane, Ruben A. Aquino, Hendel Butoy, Mark Henn and Doug Krohn. Art: Dan Hansen. More than 300 others were involved in various ways with the production. (Walt Disney, in assoc. with Silver Screen Partners/Warner.) Rel: 15 December 1989. 74 mins. Cert U.

The Package. Predictable, out-dated conspiracy thriller about an elaborate Soviet-American assassination attempt on Gorbachev, planned to preserve the nuclear arms race. Gene Hackman stars as a common-or-garden army sergeant who stumbles into the plot when a prisoner he is escorting from East Berlin to the US escapes. Cold-war clichés fly like shrapnel, but *The Package* succeeds adequately as a nuts-and-bolts thriller, with Hackman always watchable as a man alien to fear, and with some good dialogue to chew on. [JC-W]

Cast includes: Gene Hackman (Johnny Gallagher), Joanna Cassidy (Eileen Gallagher), Tommy Lee Jones (Thomas Boyette), John Heard (Col Glen Whitacre), Dennis Franz (Milan Delich), Kevin Crowley (Walter Henke), Chelcie Ross (General Hopkins), Pam Grier, Ron Dean, Nathan Davis, Joe Greco, Ike Pappas, Marco St John, Reni Santoni, Michael Skewes, Johnny Lee Davenport, Thalmus Rasulala. Dir: Andrew Davis. Pro: Beverly J. Camhe and Tobie Haggerty. Co-Pro: Andrew Davis and Dennis Haggerty. Ex Pro: Arne L. Schmidt. Screenplay: John Bishop. Ph: Frank Tidy.

The domestic rollercoaster ride of Parenthood *(Universal-UIP), with* (left to right, adults only) *Leaf Phoenix, Keanu Reeves, Martha Plimpton, Dianne Wiest* (sitting), *Harley Kozak, Rick Moranis, Mary Steenburgen, Steve Martin, Jason Robards, Eileen Ryan, Tom Hulce and, last but not least, Helen Shaw* (also sitting).

Ed: Don Zimmerman and Billy Weber. Pro Des: Michael Levesque. M: James Newton Howard. Costumes: Marilyn Vance-Straker. Sound: Scott D. Smith. (Orion–Rank.) Rel: 8 June 1990. 108 mins. Cert 15.

Parenthood. Five generations of a suburban American family are lovingly examined in this first-rate, heart-warming comedy-drama. Although shot through with sentimentality, the film offers some eye-opening truths on fatherhood, problem children, one-parent motherhood, black sheep, teenage marriage and pre-school education – but always with an entertaining flourish. Steve Martin, as a father of three, works marvellously and hilariously with the children and handles his dramatic passages superbly. Mary Steenburgen, as his wife, is excellent; while, as Martin's brother-in-law, Rick

Moranis *almost* overcomes his screen persona as America's favourite nerd. A perspicacious script shines throughout (and never scrapes the barrel for laughs), showing every aspect of parenthood (Martin: 'Woman have choices, men have responsibilities'; or Dianne Wiest: 'I can't be a grandmother – I was at Woodstock!'). A feel-good movie with warning lights. [JC-W]

Cast includes: Steve Martin (Gil), Tom Hulce (Larry), Rick Moranis (Nathan), Martha Plimpton (Julie), Keanu Reeves ('That' Tod), Jason Robards (Frank), Mary Steenburgen (Karen), Dianne Wiest (Helen), Harley Kozak (Susan), Dennis Dugan (David Brodsky), Leaf Phoenix (Garry), Eileen Ryan (Marilyn), Helen Shaw (Grandma), Jasen Fisher, Paul Linke, Alisan Porter, Zachary Lavoy, Ivyann Schwan, Alex Burrall, Lowell Ganz, Rance Howard, Clint Howard. Dir: Ron Howard. Pro: Brian Grazer. Ex Pro: Joseph M. Caracciolo. Screenplay: Lowell Ganz and Babaloo Mandel; from a story by Ganz, Mandel and Ron Howard. Ph: Donald McAlpine. Ed: Michael Hill and Daniel Hanley. Pro Des: Todd Hallowell. M: Randy Newman. Costumes: Ruth Morley. Sound: Richard S. Church. (Imagine/Universal–UIP.) Rel: 12 January 1990. 99 mins. Cert 15.

Fred Gwynne as the mysterious neighbour in Stephen King's scary Pet Sematary *(UIP).*

Patti Rocks. Yet another of those low-budget, adult American films in which the accent is on talk. Billy (Chris Mulkey) is a loud-mouthed, loose-moralled male chauvinist. He is married with two daughters and has made his mistress pregnant. Terrified of his wife finding out, Billy has to confront his girl-friend with the truth about his marriage. Persuading an old friend, Eddie (John Jenkins), to lend him moral support, he drives through the night to confront his fate. On the journey, he entertains Eddie with his sexist, poetic opinions of the weaker sex. Unfortunately, Billy is such an odious character that there is little to like in this 'serious adult comedy' (as the film is billed), until the appearance of Patti Rocks (Karen Landry), his put-upon mistress. It is Landry's performance and dialogue (which the actress wrote herself) that ultimately redeems this seedy little tale. For the record, *Patti Rocks* is a sequel to director David Burton Morris's 1975 *Loose Ends*. [JC-W]

Also with: Joe Minjares, Buffy Sedlachek, Mae Mayhew. Dir: David Burton Morris. Pro: Gwen Field and Gregory M. Cummins. Ex Pro: Sam Grogg. Story and Screenplay: Morris, Chris Mulkey, John Jenkins and Karen Landry; based on characters created by Victoria Wozniak. Ph and Ed: Gregory M. Cummins. Art: Charlotte Whitaker. M: Doug Maynard. (FilmDallas–Premier Releasing.) Rel: floating; first shown London (Everyman Cinema, Hampstead) 15 September 1989. 87 mins. Cert 18.

Pet Sematary. Stephen King unleashes a whole psychiatrist's Filofax of fears in this thoroughly nasty thriller set on both sides of a killer main road. The Creed family (nuclear, of course) moves from urban Chicago to rural Maine (Stephen King's home state) and, far from finding country bliss, instead encounter a nightmare of supernatural origin. Their son is almost mown down by a passing truck, a local schoolboy is run over, the cat is killed in the road and so on. King plays on our fears of mutilated pets, main roads, giant juggernauts and walking corpses, and defies logic in a tale that is well told but excessively silly. Incidentally, this is the first King novel (a No. 1 best-seller) that the maestro has himself adapted for the screen. [JC-W]

Cast includes: Dale Midkiff (Dr Louis Creed), Denise Crosby (Rachel Creed), Fred Gwynne (Jud Crandall), Blaze Berdahl (Ellie Creed), Miko Hughes (Gage Creed), Brad Greenquist (Victor Pascow), Susan J. Blommaert (Missy Dandridge). Dir: Mary Lambert. Pro: Richard P. Rubinstein. Ex Pro: Tim Zinnemann. Screenplay: Stephen King; based on his own novel. Ph: Peter Stein. Ed: Michael Hill, Daniel Hanley. Pro Des: Michael Z. Hanan. M: Elliot Goldenthal. Costumes: Marlene Stewart. (Paramount–UIP.) Rel: 17 November 1989. 102 mins. Cert 18.

The Phantom of the Opera. Be warned; this isn't a screen version of the stage musical that has been making millions on both sides of the Atlantic, nor has it any close relationship to the original silent film adaptation of Gaston Leroux's classic horror story (starring Lon Chaney), nor does it owe much to the 1943 and 1962 films that followed. Made in English in Budapest, obviously with a careful eye on the budget, it is competently made, takes liberties with the orginal story and has *Elm Street*'s Robert Englund in the title role. This is the first of several 'Phantom' films designed to cash in on the prodigious success of the Andrew Lloyd Webber stage show. [FMS]

Cast: Robert Englund, Jill Schoelen, Alex Hyde-White, Bill Nighy, Stephanie Lawrence, Terence Harvey, Nathan Lewis, Molly Shannon, Emma Rawson. Dir: Dwight H. Little. Pro: Harry Alan Towers. Ex Pro: Menahem Golan. Assoc Pro: Eliezer Ben Chorin. Screenplay: Duke Sandefur; based on a screenplay by Gerry O'Hara; from the Gaston Leroux novel. Ph: Elmer Ragalyi. Ed: Charles Bornstein. Art: Tivada Bertalan. M: Misha Segal. (21st Century Productions in assoc. with Breton Films–Castle Premier.) Rel: floating; first shown London (Cannon, Haymarket) 15 June 1990. 92 mins. Cert 18.

Physical Evidence. A familiar, time-worn court-case thriller with Theresa Russell as a young attorney trying to earn her stripes defending a cop accused of murder. The more guilty the cop looks, the more we believe his innocence – because it's that kind of movie. The usual suspects are rounded up, threats are made and reputations blackened by a script in search of a shred of originality. The twist is that Ms Russell has a bigger role than Burt Reynolds, the latter playing the cop as if he had a permanent migraine. Set in Boston, but filmed in Toronto and Montreal, *Physical Evidence* looks dingy and creaks with explanatory dialogue. Previously known as *Smoke*. [JC-W]

Cast includes: Burt Reynolds (Joe Paris), Theresa Russell (Jenny Hudson), Ned Beatty (James Nicks), Kay Lenz (Deborah Quinn), Ted McGinley (Kyle), Tom O'Brien (Matt Farley), Kenneth Welsh (Harry Norton), Ray Baker, Ken James, Michael P. Moran, Angelo Rizacos, Lamar Jackson, Paul Hubbard, Larry Reynolds, Peter MacNeill, Laurie Paton, Don Granbery, Angie McNab, Laurie Holden. Dir: Michael Crichton. Pro: Martin Ransohoff. Ex Pro: Don Carmody. Screenplay: Bill Phillips; from a story by Phillips and Steve Ransohoff. Ph: John A. Alonzo. Ed: Glenn Farr. Pro Des: Dan Yarhi. M: Henry Mancini. Costumes: Betsy Cox. (Rank.) Rel: floating; first shown London (Odeon, Leicester Sq) 1 September 1989. 99 mins. Cert 18.

Piravi (The Birth). An old man living in northern Kerala (India) worries about his son Raghu, a student, who should have returned from the state capital Trivandrum to attend his father's birthday celebrations. Enquiries made of Raghu's acquaintances lead to evasive comments, and it seems that only a journey all the way to Trivandrum will reveal the truth about his disappearance. To discover the facts becomes ever more urgent when a report in a newspaper suggests that the youth has been arrested. Like Mira Nair's *Salaam Bombay!*, *Piravi* arrives in London with a reputation and bearing a clutch of awards. A first feature by Shaji, the noted cinematographer, it is a remarkable debut. [MS]

Cast includes: Premji, Archana, C. V. Sreeraman, Mullene, Krishna Moorty. Dir: Shaji. Pro: Film Folk. Screenplay: S. Jayachandran and Nair. Ph: Sunny Joseph. M: G. Aravindan. (Film Folk–ICA/Contemporary.) Rel: floating; first shown London (ICA) 26 January 1990. 110 mins. No cert.

Plaff! or Too Afraid of Life. Extraordinary, slapdash satire from Cuban director Juan Carlos Tabio, who uses the story of a mentally persecuted widow and mother to express his dissatisfaction with 'troubled' times in his country. The title suggests the noise of an egg hitting a wall, but one can't help thinking that it's Tabio who has ended up with egg on his face. Still, there are some refreshing glimpses into Cuban sexual and social anxiety. [CB]

Cast includes: Daisy Granados (Concha), Thais Valdés (Clarita), Luis Alberto Garcia (José Ramón), Raúl Pomares (Tomas), Alicia Bustamante (Asunción), Jorge Cao (Contreras). Dir: Juan Carlos Tabio. Pro: Ricardo Avila. Screenplay: Daniel Chavarria and Juan Carlos Tabio. Ph: Julio Valdés. Ed: Roberto Bravo. M: Nicolàs Reynoso. Sound: Raul Garcia. (Instituto Cubano de Artes e Industrias–Metro.) Rel: floating; first shown London (ICA) 9 March 1990. 110 mins. Cert 15.

Play Me Something. An astonishingly pretentious, shoe-string budget production from artist/art critic/poet/novelist/playwright/scenarist John Berger. Berger himself plays a stranger who walks into an airport waiting room in Barra, in the Hebrides, to relate a strange Venetian love story to the

A scene from ICA/Contemporary's Piravi, *directed by Shaji.*

assembled passengers. This critic fell asleep. [JC-W]

Also with: Lucia Lanzarini (Marietta), Charlie Barron (Bruno), Hamish Henderson (electrician), Tilda Swinton (hairdresser), Stewart Ennis, Robert Carr, Liz Lochhead. Dir and (with John Berger) Screenplay: Timothy Neat. Pro: Kate Swan. Ex Pro: Colin MacCabe. Ph: Chris Cox. Ed: Russell Fenton. Art: Annette Gillies. M: Jim Sutherland. Sound: Aad Wirtz. (BFI/Film Four/Scottish Film Production Fund/Grampian TV–BFI.) Rel: floating; first shown London (Riverside, Hammersmith) 6 October 1989. 80 mins. Cert 15.

Police Academy 6: City Under Siege. With an eye possibly cocked on the British 'Carry On' record, this sixth variation on the original *Police Academy* romp suggests there is still plenty of recycling possibility there for the future. This time round the so-called plot has Commander Lassard's team of hopefuls assigned to track down a gang of clever crooks whose daring robberies have so far foxed the cops. [FMS]

Cast includes: George Gaynes, Bubba Smith, David Graf, Michael Winslow, Leslie Easterbrook, Marion Ramsey, Lance Kinsey, Matt McCoy, Bruce Mahler, G. W. Bailey, Kenneth Mars, Gerrit Graham, George R. Robinson. Dir: Peter Bonerz. Pro: Paul Maslansky. Screenplay: S. J. Cur-

Comedy cops Marion Ramsey and Bruce Mahler coolly and confidently tackling crime in City Under Siege, *sixth of Warner's* Police Academy *series.*

wick; based on the characters created by Ned Israel and Pat Proft. Ph: Charles Rosher Jr. Ed: Hubert De La Bouillerie. Pro Des: Tho E. Azzari. M: Robert Folk. (Warner.) Rel: 21 July 1989. 83 mins. Cert PG.

Powwow Highway. Lightweight but likeable road movie in which two Cheyenne Indians set off for Sante Fe, New Mexico, from their Montana reservation. Buddy Red Bow is on the warpath to free his sister from trumped-up charges of cannabis possession, while his companion, would-be warrior Philbert Bono, is on a more spiritual quest. Part-Blackfoot actor A. Martinez is Red Bow and Mohawk Gary Farmer is Philbert, both contributing an edge of authenticity long missing from American movies dealing with Indian folklore (actually, this was financed by Britain's HandMade). The film, essentially an adventure-comedy, does address some disturbing statistics – 75 per cent of American Indians live below the pov-

erty line – but cannot help trivialising the subject matter by its very format. The 'powwow highway' of the title refers to a symbolic road between ancient tradition and modern reality, *powwow* being an Algonquin word meaning 'ceremonial gathering'. [JC-W]

Also with: Joanelle Nadine Romero (Bonnie Red Bow), Wayne Waterman (Wolf Tooth), Margo Kane (Imogene), Amanda Wyss (Rabbit Layton), John Tudell, Wes Studi, Randal Patrick, Geoff Rivas, Sam Vlahos,

Mystic warrior or junk food addict? Gary Farmer in a dream sequence from Jonathan Wacks's Powwow Highway *(HandMade).*

Chrissie McDonald, Sky Seals, Rogene Not Afraid, Tony Frank. Dir: Jonathan Wacks. Pro: Jan Wieringa. Ex Pro: George Harrison and Denis O'Brien. Screenplay: Janet Heaney and Jean Stawarz; based on the novel by David Seals. Ph: Toyomichi Kurita. Ed: James Austin Stewart. Pro Des: Cynthia Sowder. M: Barry Goldberg. Costumes: Isis Mussenden. Sound: Ed Novick. (HandMade.) Rel: floating; first shown London (Electric, Portobello Road) 11 May 1990. 91 mins. Cert 15.

Pretty Woman. Divinely escapist fairy tale with Richard Gere as a smooth millionaire broker chained to endless meetings and his cellular phone. Needing a no-strings-attached escort for his week in Beverly Hills, he hires a good-looking prostitute, hands her his credit card and tells her to update her wardrobe (clothes by Cerruti). Besides $3,000, Gere's escort is given a crash course in class, but also hands out some lessons of her own. In the title role Julia Roberts is a dream on legs, turning this morally dubious fantasy into a high-concept, star-cementing vehicle. An obvious transplant and update of *Pygmalion/My Fair Lady*, the film even pays homage to the latter by slipping in an Audrey Hepburn film clip. Forget your moral politics and enjoy yourself. [JC-W]

Cast includes: Richard Gere (Edward Lewis), Julia Roberts (Vivian Ward), Hector Elizondo (hotel manager), Ralph Bellamy (James Morse), Jason Alexander (Philip Stuckey), Laura San Giacomo (Kit de Luca), Alex Hyde White (David Morse), Amy Yasbeck, Elinor Donahue, Judith Baldwin, Bill Applebaum, Frank Campanella, Larry Miller, Dey Young, Stacy Keach Sr, Lloyd Nelson, Tracy Reiner, Tom Nolan. Dir: Garry Marshall. Pro: Arnon Milchan and Steve Reuther. Ex Pro: Laura Ziskin. Screenplay: J. F. Lawton. Ph: Charles Minsky. Ed: Priscilla Nedd. Pro Des: Albert Brenner. M: James Newton Howard; numbers performed by Go West, Christopher Otcasek, Red Hot Chili Peppers, David Bowie, Robert Palmer, Natalie Cole, Richard Gere, Roy Orbison, Kenny G, Peter Cetera, etc. Costumes: Marilyn Vance-Straker. Sound: Jim Webb. (Touchstone-- Warner.) Rel: 11 May 1990. 120 mins. Cert 15.

A Private Life. Cape Town, 1950-73. A true story in which a South African woman is wrongly 'classified' as black, preventing her from seeing the man she loves. Without a birth certificate or rec-

Laura San Giacomo and Julia Roberts as hookers on Hollywood Boulevard, in Warner's Pretty Woman. *After the fairy-tale transformation: Ms Roberts as fashion queen with the man of her dreams, Richard Gere.*

ords of her mother, Stella (Jane Cilliers, perfect) fights to prove that she is white to the disbelieving authorities of Cape Town. A labour of love, *A Private Life* took ten years to reach the screen, due, in part, to its creator's insistence that the film be shot on authentic South African locations. A raw ordinariness and documentary edge combine to force home the reality of an everyday plight in a beleaguered country. [JC-W]

Also with: Bill Flynn (Jack Dupont), Kevin Smith (older Paul), Ian Roberts (Sgt Smit),

Don't mess with this dead man: Dolph Lundgren as The Punisher *(Castle Premier).*

Embeth Davidtz (older Karen), Lance Maron (older Gary), Joanna Weinberg (Andrea), Justin John, Talia Leibman, Warren Hetz, Anthony Fridjhon, Patrick Mynhardt. Dir: Francis Gerard. Ex Pro: Gerard and Roland Robinson. Assoc Pro: Moira Tuck. Screenplay: Andrew Davies. Ph: Nat Crosby. Ed: Robin Sales. Pro Des: Mark Wilby. M: Trevor Jones. Costumes: Diane Cilliers. Sound: Robin Harris. (BBC–HBO.) Rel: 24 November 1989. 95 mins. Cert 15.

The Punisher. Imagine *RoboCop* married to *Batman* – with a truly international cast – and you have a rough draft for *The Punisher*. Based on the Marvel Comic strip, the story concerns the one-man war on crime waged by Frank Castle (Dolph Lundgren), mythic avenger by night, dead cop in the record books. Frank's family was wiped out by a Mafia kingpin and he's borne a grudge ever since; to date his body-count is 125 'guilty ones'. Louis Gossett Jr, as detective Jake Berkowitz, knows the score and barks at Frank, 'What do you call a hundred and twenty-five murders in five years?'; to which Frank answers, 'Work in progress.' Yes, there's humour amid the mayhem, stunning stunts and gripping Wagnerian score. The English version was considerably trimmed of its original violence. Filmed in Sydney, of all places. [JC-W]

Also with: Jeroen Krabbe (Gianni Franco), Kim Miyori (Lady Tanaka), Bryan Marshall (Dino Moretti), Nancy Everhard (Samantha Leary), Barry Otto (Shake), Brian Rooney, Zoshka Mizak, Todd Boyce. Dir: Mark Goldblatt. Pro: Robert Mark Kamen. Co-Pro: Su Armstrong. Ex Pro: Robert Guralnick. Screenplay: Boaz Yakin; based on the comic strip. Ph: Ian Baker. Ed: Tim Wellburn. Pro Des: Norma Moricuea. M: Dennis Dreith. (New World–Castle Premier.) Rel: 1 June 1990. 88 mins. Cert 18.

Queen of Hearts. Enchanting and stylish saga that defies categorisation, about a family of Italians settled in modern-day England. Directed by Jon Amiel (BBC's *The Singing Detective*), the film eloquently traces the life-long love affair of Danilo and Rosa (Joseph Long and Anita Zagaria), and their struggle to bring up a family in London's Italian quarter. Related through the eyes of Eddie (Ian Hawkes), Danilo's youngest son, the story takes on an almost operatic quality, related in a series of truly stunning set pieces. A film to cherish. [JC-W]

Also with: Eileen Way (Mama Sibilla), Vittorio Duse (Nonno), Vittoria Amandola (Barbariccia), Tat Whalley (Beetle), Jimmy Lambert (Bruno), Ronan Vibert, Matilda Thorpe, Sarah Hadaway, Michael Mears. Dir: Jon Amiel. Pro: John Hardy. Ex Pro: Graham Benson. Assoc Pro: Caroline Hewitt. Screenplay: Tony Grisoni. Ph: Mike Southon. Ed: Peter Boyle. Pro Des: Jim Clay. M: Michael Convertino. Costumes: Lindy Hemming. Sound: Peter Glossop. (Nelson Entertainment/Enterprise/TVS Films–Enterprise.) Rel: 29 September 1989. 112 mins. Cert PG.

The Rachel Papers. Screen version of Martin Amis's celebrated, ribald bestseller which the author wrote at 24 (in 1973) to exorcise his adolescent ghosts. In the film, Charles Highway (Dexter Fletcher) keeps a file of his sexual conquests and techniques on computer, somewhat outdating the title. Nevertheless, this pop video update is stylishly directed by Damian Harris (son of Richard) in his directorial debut, backed up by a welter of fine cameos (Jonathan Pryce, James Spader, Bill

Tat Whalley and Ian Hawkes spy on the old, eccentric Nonno (Vittorio Duse) in Jon Amiel's utterly enchanting Queen of Hearts *(Enterprise).*

RELEASES OF THE YEAR

Paterson, Michael Gambon) and an excellent score. Unfortunately, neither Dexter Fletcher as the computer-age Romeo, nor Ione Skye as Rachel, his unattainable Venus, can match the material – try as they may. [JC-W]

Also with: Jonathan Pryce (Norman), James Spader (DeForest), Bill Paterson (Gordon Highway), Shirley Anne Field (Mrs Seth-Smith), Jared Harris (Geoff), Aubrey Morris, Claire Skinner, Nicola Kimber, Lesley Sharp, Michael Gambon, Pat Keen, Shirley King, Di Langford, Amanda Dickinson. Dir and Screenplay: Damian Harris; from the novel by Martin Amis. Pro: Andrew Karsh. Co-Pro: Paul Raphael. Ex Pro: Eric Fellner. Ph: Alex Thomson, Tony Spratling. Ed: David Martin. Pro Des: Andrew McAlpine. M: Chaz Jankel. Costumes: Marit Allen. Sound: Ian Voight. (Initial Film/Longfellow Pictures–Virgin.) Rel: 27 October 1989. 95 mins. Cert 18.

The Rainbow. Ken Russell first established himself as a world-class director with *Women in Love*, and now, nineteen years on, he returns to D. H. Lawrence territory. *The Rainbow* was written several years before *Women in Love*, exploring the very first stirrings of sexuality in Ursula Brangwen (played by Jennie Linden in the earlier film and here by Sammi Davis). Only the last third of Lawrence's novel told Ursula's story – which otherwise described the lives of her parents and grandparents – but Russell has opted to concentrate on the budding of adolescence and hope. Set in the Midlands at the turn of the century, the film follows Ursula's fling with her athletics teacher (Amanda Donohoe), her dalliance with a dashing soldier and her own efforts at teaching. Sammi Davis struggles manfully as Ursula, all tantrums one minute and bright-eyed and bushy-tailed the next. Clothes are shed, hearts are broken and Northern accents are trampled on in this broad, colourful adaptation in which everybody is far too busy acting. Oh, yes – and beware the heavy-handed symbolism. [JC-W]

Also with: Paul McGann (Anton Skrebensky), Amanda Donohoe (Winifred Inger), Christopher Gable (Will Brangwen), David Hemmings (Uncle Henry), Glenda Jackson (Anna Brangwen), Dudley Sutton, Jim Carter, Judith Paris, Ken Colley, Molly Russell, Alan Edmondson, Rupert Russell. Dir, Pro and (with Vivian Russell) Screenplay: Ken Russell; from the novel by David

Herbert Lawrence. Ex Pro: William J. Quigley and Dan Ireland. Line Pro: Ronaldo Vasconcellos. Ph: Billy Williams. Ed: Peter Davies. Pro Des: Luciana Arrighi. M: Carl Davis. Costumes: Arrighi. Sound: John Murphy. (Vestron.) Rel: floating; first shown London (Odeon, Haymarket) 3 November 1989. 104 mins. Cert 15.

Dexter Fletcher ponders the mysteries of the opposite sex in Virgin's film version of Martin Amis's acclaimed The Rachel Papers.

Ursula Brangwen (Sammi Davis) discovers heterosexual sex with Anton Skrebensky (Paul McGann) in Ken Russell's overblown The Rainbow *(Vestron).*

Figures in a wintry landscape: Ian McElhinney and Carol Scanlan as Reefer and the Model *in this memorable, idiosyncratic Metro release.*

Reefer and the Model. Off-beat, pointedly original saga about four drifters in present-day Ireland who turn to a life of crime. Brimming with atmosphere, this witty road movie-cum-thriller smacks of real life, shot through with streaks of the surreal and bizarre. The unknown cast are all excellent, as is the photography and music, creating a unique and entertaining nugget of cinema. [JC-W]

Cast includes: Ian McElhinney (Reefer), Eve Watkinson (mother), Carol Scanlan (the model), Sean Lawlor (Spider), Ray McBride (Badger), Birdy Sweeney, Dave Duffy, Little John Nee, Maire Chinsealach. Dir and Screenplay: Joe Comerford. Pro: Lelia Doolan. Ph: Breffni Byrne. Ed: Sé Merry. Pro Des: John Lucas. M: Johnny Duhan. (Berber Films/Bord Scannan na hÉireann/Irish Film Board/Radio Telefis Éireann/Channel Four–Metro.) Rel: floating; first shown London (Metro) 24 November 1989. 90 mins. Cert 15.

Renegades. Kiefer Sutherland and Lou Diamond Phillips, last seen together on horseback in *Young Guns*, take to the streets of Philadelphia as, respectively, an undercover cop and a Lakota Indian in search of a stolen sacred lance. Quite frankly, Sutherland looks entirely too young to play a policeman, even hidden behind a moustache (a device employed by fellow Young Gun Emilio Estevez to play a cop in *Stakeout*). However, Sutherland exudes enough rough charisma to hold the movie together, which is more than can be said for Phillips. Jami Gertz, last seen alongside Sutherland in *The Lost Boys* (all friends here), has precious little to do and deserves better than this. Still, *Renegades* (previously *Lakota*) moves along at a rate of knots – thanks to Jack Sholder's efficient direction – and has enough good car-chases and despicable villains to keep boredom well at bay. [JC-W]

Cast includes: Kiefer Sutherland (Buster), Lou Diamond Phillips (Hank), Jami Gertz (Barbara), Rob Knepper (Marino), Bill Smitrovich (Finch), Peter MacNeill (Denny Ransom), Floyd Westerman, Joe Griffin, Clark Johnson, Gary Farmer, Joseph Hieu, Heidi Von Palleske, Tom Butler, Paul Butler, Big Yank, Robert La Sardo. Dir: Jack Sholder. Pro: David Madden. Ex Pro: James G. Robinson, Joe Roth, Ted Field and Robert Cort. Screenplay: David Rich. Ph: Phil Meheux. Ed: Caroline Biggerstaff. Pro Des: Carol Spier. M: Michael Kamen. Costumes: Gina Kiellerman. Sound: Larry Kemp and Wylie Stateman. (Morgan Creek/Interscope Communications–Virgin Vision.) Rel: 9 March 1990. 105 mins. Cert 18.

Resurrected. Inspired by true events, this is the somewhat depressing story of a British soldier who returns from the dead seven weeks after going missing in action in the Falklands. 'Dead', the boy is a hero, but alive he's a potential deserter. Oddly, this raw, uneven and televisual piece won both the Catholic and Protestant awards at the 1989 Berlin Festival. [JC-W]

Cast includes: Tom Bell (Mr Deakin), Rita Tushingham (Mrs Deakin), David Thewlis (Kevin Deakin), Michael Pollitt (Gregory Deakin), Rudi Davies (Julie), Christopher Fulford (Slaven), Paul Geoffrey (vicar), Ewan Stewart, David Lonsdale, Peter Gunn, William Hoyland, Mark Wing-Davey, Kenny Ireland, Nigel Hastings. Dir: Paul Greengrass. Pro: Adrian Hughes and Tara Prem. Screenplay: Martin Allen. Ph: Ivan Strasburg. Ed: Dan Rea. Pro Des:

Together again: the formidable four musketeers, Aramis (Richard Chamberlain), Athos (Oliver Reed), d'Artagnan (Michael York) and Porthos (Frank Finlay), in Richard Lester's knockabout Warner comedy, The Return of the Musketeers.

Christopher Burke. M Ed: Andrew Glen. Costumes: Tudor George. Sound: Mike McDuffie. (Film Four Int/British Screen/St Pancras Film–HoBo.) Rel: 29 September 1989. 96 mins. Cert 15.

The Return of Swamp Thing. Jolly little piece of 'family orientated' nonsense about a friendly mutant from the bayous of Louisiana. A sequel to Wes Craven's darker original, this claptrap plays shamelessly for laughs and stocks its storyline with Southern caricatures and in-jokes (Louis Jourdan's evil Dr Arcane owns a parrot called Gigi). All this may appeal to 10-to-14-year-olds, but anybody with even a semblance of intelligence should stay clear. [JC-W]

Also with: Heather Locklear (Abby Arcane), Sarah Douglas (Dr Lana Zurrell), Dick Durock (Swamp Thing), Joey Sagal (Gunn), Ace Mask (Dr Rochelle), Chris Doyle, Daniel Taylor, Ronreaco Lee, Monique Gabrielle, Ralph Pace, Albert B. Cooper IV. Dir: Jim Wynorski. Pro: Benja-

min Melniker and Micahel E. Uslan. Ex Pro: Tom Kuhn and Charles Mitchell. Screenplay: Derek Spenser and Grant Morris; based upon characters appearing in magazines published by DC Comics Inc. Ph: Zoran Hochstatter. Ed: Leslie Rosenthal. Pro Des: Robb Wilson King. M: Chuck Cirino; 'Born On the Bayou' sung by Creedence Clearwater Revival. Costumes: Vicky Graef. Sound: Blake Wilcox. (J&M Entertainment/Lightyear Ent–Medusa.) Rel: 22 December 1989. 88 mins. Cert 12.

The Return of the Musketeers. In 1974, Richard Lester unveiled his highly individual, knockabout comedy based on the Dumas classic book *The Three Musketeers*, following it a year later with *The Four Musketeers*, which was largely made up of excess footage from the first film. Now, some fifteen years later, Lester comes up with the third 'Musketeer' movie, using much of the original cast (some of them showing their age, but others surprisingly not). It's a slaphappy affair, sometimes farcically funny, sometimes repititious and sometimes a bit tired, but those who missed the first two films may not notice. The combination of slapstick, sword fights and general swashbuckling

with spectacularly lovely backgrounds is typical of Lester, as are the starry cast and the dizzying plot. Roy Kinnear, in the thick of it all, was sadly killed during filming, which must have cast a shadow over the production. [FMS]

Cast: Michael York (D'Artagnan), Oliver Reed (Athos), Frank Finlay (Porthos), Richard Chamberlain (Aramis), C. Thomas Howell (Athos's son), Kim Cattrall (a hardworking Justine), Geraldine Chaplin (Queen Anne), Roy Kinnear (Planchet), Christopher Lee (Rochefort), Philippe Noiret (Cardinal Mazarin), Alan Howard (Cromwell), Jean Pierre Cassel (Cyrano), Bill Paterson (Charles I), David Birkin, Eusebio Lazaro, Servanne Ducorps, W. J. Fletcher, Laure Sabardin, Marceline Collard, Billy Connolly, Pat Roach, Jesus Ruyman, Fernando de Juan, Barry Burgues, Leon Greene, Agata Lys, Bob Todd, Lucy Hardwick. Dir: Richard Lester. Pro: Pierre Spengler. Ex Pro: Mario Sotela and Wayne Drizin. Screenplay: George Macdonald Fraser; based on the Dumas novel *Twenty Years After*. Ph: Bernarr Lutic. Ed: John Victor Smith. Pro Des: Gil Parrondo. M: Jean Claude Petit. (Michelle De Broca/Pierre Spengler/Timothy Burrill Oros, London-Filmdebroc/Cine 5 Paris/Iberoamericana Films, Madrid–Entertainment.) Rel: 25 August 1989. 100 mins. Cert PG.

Miou-Miou and François Methe in Pathé's The Revolving Doors – Les Portes Tournantes, *an affecting story of cinema and music.*

Revenge. Mexico, 1989. This sprawling saga of friendship, lust, infidelity and revenge is a leisurely paced, atmospheric thriller that somehow misses its mark. The initial friendship between daredevil pilot Michael Cochran (Kevin Costner) and Mexican crimelord 'Tibey' Mendez (Anthony Quinn) is an intriguing one, but is neither developed nor fully explained. When the former runs off with the latter's wife, there is no sexual chemistry between the adulterers, and the cuckold's revenge is appallingly harsh. Still, there are some excellent supporting performances (particularly from James Gammon and Miguel Ferrer), a nice score and some awe-inspiring photography. [JC-W]

Also with: Madeleine Stowe (Miryea), Sally Kirkland (rock star), Miguel Ferrer (Amador), Tomas Milian (Cesar), James Gammon (Texan), Joaquin Martinez (Mauro), Jesse Corti, Luis de Icaza, John Leguizamo, Joe Santos, Edna Bolkan, Pia Karina, Claudio Brook. Dir: Tony Scott. Pro: Hunt Lowry and Stanley Rubin. Ex Pro: Kevin Costner. Screenplay: Jim Harrison and Jeffrey Fiskin; based on Harrison's novella of the same name. Ph: Jeffrey Kimball. Ed: Chris Lebenzon. Pro Des: Michael Seymour and Benjamin Fernandez. M: Jack Nitzsche. Costumes: Aude Bronson-Howard. Sound: Sandy Berman and Randle Akerson. (New World–Columbia Tri-Star.) Rel: 22 June 1990. 124 mins. Cert 18.

The Revolving Doors – Les Portes Tournantes. Enchanting, atmospheric story (told in flashback) about a country girl bewitched by the magic of silent cinema. Taking a job as a piano accompanist, Celeste (Monique Spaziani) is made redundant by the talkies, falls in love with and marries the local rich boy, gives birth to a son and then continues to try and fulfil her musical ambitions. By turns moving and amusing, this poignant French-Canadian co-production won two prizes at the 1988 Rio de Janeiro Film Festival. [CB]

Also with: Gabriel Arcand (Blaudelle), Miou-Miou (Lauda), François Methe (Antoine), Jacques Penot, Françoise Faucher, Jean-Louis Roux, Remy Girard, Charles Reiner. Dir: Francis Mankiewicz. Pro: René Malo and Francyne Morin. Screenplay: Jacques Savoie and Francis Mankiewicz. Ph: Thomas Vamos. Ed: Andre Corriveau. Art: Anne Pritchard. M: François Dompierre. Costumes: François Barbeau. Sound: Bernard Aubouy. (Malofilm/Canal Plus/Office National du Film Canard & ACPAV-Cannon/Gala.) Rel: floating; first shown London (Cannon Premiere) 16 February 1990. 102 mins. Cert U.

RoadHouse. Macho, formula movie starring Patrick Swayze as a 'cooler' – a super-bouncer – hired to oversee the Double Deuce, a bar described as 'the sort of place where you sweep up the eyeballs after closing'. Naturally, some local rednecks take exception to Swayze's clean-up act, not least Ben Gazzara, the town's crime kingpin. All and sundry are cast by numbers (Sam Elliott is a grizzled biker who lends Swayze a hand), except for Swayze himself, who is about one foot too short to play a bouncer ('I thought you'd be bigger', everybody improvises). This is mindless, muscular entertainment, but the fight choreography is excellent and the music stands out. [JC-W]

Cast includes; Patrick Swayze (Dalton), Ben Gazzara (Brad Wesley), Kelly Lynch (Doc), Sam Elliott (Wade Garrett), Marshall Teague (Jimmy), Kevin Tighe (Tilghman), Julie Michaels, Red West, Sunshine Parker, Jeff Healey, John Doe, Kathleen Wilhoite, Sheila Caan, Jon Paul Jones, Keith David, Cheryl Baker, Jacklyn Palmer. Dir: Rowdy Herrington. Pro: Joel Silver. Ex Pro: Steve Perry and Tim Moore. Screenplay: David Lee Henry and Hilary Henkin. Ph: Dean Cundey. Ed: Frank Urioste and John Link. M: Michael Kamen; songs performed by Dion, The Jeff Healey Band, Bob Seger, Otis Redding, Wilson Pickett, Little Feat, etc. Costumes: Marilyn Vance-Straker. Sound: Bud Maffett. (United Artists–UIP.) Rel: 10 November 1989. 114 mins. Cert 18.

Roger & Me. Alternately tragic, moving and very funny documentary about Flint, Michigan, the unemployment capital of the USA. Once the vehicle centre of the world – Flint boasted more car-workers than Detroit – the city's economy collapsed when General Motors axed 35,000 jobs over a period of four years. Between February 1987 and August 1989, former gutter journalist Michael Moore patrolled the city with a small camera crew, talking to locals, filming the deputy sheriff evicting the newly unemployed and trying to set up an interview with Roger B. Smith, chairman of General Motors. Nothing makes better documentary cinema than the filming of subjects who don't want to be photographed, and here Michael Moore pulls no punches. But *Roger & Me* is more than just a *cinéma vérité* exposé; packed with news footage, film clips and star interviews (Pat Boone sings, Bob Eubank tells an anti-Semitic AIDS joke), the film is an entertaining eye-opener – a social comedy with teeth. P.S. To finance the production, Moore sold his house and practically everything he owned (after completion, his phone was cut off because he couldn't pay the bill). Winner of the Best Documentary prize from the National Board of Review, the National Society of Film Critics, the

Roger & Me; an 'auto'-biography from Warner that fires on all cylinders. Left to right: *Rabbit-skinner Rhoda Britton, film-maker Michael Moore and deputy sheriff Fred Ross.*

Los Angeles Film Critics, the New York Film Critics' Circle, etc. [JC-W]

Dir, Pro and Screenplay: Michael Moore. Ed and Assoc Pro: Wendey Stanzler. Ed and Sound: Jennifer Beman. M: Numbers performed by Pat Boone, The Beach Boys ('Wouldn't It Be Nice'), Connie Francis, Bruce Springsteen, The Michigan State University Marching Band, etc. Camera crew: Christopher Beaver, John Prusack, Kevin Rafferty and Bruce Schermer. (Dog Eat Dog Films–Warner.) Rel: 20 April 1990. 91 mins. Cert 15.

Romero. El Salvador, 1978–80. Lacking the whiplash brutality of *Salvador*, John Duigan's *Romero* drives its point home with a tenacious, slow-burn determination. Raul Julia stars as Oscar Romero, real-life Archibishop of San Salvador and spokesman on human rights. Elected for his apparent frailty and absorption in books, Romero gradually sided with the people, opposed the military government and fought 'for non-violence with the weapon of truth'. At times a little uneven and rough round the edges, this *Reader's Digest* approach to heroism in politics is well written and dominated by Julia's portrayal of dignified strength. Above all, this is a tragic and compelling story that begs to be told – the first in a series of films from Paulist Pictures, a company established by Father Ellwood Keiser solely to produce 'features about human values'. [JC-W]

Also with: Richard Jordan (Fr Rutilio Grande), Ana Alicia (Arista Zelada), Eddie Velez (Lt Columa), Alejandro Bracho (Fr Alfonzo Morantes), Tony Plana (Fr Manuel Morantes), Harold Gould (Francisco Galedo), Lucy Reina (Lucia), Al Ruscio, Tony Perez, Robert Viharo, Harold Cannon-Lopez, Claudio Brook. Dir: John Duigan. Pro: Ellwood E. Keiser, CSP. Ex Pro: Lawrence Mortorff and John Sacret Young. Screenplay: Young. Ph: Geoff Burton. Ed: Frans Vandenburg. Pro Des: Roger Ford. M: Gabriel Yared. Sound: Edward Beyer. (Paulist Pictures–Warner.) Rel: 23 February 1990. 106 mins. Cert 15.

Raul Julia, as Oscar Romero, *prays in the midst of the ruins of El Salvadorean religion, in the Warner release.*

Rooftops. The beautiful homeless of New York's Lower East Side are being dumped on by a local crack dealer, a swarthy type called Lobo with little character and no manners. To drown their sorrows, the local kids dance up a storm illegally at street corners, in their favourite terpsichorean activity called 'combat dance' (a martial arts jig specially invented for this movie). All this is strictly formula stuff, but it's executed with aplomb and conviction, while a young, largely unknown cast inject some life into their stereotypes. [JC-W]

Cast includes: Jason Gedrick (T), Troy Beyer (Elana), Eddie Velez (Lobo), Tisha Campbell (Amber), Alexis Cruz (Squeak), Allen Payne (Kadim), Steve Love, Rafael Baez, Jaimi Tirelli, Luis Guzman, Millie Tirelli, Rockets Redglare, Edouard de Soto, Paul Herman, Robert Weil. Dir: Robert Wise. Pro: Howard W. Koch Jr. Ex Pro: Taylor Hackford and Stuart Benjamin. Screenplay: Terence Brennan; based on a story by Allan Goldstein and Tony Mark. Ph: Theo Van de Sande. Ed: William Reynolds. Pro Des: Jeannine C. Oppewall. M: David A. Stewart (of Eurythmics) and Michael Kamen; songs performed by Etta James, Dave Stewart, Jeffrey Osborne, London Beat, Kisses From the Kremlin, Eurythmics, Grace Jones, etc. Choreography: John Carrafa and Jelon Vieira. Costumes: Kathleen Detoro. Sound: Tom Nelson. (New Visions–Fox.) Rel: 9 February 1990. 95 mins. Cert 15.

Rosalie Goes Shopping. The third teaming of West German director/writer Percy Adlon and his large lady star Marianne Sägebrecht (the first was *Sugarbaby*; second *Bagdad Cafe*), though still amusing, is less so that its predecessors, possibly due to a change of pace – from leisurely to hectic – and less depth. Here the ample German star plays a *hausfrau* married to an American airplane nut (Brad Davis) and living with their seven offspring in Stuttgart (Arizona). She keeps up a high standard of living by juggling a vast collection of credit cards, and when this little racket dries up she rigs a computer to steal millions of dollars from the bank. But *how* is never explained, so this satire on modern American consumer society is weak at the roots. But it's still a movie well out of the rut. (With English dialogue.) [FMS]

Rest of cast: Judge Reinhold (the priest), William Harlander (Rosalie's father), Erika

Blumberger (mother), Patricia Zehentmayr (Barbara), John Hawkes (Schnuki), Alex Winter (Schatzi), Courtney Kraus (April), David Denney, Lisa and Lori Fitzhugh, Dina Chandel, Bill Butler, Ed Gelhart, John Willia, John Galt. Dir: Percy Adlon. Pro and (with Christopher Doherty) Screenplay: Percy and Eleonore Adlon. Ph: Bernd Heinl. Ed: Heiko Hinders. Art: Stephen Lineweaver. (Pelemele–Mainline.) Rel: floating; first shown London (Cannon, Shaftesbury Ave, Screen on the Hill and Chelsea Cinema) 12 January 1990. 93 mins. Cert 15.

Roselyn and the Lions – Roselyn et les Lions. Young French stars Isabelle Pasco and Gérard Sandoz spent nine months preparing for their roles as budding lion-tamers, and their hard work would seem to have paid off. This is an authentic, believable look at the arduous, dangerous task that zoo workers and circus trainers endure, although at times it looks too much like a 'How to . . .' course for would-be circus professionals. Pasco and Sandoz play a pair of star-crossed lovers who traverse France in search of rewarding work with big cats. On the road, and in and out of the lion's den, they take a crash course in adult responsibility and may or may not find true happiness. However, the lion's share of the action goes to the bigger game. [JC-W]

Leslie Cheung and Anita Mui as the young lovers in Rouge – The Legend of Flowers *(ICA), a memorable Hong Kong production.*

Cast includes: Isabelle Pasco (Roselyn), Gérard Sandoz (Thierry), Philippe Clevenot (Bracquard), Gunter Meisner (Klint), Wolf Harnisch (Koenig), Gabiriel Monnet (Frazier), Jacques Le Carpentier (Markovitch), Hans Meyer (Rainer), Dimitri Furdui, Melih Duzenli, Carlos Pavlidis, Jacques Mathou, Jean-Jacques Scheffer, Katleen Johnsen, Marius Pujszo. Dir and Pro: Jean-Jacques Beineix. Screenplay: Beineix and Jacques Forgeas, with the technical collaboration of Thierry Le Portier. Ph: Jean-François Robin. Ed. Marie Castro-Brechignac. Art: Carlos Conti. M: Reinhardt Wagner. Sound: Pierre Befve. (Cargo Films/Gaumont–Palace.) Rel: floating; first shown London (Curzon, West End) 15 December 1989. 130 mins. Cert 12.

Rouge – The Legend of Flowers. A very superior Hong Kong Chinese film which can't be faulted in any department, well meriting the several Taiwanese Golden Horse and other awards it garnered. It's a 'Romeo and Juliet' story about a rich young man who falls in love with a beautiful prostitute and plans to marry her. His horrified family forbids the liaison, and the thwarted couple decide on joint suicide by eating raw opium, but although she dies, the young man is too scared to carry out his side of the contract. This thoroughly enjoyable film is beautiful to look at, is superbly directed and photographed, and boasts some impressive performances (notably by ex-vocalist Anita Mui as the girl, and Leslie Cheung as the young man). [FMS]

Cast also includes: Alex Man, Emily Chu, etc. Dir: Stanley Kwan. Ex Pro: Jackie and Willie Chan. Screenplay: Li Pik-wah. (Golden Harvest–ICA.) Rel: floating; first shown London (ICA) 20 October 1989. 93 mins. No cert.

Rude Awakening. This is the first green comedy, wrapped up in an affectionate homage to the groovy, peacenik Sixties. Eric Roberts and Cheech ('pass that joint') Marin play two hippies who are wanted by the FBI and have hidden out in a Central American jungle for the last twenty years. Unaltered by time, Roberts and Marin return to New York to warn the city of an impending US invasion of the peaceful, fictitious country of Managuador. But nobody will listen. While sending up the sartorial and behavioural extremes of the Sixties, *Rude Awakening* offers a chilling view of the world we live in today. Roberts (at his most watchable for ages) has to digest whole the new realities of inflation, acid rain, starvation, nuclear warheads, AIDS and a hole in the ozone layer. Mawkishness is kept at bay by a host of comic turns (particularly from Andrea Martin, Buck Henry and Cindy Williams) and a view of humanity that is ultimately rather moving. Dig it. [JC-W]

Cast includes: Cheech Marin (Hesus), Eric Roberts (Fred), Julie Hagerty (Petra), Robert Carradine (Sammy), Buck Henry (Lloyd), Louise Lasser (Ronnie), Cindy Williams (June), Andrea Martin (April), Cliff DeYoung (Brubaker), Ed Fry, Aaron Russo, Patrick John Hurley, Daniel Chapman, Dr Timothy Leary, Jerry Rubin, Tom Sizemore, Dave King. Dir: Aaron Russo and David Greenwalt. Pro: Aaron Russo. Screenplay: Neil Levy and Richard LaGravenese; from a story by Levy. Ph: Tim Sigel. Ed: Paul Fried. Pro Des: Mel Bourne. M: Jonathan Elias; songs performed by Bob Dylan, Pat Boone, Jimi Hendrix, Jefferson Airplane, The Grateful Dead, The Doors, Kim Carnes, Miami Sound Machine, Mike and the Mechanics, etc. Costumes: Peggy Farrell. Sound: Greg Sheldon. (Rank.) Rel: 23 March 1990. 101 mins. Cert 15.

Running on Empty. Protesting against the Vietnam war, Arthur and Annie Pope (Judd Hirsch and Christine Lahti) accidentally blinded a janitor when they bombed a government-funded napalm laboratory. The janitor wasn't supposed to have been there. Anyhow, the Popes were put on the FBI's 'Ten Most Wanted' list. Now, fifteen years later,

Eric Roberts and Cheech Marin visit the Eighties in the endearing Rank release, Rude Awakening.

Arthur and Annie have two sons, aged 10 and 17, and they're still living 'underground', juggling identities at the hint of discovery. Danny Pope (River Phoenix), the oldest son, wants a normal life: Lorna (Martha Plimpton), his girl-friend, wants to know his secret. Sidney Lumet's film, bleached clean of sentimentality, addresses issues seldom broached by Hollywood, and punches home its message with the force of a chop to the solar plexus. This is intelligent, informative, articulate and extremely moving drama at its most effective. For her role, Christine Lahti won the Los Angeles Film Critics' Award. [JC-W]

River Phoenix, Christine Lahti and Jonas Abry on the run in Sidney Lumet's stunning Running on Empty *(Lorimar-Warner).*

Hunter or hunted? Al Pacino in UIP's Sea of Love.

Also with; Jonas Abry (Harry Pope), Steven Hill (Mr Patterson), L. M. Kit Carson (Gus Winant), Ed Crowley (Mr Phillips), Augusta Dabney, David Margulies, Jenny Lumet. Dir: Sidney Lumet. Pro: Amy Robinson and Griffin Dunne. Ex Pro: Naomi Foner and Burtt Harris. Screenplay: Naomi Foner. Ph: Gerry Fisher. Ed: Andrew Mondshein.

Pro Des: Philip Rosenberg. M: Tony Mottola. Costumes: Anna Hill Johnstone. Sound: James Sabat. (Lorimar–Warner.) Rel: 28 July 1989. 117 mins. Cert 15.

Russicum. Embarrassing Italian conspiracy thriller about a plot to sabotage the Pope's visit to Russia. Demented camera angles, excruciating dubbing, melodramatic music and a plot as impenetrable as the Vatican assist in the torture. [JC-W]

Casti includes: F Murray Abraham (Father Carafa), Treat Williams (Mark Hendrix), Danny Aiello (George Sherman), Robert Balchus (Michael Wessling), Rita Rusic (Alexandra), Nigel Court, Leopoldo Mastelloni, Fabio Traversa and Rossano Brazzi as Marini. Dir: Pasquale Squitieri. Pro: Mario and Vittorio Cecchi Gori. Screenplay: Valerio Riva, Robert Balchus and Squitieri; from the novel *Il Martedi del Diavolo* by Enzo Russo. Ph: Mario Cimini. Ed: Mauro Bonnani. M: Renato Serio. Costumes: Blanche Cardinale. Sound: Benito Alchimede. (Cecchi Gori Group/Tiger Cinematografica/ RAI–Columbia Tri-Star.) Rel: 8 December 1989. 111 mins. Cert 15.

Farce struggle: Arnetia Walker and Ed Begley Jr over-act as newly-weds in Rank's Scenes from the Class Struggle in Beverly Hills.

Santa Sangre (Holy Blood). Alexandro Jodorowsky, the Chilean-born, Paris-based director of the cult, horrific *El Topo* (1971), returns to form with this surreal, Mexican-shot, Italian-financed mutation. As in *El Topo*, Jodorowsky fills his story with freaks – amputees, dwarfs, giants, mongols, prostitutes, strippers, clowns and the severely obese – in a bizarre story that marries *Psycho* with *The Hands of Orlac*. A young circus boy witnesses his father (an impossibly fat Guy Stockwell) cut off his mother's arms and then commit suicide. This drives the boy mad and, as an adult, he embarks on a spree of killing, substituting a ventriloquist's dummy for his armless mother, his own hands becoming hers – whether to comb her hair or to knife his girl-friends. Weird, offensive and unforgettable. [JC-W]

Cast includes: Axel Jodorowsky (Fenix), Blanca Guerra (Concha), Guy Stockwell (Orgo), Sabrina Dennison (Alma), Therma Tixou, Adan Jodorowsky, Faviola Blenka Tapia, Teo Jodorowsky. Dir: Alexandro Jodorowsky. Pro: Claudio Argento. Screenplay: Jodorowsky, Argento and Roberto Leoni. Ph: Daniele Nannuzzi. Ed: Mauro

Bonanni. Art: Alejandro Luna. M: Simon Boswell. (Intersound–Mainline.) Rel: 13 April 1990. Uncut at 123 mins. Cert 18.

Scenes from the Class Struggle in Beverly Hills. Love among the stretch limos and palm trees. Nothing subtle here, just a busy comedy desperate to shock with a stockpile of stock characters, all with rampant libidos to spill. Jacqueline Bisset, still lovely at 45, plays a has-been soap queen who is hostess to friends and relatives for her husband's wake. Not so much a rich *Big Chill* as a smutty, glossy farce of the Brian Rix kind. [JC-W]

Cast includes: Jacqueline Bisset (Clare Lipkin), Ray Sharkey (Frank), Robert Beltran (Juan), Mary Woronov (Lisabeth), Ed Begley Jr (Peter), Wallace Shawn (Howard), Paul Mazursky (Sidney Lipkin), Darren (Bojangles), Arnetia Walker, Rebecca Shaeffer, Barret Oliver, Edith Diaz, Paul Bartel, Debora Babos, Bruce Wagner. Dir: Paul Bartel. Pro: Jim C. Katz. Assoc Pro: Bruce Wagner. Ex Pro: Amir J. Malin and Ira Deutchman. Screenplay: Bruce Wagner; from a story by Bartel and Wagner. Ph: Steven Fierberg. Ed: Alan Toomayan. Pro Des: Alex Tavoularis. M: Stanley Myers. Costumes: Dona Granata. Sound: Trevor Black. (Cinecom–Rank.) Rel: 19 January 1990. 104 mins. Cert 18.

Sea of Love is a slick, well-written romantic thriller with one fatal flaw: the protagonists just aren't sympathetic. John Goodman and Al Pacino play two New York cops tracing a serial killer with a penchant for shooting her victims in the back of the head while they're lying naked on a bed. All the victims have one thing in common: they put sappy love poems in a New York singles' magazine. Goodman and Pacino track down fifty-or-so women who responded to the ads, and then act out the role of potential date. Frank Keller (Pacino), whose ex-wife has married a colleague, sniffs romance, narrows his eyes and tumbles in lust with murder suspect No. 1, the mysterious beautiful blonde Helen (Ellen Barkin, giving a performance of nuclear-powered sex appeal). This is the stuff of great drama. Richard Price's artful script subtly alters our opinion of Barkin's guilt from scene to scene, but ultimately this is a one-premise situation. Is she or isn't she? Also, Pacino, good as he is, turns into such an obnoxious

Richard Pryor and Gene Wilder team up as the blind and the deaf in the successful See No Evil, Hear No Evil *(UIP).*

bore that, by the film's conclusion, we don't even *care* if he too ends up naked and dead. Forget the credibility gaps, concentrate on the sparks that the stars engender. [JC-W]

Also with: John Goodman (Sherman), Michael Rooker (Terry), William Hickey (Frank, Sr), Richard Jenkins (Gruber), Christine Estabrook (Gina Gallagher), Paul Calderon, Gene Canfield, Larry Joshua, John Spencer, Barbara Baxley, Patricia Barry, Mark Phelan, Michael O'Neill, Jacqueline Brookes, Brian Paul. Dir: Harold Becker. Pro: Martin Bregman and Louis A. Stroller. Screenplay: Richard Price. Ph: Ronnie Taylor. Ed: David Bretherton. Pro Des: John Jay Moore. M: Trevor Jones; 'Sea of Love' performed by Phil Phillips and the Twilights, also by Tom Waits; other songs by Sade, Bobby Darin, Branford Marsalis. Costumes: Betsy Cox. Sound: Keith Wester. (Universal–UIP.) Rel: 16 February 1990. 113 mins. Cert 18.

See No Evil, Hear No Evil. Richard Pryor and Gene Wilder team up as a blind man and deaf actor who 'witness'

a murder and are then blamed for it. On the run in New York, the duo can only clear their name if they apprehend the real killer – a beautiful woman (Joan Severance). Neither Pryor nor Wilder have had much solo success recently, but they work well together in this, their third joint outing (following *Silver Streak* and *Stir Crazy*). The film was a hit in the States and does have its funny moments (Pryor, belatedly discovering that he is black: 'Does dad know?') while never laughing *at* the disabilities it portrays. [JC-W]

Cast includes: Richard Pryor (Wally), Gene Wilder (Dave), Joan Severance (Eve), Kevin Spacey (Kirgo), Alan North (Braddock), Anthony Zerbe (Sutherland), Louis Giambalvo (Gatlin), Kirsten Childs (Adele), Audrie Neenan, Lauren Tom, Alexandra Neil, Tonya Pinkins, Alan Pottinger, Pirie MacDonald. Dir: Arthur Hiller. Pro: Marvin Worth. Ex Pro: Burtt Harris, Earl Barret and Arne Sultan. Screenplay: Barret, Sultan, Eliot Wald, Andrew Kurtzman and Gene Wilder; from a story by Barret, Sultan and Marvin Worth. Ph: Victor J. Kemper. Ed: Robert C. Jones. Pro Des: Robert Gundlach. M: Stewart Copeland. Costumes: Ruth Morley. Sound: Dennis Maitland. (Columbia Tri-Star.) Rel: 1 September 1989. 107 mins. Cert 15.

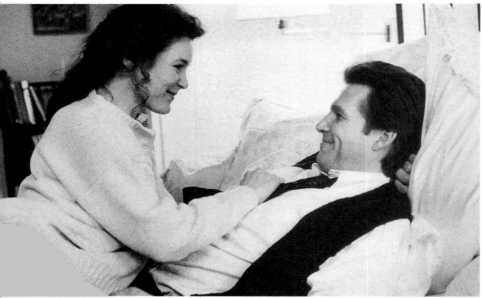

Alice Krige and Jeff Bridges attempt to start their lives afresh – with each other – in Alan J. Pakula's thoughtful and mature comedy-drama, See You in the Morning *(Warner).*

Latent sexuality: Andie MacDowell unveils the truth in Steven Soderbergh's brilliant sex – lies and videotape *(Virgin).*

two children. But both characters have developed too many jagged edges to fit together neatly, and it's no fun playing a second parent when your own children are suffering. *See You in the Morning* is particularly remarkable as this is the first screenplay director-producer Alan J. Pakula has written, based on a handful of semi-autobiographical notes collected over the years. To get under the skin of his characters, Pakula worked extensively with his cast, allowing his performers four weeks of rehearsal before a single camera turned. A well-made, thought-provoking drama with a stand-out performance from South Africa's Alice Krige. [JC-W]

Cast includes: Jeff Bridges (Larry Livingston), Alice Krige (Beth Goodwin), Farrah Fawcett (Jo Livingston), Drew Barrymore (Cathy), Lukas Haas (Petey), David Dukes (Peter Goodwin), Frances Sternhagen (Neenie), George Hearn (Martin), Theodore Bikel (Bronie), Linda Lavin (Sidney), Heather Lilly, Macauley Culkin, William LeMassena, Tom Aldredge, Dorothy Dean, Alixe Gordin, Christopher Curry, Christopher Murray, Corky (as George, the dog). Dir and Screenplay: Alan J. Pakula. Pro: Pakula and Susan Holt. Ph: Donald McAlpine. Ed: Evan Lottman. Pro Des: George Jenkins. M: Michael Small; songs performed by Nat King Cole, Jeanette MacDonald, etc. Costumes: John Boxer. Sound: Chris Newman. (Lorimar–Warner.) Rel: 4 May 1990. 118 mins. Cert 12.

See You in the Morning. Heart-felt and extremely well-acted comedy-drama about musical-family relationships. Jeff Bridges plays a successful New York psychiatrist, divorced with two children, falling in love with photographer Alice Krige, widowed with

sex – lies and videotape. An intimate, adult drama set in Baton Rouge, Louisiana, in which a quartet of young, yuppie adults come to terms with their shifting sexuality. Winner of the Palme d'Or at Cannes, the picture dares to pry into places barely touched by cinema before, while eschewing the gratuitous display of nudity. Filmed on an economical budget of $1.2 million, the film's production values are to be applauded, the performances are wonderful (particularly newcomer Laura San Giacomo) and the dialogue sparkles ('women become attracted to the men they love and men fall in love with the women they're attracted to'). First time director Steven Soderbergh is headed for greatness. [JC-W]

Cast: James Spader (winner of the Best Actor award at Cannes, as Graham), Andie MacDowell (Ann), Peter Gallagher (John), Laura San Giacomo (Cynthia), Ron Vawter (therapist), Steven Brill (barfly), Alexandra

John Cusack, Dwight Schultz (as Oppenheimer) and Paul Newman playing God on an explosive government project – in Roland Joffé's erudite Shadow Makers *(UIP).*

Root, Earl T. Taylor. Dir, Screenplay and Ed: Steven Soderbergh. Pro: Robert Newmyer and John Hardy. Ex Pro: Nancy Tenenbaum, Nick Wechsler and Morgan Mason. Ph: Walt Lloyd. Art: Joanne Schmidt. M: Cliff Martinez. Costumes: James Ryder. Sound: Paul Ledford. (Outlaw–Virgin.) Rel: 8 September 1989. 100 mins. Cert 18.

Shadow Makers (US: *Fat Man and Little Boy*). When the US dropped their bombs on Hiroshima and Nagasaki, the war with Germany was already over and the Japanese had proposed terms for surrender. The combined impact of the two atomic weapons – 'Fat Man' and 'Little Boy' – annihilated 200,000 people. Two cities vanished in a matter of seconds. Roland Joffé and Bruce Robinson's chilling, eloquent film examines why and how this came about. The US government invested

two *billion* dollars and three years to build the ultimate Armageddon 'gadget' (their word) and employed a platoon of the world's top scientists – headed by J. Robert Oppenheimer. A project of this importance, however evil, simply had to reach its conclusion and be 'big enough to stop all war for ever', in the words of General Leslie 'Dick' Groves. And so Oppenheimer became the Lord of the earth's atmosphere, unleashing an energy never before realised or even believed possible. For some, *Shadow Makers* may be on the talky side, but nevertheless it's an articulate and terrifying history lesson. [JC-W]

Cast includes: Paul Newman (General Leslie R. Groves), Dwight Schultz (J. Robert Oppenheimer), John Cusack (Michael Merriman), Laura Dern (Kathleen Robinson), Ron Frazier (Peer de Silva), John C. McGinley (Richard Schoenfield), Natasha Richardson (Jean Tatlock), Ron Vawter (Jamie Latrobe), Michael Brockman (William 'Deke' Parsons), Todd Field (Robert Wilson), Del Close, John Considine, Alan Corduner, Joseph d'Angerio, Ed Lauter, Logan Ramsey, Fred Dalton Thompson,

Tom McFarlane, John Williams, Alan Oppenheimer (voice only). Dir: Roland Joffé. Pro: Tony Garnett. Ex Pro: John Calley. Screenplay: Bruce Robinson and Roland Joffe; based on Robinson's story. Ph: Vilmos Zsigmond. Ed: Francoise Bonnot. Pro Des: Gregg Fonseca. M: Ennio Morricone. Costumes: Nick Ede. Sound: William J. Randall. (Paramount–UIP.) Rel: 9 March 1990. 127 mins. Cert PG.

She-Devil. High-octane, highly Hollywood version of the BBC's brilliant, black dramatisation of Fay Weldon's bitter, feminist novel, *The Life and Loves of a She-Devil.* Meryl Streep, mistaking over-acting for comedy, takes over the role, first played by Patricia Hodge, of the rich, beautiful and fashionably thin romantic novelist who lures an accountant away from his impoverished, unattractive and overweight wife. The wife, fleshed out by stand-up comic Roseanne Barr, lacks the necessary menace, making this ugly dumpling a somewhat shallow reactionary. At its worst, Orion's *She-Devil* is broad farce with nowhere to go, at its best an excuse for the conscientious Ms

Little does Mary Fisher (Meryl Streep) realise what's in store for her after her first introduction to the gross, scheming Ruth Patchett (Roseanne Barr) in Susan Seidelman's unsuccessful realisation of Fay Weldon's She-Devil *(Rank).*

Streep to let her hair down. Either way, it's a misguided vehicle without wheels. [JC-W]

Cast includes: Meryl Streep (Mary Fisher), Roseanne Barr (Ruth Patchett), Ed Begley Jr (Bob Patchett), Sylvia Miles (Mrs Fisher), Linda Hunt (Hooper), A. Martinez (Garcia), Maria Pitillo (Olivia Honey), Elisebeth Peters, Bryan Larkin, Mary Louise Wilson, Susan Willis, Jack Gilpin, Deborah Rush, Sally Jessy Raphael. Dir: Susan Seidelman. Pro: Jonathan Brett and Susan Seidelman. Screenplay: Barry Strugatz and Mark R. Burns; based on the novel *The Life and Loves of a She-Devil* by Fay Weldon. Ph: Oliver Stapleton. Ed: Craig McKay. Pro Des: Santo Loquasto. M: Howard Shore; songs performed by Chubby Checker, The Fat Boys, Yello, D. Mob, Jermaine Stewart, Elvis Presley, Carmel, etc. Costumes: Albert Wolsky. Sound: Tod A. Maitland. (Orion–Rank.) Rel: 11 May 1990. 99 mins. Cert 15.

She's Been Away. Powerful, absorbing drama starring Peggy Ashcroft as an old dear rescued from a mental home after 60 years of being institutionalised. James Fox and Geraldine James play the rich, upmarket couple who take her into the family bosom, where her madness becomes disastrously infectious. A terrifying and intelligent look at both mental instability and a sterile marriage, *She's Been Away* was scripted by Stephen Poliakoff and partly inspired by the fate of the Queen Mother's cousin. Dame Peggy and Miss James

jointly won the best actress prize at the Venice Film Festival, little compensation for the shabby distribution that this superb film was afforded before its death on television. [JC-W]

Cast includes: Peggy Ashcroft (Lillian Huckle), Geraldine James (Harriet Ambrose), James Fox (Hugh Ambrose), Jackson Kyle (Dominic Ambrose), Rosalie Crutchley (Gladys), Rachel Kempson (Matilda), Rebecca Pidgeon (young Lillian), Hugh Lloyd (George), Cryss Jean Healey (young Margaret), Leslie Goodall, Edgar Goodall, Barnaby Holm, Brid Brennan, David Hargreaves, Hugh Ross, Claire Williamson, Robyn Moore, Richard Huw. Dir: Peter Hall. Pro: Kenith Trodd. Screenplay: Stephen Poliakoff. Ph: Philip Bonham-Carter. Ed: Ardan Fisher. Pro Des: Gary Williamson. M: Stephen Edwards. Costumes: Anushia Nieradzik. Sound: Clive Derbyshire. (BBC.) Rel: London (Riverside Studios) only, 22–28 September 1989. 103 mins. Cert PG.

Shirley Valentine. British actress Pauline Collins was rightly nominated for an Oscar this year for her magnificent performance in this lovely comedy – though sadly she didn't win the award. Plump, vivacious and attractive, she plays a suburban housewife who suddenly rebels against her situation, and a husband who takes her for granted, and decides to realise her long-held dream of a holiday in Greece. Tom Conti is splendid, too, as the Greek hotelier who sexually liberates her. Very funny, tender and true, this is magnificent entertainment. British, too. [FMS]

Rest of cast: Julia McKenzie (neighbour Gillian), Alison Steadman (friend Jane), Joanna

Lumley (Marjorie), Bernard Hill (husband Joe), Sylvia Syms (headmistress), George Costigan (Dougie), Anna Keaveney (Jeanette), Tracie Bennett (Milandra), Ken Sharrock (Sydney), Karen Craig (Thelma), Gareth Jefferson (Brian), Gillian Kearney, Catharine Duncan, Cardew Robinson, Honora Burke, Marc Zuber. Dir and Pro: Lewis Gilbert. Ex Pro: John Dark. Screenplay: Willy Russell (who also wrote the music, orchestrated by Chris Palmer and Chris Walker); adapted from his one-woman play success *The Wit and Wisdom of Shirley Valentine* with Miss Collins, for which she won a 'Tony' and other awards. Ph: Alan Hume. Ed: Lesley Walker. Pro Des: John Stoll. Pro Supervisor: Roy Stevens. Greek music: George Matzinassios. Costumes: Sandy Paterson. (Paramount–UIP.) Rel: 27 October 1989. 109 mins. Cert 15.

Shocker. Routine blood-splattered 'slasher' thriller about a mass killer; though you have to be pretty clever to follow the story as it lurches from one by-now conventional incident to another. And yet the director was *Elm Tree* specialist Wes Craven . . . [FMS]

Cast: Mitch Pileggi (killer), Peter Berg (Jonathan Parker), Michael Murphy (Lt Don Parker), Cami Cooper, Richard Brooks, Theodore Raimi, John Tesh, Dr Timothy Leary, Heather Lagenkamp, Bingham Ray. Dir, Screenplay and Co-Ex Pro: Wes Craven. Pro: Marianne Maddalena and Barin Kumar. Co-Pro: Peter Foster and Bob Engelman. Co-Ex Pro: Shep Gordon. Ph: Jacques Maitkin. Ed: Andy Blumenthal. Pro Des: Cynthia Kay Charette. Art: Randy Moore. Costumes: Isis Mussenden. M: William Goldstein. (Alive Films-Universal–Guild.) Rel: floating; first shown London (Cannon, Panton St) 20 April 1990. 110 mins. Cert 18.

Shohei Imamura's Black Rain – Kuroi Ame. The ominous rain of the title is the lethal radiation emitted by the atom bomb dropped on Hiroshima. The director Shohei Imamura examines the phenomenon through one family, and in particular through Yasuko (Yoshiko Tanaka), a 25-year-old Japanese girl who is rejected by a series of suitors due to the possibility of her succumbing to the disease. By examining the catastrophe of the bombing through the details of human suffering, Imamura has realised a film of untold power. He shows that years after Hiroshima, Japan is still suffering, both physically and spiritually. [CB]

One of the most delightful comedies of the year, Paramount/UIP's Shirley Valentine *was memorable for Pauline Collins's performance in the title role, supported by Tom Conti as the Greek who sexually liberates her.*

Also with: Kazuo Kitamura (Shigematsu), Etsuko Ichihara (Shigako), Shoichi Ozawa, Norihei Miki, Kaisuka Ishide. Dir: Shohei Imamura. Pro: Hisa Iino. Screenplay: Imamura and Toshiro Ishido; based on the novel by Masuji Ibuse. Ph: Takashi Kawamata. Ed: Hajime Okayusu. Art: Hisso Inagaki. M: Toru Takemitsu. Sound: Ken'-ichi Benitani. (Imamura/Hayashibara Group/Tohokushinsha Film Co.–Artificial Eye.) Rel: floating; first shown London (Renoir) 29 June 1990. 123 mins. Cert PG.

A Short Film About Killing – Krotki Film o Zabijaniu is Polish director Krzysztof Kieslowski's opening shot in his formidable plan to make ten feature films, each based on one of the Biblical Commandments. It's a painfully grim and disturbing story about a mindless vagrant youth in Warsaw who, for no good reason, horribly and lingeringly kills an admittedly unpleasant taxi driver without bothering about the consequences. Inevitably caught, he is

condemned to hang – a ghastly, detailed sequence, as stomach-turning as the murder. Cold and detached, it shows crime and punishment as equally vile, but leaves many questions unanswered. For all the horror of the content, this is a remarkable piece of movie-making. If you *do* have the stomach to watch it, don't see it just before – or after – dinner! [FMS]

Cast: Miroslaw Baka (the killer), Jan Tesare (the victim), Krzysztof Globisz. Dir and (with Krzysztof Piesiewcz) Screenplay: Kryzsztof Kieslowski. Pro Manager: Rysz-

The police catch up with the moronic murderer (Miroslaw Baka) in Gala's release of A Short Film About Killing – Krotki Film o Zabijaniu, *the first of ten films by Polish director Kzrysztof Kieslowski based on the Ten Commandments.*

For some reason Michael (Patrick Dempsey) attracts women – not least Jennifer Connelly's Gabriella. However, audiences weren't attracted to Sisters, *a UIP release.*

ard Chutkowski. Ph: Slawomir Idziak. Ed: Ewa Smal. Set Des: Halina Dobrowolska. M: Zbigniew Preisner. Sound: Malgorzata Jaworska. (Polish Corp for Film Pro 'Zespoly Filmowe'/Film Unit 'Tor'–Gala.) Rel: floating; first shown London (Cannon Pre miere) 17 November 1989. 85 mins. Cert 18.

A Short Film About Love – Krotki Film o Miloski Mesmerising account of a 19-year-old voyeur's obsession with a 30-year-old beauty living across from his block. Nothing so sinister as a

Polish re-make of *Rear Window*, or indeed *Body Double*, but the second episode in Krzysztof Kieslowski's ode to the Ten Commandments, following on from the award-winning *A Short Film About Killing*. This, too, picked up some trophies (winner of the Grand Prix at the Gdansk Film Festival, to name one), and is, as minimalist narration goes, a powerfully erotic examination of love and sexuality, persuasive in its simplicity and always unexpected. [JC-W]

John Ritter, as womaniser Zach Hutton, tries to keep up with the women in his life in Blake Edwards's awful Skin Deep *(Fox).*

Cast includes: Grazyna Szapolowska (Magda), Olaf Lubaszenko (Tomek), Ste Fania Iwinski (Vermieterin), Piotr Machalica (Roman). Dir: Krzysztof Kieslowski. Pro: Polish Film Producers' Corp. '88. Prod Ex: Ryszard Chutkowski. Screenplay: Krzysztof Piesiewicz and Krzysztof Kieslowski. Ph: Witold Adamek. Ed: Ewa Smal. Art: Halina Dobrowolska. M: Zbigniew Preisner. Sound: Nikodem Wolk-Laniewski. (Polish Film Corp.–Cannon/Gala.) Rel: floating; first shown London (Cannon Premiere) 30 March 1990. 90 mins. Cert 18.

Sisters. British screenwriter Rupert Walters confessed that 'whenever I go and stay with someone I'm always afraid a member of the family will die and I'll be blamed for it' – out of which evolved his script for *Sisters* (formerly *Some Girls*). Patrick Dempsey top-bills as Michael, a student who follows his girl-friend (Jennifer Connelly) to her family home in Quebec city. There Michael undergoes a nightmarish Christmas as he gets to know the various members of the eccentric d'Arc family, including the childlike, moribund 'Granny' (Lila Kedrova). More than just a romantic comedy, *Sisters* attempts to be many things but tries too hard for its own good. Dempsey is not cut from the cloth of cinematic charisma and engenders little sympathetic response, although Andre Gregory makes the most of the nude biographer, Mr d'Arc. Surprisingly, *Sisters* was cofinanced by Robert Redford's Sundance Institute. [JC-W]

Also with: Florinda Bolkan (Mrs d'Arc), Jennifer Connelly (Gabriella), Lance Edwards (Nick), Sheila Kelley (Irenka), Ashley Greenfield (Simone), Jean-Louis Millette, Sanna Vraa. Dir: Michael Hoffman. Pro: Rick Stevenson. Ex Pro: Robert Redford. Screenplay: Rupert Walters. Ph: Ueli Steiger. Ed: David Spers. Pro Des: Eugenio Zanetti. M: James Newton Howard; songs performed by Julia Fordham ('Comfort of Strangers'), Ziggy Marley & the Melody Makers, etc. Sound: Martin Evans. (MGM/Wildwood Enterprises–UIP.) Rel: 19 January 1990. 94 mins. Cert 15.

Ski Patrol. From the producer of *Police Academy*, this action-packed ski comedy could have been a lot worse. Old cowboy Ray Walston runs the Snowy Peaks Lodge, but sees his dream threatened by land developer Martin Mull. Zany characters abound, but they're better drawn than usual, and

Bernadette Peters, as Eleanor, is led astray in Manhattan's Bohemian art world, in James Ivory's splendid Slaves of New York *(Columbia Tri-Star).*

the ski stunts are fabulous, as is the scenery. [CB]

Cast includes: Roger Rose (Jerry Kramer), Yvette Nipar (Ellen), T. K. Carter (Iceman), Ray Walston (Pops), Cory Timbrook (Lance), Martin Mull (Maris), Leslie Jordan, George Lopez, Paul Fieg, Tess, Sean Gregory Sullivan. Dir: Richard Correll. Pro: Don West and Phillip Goldfine. Ex Pro: Paul Maslansky. Screenplay: Steven Long Mitchell and Craig W. Van Sickle. Ph: John Stephens. Ed: Scott Wallace. Pro Des: Fred Weiler. M: Bruce Miller. Costumes: Angee Beckett. Sound: John Earl Stein. (Epic Prods–Entertainment.) Rel: 15 June 1990. 91 mins. Cert PG.

Skin Deep. Zach Hutton (John Ritter), a successful novelist, is thrown out of his Los Angeles home when his wife catches him in bed having an argument with his mistress over an affair he's having with his wife's hairdresser. Plunged into writer's block, Zach endures a rollercoaster ride of sexual

disaster, aggravated by his alcoholism, that leads to terminal depression. All this is aimed for hysterics, but plays more like *That's Blake Edwards!*, a sort of compilation of the director's favourite scenes from his past movies. Worse still, John Ritter is neither sympathetic nor charismatic, let alone funny. [JC-W]

Also with: Vincent Gardenia (Barnie, the bartender), Alyson Reed (wife Alex), Joel Brooks (Jake), Julianne Phillips (Molly), Chelsea Field (Amy), Peter Donat (Sparky), Don Gordon (Curt), Nina Foch (Alex's mother), Denise Crosby, Michael Kidd, Dee Dee Rescher, Bryan Genesse, Raye Hollit, Jean Marie McKee, Brenda Swanson, Heidi Paine, Diana Barton, Sheryl Lee Ralph. Dir and Screenplay: Blake Edwards. Pro: Tony Adams. Ex Pro: Joe Roth and James G. Robinson. Ph: Isidore Mankofsky. Ed: Robert Pergament. Pro Des: Rodger Maus. Costumes: Nolan Miller. Sound: Milton C. Burrow. (Fox.) Rel: 7 July 1989. 101 mins. Cert 18.

Slaves of New York. Director James Ivory sheds his image as a classical director (*Heat and Dust, A Room with a View*) to grapple with Tama Janowitz's

cult novel about sex and art in New York. A sort of Bohemian *After Hours*, the comedy-drama zips along at a playful clip, introducing a kaleidoscope of colourful characters at the rate of one new eccentric every five minutes or so. At the centre of this merry whirlwind clambers Bernadette Peters as a socially ostracised misfit and creator of bizarre hats. Ms Janowitz adapted her own novel and the result is a stylish, often very amusing romp. [JC-W]

Cast includes: Bernadette Peters (Eleanor), Chris Sarandon (Victor Okrent), MaryBeth Hurt (Ginger Booth), Madeleine Potter (Daria), Adam Coleman Howard (Stash Stotz), Nick Corri (Marley), Charles McCaughan (Sherman), John Harkins (Chuck Dade Dolger), Mercedes Ruehl (Samantha), Steve Buscemi (Wilfredo), Michael Schoeffling (Jan), Bruce Peter Young (Mikell), Betty Comden, Tammy Grimes, Paul Jabara, Sakina Jaffrey, Tama Janowitz (Abby), Anna Katarina, Joe Leeway. Dir: James Ivory. Pro: Ismail Merchant and Gary Hendler. Screenplay: Tama Janowitz; from her own novel. Ph: Tony Pierce-Roberts. Ed: Katherine Wenning. Pro Des: David Gropman. M: Richard Robbins. Costumes: Carol Ramsey. Sound: Tom Nelson. (Columbia Tri-Star.) Rel: floating;

Owner Marcello Mastroianni and his faithful projectionist Massimo Troisis count up the night's takings in Ettore Scola's wistful salute to the early cinemas in Splendor *(Warner).*

first shown London (Curzon, West End) 18 August 1989. 125 mins. Cert 15.

Society. Bearing in mind that this was described as the sickest movie of 1990 and the most revolting film ever made, *Society* is a lot of fun. A depiction of the Beverly Hills rich feeding (literally) off the poor, the film follows the apparent hallucinations of Billy Whitney, a clean-cut, 17-year-old Californian jock. All sorts of yucky things start to occur: Billy bites into an apple seething with worms, his sister's back sweats and swells – you know the sort of stuff. Naturally, Billy is in therapy, but his doctor suspects nothing more than paranoia. We know better. As low-budget genre pictures go, this is a slick production, brimming with imagination and sick to its very core. Thank-

fully, it doesn't take itself seriously for a minute, allowing the over-the-top special effects (by Screaming Mad George) to wander into Mel Brooks territory. [JC-W]

Cast includes: Billy Warlock (Billy Whitney), Devin DeVasquez (Clarisa), Evan Richards (Milo), Ben Meyerson (Ferguson), Ben Slack (Dr Cleveland), Patrice Jennings (Jenny), Heidi Kozak (Shauna), Pamela Matheson (Mrs Carlyn), Connie Danese, Tim Bartell, Charles Lucia, David Wiley, David Wells. Dir: Brian Yuzna. Pro: Keith Walley. Ex Pro: Paul White, Keizo Kabata and Terry Ogisu. Screenplay: Woody Keith and Rick Fry. Ph: Rick Richter. Ed: Peter Teschner. M: Mark Ryder and Phil Davies. (Wild Street Pictures–Medusa.) Rel: 6 April 1990. 99 mins. Cert 18.

Speaking Parts. Sex vies with videotape in this self-important, stylised Canadian drama that focuses on the lives of three lonely people floating around Toronto. Lisa checks out videos of Lance, a film extra with whom she's in

love, while Lance auditions – on video – for a speaking part in a movie. Other characters flit on and off various video screens, or appear behind cameras, helping to blur the line between reality and techno-fantasy. This is the sort of tricksy, clever-clever pretension that a director like Alan Rudolph *could* have made compelling. [JC-W]

Cast includes: Michael McManus (Lance), Arsinee Khanjian (Lisa), Gabrielle Rose (Clara), Tony Nardi (Eddie), David Hemblen (the producer), Patricia Collins (hotel employer). Dir and Screenplay: Atom Egoyan. Ex Co-Pro: Don Ranvaud. Ph: Paul Sarossy. Ed: Bruce McDonald. Art: Linda Del Rosario. M: Mychael Danna. (Ego Film Arts/Telefilm Canada/The Ontario Film Development Corporation/Academy Pictures, Rome/Film Four International–Recorded Releasing.) Rel: 15 September 1989. 92 mins. Cert 18.

Splendor is Ettore Scola's gentle, wistful and nostalgic – and somewhat uneven – salute to the cinema of the

Two people trying to communicate: Jane Fonda and Robert De Niro in Martin Ritt's beautifully touching Stanley & Iris, *from UIP.*

past, presented as the story of Jordan (Marcello Mastroianni) the owner-manager of a small Italian cinema with a gradually decreasing audience and gradually mounting debts. He struggles to keep the place going, but eventually sells out to a local furniture store. As he watches the workmen move in he looks back, in a series of flashbacks (some in colour and some in black-and-white), to the time when as a child he helped his travelling showman father, then to the purchase of the 'Splendor' and the years when he ran it with the faithful help of his loquacious projectionist (Massimo Troisi) and ex-showgirl usherette (Marina Vlady). Notable are the interpolated sequences from screen classics of the past by Fellini, Truffaut, De Sica, Capra, Olmi, Bergman and others. And the ending

is pure Capra: at the last moment, the villagers sweep in to fill the seats and stop the sale, bringing a somewhat bloodless film to pulsating and moving life. [FMS]

Others in the cast: Paolo Panelli, Pamela Villoresi, Giacomo Piperno, Massimo Bartocini, Mauro Bosco, Ferruccio Castronuovo, Fillipo Greco (Jordan aged 11) and Antonio Silvano (Jordan aged 6). Dir and Screenplay: Ettore Scola. Pro: Mario and Vittorio Cecchi Gori and Studio EL. Ph: Luciano Tovoli. Ed: Francesco Malvestito. Art: Luciano Ricceri. M: Armando Trovaioli. (Cecci Gori Group-Tiger Cinematografica/ Studio EL, Rome/Gaumont Pro. Generale d'Images, Paris, in collaboration with RAI--Warner.) Rel: floating; first shown London (Camden Plaza and Chelsea Cinema) 4 August 1989. 110 mins. Cert PG.

Stanley & Iris. (Previously known as *Union Street* and *Letters.*) Connecticut, 1990. Stanley Cox is an illiterate mashed-potato cook in a factory canteen. Iris King is a widowed produc-

tion-line worker living in a house of domestic friction. Stanley cannot drive or catch a bus because he cannot read, just like 27 million other American adults. Iris lives a dead-end life, but her values are important ones – up to a point. 'You're smart,' Stanley tells her, 'but you're not sensible.' Stanley and Iris are genuine, complex and simple people and they can learn from each other. Martin Ritt's tender, adult love story was not admired by the critics but is a work of enormous humanity and love, superbly played by Robert De Niro and Jane Fonda in the title roles. A mature, moving piece of cinema. [JC-W]

Also with: Swoosie Kurtz (Sharon), Martha Plimpton (Kelly), Harley Cross (Richard), Jamey Sheridan (Joe), Feodor Chaliapin (Leonides Cox), Zohra Lampert, Loretta Devine, Julie Garfield, Karen Ludwig, Kathy Kinney, Laurel Lyle, Marty Testa, Katherine Cortez, Stephen Root. Dir: Martin Ritt. Pro: Arlene Sellers and Alex Winitsky. Ex Pro: Patrick Palmer. Screen-

Mr Spock (Leonard Nimoy) visits Captain Kirk (Willliam Shatner) on a dangerous climbing expedition in UIP's disappointing Star Trek V – The Final Frontier. *William Shatner directed.*

play: Harriet Frank Jr and Irving Ravetch; based on the novel *Union Street* by Pat Barker. Ph: Donald McAlpine. Ed: Sidney Levin. Pro Des: Joel Schiller. M: John William. Costumes: Theoni Aldredge. Sound: Richard Lightstone. (Lantana/MGM–UIP).) Rel: 22 June 1990. 104 mins. Cert 15.

Star Trek V – The Final Frontier. Taken over by an omnipotent brainwasher, the Starship *Enterprise* boldly goes where no man has gone before – to Heaven itself. This outrageous premise, in which the dreaded Klingons do battle with God, is a conceit of awesome proportions, coated with predictable sentimentality but lacking either a sense of dread or wonder. The *Enterprise* itself creaks and groans with old age, as does the paunchy cast. This 'final' (?) entry in the Star Trek log was generally considered to be the weakest. [JC-W]

Cast includes: William Shatner (Kirk), Leonard Nimoy (Spock), DeForest Kelley (McCoy), James Doohan (Scotty), Walter Koenig (Chekov), Nichelle Nichols (Uhura), George Takei (Sulu), David Warner (St John Talbot), Laurence Luckinbill (Sybok), George Murdock (God), Charles Cooper, Cynthia Gouw, Todd Bryant, Spice Williams, Rex Holman, Harve Bennett, Melanie Shatner. Dir: William Shatner. Pro: Harve Bennet. Ex Pro: Ralph Winter. Screenplay: David Loughery; from a story by Shatner, Bennett and Loughery, based on characters created by Gene Roddenberry. Ph: Andrew Laszlo. Ed: Peter Berger. Pro Des: Herman Zimmerman. M: Jerry Goldsmith; 'The Moon's a Window to Heaven' performed by Hiroshima. Costumes: Nilo Rodis-Jamero. Sound: David Ronne. (Paramount–UIP.) Rel: 20 October 1989. 102 mins. Cert PG.

Steel Magnolias. There are two ways of approaching this: you can either close your eyes to the Southern melodrama (i.e. screaming matches) and muffle your ears to the syrupy music, *or* – you can just sit back and *indulge. Steel Magnolias* – based on the successful play by Robert Harling – is broad, manipulative entertainment, but fires on all cylinders. A cast of staggering

talent take turns to chew the scenery, but it is Dolly Parton who shines brighter than all with her sunny smile and throwaway *bon mots* ('Sammy's so confused, he doesn't know whether to scratch his watch or wind his butt'). Several generations of women scream, laugh, cry and fall in love over a period of several years, colliding into each other at Easter, Hallowe'en, Mardi Gras, and so on. Verdict: Heart-warming, gut-wrenching, top-class escapism. The jewel in the crown, Julia Roberts, was nominated for an Oscar for her role. [JC-W]

Cast includes: Sally Field (M'Lynn Eatenton), Dolly Parton (Truvy Jones), Shirley MacLaine (Ouiser Boudreaux), Daryl Hannah (Annelle Dupuy Desoto), Olympia Dukakis (Clairee Belcher), Julia Roberts (Shelby Eatenton Latcherie), Tom Skerritt (Drum Eatenton), Dylan McDermott (Jackson Latcherie), Kevin J. O'Connor (Sammy Desoto), Sam Shepard (Spud Jones), Bill McCutcheon, Ann Wedgeworth, Knowl Johnson, Jonathan Ward, Bibi Besch, Ronald Young, Nancy Parsons, Robert Harling. Dir: Herbert Ross. Pro: Ray Stark. Ex Pro: Victoria White. Screenplay: Robert Harling; based on his own play. Ph: John A. Alonzo. Ed: Paul Hirsch. Pro Des: Gene

Callahan and Edward Pisoni. M: Georges Delerue; 'I Got Mine' written and performed by Ry Cooder. Costumes: Julie Weiss. Sound: Al Overton. (Rastar/Tri-Star–Columbia Tri-Star.) Rel: 9 February 1990. 117 mins. Cert 15.

A Strange Place to Meet – Drôle d'Endroit pour une Rencontre. On a winter night outside Paris a woman (Catherine Deneuve) is abandoned by her husband on the side of a road, disturbing a man (Gérard Depardieu) repairing his car. At first hostile, the man gradually becomes obsessed by the woman, the latter waiting in desperation for her husband to return. At times intriguing and at others equally irritating, *A Strange Place to Meet* is marginally redeemed by its two stars and our nagging desire to know what'll happen next. [JC-W]

Cast includes: Catherine Deneuve (France), Gérard Depardieu (Charles), Nathalie Cardone (Sylvie), André Wilms (Georges), Jean-Pierre Sentier (Pierrot). Dir and (with Dominique Faysse) Screenplay: François Dupeyron. Ex Pro: René Cleitman. Ph: Charlie Van Damme. Art: Carlos Conti. M: Richard Strauss. Costumes: Caroline de Vivaise. Sound: Pierre Gamet and Jean-Paul Loublier. (Hachette Premiere & Cie/Hachette Productions/Films A2/DD Prod/ Deneuve SA/Orly Films/ Editions Sidonie –Artificial Eye.) Rel: 8 September 1989. 97 mins. Cert 15.

Strapless is a love story for real people. Lovers reply with authentic answers and hide behind real questions. An American radiotherapist living in London, Lillian Hempel (Blair Brown), is courted by a rich, enigmatic European (Bruno Ganz) while on holiday in Lisbon. He follows her to England and showers her with expensive gifts, quizzing her but revealing little about himself. Meanwhile, Lillian's relationship with her younger sister, the wayward Amy (Bridget Fonda), is becoming increasingly strained. Pressure at work – St Mary's Hospital – adds to the conspiracy to change Lillian Hempel for good. Writer-director David Hare (*Wetherby, Paris by Night*) wanted to make a film that could 'balance romance and realism in a way which is actually true to life'. Shedding the pretension that engulfed *Paris by Night*, Hare has injected an eloquent optimism into a fragile emotional make-up. *Strapless* is

Love among the intellectuals: Blair Brown topples in love with Bruno Ganz in David Hare's literate Strapless *(Virgin Vision).*

compelling narrative, beautifully written and produced, and peopled with characters that are in us all. [JC-W]

Also with: Hugh Laurie (Colin), Gary O'Brien (Mr Clark), Alan Howard (Mr Cooper), Suzanne Burden (Romaine Salmon), Cyril Nri (Harold Sabola), Rohan McCullough (Annie Rice), Billy Roch, Camille Coduri, Spencer Leigh, Constantin Alexandrov, Dana Gillespie, Jeremy Gagan, Alexandra Pigg, Helen Lindsay, Michael Gough, Ann Firbank, Joe Hare, Melanie Roe. Dir and Screenplay: David Hare. Pro: Rick McCallum. Co-Pro: Patsy Pollock. Ph: Andrew Dunn. Ed: Edward Marnier. Pro Des: Roger Hall. M: Nick Bicat; 'When I Fall in Love' sung by Nat King Cole. Costumes: Penny Rose and Rebecca Hale. Sound: Clive Winter. (Granada/Film Four-- Virgin Vision.) Rel: floating; first shown London (Curzon, West End) 23 March 1990. 99 mins. Cert 15.

The Summer of Aviya – Hakayitz Shel Aviya. Israel, 1951. Based on the childhood memoirs of Gila Almagor, this is a touching, occasionally overwrought tale of an Auschwitz survivor who spends a summer with her 9-year-old daughter – following her release from a mental institution. Almagor plays her own mother, while young Kaipo Cohen as the daughter is a remarkable discovery. Winner of the Silver Bear at

the 1989 Berlin Film Festival. With Hebrew dialogue and English subtitles. [CB]

Cast includes: Gila Almagor (Henya), Kaipo Cohen (Aviya), Eli Cohen (Mr Gantz), Marina Rossetti (Mrs Gantz), Avital Dicker (Maya), Dina Avrech (Mrs Abramson), Ya'kov Ayali (the refugee). Dir: Eli Cohen. Pro: Eitan Evan and Gila Almagor. Screenplay: Eli Cohen, Gila Almagor and Chaim Buzaglo; based on the novel and play by Almagor. Ph: David Gurfinkel. Ed: Tova N'eman. Art: Yoram Shayer. M: Shem-Tov Levi. Costumes: Rona Doron. (Mutual.) Rel: floating; first shown London (Phoenix, East Finchley) 9 March 1990. 96 mins. Cert PG.

Summer Vacation 1999 – 1999: Nen No Natsu Yasumi. A Japanese film about boys aged between 13 and 16, *Summer Vacation* is set in a boarding school after term has ended. Instead of returning home, three boys stay on and are later joined by a newcomer, who bears an uncanny resemblance to a youth who had been close to all three before his sudden, unexplained disappearance. As hauntingly atmospheric as *Picnic at Hanging Rock*, as sensual as *Black Narcissus* and as far from naturalism as the most surreal scenes in Lindsay Anderson's *If . . .* , this is a poetic and often enigmatic study of the emotional strains of adolescence. Its particularly unusual claim to fame, however, is that the boys are all played by actresses. [MS]

Cast includes: Eri Miyajima (Yu/Kaoru), Tomoko Otakara (Kazuhiko), Miyuki Nakano (Naota), Rie Mizuhara (Noira). Dir: Shusuke Kaneko. Pro: Naoya Narita and Mitsuhisa Hida. Ex Pro: Yutaka Okada and Eiji Kishi. Screenplay: Rio Kishida. Ph: Kenji Takama. Ed: Isao Tomita. Art: Shu Yamaguchi. M: Yuriko Nakamura. (New Century producers/CBS-Sony Group–ICA.) Rel: floating; first shown London (ICA) 16 February 1990. 90 mins. Cert 15.

Sur. Buenos Aires, 1983. Floreal (Miguel Angel Sola) is a former subversive released after the fall of the military dictatorship. The fate of others who disappeared cannot be forgotten, but much of the film's emphasis is on the response of Floreal to the discovery that his wife had taken a Corsican lover after his own disappearance. It is easy to admire this strikingly individual film, but not so easy to be touched by it – feeling is communicated less through the central drama than in those moments when the film is graced by a poetry close to melancholy. Winner of the Best Director award at the 1988 Cannes Film Festival. [MS]

Also with: Susu Pecoraro (Rosi Echegoyen), Philippe Leotard (Roberto), Lito Cruz (El Negro), Ulises Dumont, Roberto Goyeneche, Gabriela Toscano. Dir and Screenplay: Fernando E. Solanas. Line Pro: Envar

Genevieve Lemon in her extraordinary film debut as Sweetie (Electric), *which won her the Best Actress Award from the Australian critics.*

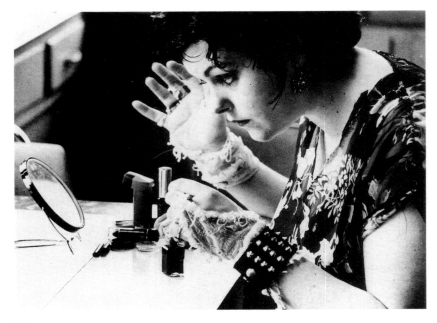

El Kadri, Fernando E. Solanas, Patricia Novat and Pierre Novat. Ex Pro: Sabina Sigler and Djamila Olivesi. Ph: Felix Monti. Ed: Juan Carlos Macias and Pablo Mari. Pro Des: Fernando E. Solanas. M: Astor Piazzolla. Sound: Anibal Libenson. (Cinesur S. A. (Argentina)/Productions Pacific/-Canal Plus Productions (France)–Gala.) Rel: floating; first shown London (Cannon Premiere) 2 February 1990. 119 mins. Cert 15.

Sweetie does not live up to her name. In fact, she is an absolute horror, a selfish, over-fed Australian abomination and would-be entertainer. Like the main character in Alex van Warmerdam's *Abel*, this demented baggage is a thorn in her family's side and won't go away. A darkly witty examination of suburban paranoia, *Sweetie* is far more than just a bizarre character study. And any film that concludes that love is just 'sex and courage' is out to raise a few eyebrows. A remarkable feature debut from short film maker Jane Campion and a favourite at the 1989 Cannes Film Festival. [JC-W]

Cast includes: Genevieve Lemon (Sweetie), Karen Colston (Kay), Tom Lycos (Louis), Jon Darling (Gordon), Dorothy Barry (Flo), Michael Lake (Michael Lake), Andrew Pataczek (Clayton). Dir: Jane Campion. Pro: John Maynard. Co-Pro: William MacKinnon. Screenplay: Gerard Lee and Jane Campion; from an idea by Campion. Ph: Sally Bongers. Ed: Veronika Haussler. Art: Peter Harris. M: Martin Armiger. Costumes: Amanda Lovejoy. Sound: Leo Sullivan. (Arenafilm–Contemporary/Electric.) Rel: 4 May 1990. 90 mins. Cert 15.

A Tale of Springtime – Conte de Printemps. Practically nobody can direct young actresses as well as Eric Rohmer. Without exception he can elicit the most natural, spontaneous performances from the inexperienced (who are invariably too pretty for their own good). Not only that, but he writes intelligent, lifelike dialogue that both provokes and delights. After his sextet of Comedies and Proverbs, Rohmer has embarked on a new set of romantic stories, Tales of the Four Seasons. This springtime anecdote examines the relationship between a student, Natasha, and a teacher of philosophy, Jeanne, who befriend each other in a matter of minutes, and shows how the former tries to manipulate the latter to fall in love with her father. [JC-W]

Cast includes: Anne Teyssedre (Jeanne), Hugues Quester (Igor), Florence Darel (Natasha), Eloise Bennett (Eve), Gaelle (Sophie Robin). Dir and Screenplay: Eric Rohmer. Pro: Margaret Menegoz. Ph: Luc Pages. Ed: Maria-Luisa Garcia. M; Beethoven, Schumann. Sound: Pascal Ribier. (Roissy Films/Films du Losange-Artificial Eye.) Rel: floating; first shown London (Chelsea Cinema and Camden Plaza) 15 June 1990. 112 mins. Cert U.

Talk Radio. Hard-hitting, muscular film version of Eric Bogosian's off-Broadway play about a tough-talking Dallas radio host. Barry Champlain (Bogosian), who worships his own voice, is the man Texans love to hate – and Champlain hates them right back. There's nothing more boring than 'people who love you', he snarls into his mike, cutting a fan off the air. Inspired by the life and mouth of murdered Denver DJ Alan Berg (previously played by Richard Libertini in Costa-Gavras's *Betrayed*), *Talk Radio* is a *tour de force* for Bogosian who stars in his own screenplay, co-written with Oliver Stone (*Platoon, Wall Street*). Stone claims Bogosian 'has the potential for a Dustin Hoffman-like career' and, as director, he unleashes an enormous energy from his star. This is mesmerising cinema from a compelling filmmaker which, as a screen adaptation of a claustrophobic play, is no mean achievement. The words sting, but the images glue them in the mind. [JC-W]

Also with: Ellen Greene (Ellen), Leslie Hope (Laura), John C. McGinley (Stu), Alec Baldwin (Dan), John Pankow (Dietz),

Words can kill: the sensational Eric Bogosian as Barry Champlain in Oliver Stone's stunning radio epic Talk Radio *(Rank).*

Michael Wincott (Kent), Linda Atkinson, Robert Trebor, Zach Grenier, Rockets Redglare. Dir and (with Eric Bogosian) Screenplay: Oliver Stone; based on the play by Bogosian and Tad Savinar, and the book *Talked to Death: The Life and Murder of Alan Berg* by Stephen Singular. Pro: Edward R. Pressman and A. Kitman Ho. Ex Pro: Greg Strangis and Sam Strangis. Ph: Robert Richardson. Ed: David Brenner. Pro Des: Bruno Rubeo. M: Stewart Copeland. Costumes: Ellen Mirojnick. Sound: Tod A. Maitland. (Cineplex Odeon Films–Fox.) Rel: 15 September 1989. 108 mins. Cert 18.

Tango and Cash-in-the-bank. Sylvester Stallone makes a valiant attempt to change his image, wearing specs with his pecs – *and* an Armani wardrobe. However, even if you can change the man you can't change the formula. This is predictable, thick-skulled, cornball action entertainment, but it does fire on all cylinders. Stallone is Tango ('Armani with a badge'), an LA cop on the trail of crime kingpin Yves Perret

(Jack Palance). Kurt Russell is Cash, an alimony-paying slob, in line with Mel Gibson's cop in *Lethal Weapon*. He, too, is on the trail of Perret, who successfully frames the duo, packing them off to maximum-security hell and sitting back to watch the fireworks.

(Naturally, half the brickhouse inmates have been put away by Cash and Tango.) The plot is familiar, the dia-

Suits me: Sylvester Stallone and Kurt Russell in the wham-bang Tango and Cash, *from Warner.*

Amanda Donohoe and Ray Winstone in the enterprising, stylish thriller, 'Tank' Malling.

logue terrible, but the stunts are sensational, the photography above average for this sort of thing, and Stallone and Russell are obviously having a whale of a time. Historical note: this heralded Stallone's return to box-office popularity. [JC-W]

Also with: Teri Hatcher (Kiki/Kate), Brion James (Courier/Requin), James Hong (Quan), Marc Alaimo (Lopez), Phillip Tan (Chinese gunman), Michael J. Pollard (Owen), Robert Z'Dar, Lewis Arquette, Richard Fancy, Bing Russell (Kurt's father), Clint Howard, Shabba-Doo, Glenn Morshower, Geoffrey Lewis (Capt. Shroeder). Dir: Andrei Konchalovsky (with uncredited direction from Peter MacDonald and Albert Magnoli). Pro: Jon Peters and Peter Gruber. Ex Pro: Peter MacDonald. Screenplay: Randy Feldman. Ph: Donald E. Thorin. Ed: Stuart Baird, with Hubert De La Bouillerie and Robert Ferretti. Pro Des: J. Michael Riva. M: Harold Faltermeyer; songs performed by Bad English, Yaz, Alice Cooper, etc. Costumes: Bernie Pollack. Sound: Charles Wilborn. (Warner.) Rel: 23 March 1990. 104 mins. Cert 15.

'Tank' Malling. Hard-hitting London thriller put together by a trio of English actors, best known as three of the stars of LWT's *London's Burning*. James Marcus (Georgie in *A Clockwork Orange*) directs, Jamie Foreman and Glen Murphy both produce and co-star. Ray Winstone (*Scum*) top-bills as 'Tank', a hard-boiled Fleet Street reporter protecting the sole witness to the shenanigans of a powerful but corrupt charity organisation. Sir Robert Knights (Peter Wyngarde), a public benefactor, talks of moral bankruptcy but is the power behind a series of vicious Soho killings. It's a race against time for 'Tank', and every cop, judge and journalist is out to stop him. Hardly new territory, this – and explored with more intelligence in *Defence of the Realm* – but Marcus displays a certain style and verve, creating some spine-chilling suspense. Unfortunately, not all the acting is up to scratch. [JC-W]

Also with: Jason Connery (Dunboyne), Amanda Donohoe (Helen), Glen Murphy (Cashman), Marsha Hunt (Salena), Jamie Foreman (Danny), John Bett (Campbell Sinclair), Melissa Wilks, Glen Murphy Jr,

John Conteh, Maria Whittaker, Don Henderson, Gordon Fleming, Tristram Wymark, Sean Blowers, Nick Brimble, Liz Hickling, Paula Anne Bland, Carol Lynn Cortez, Nick Berry, Jess Conrad, Debbie Killingback, etc. Dir and (with Mick Southworth) Screenplay: James Marcus. Pro: Glen Murphy and Jamie Foreman. Ex Pro: Terence Murphy. Ph: Jason Lehel. Ed: Brian Peachey. Pro Des: Geoffrey Sharpe. M: Rick Fenn and Nick Mason. Costumes: Liz Da Costa. Sound: John Beaton. (Pointlane Films–Parkfield Entertainment.) Rel: 24 November 1989. 108 mins. Cert 18.

That Summer of White Roses. Yugoslavia, and the last summer of World War II. Tom Conti is Andrija, a simple lifeguard, paid to keep a lopsided eye on the local bathing community. His is an idyllic existence, in a picturesque setting, and he is required to do little. Occasionally, when someone is drowning, he will turn a blind eye. But soon the status quo is threatened by unforeseen events. Andrija is forced to marry a widowed young mother fleeing from the Nazis, momentarily becomes a heroic figure to his new stepson, and is relieved of his duties when it is discovered that he has never saved anyone from drowning in his life. They say that good intentions pave the way to hell. Well, there are plenty of good intentions heaped on this simple, honest tale, which might actually have thrived in a foreign language. As it is, the supporting players are poorly dubbed and Conti's accent wavers dramatically over several continents, while New York's

Susan George and Nitzan Sharron in the earnest, Yugoslav-set That Summer of White Roses *(Castle Premier). Ms George also produced.*

Rod Steiger – as a local partisan – sticks out like a sore tongue. [JC-W]

Also with: Susan George (Ana), Rod Steiger (Martin), Nitzan Sharron (Danny), Alun Armstrong (Zemba), John Gill (the doctor), John Sharp (the mayor), Geoffrey Whitehead (the clerk), Miljenko Brlecic, Vanja Drach, Slobodan Sembera, Stanka Gjuric. Dir: Rajko Grlic. Pro: Simon MacCorkindale and Mike Mihalic. Ex Pro: Susan George and Sulejman Kapic. Screenplay: Borislav Pekic, Rajko Grlic and Simon MacCorkindale. Ph: Tomislav Pinter. Ed: Damir German. Pro Des: Dinka Jericevic. M: Brane Zivkovic, Junior Campbell and Mike O'Donnell. Costumes: Vjera Ivankovic. Sound: Louis Kramer. (Amy International/Jadran–Castle Premier.) Rel: 16 February 1990. 104 mins. Cert 15.

Thelonius Monk: Straight No Chaser. A 90-minute treat for jazz fans in general and Monk fans in particular: the result of paring down some fourteen hours of previously unseen footage shot in the late 1960s. This comprehensive documentary on the man and his music was left on the shelf for years, and was only recently completed thanks to Clint Eastwood stepping in with the necessary finance. [FMS]

With: Charlie Rouse, Harry Colomby, Barry Harris, Tommy Flanagan, Thelonius Monk Jr, Bob Jones. Narrator: Sam E. Wright. Also with the voice of Baroness de Koenigswarter who – as she did with Charlie Parker – took a vital interest in Monk's career. Dir: Charlotte Zwerin. Pro: Zwerin and Bruce Ricker. Pro Ex: David Valdes. Ex Pro: Clint Eastwood. Ph: Christian Blackwood, Joan

Martin Short and Nick Nolte as incongruous allies in the Touchstone-Warner comedy, Three Fugitives.

Churchill and Stuart Math. (Malpaso Pro. in assoc. with Michael Blackwood Co.–Warner.) Rel: floating; first shown London (Metro) 29 September 1989. 89 mins. Cert PG.

Three Fugitives. Yet another attempt to achieve the impossible and successfully Americanise a French comedy (the original, Francis Veber's *Les Fugitives*, was shown in late 1986). The story is about the comic misadventures of an ex-bank robber (a sadly miscast Nick Nolte) trying to keep out of trouble, but continually thrown into situations which keep him in it. The villain's autistic young daughter (Sarah Rowland Doriff) introduces a touch of schmaltz into the proceedings. (It's ironic that the American film is written and directed by the writer-director of the French original!) [FMS]

Also with: James Earl Jones (Dugan), Alan Ruck (Tener), Kenneth McMillan (Horvath), David Arnott (bank clerk), Bruce McGill, Lee Garlington, Sy Richardson, Rocky Giordani, Rick Hall, Bill Cross, Stanley Brock. Dir, Ex Pro and Screenplay: Francis Veber. Pro: Lauren Shuler-Donner. Assoc Pro: Karen Kovacevich, Duncan Henderson and James R. Van Wyck. Pro Associates: Bill Cross and Kristine Weaver. Ph: Haskell Wexler. Ed: Bruce Green. Pro Des: Rick Carter. Art: Marjorie Stone McShirley. M: David McHugh. (Touchstone Pictures in assoc. with Silver Screen Partner IV–Warner.) Rel: 25 August 1989. 97 mins. Cert PG.

3 Women in Love. (Previously known as *The Philosopher.*) Three women, claiming to be goddesses, fall in love with an unassuming 30-year-old virgin,

Aristocrat as romantic fool: Timothy Hutton in Jerzy Skolimowski's enjoyably gushing Torrents of Spring *(Curzon).*

because he demands nothing of them. An ironic and solemn comedy, *3 Women* is an entertaining indulgence from writer-director Rudolf Thome, part of a West German trilogy of films concerning the mating ritual. [CB]

Cast includes: Johannes Herrschmann (Georg Hermes), Adriana Altaras (Franziska), Friederike Tiefenbacher (Beate), Claudia Matschulla (Martha), Jürgen Wink, Werner Gerber, Anton Rey. Dir, Pro and Screenplay: Rudolf Thome. Ph: Reinhold Vorschneider. Ed: Dörte Völz-Mammarella. Art: Eve Schaenen. M: Hanno Rinne. Costumes: Gioia Raspe. Sound: Frank Behnke. (Mainline.) Rel: floating; first shown London (Cannon, Tottenham Ct Rd and Cannon, Piccadilly) 8 June 1990. 83 mins. Cert 18.

Torrents of Spring. Sumptuous adaptation of Ivan Turgenev's 1872 tragic romance about a Russian aristocrat who suddenly and violently falls in love with two women. Opening with Timothy Hutton in yet another of his 'I can play

Rhonda LeBeck (Finn Carter) is attacked by deadly creatures from beneath the earth, in Tremors *(UIP).*

older than I am' moods, Dimitri Sanin is seen as an old man in Venice, looking back on his wasted life. Cut to Germany several decades earlier, and the time of passionate looks begins. Director Jerzy Skolimowski truly indulges himself with the smouldering subtext and is almost swept away by Stanley Myers's opulent score and his own lush set pieces. Although some found the pace terminally sluggish, this critic enjoyed the emotional aerobics and the wallowing in period detail. Hutton in particular took his role to heart, adopting a thick Russian accent, learning to dance Russian style, riding, playing the piano, and indulging in no end of un-American activities. Nastassja Kinski – post-*Revolution* and post-baby – is as lovely as ever. [JC-W]

Also with: Nastassja Kinski (Maria Polozov), Valeria Golino (Gemma Rosselli), William Forsythe (Polozov), Urbano Barberini (von Doenhof), Francesca de Sapio (Signora Rosselli), Jacques Herlin, Antonio Cantafora, Christopher Janczar, Christian Dottorini, Jerzy Skolimowski. Dir: Jerzy Skolimowski. Pro: Angelo Rizzoli. Ex Pro: Mario Cotone. Screenplay: Skolimowski and Arcangelo Bonaccorso; based on the novel by Ivan Turgenev. Ph: Dante Spinotti and Witold Sobocinski. Ed: Cesare d'Amico. Pro Des: Francesco Bronzi. M: Stanley Myers; conducted by Carlo Savina. Costumes: Theodor Pistek. Sound: Andre Hervee. (Erre/Reteitalia/Les Films Ariane/Films A2–Curzon Film Distributors.) Rel: floating; first shown London (Curzon, West End) 18 May 1990. 101 mins. Cert PG.

Treasure Island. Lumbering, over-long but occasionally spirited version of the Robert Louis Stevenson tale of pirates and hidden loot in the eighteenth century. Charlton Heston follows in the footstep of Wallace Beery, Robert Newton, Orson Welles and Kirk Douglas as the peg-legged Long John Silver, lending the old salt a certain sly charm. The actor's son, Fraser C. Heston, directs on Caribbean locations. [CB]

Also with: Christian Bale (Jim Hawkins), Oliver Reed (Capt. Billy Bones), Christopher Lee (Blind Pew), Julian Glover (Dr Livesey), Richard Johnson (Squire Trewlawney), Clive Wood (Capt. Smollett), John Benfield, Isla Blair, Robert Putt, Peter Postlethwaite. Dir, Pro and Screenplay: Fraser C. Heston. Ex Pro: Peter Snell. Ph: Robert Steadman. Ed: Eric Boyd-Perkins. Pro Des: Tony Woollard. M: Paddy Maloney; performed by The Chieftains. (Turner/Agamemnon Films/British Lion–Warner.) Rel: 15 June 1990. 132 mins. Cert PG.

Tremors. Deep in the back pocket of Nevada, the sleepy town of Perfection (*sic*) is being attacked by something from Beneath the Earth. Now, there ain't nothin' original about this horror-comic, but it's directed at such a clip, and the performances are so engaging, that it must be the most endearing monster pic for years. The gory special effects aren't half bad either. [JC-W]

Willem Dafoe in yet another extraordinary performance, in Robert M. Young's distressing Triumph of the Spirit *(Guild).*

Cast includes: Kevin Bacon (Valentine McKee), Fred Ward (Earl Basset), Finn Carter (Rhonda LeBeck), Michael Gross (Burt Gummer), Reba McEntire (Heather Gummer), Bobby Jacoby (Melvin Plug), Charlotte Stewart, Richard Marcus, Victor Wong, Conrad Bachmann, Bibi Besch. Dir: Ron Underwood. Pro and Screenplay: Brent Maddock and S. S. Wilson; from a story by Underwood, Maddock and Wilson. Ex Pro: Gale Ann Hurd. Ph: Alexander Gruszynski. Ed: O. Nicholas Brown. Pro Des: Ivo Cristante. M: Ernest Troost. Sound: Walt Martin. Dirt Wrangler: Dale R. Newell. (No Frills/Universal–UIP.) Rel: 29 June 1990. 95 mins. Cert 15.

Triumph of the Spirit. Harrowing drama about a Greek Jewish boxer fighting to stay alive in Auschwitz. As yet unbeaten in the ring, Salamo Arouch (Willem Dafoe) entertains SS officers by fighting selected opponents (who are executed when they lose), enabling his father and brother to share

Gérard Depardieu with his too-beautiful wife Carole Bouquet in Bertrand Blier's wicked examination of men and women, 'Trop Belle Pour Toi' (Too Beautiful for You).

in his edible winnings. Compulsive human drama inspired by real events, although the story is dually credited to co-producer Shimon Arama and someone called Zion Haen. Although a few of the Nazis are of the comic-strip variety, the acting is generally excellent, particularly Robert Loggia as Salamo's dignified, loving father. Unfortunately, the music is a little too polished and operatic for a place like Auschwitz. [JC-W]

Also with: Edward James Olmos (Gypsy), Wendy Gazelle (Allegra), Kelly Wolf (Elena), Costas Mandylor (Avram), Hartmut Becker (Major Rauscher), Kario Salem, Edward Zentara, Burkhard Heyl, Sofia Saretok. Dir: Robert M. Young. Pro: Arnold Kopelson and Shimon Arama. Screenplay: Andrzej Krakowski and Laurence Heath. Ph: Curtis Clark. Ed: Arthur Coburn. Art: Krystyna Maslowska. M: Cliff Eidelman. Costumes: Hilary Rosenfeld. Sound: Eli Yarkoni. (Nova International–Guild.) Rel: 22 June 1990. 120 mins. Cert 15.

Troop Beverly Hills. A worried wife decides to save her rocky marriage (her husband accuses her of having 'lost her spark') by volunteering to revitalise the

scorned and despised Beverly Hills troop of 'The Wilderness Girls of America'. By using some fairly unconventional methods, she eventually succeeds. Shelley Long in the central role does in fact send plenty of fun sparks flying, and she's got a good foil in Betty Thomas as her rival. Teen fodder. [FMS]

Cast: Shelley Long, Craig T. Nelson, Betty Thomas, Mary Gross, Stephanie Beacham, Audra Lindley, Edd Byrnes, Jenny Lewis, Tasha Scott, Ami Foster, Carla Gugino, Heather Hopper, Aquilina Soriano. Dir: Jeff Kanew. Pro: Ava Ostern Fries. Ex Pro: Charles Fries. Screenplay: Pamela Norris and Margaret Grieco Oberman; based on a story by Ava Ostern Fries. Ph: Donald E. Thorin. Ed: Mark Melnick. Pro Des: Robert Boyle. Art: Jack G. Taylor. Costumes: Theodora Van Runkle. (Fries Entertainment and Avanti Pro.–Columbia.) Rel: floating. 105 mins. Cert PG.

'Trop Belle Pour Toi!' (Too Beautiful for You). Bernard (Gérard Depardieu) is a prosperous car salesman married to a remarkable beauty (Carole Bouquet) and with two children. He has a large

Master and mastiff: Tom Hanks and Beasley as Turner and Hooch, *from Touchstone-Warner.*

circle of friends, a splendid house in the south of France – in fact, everything a man could desire. Except a mistress. When he falls head over heels in love with his frumpy, middle-aged secretary (Josiane Balasko), his life changes dramatically for the worse. If only she had been beautiful! An intriguing concept this (ripe for an American re-make), but mangled by fussy execution that combines flashbacks, flashforwards and fantasy sequences with the desperation of a director trying to disguise a one-joke film. Nevertheless, *'Trop Belle Pour Toi!'* tied with *Cinema Paradiso* for the Special Jury Prize at the 1989 Cannes Film Festival. [JC-W]

Also with: Josiane Balasko (Colette), Carole Bouquet (Florence), Roland Blanche (Marcello), Francois Cluzet (Pascal), Didier Benureau (Leonce), Philippe Loffredo, Sylvie Orcier, Myriam Boyer. Dir and Screenplay: Bertrand Blier. Ph: Philippe Rousselot. Ed: Claudine Merlin. Set Design: Theobald Meurisse. M: Franz Schubert. Costumes: Michele Marmande-Cerf. Sound: Louis Gimel and Paul Bertault. (Cine Valse/DD Productions/Orly Films/SEDIF/TF1/Films Productions–Artificial Eye.) Rel: 2 March 1990. 91 mins. Cert 18.

Turner and Hooch. Amiable, vaguely predictable cop-and-his-dog comedy-drama, released on the tail of *K–9*. Tom Hanks is Turner, a neat, finicky, small-town cop, and Beasley is Hooch, a massive, drooling, beer-swilling, farting mastiff. There's a love story (of course), and a side plot about drug money (naturally), but Hanks is in good form (after his dreary perform-

ance in *The 'Burbs*) and Reginald Vel-Johnson is excellent as his hearty colleague. [JC-W]

Cast includes: Tom Hanks (Scott Turner), Mare Winningham (Emily Carson), Craig T. Nelson (Chief Hyde), Reginald VelJohnson (David Sutton), Scott Paulin (Zack Gregory), J. C. Quinn (Walter Boyett), John McIntire (Amos Reed), David Knell, Ebbe Roe Smith, Kevin Scannell, Clyde Kusatsu, Scott Stevens. Dir: Roger Spottiswoode. Pro: Raymond Wagner. Ex Pro: Daniel Petrie Jr. Screenplay: Dennis Shryack, Michael Blodgett, Daniel Petrie Jr, Jim Cash and Jack Epps Jr; from a story by Shryack, Blodgett and Petrie. Ph: Adam Greenberg. Ed: Paul Seydor, Mark Conte, Kenneth Morrisey and Lois Freeman-Fox. Pro Des: John DeCuir. M: Charles Gross. Sound: Jim Webb. (Touchstone–Warner.) Rel: 12 January 1989. 99 mins. Cert PG.

Twilight City. 'Meditative' partly fictionalised documentary shown as part of the New Black British Cinema season; about an investigative journalist preparing a feature about 'New London

Dear old Uncle Buck: *John Candy surrounded by his wards, Macaulay Culkin, Jean Kelly and Gaby Hoffman – from UIP.*

and the Creation of Wealth' and at the same time involved in the personal problem of a ten-year separation from her mother, who now regrets the rift. As the journalist's feature suggests, the film is fundamentally concerned with those most at risk from the 'New London' – vulnerable minorities such as lesbians and gays, and the inhabitants of the 'cardboard city'. [FMS]

Dir: Reece Aguiste. Pro: Black Audio Film Collective. (ICA.) Rel: floating; first shown London (ICA) 23 October 1989. 52 mins. No cert.

Two Moon Junction. Unbearably slow and pretentious, predominantly waist-up soft porn set in the Deep South. April Delongpre, a dream on two legs, is being put through the plantation wedding machine, but is derailed by Perry (Richard Tyson), an itinerant, snub-nosed runt with a D-cup chest. She knows she hates Perry really, but her marriage to handsome, wet Chad looks less and less likely. Will she? Won't she? Do we care? Louise Fletcher, matriarch of the B-movie, pumps humour into her lines as Grandma, but

Gone but not forgotten: Johanna Ter Steege in Metro's fascinating thriller, The Vanishing – Spoorloos/L'Homme Qui Voulait Savoir.

the rest of the cast are desperately at sea. Even with the presence of Burl Ives, Tennessee Williams this ain't. [JC-W]

Also with: Sherilyn Fenn (April Delongpre), Burl Ives (Sheriff Earl Hawkins), Kristy McNichol (Patti Jean), Martin Hewitt (Chad), Juanita Moore, Don Galloway, Millie Perkins, Milla Loginova, Nicole Rosselle, Kerry Remsen, Herve Villechaize, Harry Cohn, Nancy Fish, Sharon Madden, Screamin' Jay Hawkins, Ellen Geer. Dir and Screenplay: Zalman King; from a story by King and MacGregor Douglas. Pro: Donald P. Borchers. Ex Pro: Mel Pearl and Don Levin. Ph: Mark Plummer. Ed: Marc Grossman. Pro Des: Michelle Minch. M: Jonathan Elias; songs performed by George Thorogood, Screamin' Jay Hawkins, Notre Dame Glee Club, Jerry Harrison, etc. Costumes: Maria Mancuso. Sound: Stephen Halbert. (Samuel Goldwyn–Recorded Releasing.) Rel: 3 November 1989. 104 mins. Cert 18.

Uncle Buck. John Candy is a mountainous, no-good clumsy oaf who'll do anything to get out of working at his girl-friend's tyre shop. One such excuse is babysitting indefinitely for his brother's three kids – aged 6 to 15. You know exactly what's going to happen after the first ten minutes, but the film glides from A to Z by a stylish and often surprising route. Candy is at his funniest and most likeable yet, but (almost) has the film stolen from under his feet by his infant and adolescent co-stars. Jean Louisa Kelly in particular unveils a remarkable talent, making her troubled teenager believable, funny and sexy all at the same time. Sentimental, yes; predictable, of course; but don't knock this well-directed gateau – it's got heart, and it's funny, too. [JC-W]

Also with: Amy Madigan (Chanice Kobolowski), Jean Louisa Kelly (Tia Russell), Gaby Hoffman (Maisy Russell), Macaulay Culkin (Miles Russell), Elaine Bromka (Cindy Russell), Garrett M. Brown (Bob Russell), Laurie Metcalf (Marcie Dahlgren-Frost), Suzanne Shepherd (Mrs Hoargarth), Dennis Cockrum (Pal), Jay Underwood (Bug), Patricia Arquette (voice only), Brian Tarantina, Mike Starr, Mark Rosenthal. Dir and Screenplay: John Hughes. Pro: Hughes and Tom Jacobson. Ph: Ralf Bode. Ed: Lou Lombardo, Tony Lombardo and Peck Prior. Pro Des: John W. Corso. M: Ira Newborn; songs performed by Perry Como, Young MC, Flesh for Lulu, etc. Costumes: Marilyn Vance-Straker. Sound: James Alexander. (Universal–UIP.) Rel: 13 April 1990. 100 mins. Cert 12.

The Vanishing – Spoorloos/ L'Homme Qui Voulait Savoir. There can be few things in life as emotionally destroying as the unexplained disappearance of one's partner. With stylish detachment, French film-maker George Sluizer explores the escalating obsession of a Dutch tourist with finding his girl-friend after she has 'vanished' at a road stop in France. A parallel story follows the ordered life of a man obviously responsible for the disappearance, but we – the audience – are left in suspense until the film's conclusion, when the two stories converge in a chilling Hitchcockian (or Chabrolian) finale. Compelling cinema, and artfully realised. Winner of innumerable international awards, including trophies for best film from the Dutch and Australian film critics. [JC-W]

115

Cast includes: Bernard-Pierre Donnadieu (Raymond Lemorne), Gene Bervoets (Rex Hofman), Johanna Ter Steege (Saskia), Gwen Eckhaus (Lieneke), Bernadette Le Saché, Tania Latarjet, Lucille Glenn, Roger Souza, Doumée, Linda Wise, Ian Magilton, Ghislaine Gazaix. Dir: George Sluizer. Pro: Anne Lordon and George Sluizer. Screenplay: Tim Krabbé; based on his novel *The Golden Egg*. Ph: Toni Kuhn. Ed: Sluizer and Lın Friedman. Pro Des: Santiago Isidro

Peter sadly contemplates his father's decision to sell the fishing vessel Venus Peter *to the breakers. And an unusual scene* (left), *in which the local verger gives Princess Paloma (Juliet Cadzow) a rough sort of bath.*

Pin. M: Henny Vrienten. Sound: Piotr Van Dijk. (Golden Egg *Amsterdam*/Ingrid *Paris*—Metro). Selected release: 1 June 1990. 107 mins. Cert 12.

Venus Peter. In spite of its occasional ambiguities (for instance, why does the priest wash down the naked gypsy girl hermit?) this promisingly crafted film by tyro director Ian Sellar has a lot to offer. Filmed on location under the bleak, angry skies of the Orkneys, it tells of a small boy whose dreams of his sea captain father are shattered when dad returns to the island to reveal a more mundane reason for his absence; unable to stand the hard life he has fled home and family for the easier, more affluent mainland. The boy, a sturdy little lad with great appeal, was taken from the local school; his fisherman grandfather is played with quiet conviction by Ray McAnally. And the fishing boat of the film's title has a major role,

too. *Venus Peter* comes to the screen like a breath of fresh, healthy, sea-tinged air. [FMS]

Cast: Ray McAnally, Gordon Strachan (Peter, the boy), Juliet Cadzow (the hermit Princess Paloma), David Hayman (preacher), Sheila Keith (Epp), Mary MacLeon (old teacher), Sinead Cusack (new teacher), Peter Caffrey (Peter's father), Caroline Paterson (mother), Alex McAvoy, Emma Dingwall, Robin McCaffrey, Louise Breslin, George Anton, Alan Tall. Dir: Ian Sellar. Pro: Christopher Young. Assoc Pro: Alan J. Wands. Ex Pro: Colin MacCabe. Screenplay: Ian Sellar and Christopher Rush. Ph: Gabriel Beristain. Ed: David Spiers. Pro Des: Andy Harris. M: Jonathan Dove. Sound: David Stephenson. Costumes: Sandy Powell. (British Film Institute in assoc. with Channel Four TV Co., The Scottish Film Pro. Fund, Orkney Island Council and British Screen–Recorded Releasing.) Rel: floating; first shown London (Cannon, Tottenham Ct Rd and Chelsea Cinema), 1 December 1989. 94 mins. Cert 12.

Vincent & Theo. Slow-moving, overlong, but intelligent and literate portrait of Van Gogh and his art-dealing brother Theo. Tim Roth bears an uncanny resemblance to the self-portraits that Van Gogh painted, and convincingly reveals the yobbo prodigy of art history – a pathetic, gnarled figure one minute, and a passionate genius the next. Wisely, director Robert Altman takes a naturalistic approach, while imbuing his screen with some striking visuals. This is undoubtedly the director's best work for ages, once again revealing his eye for telling detail. He also establishes the real truth about Van Gogh's ear! Following on the heels of Paul Cox's *Vincent* and Akira Kurosawa's *Dreams* (in which Martin Scorsese plays the painter), *Vincent & Theo* will itself be pursued by Maurice Pialat's *Van Gogh*. [JC-W]

Also with: Paul Rhys (Theo Van Gogh), Johanna Ter Steege (Jo Bonger), Wladimir Yordanoff (Paul Gauguin), Jip Wijngaarden (Sien Hoornik), Anne Canovas (Marie), Hans Kesting (Andries Bonger), Jean-Pierre Cassel (Dr Paul Gachet), Marie-Louise Stheins (Jet Mauve), Vincent Souliac (Paul Millet), Feodor Atkine (Dr Peyron), Bernadette Giraud (Marguerite Gachet), Jean-Francois Perrier, Adrian Brine, Peter Tuinman, Annie Chaplin. Dir: Robert Altman. Pro: Ludi Boeken. Ex Pro: David Conroy. Screenplay: Julian Mitchell. Ph: Jean Lepine. Ed: Francoise Coispeau and Geraldine Peroni. Pro Des: Stephen Altman. M: Gabriel Yared. Costumes: Scott Bushnell. (Belbo/Arena–Blue Dolphin.) Rel: 22 June 1990. 140 mins. Cert 15.

The War of the Roses. Terrifying romantic comedy-cum-horror film in which the civilised, charming Barbara and Oliver Rose fight to the death for the possession of their house in a spine-chilling divorce. Kathleen Turner, afraid that her character was unbelievably malevolent, turned the role down twice before finally accepting the part (after insisting that the Rose children were made older). Danny DeVito, who appears as Oliver's lawyer and as Hitchcockian narrator, directs with considerable flair, anchoring his highly emotional film to the guy posts of realism, comedy and thrills. With Michael Douglas rounding off the star names as Oliver, *The War of the Roses* marks the third occasion that the trio have worked together (previously in *Romancing the Stone* and *The Jewel of the Nile*). Unhappily-marrieds and animal-lovers beware . . . [JC-W]

Also with: Marianne Sägebrecht (Susan), Sean Astin (Josh at 17), Heather Fairchild

(Carolyn at 17), G. D. Spradlin (Harry Thurmont), Peter Donat (Larrabee), Dan Castellaneta, Gloria Cromwell, Susan Isaacs, Jacqueline Cassell, Prince Hughes, Danitra Vance, David Wohl, with Popeye (Bennie) and Tyler (Kitty Kitty). Dir: Danny DeVito. Pro: James L. Brooks and Arnon Milchan. Ex Pro: Polly Platt and Doug Claybourne. Co-Pro and Screenplay:

Tim Roth in his best screen performance yet, as the rural genius Van Gogh in Robert Altman's Vincent and Theo *(from Blue Dolphin).*

The battle of Barbara (Kathleen Turner) and Oliver Rose (Michael Douglas) in Danny DeVito's nightmarish, uncompromising and bitterly hilarious horror-comic-romance, The War of the Roses *(Fox).*

Whose line is it anyway? Alan Bates and Betsy enjoy a telephone conversation in Colin Gregg's We Think the World of You, *from Recorded Releasing.*

Michael Leeson; based on the novel by Warren Adler. Ph: Stephen H. Burum. Ed: Lynzee Klingman. Pro Des: Ida Random. M: David Newman; 'Only You' performed by The Platters. Costumes: Gloria Gresham. Sound: Leslie Shatz. (Fox.) Rel: 9 March 1990. 111 mins. Cert 15.

We the Living – Noi Vivi. Made in Italy in 1942, this fascinating marathon museum piece (nearly three hours long) was quickly suppressed by the fascist authorities when they realised the film's subversive implications. How delightful it is to see a 21-year-old Alida Valli and a 26-year-old Rossano Brazzi in action, along with the lesser-known Fosco Giachetti, in a full-blooded romantic triangle, leading to a highly dramatic confrontation. Made on the grand scale, against stirring political backgrounds, ably directed and gener-

Jonathan Silverman, the corpse and Andrew McCarthy go on holiday in Ted Kotcheff's dead lively Weekend at Bernie's *(Rank).*

ally splendidly acted, this elderly black-and-white film shows few signs of its age and well deserves this resuscitation. [FMS]

Also with: Giovanno Grasso, Emilio Cigoli, Cesarina Gheraldi, Mario Pisu. Dir: Goffredo Alessandrini. Screenplay: Anton Giulio Majano; based on the novel by Ayn Rand; adapted by Corrado Alvaro and Orio ergani. Ph: Giuseppe Caracciolo. Ed: Eraldo Da Roma. Art: Andrea Beloborodoff, Giorgio Abkaasi and Amleto Bonetti. M: Renzo Rosselini. (Scalara Films, Rome–Everyman/Mutual.) Rel: floating; first shown London (Everyman) 21 July 1989. 174 mins. Cert PG.

We Think the World of You. Unusual, small-scale drama set in London in the Fifties, about a civil servant's obsession with an Alsatian dog. Frank Meadows (Alan Bates) is comfortably off, middle-aged and a spectator of events around him. When the former 'love' of his life, Johnny (Gary Oldman), goes to prison for burglary, Frank becomes increasingly concerned for the welfare of Johnny's dog Evie. Slow-moving at times and rather bleak, Colin Gregg's film (based on a true story) is nevertheless buoyed by some fine performances, wonderful dialogue and a wry sense of humour. Also, a welcome return to form by Alan Bates. [JC-W]

Also with: Max Wall (Tom), Liz Smith (Millie), Frances Barber (Megan), Sheila Ballantine, Ryan Batt, and Betsy as Evie. Dir: Colin Gregg. Pro: Tommaso Jandelli and Paul Cowan. Screenplay: Hugh Stoddart; from the novel by Joseph R. Ackerley. Ph: Mike Garfath. Ed: Peter Delfgon. Pro Des: Jamie Leonard. M: Julian Jacobson. Costumes: Doreen Watkinson. Sound: Tony Dawe. (Film Four/British Screen/Cinecom Entertainment/Goldscreen Films–Recorded Releasing.) Rel: 22 September 1989. 91 mins. Cert PG.

Weekend at Bernie's. Frenetic farce about two New York yuppies with a body on their hands – the corpse of their boss. As long as they can prove he's alive, they're safe, but should the threat of his demise leak out . . . all sorts of things might happen. In spite of itself, this nonsense proves to be on the likeable side, although it's leagues away from Hitchcock's similar and superior *The Trouble with Harry*. As the corpse, Terry Kiser gives an engaging performance, but everybody else tries a little too hard – energy never was a

Robert De Niro and Sean Penn as funny convicts dressed up as priests in Neil Jordan's excruciating We're No Angels *(UIP). Pass.*

substitute for wit. Surprisingly, *First Blood*'s Ted Kotcheff was at the helm. [JC-W]

Also with: Andrew McCarthy (Larry Wilson), Jonathan Silverman (Richard Parker), Catherine Mary Stewart (Gwen Saunders), Don Calfa, Catherine Parks, Eloise Broady, Gregory Salata, Louis Giambalvo, Ted Kotcheff. Dir: Ted Kotcheff. Pro: Victor Drai. Ex Pro: Robert Klane and Malcolm R. Harding. Screenplay: Klane. Ph: Francois Protat. Ed: Joan E. Chapman. Pro Des: Peter Jamison. M: Andy Summers (of The Police); songs performed by Jermaine Stewart, etc. Sound: Walter S. Hoylman. (Gladden–Rank.) Rel: 16 March 1990. 99 mins. Cert 12.

Welcome Home. Glacier-paced story about a Vietnam vet, Jake Robbins (Kris Kristofferson), who returns to his family after being presumed dead for seventeen years. His wife, who has come to terms with Jake's passing, now lives in harmony with her new husband and Jake's son. Needless to say, the soldier's return stirs up a right conflict

of emotions. Everybody stares meaningfully into the distance as the minutes tick by, but act and talk in the unlikeliest of ways. Little passion is spent and remarkably little happens; certainly scant light is shed on the false concept of heroism. A far more effective film on the subject, if cruder in execution, was the British *Resurrected* (also reviewed here), dealing with an MIA from the Falklands war. Sadly, *Welcome Home* was director Franklin J. Schaffner's last film before he died. [JC-W]

Also with: JoBeth Williams (Sarah), Sam Waterston (Woody), Brian Keith (Harry Robbins), Thomas Wilson Brown (Tyler), Trey Wilson, J. J., Ken Pogue, Kieu Chinh, Larry Reynolds, Gene Clark. Dir: Franklin J. Schaffner. Pro: Martin Ransohoff. Ex Pro: Don Carmody. Screenplay: Maggie Kleinman. Ph: Fred J. Koenekamp. Ed: Robert E. Swink. Pro Des: Dan Yarhi. M: Henry Mancini; theme song performed by Willie Nelson, 'Your Song' by Elton John. Costumes: Wendy Partridge. Sound: Peter Shewchuk. (Rank.) Rel: 19 January 1990. 92 mins. Cert 15.

We're No Angels. From the director of *Mona Lisa*, the producer of *The Untouchables*, the writer of *House of*

Games, the cinematographer of *The Bear* and the composer of *Gandhi* comes a farce of bewildering ineptitude. Even more inexplicable is that Robert De Niro turns producer with this remake of a so-so Humphrey Bogart vehicle of 1955. De Niro and Sean Penn team up as a couple of dimwitted escaped convicts who hide out as priests on the Canadian border in order to evade capture. In spite of Penn's bumbling inarticulateness, he is mistaken for an orator of great wisdom, only one of several improbabilities that mangle this story. De Niro and Penn mug hopelessly at the camera, while Demi Moore – as the so-called 'romantic interest' – is strident and unattractive. Somewhere in the boardroom, Mr De Niro, this film went terribly, terribly wrong. An expensive embarrassment for all concerned. [JC-W]

Cast includes: Robert De Niro (Ned), Sean Penn (Jim), Demi Moore (Molly), Hoyt Axton (Father Levesque), Ray McAnally (warder), James Russo (Bobby), Bruno Kirby, Wallace Shawn, John C. Reilly, Jay Brazeau, Ken Buhay, Elizabeth Lawrence, Bill Murdoch, Jessica Jickels, Antony Holland. Dir: Neil Jordan. Pro: Art Linson. Co-Pro: Fred Caruso. Ex Pro: Robert De

Jessica Lange and Dennis Quaid in Taylor Hackford's elephantine When I Fall in Love *(Warner).*

Niro. Screenplay: David Mamet. Ph: Philippe Rousselot. Ed: Mick Audsley and Joke Van Wuk. Pro Des: Wolf Kroeger. M: George Fenton. Costumes: Theoni V. Aldredge. Sound: Kant Pan. (Paramount–UIP.) Rel: 1 June 1990. 106 mins. Cert 15.

What Have I Done to Deserve This? – ?Que He Hecho Yo Para Merecer Esto!! Frantically busy incident- and character-packed Spanish comedy/drama (even the director is reported as saying that he didn't know which it was), set in an overcrowded family flat in Madrid. Following the *The Law of Desire* and *Women on the Edge of a Nervous Breakdown*, this is the third of Pedro Almodóvar's movies to be shown in the UK in just over a year, although it was in fact the first to be made. Sharp and serious comment on the position of the Spanish housewife and the disintegration of family life is offset by a great deal of fairly tasteless comedy which certainly won't appeal to everyone. [FMS]

Cast: Carmen Maura (outstanding as housewife Gloria), Luis Hostalot (Polo), Angel de Andres-Lórez (husband Antonio), Juan Martinez (son Toni), Miguel Angel Herranz (son Miguel), Gonzalo Suarez (Lucas), Verónica Forqué (Cristal), Chus Lampreave (grandma), Kiti Manver (Juani), Sonia Anabela Hilomann, Katia Loritz, Cecilia Roth, Diego Caretti, Ryo Hiruma, Amparo Soler Leal. Dir and Screenplay: Pedro Almodóvar. Pro: Tadeo Villalba. Ex Pro: Hervé Hachuel. Ph: Angel Luis Fernandez. Ed: José Solcedo. M: Bernardo Bonezzi. (Tesauro/Kaktus Films–Metro Pictures.) Rel: floating; first shown London (Metro) 4 August 1989. 100 mins. Cert 18.

When I Fall in Love (US: *Everybody's All-American*). This is the all-American film that Warner Bros were afraid to release in Britain – because of its American Football background. But, due to the enormous interest in its video release, Warner's changed their mind and here we are. With a cast comprising Jessica Lange, Dennis Quaid, Timothy Hutton and John Goodman, you can see why the video would have stirred up so much interest. Dennis Quaid (in a typically extrovert performance) plays Gavin Grey, an arrogant jock and foot-ball star, joined at the hip to Jessica Lange. Lange is Babs Rogers, a teenage beauty royal (the Magnolia Queen) who, questioned on her educational future, proclaims 'I'm majoring in Gavin and me'. Spanning 25 years, the film follows the ups and downs of this vibrant Southern couple, viewed with adulation, affection and eventually anxiety by Gavin's nephew, Donnie (Timothy Hutton). It is Hutton, in the back-seat role of spectator, who has the most difficult task, but who is, perhaps, the most effective (even though Quaid put on forty pounds to make his ageing character more authentic). Romance, tragedy and betrayal flit on and off the screen, and we are kept suitably glued to the action thanks to some above-average thespian duty. Sentimental, yes; crass, even; but this is high-grade soap. [JC-W]

Also with: John Goodman (Lawrence), Carl Lumbly (Narvel Blue), Ray Baker (Bolling Kiely), Savannah Smith Boucher (Darlene Kiely), Patricia Clarkson (Leslie Stone), J. Kevin Brune, Roy B. Stewart Jr, Pat Pierre Perkins, Aaron Neville, J. C. Sealy, Tom Rickman, Melissa Massey, Sherrod Auxt, Jeb Quaid. Dir: Taylor Hackford. Pro:

Hackford, Laura Ziskin and Ian Sander. Ex Pro: Stuart Benjamin. Screenplay: Tom Rickman; based on the novel by Frank Deford. Ph: Stephen Goldblatt. Ed: Don Zimmerman. Pro Des: Joe Alves. M: James Newton Howard; songs performed by Nat King Cole, Dean Martin, Chubby Checker, Johnny Mathis, Lee Dorsey, Steely Dan, etc. Costumes: Theadora Van Runkle. Sound: Jeff Wexler. (New Visions–Warner.) Rel: 16 February 1990. 127 mins. Cert 15.

When the Whales Came. 'They don't make films like that any more . . .' But they can and, just occasionally, they do, as *When the Whales Came* proves. Technically magnificent, this simple, heartwarming and finally very moving film, made wholly on Bryher (the smallest of the inhabited Scilly Isles), has the now-rare U certificate and not a foul word in the script. Set in 1914 at the outbreak of World War I, the story adapts a Viking fable about the narwhale: two small children befriend a stone-deaf hermit and join with him to save a shoal of whales in danger of being beached by the tide and slaughtered by the local fishing community. A lovely film, and 'green' to boot. [FMS]

Cast: Paul Scofield (the hermit), Max Rennie and Helen Pearce (the children), David Threlfall and Helen Mirren (the girl's parents), John Hallam (the boy's father), Nicholas Jones (vicar), Jeremy Kemp (schoolteacher), Irene Wilson, Fergus Rees, Frederick Warder, Kerra Spowart, Barbara Ewing, Keith Low, David Suchet, Barbara Jefford, Dexter Fletcher, Blue Philpott, Penny Rogers, Derek Pearce, Susan Curnow, James Stedeford, Paul Thomas, David Sherris, Joanna Bartholomew, Stephen Dan, David Quilter. Dir: Clive Rees. Pro: Simon Channing Williams. Assoc Pro: Alexander Myers. Ex Pro: Geoffrey Wansell. Screenplay: Michael Morpurgo; based on his novel *Why the Whales Came*. Ph: Robert Paynter. Ed: Andrew Boulton. Pro Des: Bruce Grimes. M: Christopher Gunning. Add M: Ruth Rennie. (Golden Swan Pro in assoc. with Central Independent Television–Fox.) Rel: floating; first shown London (Cannon, Shaftesbury Ave) 8 September 1989. 100 mins. Cert U.

Who's Harry Crumb? Disastrously unfunny comedy about a clumsy and moronic private detective (John Candy) assigned a kidnapping case. As Harry Crumb is so unremittingly stupid, it is difficult to find him even remotely funny as surely the most basic comedy must be rooted in *some* reality? Annie

The hermit (Paul Scofield) who teams up with two local youngsters in the Scilly Isles to save the stranded whales, in Fox's When the Whales Came.

Potts (as a scheming nymphomaniac) is always good value, but even this talented comedienne is on a losing wicket with such obvious material. [JC-W]

Also with: Jeffrey Jones (Eliot Draisen), Tim Thomerson (Vince Barnes), Barry Corbin (P. J. Downing), Shawnee Smith (Nikki Downing), Valri Bromfield (Detective Casey), Doug Steckler, Renee Coleman, Wesley Mann, Tamsin Kelsey, Joe Flaherty (the director's brother in real life), Fiona Roeske, James Belushi. Dir: Paul Flaherty. Pro: Arnon Milchan. Co-Pro: George W. Perkins. Ex Pro: John Candy. Screenplay: Robert Conte and Peter Martin Wortmann. Ph: Stephen M. Katz. Ed: Danford B. Greene. Pro Des: Trevor Williams. M: Michel Colombier; songs by Richard Martin Ross, The Temptations, Bonnie Tyler, Sonny Bono, James Brown. Costumes: Jerry R. Allen. Sound: Rick Patton. (Columbia Tri-Star.) Rel: 7 July 1989. 95 mins. Cert PG.

Wilt. There is nothing in the least wrong with Tom Sharpe's novel, on which this is based, while – cinematically – Griff Rhys Jones and Mel Smith have never been used to better effect. But the film just isn't *enough*. It's not real enough, it's not chilling enough and it's certainly not funny enough – although some scenes, taken on their own, are hilarious. What the film lacks

Griff Rhys Jones and Mel Smith as suspect and thick copper in the intermittently amusing Wilt, *from Rank.*

Tales of the frontier: Kelly McGillis and Kurt Russell fight clan and cold in Ted Kotcheff's detailed drama, Winter People *(Rank).*

is comic momentum. Griff is Henry Wilt, an uninspiring teacher of Liberal Studies at an East Anglia technical college who is suspected by a promotion-hungry copper (Mel) of killing his wife. Unfortunately, Wilt is such a damp squib that he deserves everything he gets. [JC-W]

Also with: Mel Smith (Flint), Alison Steadman (Eva Wilt), Diana Quick (Sally), Jeremy Clyde (Hugh), Roger Allam, David Ryall, Roger Lloyd Pack, Dermot Crowley, John Normington, Tony Mathews, Barbara Hicks, Adam Bareham, Josephine Tewson, Ken Drury, Imogen Claire. Dir: Michael Tuchner. Pro: Brian Eastman. Ex Pro: Nick Elliott and Peter Fincham. Screenplay: Andrew Marshall and David Renwick; from the novel by Tom Sharpe. Ph: Norman Langley. Ed: Chris Blunden. Pro Des: Leo Austin. M: Anne Dudley. Costumes: Liz Waller. Sound: Christian Wangler. (LWT–Rank.) Rel: 3 November 1989. 91 mins. Cert 15.

Windprints. The story of a young South African news cameraman (Sean

Bean) forced to come to terms with history as it is happening around him. [FMS]

Also with: John Hurt, Marius Weyers, Eric Nobbs, Lesley Fong, Kurt Egelhof, Dana Niehaus, Trudie Taljaard, Goliath Davids, Johan Kruger. Dir, Screenplay and Ex Pro: David Wicht. (Virgin Vision/ICA.) Rel: floating; first shown in London (ICA) 29 June 1990. 100 mins. No cert.

Winter People. Old-fashioned adventure/love story set in the Appalachian mountains in 1934. A widowed clockmaker, Wayland Jackson (Kurt Russell), and his young daughter find themselves stranded in the Carolina hills when their car breaks down. Forced to find shelter with a local woman, Collie (Kelly McGillis), Wayland is plunged into a war between neighbouring clans. A vivid sense of time and place helps this story of pioneering people find its dramatic footing, although the dialogue does, occasionally, stick in the actors' mouths. Overall, a worthy, interesting effort. [JC-W]

Also with: Lloyd Bridges (William Wright), Mitchell Ryan (Drury Campbell), Amelia Burnette (Paula Jackson), Eileen Ryan

(Annie Wright), Lanny Flaherty (Gudger Wright), Don Michael Paul (young Wright), David Dwyer, Jeffrey Meek, Bill Gribble, Wallace Merck, Walker Averitt, Dashiell Coleman, Judy Simpson Cook. Dir: Ted Kotcheff. Pro: Robert H. Solo. Screenplay: Carol Sobieski; from the novel by John Ehle. Ph: Francois Protat. Ed: Thomas Nelson. Pro Des: Ron Firestone. M: John Scott. Costumes: Ruth Morgan. Sound: Robert Gravenor. (Nelson–Rank.) Rel: 23 February 1990. 111 mins. Cert 15.

A Winter Tan. Or, Shirley Valentine goes to Acapulco and finds true sexuality. Like Ambrose Bierce – played by Gregory Peck in *Old Gringo* – Maryse Holder was a North American writer who disappeared under mysterious circumstances in Mexico. Here, her story is related through the letters she sent home to her best friend, a Canadian teacher. As Maryse explains it, she is 'on vacation from feminism' and is out to sample the beaches, bars and beds of the Mexican fast lane. Startlingly frank, *A Winter Tan* plays like a docudrama on a G-string budget, enriched by a performance of extraordinary selflessness and commitment by Jackie Burroughs, who dominates the film in

Jackie Burroughs in the performance of her lifetime, as raunchy feminist writer Maryse Holder, in the ICA's Canadian oddity, A Winter Tan.

virtually a solo turn. Some may be shocked by Maryse's blunt confessions, but few could forget them. [JC-W]

Also with: Erando Gonzalez (Miguel Novaro), Javier Torres Zarragoza (Lucio Salvador), Anita Olanick (Pam), Diane D'Aguila (Edith), Fernando Perez de Leon (Andres). Dir: Jackie Burroughs, Louise Clark, John Frizzell, John Walker, Aerlyn Weissman. Screenplay: Burroughs; based on the books *Give Sorrow Words* and *Maryse Holder's Letters from Mexico* by Maryse Holder. Pro: Louise Clark. Ph: John Walker. Ed: Alan Lee. M: Ahmed Hassan and John Lang. Sound: Aerlyn Weissman. (Ontario Film Development Corp/Telefilm Canada/Canada Council/Ontario Arts Council–Films Transit.) Rel: floating; first shown London (ICA) 24 November 1989. 91 mins. Cert 18.

Wired. Not so much a film version of Bob Woodward's biography of John Belushi as a self-indulgent casserole of skits and ideas. As Woodward (J. T. Walsh) investigates Belushi's death, the comedian himself unzips his body bag and is taken on a tour of his life by a Puerto Rican cab driver (Ray Sharkey). Offering precious little insight into Belushi's family background or film career, the picture concentrates on his gross character traits and drug habits. However, people are constantly telling him that they love him, although the film refuses to show the slightest reason why they should. Unknown stage actor Michael Chiklis does his damnedest to impersonate the star, but even after putting on 30 pounds in weight he is far too flimsy a substitute. Belushi would have been sorely embarrassed. [JC-W]

Also with: Patti D'Arbanville (Cathy Smith), Lucinda Jenney (Judy Belushi), Gary Groomes (Dan Aykroyd), Alex Rocco (Arnie Fromson), Jerre Burns, Clyde Kusatsu, Tom Bower, Earl Billings, Dakin Matthews, J. C. Quinn, Matthew Faison, Amy Michelson, Diane Behrens, Drew Pillsbury, Billy Preston, with Pete Willcox (Elvis impersonator) and A. C. Meadows (colonel impersonator). Dir: Larry Peerce. Pro: Edward S. Feldman and Charles P. Meeker. Ex Pro: P. Michael Smith and Paul Carran. Screenplay: Earl Mac Rauch; from the book by Bob Woodward. Ph: Tony Imi. Ed: Eric Sears. Pro Des: Brian Eatwell. M: Basil Poledouris, with songs performed by The Ventures, Joe Strummer and Richie Havens ('Still Looking For a Way To Say Goodbye'). Sound: Robert Wald. (Lion Screen–Entertainment.) Rel: 6 October 1989. 100 mins. Cert 18.

The Witches. Near-perfect screen adaptation of Roald Dahl's sinister children's novel, the story of the Grand High Witch and her dastardly plot to turn all English children into mice. Nicolas Roeg may have been a surprising choice as director, but he never underestimates or underrates his preteen audience. As children's screen entertainment goes, this could well become a classic of its genre. Relish Rowan Atkinson's officious, terminally cross hotel manager and admire the late Jim Henson's superbly imaginative (and realistic) puppet creations. Enormous, creepy fun. [JC-W]

Cast includes: Anjelica Huston (Miss Ernst/Grand High Witch), Mai Zetterling (grandmother), Jasen Fisher (Luke), Charlie Potter (Bruno Jenkins), Rowan Atkinson (Mr Stringer), Bill Paterson (Mr Jenkins), Brenda Blethyn (Mrs Jenkins), Jane Horrocks (Miss Ernst's assistant), Jenny Runacre, Rosamund Greenwood. Dir: Nicolas

And this little boy went into the skirting board: Anjelica Huston as the Grand High Witch and Charlie Potter as imminent victim in Nicolas Roeg's hugely enjoyable The Witches *(Warner).*

Roeg. Pro: Mark Shivas. Ex Pro: Jim Henson. Screenplay: Allan Scott; based on the book by Roald Dahl. Ph: Harvey Harrison. Ed: Tony Lawson. Pro Des: Andrew Saunders. M: Stanley Myers. Costumes: Marit Allen. (Lorimar–Warner.) Rel: 25 May 1990. 92 mins. Cert PG.

The Wolves of Willoughby Chase. Stephanie Beacham returns to the screen after an absence of nine years (remember *Inseminoid*, 1980?) to star in this idiotic children's film. The wolves – which resemble dogs in blackface – have little to do in this story of a wicked nanny (Beacham) who hatches a plot to take over Willoughby Chase, a Gothic stately home. There are rats, secret passageways and even a Dickensian workhouse to add a little atmosphere, but nothing can overshadow the enormity of the over-acting, particularly of Geraldine James's Mrs Brisket, tyrant of the orphanage. Filmed in Czechoslovakia. [JC-W]

Cast includes: Stephanie Beacham (Sligh-carp), Mel Smith (Grimshaw), Richard O'Brien (James), Jane Horrocks (Pattern), Eleanor David (Lady Willoughby), Jonathan Coy (Lord Willoughby), Emily Hudson (Bonnie), Aleks Darowska (Sylvia), Lynton Dearden (Simon), Dyllis Hamlett (aunt). Dir: Stuart Orme. Pro: Mark Forstater. Screenplay: William N. Akers; from the novel by Joan Aiken. Ph: Paul Beeson. Ed: Martin Walsh. Pro Des: Christopher Hobbs. M: Colin Towns. Costumes: Hobbs. Sound: Peter Glossop. (Zenith–Entertainment.) Rel: 15 December 1989. 93 mins. Cert PG.

Yaaba. Two children run across a desert, figures in an African landscape. This vision both opens and closes Idrissa Ouedraogo's highly sympathetic, prize-winning second feature. Between times we see how these two, the boy Bila and his female cousin Nopoko, play vital roles in events concerning an old woman who is regarded by the villagers as a witch. Viewed in the context of other African movies, *Yaaba* is very clearly the archetypal village tale. But what it lacks in originality it makes up for in human feeling. [MS]

Cast includes: Fatima Sanga (Yaaba), Noufou Ouedraogo (Bila), Roukietou Barry (Nopoko), Adama Ouedraogo, Sibidou Ouedraogo, Rasmané Ouedraogo, Assita Ouedraogo, Zenabou Ouedraogo, etc. Dir and Screenplay: Idrissa Ouedraogo. Pro: Freddy Denaes, Pierre-Alain Meier and Idrissa Ouedraogo. Ph: Matthais Kälin. Ed: Loredana Cristelli. M: Francis Bebey. Sound: Dominique Dalmasso. (Arcadia Films/Les Films de l'Avenir/Thelma Film AG–Oasis.) Rel: floating; first shown London (Renoir) 26 January 1990. 90 mins. Cert PG.

Young Einstein. Astonishingly, *Young Einstein* is the second most successful Aussie film ever (after *Crocodile Dundee*). First released this year, it was actually unveiled at the 1986 Australian Film Awards, but it's been tinkered with since then. Its star and maker (story editor, director, co-producer and co-scenarist) is the Australian scenarist Yahoo Serious (real name Greg Pead) and the wild story is – loosely – about his discovery, while trying to perk up his home-made beer, of how to split the atom. But how you feel about this movie depends entirely on your reaction to the zany clown who dominates it. [FMS]

Cast: Yahoo Serious (Einstein), Odile Le Clezio (Marie Curie), John Howard (Preston Preston), Pee Wee Wilson (Mr Einstein), Su Cruickshank (Mrs Einstein), Basil Clarke (Charles Darwin), Esben Storm (Wilbur Wright), Lulu Pinkus (the blonde), Kaarin Fairfax (the brunette), Jonathan Coleman (Wolfgang Bavarian), Roger Ward (cat pie cook), Adam Bowen (Marconi), Tim McKew (Sigmund Freud), Ian James Tait (Thomas Edison), etc. Dir, Story, Screenplay (with David Roach), Pro (with Warwick Ross and David Loach): Yahoo Serious. Assoc Pro: Lulu Pinkus. Ex Pro: Graham Burke and Ray Beattie. Ph: Jeff Darling. Pro Des: Steve Marr, Laurence Faen and Colin Gibson. M: William Motzing, Martin Armiger and Tommy Tycho. (Serious Films–Warner.) Rel: 13 October 1989. 91 mins. Cert PG.

Young Einstein *having a relaxing bath, in the Warner release of the most successful movie ever to be made and screened in Australia.*

Letter from Hollywood

ANTHONY SLIDE

As with any year in Hollywood, there has been the typical amount of silliness. On 14 June 1989, Zsa Zsa Gabor was arrested for slapping a Beverly Hills cop – it proved to be a slap heard around the world, and a slap which made the ageing Hungarian nonentity (at least according to *The National Enquirer*) the most unpopular woman in America. Upon hearing of her sentence to perform community service, comedian Robert Klein opined that the greatest service Zsa Zsa Gabor could do for any community would be to leave it. Undaunted, Miss Gabor decided to appear in the annual New Year's Day Rose Parade in Pasadena, and was booed by a capacity crowd. She was signed for a Dreyer's ice cream commercial, but the company allegedly received so many complaints from television viewers that the spot had to be withdrawn. It would appear that one slap has done more than a lifetime of bad reviews – it has ended Gabor's career. Now, if only we could get Pia Zadora to slap a cop!

Unfortunately, Pia Zadora is still a part of the Hollywood community, and, as if to prove her self-importance, she arranged for the demolition of Pickfair (the former home of Mary Pickford and Douglas Fairbanks), which her husband had generously acquired for her.

Following in Miss Gabor's shadow, actor Rob Lowe managed to make a fool of himself by having sex with a sixteen-year-old girl and taping the entire event. He was tried on charges of sexual exploitation of a minor in July 1989, and the tape became a best-seller, being perhaps more widely distributed than many of Mr Lowe's films.

The most important Hollywood anniversary, although it took place in Anaheim, was the 35th anniversary of Disneyland, celebrated on 12 January 1990. Present were the three men who co-hosted the original live television broadcast which opened the amusement park on 17 July 1955: Ronald Reagan, Art Linkletter and Bob Cummings. Ex-President Reagan noted, 'They say one man of vision can change the world. Maybe Walt Disney did not alter the globe, but he made one section a happier place.'

The Walt Disney Company has been busy restoring the 65-year-old Paramount Theater, located across the street from the Chinese Theater in Hollywood. It's a worthwhile and commendable project, although it is doubtful it will be completed, as planned, to host the premiere of *Dick Tracy*.

Another worthwhile Disney event took place at the studio on 19 July 1989, when company head Michael Eisner honoured ten of the studio's animators with Disney Legend Awards. The lucky ten were Ub Iwerks, Les Clark, Milt Kahl, Eric Larson, Wolfgang Reitherman, Marc Davis, Ollie Johnston, Ward Kimball, John Lounsbery and Frank Thomas. Eisner described the awards as a demonstration of the importance of the studio's heritage. Other than that, it has been a bad year for animation, with the Disney event taking place less than a month after the death of Mel Blanc, and little less than three months before the demise of 'Bullwinkle' creator Jay Ward.

The Palm Springs Film Festival made its debut in January 1990, with Mayor Sonny Bono (of Sonny and Cher fame) as the guiding light behind the event. A month later, the Hollywood Walk of Fame celebrated its 30th anniversary, and announced that the cost of 'buying' a star on Hollywood Boulevard had risen from $3500 to $4800. In April 1990, the Hollywood Chamber of Commerce, the organisation behind one of the sleazier Hollywood attractions, announced that a replica of the Walk of Fame, but with only 25 stars, was to be dedicated in Nagoya, Japan, a sister city to Los Angeles.

The American Film Institute announced it was celebrating its 25th anniversary on 26 September 1989, with a fundraising celebration at the White House. However, after it was pointed out that the Institute had not been in existence for that length of time – it just seems like 25 years – the event was retitled a celebration to 'reaffirm the commitment' made by then-President Lyndon Johnson in pledging to create the AFI back in 1964. Forty-three film and television personalities, including Steven Spielberg, Gene Kelly, Charlton Heston, Goldie Hawn, Steve Martin and Brooke Shields, were on hand for the event, at which President Bush reminded the guests that 'Films are the mirror and conscience of America.'

The Hollywood community apparently has a conscience as far as saving the rain forests is concerned, and a benefit in Beverly Hills on 12 February 1990 raised $1.2 million for the cause. Of course, in Hollywood there is conscience and conscience, and rock star Don Henley was quick to point out 'a half-million dead animals' in the cloakroom at the benefit. Regrettably, neither he nor Sting carried out their threat to burn all the fur coats!

Happily, fur is dead as far as many in Hollywood are concerned, and three of the biggest supporters of the Animal Rights movement are Golden Girls Rue McClanahan, Bea Arthur and Betty White. Betty is one of the few visitors to my home who has got down and rolled around on the floor with my labrador retriever – in fact, the only other celebrity visitor who has behaved in a similar fashion was, surprisingly, Hurd Hatfield.

1989 was the 50th anniversary of the opening of *Gone with the Wind*, and the big celebration took place in Atlanta on 10–12 December, with ten of the twelve surviving cast members present to enjoy Ted Turner's unveiling of a new print, lovingly restored by the Burbank-based YCM Laboratory. Butterfly McQueen and Ann Rutherford were among the guests, but, sadly, Olivia de Havilland failed to turn up. A 50th anniversary celebration also took place at what is now called the Culver Studios, where *Gone with the Wind* was shot. The 'happening' on Sunday, 16 July included a Clark Gable lookalike contest, judged by Jane Withers, and appearances by some of the minor members of the cast, such as Patrick Curtis, Fred Crane, Mary Anderson, Rand Brooks, Frank Coghlan and Johnny Albright.

The Annual Golden Boots Awards took place on 5 August 1989, with Johnny Cash as the principal guest. He told a cheering audience, 'I thank God for the freedoms that we have in this country – including the freedom, the right, to burn the flag. I also thank God for the right to bear arms. And if you burn my flag, I'll shoot you.' The event, which also honoured John Ireland, Ellen Corby and Casey Tibbs, raised $250,000 for the Motion Picture and Television Fund, an organisation committed to saving lives – presumably even those of flag burners shot by Cash.

On 18 July 1989, groundbreaking ceremonies took place for the new library of the Academy of Motion Picture Arts and Sciences, which is to be located in what is called the Waterworks Buildings on the eastern edge of Beverly Hills. When the new building opens in the autumn of 1990, one of its first acquisitions will be the papers of Cary Grant. The actor's personal effects were donated to, and sold by, the Motion Picture and Television Fund. It was a wonderful opportunity to acquire a Cary Grant tie for only $12. More than $3 million has already been raised towards the new library building through the generosity of ABC Television (coincidentally the network which airs the Oscar show), Eastman Kodak, Columbia, Paramount, Warner Bros, Walt Disney, Twentieth Centu-

ry-Fox, and Universal. That was the good news for the Academy. The bad news was that a US District Court judge ruled that the Oscar is in the public domain, and anyone is free to use the name and the image. The Academy is appealing against the verdict.

Nothing proliferates more in Hollywood than awards, and this year there were plenty of which you may not have heard. In November 1989, Ralph Bellamy received the first annual Hal Roach Entertainment Award from Loyola Marymount University. Stanley Cortez, responsible for the magnificent photography of *The Magnificent Ambersons*, received the Lifetime Achievement Award from the American Society of Cinematographers on 25 February 1990. On 12 December 1989, Kirk and Michael Douglas were joint recipients of the Sheba Humanitarian Award from the Friends of Tel Hashomer. (Don't ask me what that is – I just report the awards.) Two days earlier, Jack Lemmon had received the Screen Actors' Guild's highest honour, the Annual Achievement Award. Actress/director Lee Grant received an award at the fifth annual Women in Film Festival in October 1989; Michael Douglas did the honours. On 3 December, Billy Crystal (who did such a great job as master of ceremonies of the 1990 Oscar show) received the Artist of the Year Award from the Anti-Defamation League of B'nai B'rith. He joked, 'I've had such an amazing year. I'd like to tell you it's fun spending time with me. Just the other day I was talking to me and I said, "You're OK." So I said thanks and we had lunch.'

David Lean was the first Englishman to be honoured by the American Film Institute, receiving its 1990 Lifetime Achievement Award on 8 March 1990. A couple of weeks later, the American Cinematheque presented its annual award to Ron Howard, at the annual fundraising event, The Moving Picture Ball. The Hollywood Entertainment Museum (formerly known as the Hollywood Exposition, and really the new Hollywood Museum) got into the awards game with its first Legacy Awards, presented at Hollywood's Holiday Inn (not the most glamorous of locations) in December 1989. Of course, it was also a fundraiser.

On 2 November 1989, some 350 invited guests gathered on Stage 18 of the Burbank Studios to pay posthum-

ous tribute to Bette Davis, six of whose films had been shot there. Present were Clint Eastwood, Glenn Ford, Robert Wagner, Anna Lee, Vincent Price, Roddy McDowall, Lionel Stander, Kim Carnes (who had enjoyed a hit with the song 'Bette Davis Eyes') and female impersonator Charles Pierce (noted for his devastating portrayals of Miss Davis).

Master of ceremonies James Woods summed up the feelings of those present when he remarked, 'I guarantee that up in heaven they are saying, "Buckle your seat belts, it's going to be a bumpy eternity." '

Sammy Davis Jr made his last public appearance at a tribute at the Shrine Auditorium on 13 November 1989. Videotaped for later presentation as a television special, the event was held to establish scholarships in Davis's name, to be administered through the United Negro College Fund. Present were many of the entertainer's friends and colleagues, including Eddie Murphy, Frank Sinatra, Clint Eastwood, Bob Hope, Michael Jackson, Shirley MacLaine and Ella Fitzgerald.

The last year also saw some unusual studio jumping, not by executives but by entire production companies. Columbia Pictures, which had shared the Burbank Studios lot with Warner Bros, moved over to the old MGM studios, which had formerly been occupied by Lorimar. The latter, which is now owned by Warner Bros, moved its operations to the Burbank Studios, and in June of 1990, Warner Bros had an official rededication of the Burbank Studios as the Warner Bros Studio (which, in actuality, it had been until 1972). Unfortunately, the sad news is that the Metrocolor Labs, which had been part of the MGM lot for so many years, closed in August 1989, leaving only two major laboratories in Los Angeles; Technicolor and De Luxe.

On a more serious level, there has been considerable activity in the field of film preservation. The big event of the year took place not in Los Angeles, but in New York, where on 2 October 1989, the Museum of Modern Art presented its new and restored version of *Intolerance*, a major undertaking by that organisation's film preservationist, Peter Williamson.

With financial support from AT&T, the Museum of Modern Art organised a multi-film tribute to Vitaphone, the

Dolores Costello and George O'Brien in Michael Curtiz' Noah's Ark (1928), restored by Robert Gitt of the UCLA Film and Television Archive.

early sound process. Among the films screened as part of the series, which opened in New York in October 1989 and subsequently toured the country, were *Viennese Nights, Don Juan, Lights of New York, Under a Texas Moon* and *The First Auto.* The majority of the films were restored by Robert Gitt of the UCLA Film and Television Archive, and perhaps the most ambitious of his projects were *Noah's Ark* and *The Divine Lady.* The latter is a delightful Corinne Griffith vehicle from 1929, in which the actress plays Emma Hamilton to Victor Varconi's Lord Nelson. (It's interesting to see a Hungarian playing the great British hero, and Varconi acquits himself well, perhaps because he is not required to speak.) Michael Curtiz' 1928 epic has only been available in recent years in a truncated and revised version compiled in the 1950s by Robert Youngson. The new restoration is a revelation in terms of the scope of the production, which moves from contemporary New York to World War I and just before, and, finally, to Biblical times. The talkie sequences between leading players Dolores Costello and George O'Brien are somewhat incongruous, but certainly in no way as bad as many similar talking sequences in other films of the period.

The big news on the preservation front came in Los Angeles on 1 May 1990, with the announcement that Steven Spielberg, Martin Scorsese, George Lucas, Sydney Pollack, Woody Allen, Francis Coppola, Stanley Kubrick and Robert Redford have formed The Film Foundation, which plans to raise some $30 million for a joint preservation effort between US archives and the major studios. It is an exciting idea, but many questions remain unanswered, such as whether the films to be restored will be the major features, selected by the board members, or the small B pictures which are rotting away in the nation's archives, with no monies in sight for their salvation. Universal immediately announced it was making $1 million available to restore 50 of the films which it owns, but 'restoration' by the studios has not always proved to be up to archival standards, and Universal would probably have spent that money as a matter of course in protecting its assets.

Whatever the outcome, the group has helped raise public interest and public consciousness over the need for film preservation – and that cannot be bad.

Movie Quotations of the Year

'The last time I was inside a woman was when I visited the Statue of Liberty.'
Woody Allen in *Crimes and Misdemeanors*

'I remember reading somewhere that men learn to love the person that they're attracted to, and that women become more and more attracted to the person they love.'
James Spader in *sex – lies and videotape*

Mrs Devereaux to son: 'Mr Parker is vision-impaired.' Mr Parker: 'Not to mention blind as a bat.'
Meg Foster and Rutger Hauer in *Blind Fury*

'We need boys so that they can grow up, get married and turn into shadows.'
Jean Louisa Kelly in *Uncle Buck*

'Marriage is like the Middle East, isn't it? There's no solution.'
Pauline Collins in *Shirley Valentine*

'I like you, Iris, just about as much as I love you.'
Robert De Niro to Jane Fonda in *Stanley & Iris*

'Cars don't behave, they are behaved upon.'
Dan Aykroyd to mother Jessica Tandy in *Driving Miss Daisy*

'This is the Eighties: if you can achieve puberty you can achieve a past.'
Dolly Parton in *Steel Magnolias*

'Carpe diem, lads. Seize the day. Make your lives extraordinary.'
Robin Williams in *Dead Poets Society*

'Justice and law are distant cousins. They're not on speaking terms at all.'
Marlon Brando as lawyer Ian McKenzie in *A Dry White Season*

'I have the willpower of a woman half my age.'
Olympia Dukakis in *Dad*

'Sticks and stones may break your bones, but words cause permanent damage.'
DJ Eric Bogosian in Oliver Stone's *Talk Radio*

'There is something down there – something not us.'
Mary Elizabeth Mastrantonio in *The Abyss*

'If you build it, He will come.'
The Voice in *Field of Dreams*

'I was a single mother long before they talked about it on Oprah Winfrey.'
Dianne Wiest in *Cookie*

'I hear the sewers of Paris are beautiful at this time of year.'
Barry Otto in *The Punisher*

'I look like a Russ Meyer movie.'
A pregnant Kirstie Alley in *Look Who's Talking*

'Rambo is a pussy.'
Sylvester Stallone in *Tango and Cash*

'I ain't ex-governor material.'
Paul Newman as Louisiana Governor Earl K. Long in Ron Shelton's *Blaze*

'Dying's not a sin. Not living is.'
Jack Lemmon to Olympia Dukakis in *Dad*

The year's most popular line:
'There was blood everywhere.'

The year's second most popular line:
'Welcome to Hell.'

The year's worst line:
'This is hell, and I'm going to give you the guided tour.'
Warder Donald Sutherland to Sylvester Stallone in *Lock Up*

'It's great to be young and insane.'
Michael Keaton in *The Dream Team*

TV Feature Films of the Year

In this section you will find all the made-for-television movies shown on BBC1 and BBC2, ITV and Channel 4, during the period covered by this edition of *Film Review*. (When a film made for US TV had a cinema release in Britain, this is noted.) The date given in brackets after each title is the year the movie was made or originally shown (often in the US). Films reviewed in previous editions of *Film Review* are listed at the end of the feature, with dates of the repeat and the previous showings, and the edition of *Film Review* in which the detailed note was included.

The Accountant (1989). Drama with some black comedy, about an accountant unfortunate enough to get mixed up with the Mafia and not finding it funny! Alfred Molina is very good as the worried victim. A large supporting cast includes Tracie Hart, George Mitchell and Clive Panto. Dir: Les Blair. Screenplay: Geoffrey Case. BBC1, 24 September 1989.

Across the Lake (1988). The last 60 days in the life of Sir Malcolm Campbell's son Donald, leading up to his brave but fatal attempt to break the water speed record with *Bluebird* on Lake Coniston which ended with the boat flipping him to his death. A very worthwhile and well-made reconstruction of the end of a sad crusade. With Anthony Hopkins. BBC1, 27 July 1989.

Act of Vengeance (1986). Sterling performances by Charles Bronson (not *Death Wish*-ing for once), Ellen Burstyn, Wilford Brimley and Ellen Barkin save this 'true-life' drama – about a mining union official who risks his life by standing up to his president – from mediocrity. Dir: John Mackenzie. Screenplay: Scott Spencer. BBC1, 9 September 1989.

An Affair in Mind (1988). A superior adaptation of Ruth Rendell's story about a fatal obsession. With Amanda Donohoe, Stephen Dillon. Dir: Colin Luke. Screenplay: Michael Baker. BBC1, 10 August 1989.

Agatha Christie's 'A Caribbean Mystery' (1983). After Margaret Rutherford and Joan Hickson, Helen Hayes takes on the mantle of Miss Christie's famous amateur sleuth Miss Marple, as she tries to prevent a third murder at her holiday hotel. Dir: Robert Lewis. Screenplay: Sue Grafton and Steven Humphrey. ITV, 9 December 1989.

All Quiet on the Western Front (1979). A quite superior TV remake of the famous Remarque anti-war play and film about life in the trenches during World War I. With Richard Thomas, Ernest Borgnine. Dir: Delbert Mann. BBC2, 19 May 1990.

Aloha Means Goodbye (1974). You'd need more than a pinch (more like a ton) of salt to swallow this preposterous plot about the nightmare experience of a young girl suffering from a rare disease, and treated by horrid doctor James Franciscus. But those Hawaiian backgrounds are lovely. With Sally Struthers, Joanna Miles. Dir: David Lowell Rich. Screenplay: Joseph Stefano; based on the novel by Naomi Hitze. ITV, 28 April 1990.

The Alpha Caper (1973). Made for American TV, and shown on TV both in the US and UK as *The Alpha Game*, this feature was released in Britain in October 1984 as a cinema film with the new title of *Inside Job*, and as such was fully reviewed in the 1975–6 *Film Review*. ITV, 14 March 1990.

As Summers Die (1986). Though long available on video, this is the first British TV showing of a strongly cast story about the struggle between rich whites and a black woman (helped by white lawyer Scott Glenn), over the property she is determined to keep. Set in Louisiana in the 1950s – and you can watch the steam rising as passions are unleashed. Also with Bette Davis, Jamie Lee Curtis. (Specially collectable for being Miss Davis's penultimate performance – what an actress!) Dir: Jean-Claude Tramont. No screenplay credit. BBC2, 23 October 1989.

Assault and Matrimony (1987). Lively, crazy comedy about a husband and wife each ineptly trying to murder the other. With real-life husband and wife Jill Eikenberry, Michael Tucker. Dir: Jim Frawley. Screenplay: John Binder; from the novel by James Anderson. ITV, 18 June 1990.

Assault on the Wayne (1970). Routine but well-made thriller about agents trying to steal a secret device from a nuclear sub . . . and you won't believe one moment of it! With Joseph Cotten, Leonard Nimoy, Keenan Wynn. Dir: Marvin Chomsky. Screenplay: Jackson Gillis. ITV, 13 November 1989.

Ball Trap on the Cote Sauvage (1989). Highly commendable British TV comedy about British families on their seaside holidays in France. With Jack

Shepherd, Zoe Wanamaker, Jamie Grove. Dir: Jack Gold. Screenplay: Andrew Davies. BBC1, 27 December 1989.

Baywatch: Panic at Malibu Pier (1989). Pilot feature for the series that followed, about lifeguard life on Malibu beach. With David Hasselhoff, Parker Stevenson, Shawn Weatherly. Dir: Richard Compton. Screenplay: Douglas Schwartz and Michael Berk. ITV, 6 January 1990.

The Betty Ford Story (1987). Almost wholly dependent on Gena Rowlands's performance as the First Lady once infamous for her tippling and drug addiction, but later renowned for her triumph over both and founding the clinic that bears her name. Also with Josef Sommer, Nana Woods. Dir: David Greene. Screenplay: Karen Hall. BBC2, 27 November 1989.

Beverly Hills Madam (1986). Soap-opera stuff as Faye Dunaway's stable of $1000-a-night chicks find they have become involved in murder. Fairly steamy, too. Also with Robin Givens, Louis Jourdan. Dir: Harvey Hart. Screenplay: Nancy Sackett. ITV, 2 September 1989.

Black Arrow (1984). Robert Louis Stevenson's story of high adventure in the England of the fifteenth century, with Oliver Reed a really splendid villain. Entertainment value guaranteed in this Disney studio version. Also with Donald Pleasance, Fernando Rey. Dir: John Hough. Screenplay: David Pursall and Peter Welbeck. ITV, 28 December 1989.

Blore MP (1989). Black farce about an MP blackmailed into spying for the Soviets. Timothy West pulls out every last stop, and gives us top-class ham. Also with Jill Baker, Stephen Moore, Maggie O'Neill, Paul Daneman. Dir: Robert Young. Screenplay: Robin Chapman; based on the book by A. N. Wilson. BBC1, 22 October 1989.

Broken Vows (1987). Tommy Lee Jones as a parish priest who finds his vows increasingly difficult to keep when he becomes involved with the girl-friend of a man he did his best to help die. A neatly plotted thriller. Also with

Annette O'Toole, M. Emmet Walsh, Milo O'Shea. Dir: Jud Taylor. Screenplay: James Costigan; based on the Salisbury Davis thriller *Where the Dark Streets Go*. BBC1, 30 October 1989.

The Cat Creature (1973). Mediocre horror film about a supernatural feline, a stolen ancient Egyptian amulet, and an elderly detective and a young archaeologist who set out to solve the mystery. With David Hedison, Stuart Whitman, John Carradine, Gale Sondergaard and Peter Lorre Jr – quite a formidable team. Dir: Curtis Harrington. Screenplay: Robert Bloch. ITV, 29 March 1990.

CAT Squad – Stalking Danger (1986). Well-directed but pretty wild and woolly thriller about an American counter-terrorist quartet foiling a ruthless gang's attempts to steal laser secrets. With Joe Cortese, Jack Youngblood, Patricia Charbonneau. Dir: William Friedkin. Screenplay: Gerald Petievich. ITV, 28 April 1990.

Caught on a Train (1980). Perfect short-story-style film about a young and ambitious publisher who becomes increasingly and unwillingly involved with a very haughty, demanding old lady, a fellow passenger on the night train to Austria, who gets him into one nightmare situation after another. Superbly acted by Peggy Ashcroft, most ably supported by Michael Kitchen and Wendy Raeback. A very superior TV movie indeed. Dir: Peter Duffel. Screenplay: Stephen Poliakoff. BBC2, 18 September 1989.

Children Crossing (1990). Another in the minor flood of BBC feature films premiered this year: this one is an adaptation of the Verity Bargate novel about the tragic consequences of a husband's real or imagined infidelity. With Peter Firth, Saskia Reeves. Dir: Angela Pope. Screenplay: Trevor Preston. BBC2, 25 March 1990.

A Christmas Carol (1984). Though made as a feature for American TV, this very superior adaptation of Charles Dickens's wonderful Christmas classic was quite deservedly originally shown in the UK as a cinema film, released in 1985. A full review appears in the 1985–6 *Film Review*. ITV, 24 December 1989.

Close Relatives (1990). New BBC film based on a tricky theme: incest. A long-distance lorry driver meets the sister he has never previously known about and falls in love with her . . . strong, thought-provoking stuff, played by a good, restrained cast. With James Hazeldine, Rosalind March, Clare Holman. Dir: Adrian Shergold. Screenplay: Stanley Price. BBC2, 4 February 1990.

Code Name: Diamond Head (1977). Routine spy stuff, set in Honolulu, about an American agent trailing a spy (a man of many disguises) who is after the secret of a new explosive. With Roy Thinnes, France Nuyen, Ian McShane. Dir: Jeannot Szwarc. Screenplay: Paul King. ITV, 10 June 1990.

Columbo: Forgotten Lady (1975). Columbo (Peter Falk), that sartorial disgrace to the New York detective force, persistently plagues ex-actress Janet Leigh into finally admitting she killed her hubbie for his money. Also with John Payne. Dir: Harvey Hart. No screenplay credit. BBC1, 20 June 1990.

Columbo: Last Salute to the Commodore (1976). The shabby Columbo investigates the suspicious death of the boss of a boat builder's. A routine voyage. With Peter Falk, Robert Vaughn, Wilfrid Hyde-White, John Dehner, Diane Baker. Dir: Patrick McGoohan. No script credit. BBC1, 13 June 1990.

Coming Out of the Ice (1982). Miserably 'true story' of American athlete Victor Herman whose residence in Russia led to his being arrested on a spy charge and eighteen years in Siberian labour camps. Well-made (it won awards) but a bit depressing. With John Savage, Willie Nelson, Francesca Annis, Frank Windsor. Dir: Waris Hussein. Screenplay: Alan Sharp; based on the book *Victor Herman*, by Herman himself. BBC1, 12 January 1989.

Dark Victory (1976). A very wan TV re-make of the famous Bette Davis weepie about a woman who finds she is dying from a brain tumour, with Elizabeth Montgomery up against memories of that performance. (The 1965 TV re-make – titled *Stolen Hours* – fared no better.) Also with Anthony Hopkins. Dir: Robert Butler. Screenplay: Charles Cohen; based on the original play by George Emerson Brewer Jr and Bertram Bloch. ITV, 12 September 1989.

The Deadly Triangle (1977). Minor crime melodrama set against the spectacular snow of California's Sun Valley, where the sheriff's badge is worn by an Olympic skier! With Dale Robinette, Taylor Larcher, Linda Scruggs Bogart. Dir: Charles S. Dubin. Screenplay: Carl Gottlieb. ITV, 1 May 1990.

Death of a Salesman (1985). Though made in the US as a telefeature, this had its first British showing (at the Camden Plaza on 26 August 1988) as a cinema film, and as such got a detailed review in the 1989–90 *Film Review*. BBC2, 5 May 1990.

Death Scream (1975). Sad and unfortunately true story of a woman who was stabbed to death while her neighbours, nervous of involvement, did nothing to help. With Lucie Arnaz, Raul Julia, John Ryan. Dir: Richard T. Heffron. Screenplay: Stirling Silliphant. ITV, 22 December 1989.

Dempsey (1983). Treat Williams making his TV feature-film debut in the role of the world-beating bruiser who ruled the ring in the 1920s. Based on Jack Dempsey's autobiography. A good supporting cast includes Sam Waterston and Sally Kellerman. It's always tough at the top but it's tougher in the fight business, as this film proves. Dir: Gus Trikonis. Screenplay: Edward Dilorenzo. BBC1, 9 March 1990.

The Devil's Daughter (1972). Shelley Winters, in usual all-stops-out style, in a black magic, mumbo-jumbo story about a girl who discovers her mother has sold her soul to the devil. Miss Winters miraculously makes it almost credible. Also with Martha Scott, Joseph Cotten. Dir: Jeannot Szwarc. Screenplay: Colin Higgins. ITV, 12 July 1989.

The Dirty Dozen – The Fatal Mission (1987). Yet another below-standard TV feature follow-up to the original cinema movie. Made watchable, though, by Telly Savalas and Ernest Borgnine as leaders of the mission to thwart Hitler's plan to ensure that the Nazis will rise again. Also with Alex Cord. Dir: Lee H. Katzin. Screenplay: Valerie Curtin and Barry Levinson. ITV, 1 July 1989.

Doctor Franken (1980). The bloodsucker Baron is transplanted to modern New York – and the transplant team have done a surprisingly good job of it! With Robert Vaughn, Teri Garr. Dir: M. J. Chomsky and J. Lieberman. Screenplay: Lee Thomas. ITV, 31 March 1990.

Doubletake (1985). Grisly murder mystery with Richard Crenna determined to find the killer who switches the heads and bodies of his victims. Based on a novel, but impressively credible: well worth watching. Also with Beverly d'Angelo, Paul Gleason, Lee Richardson. Dir: Jud Taylor. Screenplay: John Gay; based on the William Bayer novel *Switch*. ITV, 23 September 1989.

Down the Long Hills (1987). A couple of kids survive a redskin raid and struggle through the wilderness towards civilisation and safety. Leisurely but sometimes magical stuff, made by the Disney studio and directed by ace Western director Burt Kennedy. And watch bear Bart steal the acting honours! With Bruce Boxleitner, Jack Elam. Screenplay: Jon and Ruth Povare. ITV, 21 October 1989.

Drowning in the Shallow End (1990). Premiere showing of a new BBC feature film: a sharp and often witty satire on the media with Paul McGann as the scriptwriter who finds everything in his life going sour and can't understand why. Can he survive this crisis or will he go under? Also Phoebe Nicholls, Adrian Dunbar. Dir: Colin Gregg. Screenplay: Leigh Jackson. BBC2, 28 January 1990.

Earthbound (1981). A family from outer space force-land their spaceship in America and don't find anyone to help them until burly Burl Ives takes them under his ample wing. Dir: James L. Conway. Screenplay: Michael Fisher. BBC1, 9 September 1989.

Elvis – The Movie (1979). The shortened British version of the big American TV feature success *Elvis*; a well-made biopic about the King. With Kurt Russell (Elvis), Shelley Winters, Season Hubley. Dir: John Carpenter. Screenplay: Anthony Lawrence. BBC2, 11 November 1989.

Escape (1971). Another feature pilot for a series that – understandably – never happened. Daft comic-strip stuff about a Houdini-like escapologist (Christopher George) who becomes a spy, and takes on an evil mastermind character in a battle of wits. But the all-action finale is fun. (Note: don't let the title confuse you; there have been other films – in 1973 and 1980 – with the same title.) Also with Marlyn Mason, Gloria Grahame. Dir: John Llewellyn Moxey. Screenplay: Paul Playdon. ITV, 31 August 1989.

The Executioner's Song (1982). A two-part feature (three hours long in total) dramatising the true story of vicious Utah killer Gary Gilmore (Tommy Lee Jones, who won an Emmy for his performance), who ran a campaign to be killed by a firing squad rather than continue his life sentence. A good performance, too, by Rosanna Arquette as the killer's girl-friend. Dir: Lawrence Schiller. Screenplay: Norman Mailer; based on his book. BBC2, 12 March 1990.

Family Flight (1972). Familiar melodrama about a family forced by a plane crash to take stock of themselves. With Rod Taylor, Dina Merrill, Janet Margolin. Dir: Marvin Chomsky. Screenplay: Guerdon Trueblood. ITV, 5 June 1990.

The Final Frame (1989). Pop singer Graham 'Suggs' McPherson makes his acting debut with Nick Reding (his first 'star' role) in a routine thriller about a movie director in fear for his life after recording a murder on film and becoming the only witness to the crime. Dir: Paul Oremland. Screenplay: Howard Wakeling. Channel 4, 12 April 1990.

First Affair (1983). Stickily soapy feature about a young girl infatuated with a married man. With Loretta Swit, Melissa Sue Anderson. Dir: Gus Trikonis. No screenplay credit. ITV, 15 July 1989.

First and Last (1989). Sad, warm-hearted tale of a man in his sixties who decides to break out of his rut and walk (against all the odds) the length of Britain; and of the impact this has on his family and those he meets along the way. With Joss Ackland, Pat Heywood, Lionel Jeffries, Patricia Routledge. Dir: Alan Dossor. Screenplay: Michael Frayne. BBC1, 12 December 1989.

The Five of Me (1981). About a boy who develops five different personalities – one of them a psychotic – and if that sounds nutty, the makers of the movie assure us it is a true story. This develops into a moving drama about a man fighting his other selves. With David Birney, John McLiam, James Whitmore Jr. Dir: Paul Wendkos. Screenplay: L. B. Marcus; based on the book by Ted Schwarz and Henry Hawksworth. BBC2, 11 December 1989.

Frankenstein (1973). Don't let the title throw you. Though made the same year as another TV feature (*Frankenstein: The True Story*) there's no other relationship between the two. So-called 'King of TV Terror' director Dan Curtis produced this version of the old tale about the Bad Baron. With Robert Foxworth, Susan Strasberg, Bo Svenson (as the monster). Dir: Glenn Jordan. Screenplay: Sam Hall and Richard Landaur; based on the book by Mary Shelley. ITV, 9 January 1990.

Getting Physical (1984). Promising, pleasant Alexandra Paul as the unfit girl in a job rut who gets a kick and a new interest in life when she becomes interested in bodybuilding. The disco-music score may be a major asset to some viewers. Also with Sandahl Bergman, David Naughton. Dir: Steven H. Stern. Screenplay: Laurian Leggett. ITV, 8 July 1989.

The Ghost of Cyprus Swamp (1977). Historically interesting as the first-ever Disney venture into TV feature production: the adventures of a boy, a black panther and an old hermit in the beautifully photographed Florida swamplands. With Vic Morrow, Noah Beery, Jeff East (the boy). Dir: Vincent McEveety. Screenplay: Ken Price and Ronald Saunders. ITV, Part 1; 6 May 1990: Part 2; 13 May 1990.

The Hanged Man (1964). One of the first-ever features made specially for TV: a somewhat bloodless re-make of that splendid 1947 Robert Montgomery thriller *Ride the Pink Horse*. With Edmond O'Brien, Vera Miles, Robert Culp, Gene Raymond. Dir: Don Siegel. Screenplay: Jack Laird and Stanford Whitmore; based on the novel *Ride the Pink Horse* by Dorothy B. Hughes. ITV, 6 May 1990.

The Happy Valley (1987). A TV counterpart to the cinema's *White Mischief*, with Denholm Elliott (invariably worth the money on large or small screen) as the hopeless newcomer to Nairobi losing his new young wife (Amanda Hillwood) to the notorious womaniser Lord Erroll (Peter Sands). A 'true' story, set in Kenya in the 1940s. Dir: Ross Devenish. Screenplay: David Reid. BBC1, 13 July 1989.

Harry's Kingdom (1986). Brilliantly acted – by Timothy West – British, blackish comedy about the world of double-glazing! Also with Jill Baker, Larry Lamb. Dir: Robert Young. Screenplay: Ron Pearson. BBC1, 20 July 1989.

He's Asking for Me (1990). New BBC feature film: a cross between a thriller and a love story about a girl who falls for her lawyer boss and then begins to suspect this quiet man may be pestering her with dirty phone calls. Nice performances. With Maggie O'Neill, David Threlfall, Thorley Walters. Dir: Withold Starecki. Screenplay: Boleslaw Sulik. BBC2, 18 February 1990.

Home Run (1989). Throwing everything into his performance, Michael Kitchen is the East End boy made good who comes back to his much-changed Thames-side roots to find them driving him right off his trolley in this enigmatic psychological thriller. It's worth trying to work it out - if you've the patience, time and curiosity! Also with Corinne Decla, Anne Carroll, Keith Barron. Dir: Nicholas Renton. Screenplay: Andy Armitage. BBC1, 1 October 1989.

Hot Ice, Cold Hearts (1976). Pathologist Quincy (Jack Klugman) suspects that something larger than a killer fish was the cause of the death of a young Mexican, and sets out to prove his case.

Also with Robert Ito, Fernando Lamas, Robert Alda. Dir: Bruce Kessler. Screenplay: Lou Shaw and Sean Baine. ITV, 19 August 1989.

Humanoid Defender (1985). SF TV feature about an army-trained part-machine, part-human, who upsets the military apple cart when he refuses to accept the killing role allotted to him. With Terence Knox, Gary Gaspar, William Lucking, Gail Edwards. Dir: Ron Satlof. Screenplay: Nicholas Corea. BBC2, 15 December 1989.

I Dream of Jeannie: 15 Years Later (1985). Looking not a day older than when she made the original TV feature, Barbara Eden – as the wife of a former astronaut who decides to come out of retirement – just about saves this pallid drama. Also with Wayne Rogers. Dir: William Asher. Screenplay: Irma Kalish. Channel 4, 1 January 1990.

The Impossible Spy (1987). BBC's biopic about Eli Cohen (John Shea), an incredibly dedicated Israeli espionage agent who dared anything and everything to help his country during the Six Day War. An exciting addition to the truth-is-sometimes-stranger-than-fiction genre. Also with Eli Wallach. Dir: Jim Goddard. Screenplay: Marty Ross and Douglas Livingstone. BBC2, 11 February 1990.

An Innocent Woman (1986) In this French TV feature, four short stories are united by a fifth, about a young girl who imagines the various ways in which a dangerous situation might develop. With Catherine Wilkening, Jacques Dufilho. Dir: Pierre Boutron. Screenplay adapted by the director from stories by various authors. ITV, 11 December 1989.

The Karen Carpenter Story (1988). Another tragic showbiz biopic, this time the life story of singer Karen, whose brother helped her rise, and who was destroyed by overwork, worry and dope. With Cynthia Gibb, Mitchell Anderson. Dir: Joseph Sargent. Screenplay: Barry Morrow. ITV, 31 December 1989.

Kremlin Farewell (1990). Set in Russia, this drama of the Stalin era shows an orphanage boy learning the truth about the man behind the kindly

133

mask. With Freddie Jones, Kenneth Colley. Dir: Tristram Powell. Screenplay: Nigel Williams. BBC2, 1 April 1990.

Lacy and the Mississippi Queen (1978). No wonder that this dismal, uninspired pilot never led to a series. Two tough sisters travel the West seeking revenge on the killers of their dad. With Kathleen Lloyd, Debra Feuer, Jack Elam. Dir: Robert Butler. Screenplay: Kathy Donnell and Madeline Dimaggio-Wagner. ITV, 6 November 1989.

Ladykillers (1988). Bearing no relationship to the almost identically titled Ealing comedy, this is about a cute lady cop trying to work out who in the audience at a male strip show in a seedy night-club is the brutal killer. With Marilu Henner, Lesley-Anne Down, Thomas Calabro, Susan Blakely. Dir: Robert Lewis. No writing credit. BBC1, 25 May 1990.

The Last Five Minutes: Author's Disappointment (1986). Cops-and-killer stuff imported from France, centred on a murder case puzzle for the woman chief and her merry men of the 13th Paris precinct. With Jacques Debary, Caroline Sihol, Marc Eyraud. Dir: Roger Pigault. Screenplay: Alain Demouzon. ITV, 16 October 1989.

The Last Five Minutes: The Ballad of Menardeau (1986). From French TV, another case to be solved by Gallic cop Cabrol (Jacques Debary). Not much mystery but a fair ration of thrills. Dir: Maurice Fyiedland. Screenplay: François Debre. ITV, 30 October 1989.

The Last Five Minutes: Mystery of the Pine Cone (1986). A headless body found in the Landes in South-West France brings Inspector Cabrol (Jacques Debary) from Paris to investigate. One of a French TV series about crime investigation; and for our convenience they all speak English. Interesting settings. Also with Marc Eyraud, Francine Berge. Dir: Jean-Pierre Desagnat. Screenplay: Charles Maitre. ITV, 23 October 1989.

Lawman Without a Gun (1979). Minor anti-racist melodrama set in the deep South. With Louis Gosset, Clu

Gulager. Dir and Screenplay: Jerrold Freedman. BBC1, 3 November 1989.

The Legend of Walks Far Woman (1982). A TV film with a production history as interesting as the movie itself. Raquel Welch made her TV debut in this highly personal project about an American Indian woman who becomes mixed up with tribal wars, is ousted from her Blackfoot tribe, and wanders off across the plains until the Sioux pick her up. Made in 1979, it remained on the shelf until released – cut from 2½ to 2 hours – in 1982. Also with Bradford Dillman, Nick Mancuso. Dir: Mel Damski. Screenplay: Evan Hunter. BBC2, 13 January 1990.

A Long Way Home (1989). An emotion-charged little drama about the 'difficult' son of a single-parent journalist, and the au pair who gains his confidence and makes Ma jealous. With Kate Buffery, Melinda Kinnaman, Alexander Goodman. Dir: Colin Nutley. Screenplay: Michael Baker. ITV, 27 December 1989.

The Lorelei (1990). Yet another new BBC feature film, this acceptable thriller relates the horrifying experience of a lonely female teacher when she stays in a house ('The Lorelei') in remote North Wales. Neatly tailored spine-shiverer. With Amanda Redman, Michael Maloney, John Nettleton. Dir: Terry Johnson. Screenplay: Nick Dunning. BBC2, 18 March 1990.

McCloud: The Day New York Turned Blue (1976). The New Mexican marshal continues to find plenty of puzzles to solve in New York; this time it's the odd mystery of a prostitute who makes her clients literally blue. And he finds himself protecting a union member who knows more than is healthy about the Union-Mobster connection. With Dennis Weaver, Gig Young, Bernadette Peters. Dir: E. W. Swackhammer. Screenplay: Glen Larson. ITV, 3 June 1990.

McCloud: Fifth Man in a String Quartet (1972). Investigating the case of a music student accused of murdering his tutor, Mac (Dennis Weaver) finds the trail leading to gang killings, political ambitions and eventually the real killer. Also with Ric Weaver (Dennis's son),

Neville Brand, Jo Wiseman. Dir: Russ Mayberry. Screenplay: James Buchanan and Ronald Austin. ITV, 6 May 1990.

McCloud: Fire! (1976). This time, detective McCloud (Dennis Weaver) has to winkle out an arsonist who's guilty of murder. And the firelighter is played by Weaver's son, Robert. Hot stuff! Dir: Lou Antonio. Screenplay: Lou Shaw and Robert Hamilton. ITV, 8 October 1989.

McCloud: Give My Regrets to Broadway (1972). Another adventure for out-of-town Marshal McCloud (Dennis Weaver), fighting crime in the big city his own way. A deservedly popular cops-and-robbers series. Also with J. D. Cannon, Diana Muldaur. Dir: Lou Antonio. Screenplay: Peter Allen Fields. ITV, 4 February 1990.

McCloud: A Little Plot at Tranquil Valley (1971). McCloud has some nasty moments investigating a drug-running plot centred on a local cemetery. The well-handled story gives Burgess Meredith plenty of scene-stealing chances as the sly old villain. Also with Dennis Weaver, Vic Morrow, Joyce Van Patten. Dir: Jack Smight. Screenplay: Allan Fields. ITV, 1 April 1990.

McCloud: Our Man in the Harem (1975). A beauty queen goes missing and McCloud, called in to find her, picks up clues that lead to a Middle East villain and the off-limits territory of a harem. A pinch of salt needed here, but plenty of fun. With Dennis Weaver, Anne Archer, Michael Ansara. Dir: E. W. Swackhammer. Screenplay: Glen Larson and Lou Shaw. ITV, Part 1; 13 May 1990: Part 2; 20 May 1990.

McCloud: Park Avenue Pirates (1973). Leaving his tell-tale uniform in the drawer, the marshal in civilian guise sniffs out and brings the music business crooks to justice. Nice work by Dennis Weaver as the cop, with pleasant support from Jessica Walter, Lorna Luft and Barbi Benton. Dir: Bruce Kessler. Screenplay: R. P. Hillyard. ITV, 24 September 1989.

McCloud: Portrait of a Dead Girl (1970). Dennis Weaver as the Western marshal assigned to bring a very important witness (Shelly Novak) to a New York courtroom, but who ends up in handcuffs a long way from the city and his charge. The pilot feature that introduced the McCloud series. Also with Craig Stevens, Mark Richman. Dir: Richard A. Colla. Screenplay: Stanford Whitmore, Richard Levinson and William Link. ITV, 17 September 1989.

McCloud: Showdown at Times Square (1975). Out-of-town Marshal Mac is back in New York action, throwing in his badge after a row with his superior in order to carry on helping Chief Dan George locate his mysteriously missing grandson. Dir: Ron Satlof. Screenplay: Sidney Ellis and Lou Shaw. ITV, 1 October 1989.

McCloud: Somebody's Out to Get Jenny (1971). Clever juggling with three different stories makes this one of the better examples of this series about the out-of-town 'tec solving the big city's crimes. With Dennis Weaver, Julie Sommars, Barry Sullivan, Cameron Mitchell. Dir: Jack Smight. Screenplay: Robert Presnell Jr. ITV, 11 February 1990.

McCloud: Three Guns for New York (1976). Veteran baddie Neville Brand is the leader of a trio of ex-cons who face up to deceptively simple cop McC. and find he's tougher than they thought. Routine, but better than many of its kind. Dir: Bruce Kessler. Screenplay: Nicholas Baehr. ITV, 15 October 1989.

McCloud: Top of the World, Ma! (1972). On the trail of a medium-sized crook, Dennis (McCloud) Weaver finds himself led right into the big crime boss's lair! And how's this for a value-for-money cast: Joan Blondell, Bo Svenson, Stefanie Powers, J. D. Cannon, Robert Webber, Vincent Gardenia and Terry Carter. Dir: Alex March. Screenplay: Ray Danton. ITV, 22 April 1990.

Madame X (1980). Poser: with all the movie versions available of this old celluloid chestnut, why on earth did they make a TV version? Tuesday Weld plays the tear-jerking woman who kills her blackmailer and is then defended in court by her daughter, who is unaware of their relationship. Also with Eleanor Parker, Granville Van

Duzen. Dir: Robert E. Miller. Screenplay: Albert Anhalt. ITV, 13 May 1990.

The Man from the Pru (1990). A true-life 1931 murder story which brought a quiet little insurance man into the dock to face a 'guilty' verdict and has left a lot of questions unanswered to this day. Fascinating. With Jonathan Pryce, Anna Massey, Susannah York, Richard Pasco. Dir: Rob Rohrer. Screenplay: Robert Smith. BBC2, 21 January 1990.

The Man in the Brown Suit (1988). An Agatha Christie whodunnit – see how soon you can spot the killer/thief on board the cruise liner sailing in Middle Eastern waters. A star cast, all giving good performances, with top-flight direction of a good script make this TV movie an unusually good example of its kind. With Edward Woodward, Tony Randall, Stephanie Zimbalist. Dir: Alan Grint. Screenplay: Carla Jean Wagner; based on Agatha Christie's novel. ITV, 23 April 1990.

Man on a String (1971). Routine, familiar story of undercover cop *v.* the Mob. With Keith Carradine, Christopher George. Dir: Joseph Sargent. Screenplay: Ben Maddow. ITV, 3 April 1990.

The March (1990). Another in the series of BBC-financed TV feature films, this one is a major effort about a saint-like character who leads a march of some quarter-million starving Africans from their homes in the Sudan to Europe. Certainly it makes you think. With Juliet Stevenson, Malick Bowens, Mohamed Naime, Mohamed Bel Lafkih. Dir: David Wheatley. Screenplay: William Nicholson. BBC1, 20 May 1990.

Midnight Offering (1981). Silly – if not downright barmy – thriller about an American college girl who is prepared to murder a fellow student to get her own way and win the boy-friend she's set her black heart on. With Melissa Sue Anderson, Patrick Cassidy, Mary Beth McDonough. Dir: Rod Holcomb. Screenplay: Juanita Bartlett. ITV, 20 December 1989.

The Mountain and the Molehill (1988). Fascinating mystery about how

a school headmaster used D-Day secrets as clues in a *Daily Telegraph* crossword puzzle just prior to the D-Day landings. Based on fact. Splendid performance, notably by Michael Gough. Also with Michael Quill, Demetri Jagger, Jacob Krichefski. Dir: Moira Armstrong. Screenplay: David Reid. BBC1, 15 October 1989.

The Murder of Mary Phagan (1988). A polished, very well-achieved two-part TV feature about a famous American murder case of 1913, when a factory girl's body was found and her boss arraigned for her killing. The State Governor (played by Jack Lemmon) puts his career on the line when he decides to fight the court's 'guilty' verdict, and uncovers something very nasty in the process. Also with Peter Gallagher, Richard Jordan, Kathryn Walker. Dir: Billy Hale. Screenplay: Jeffrey Lane and George Stevens Jr. BBC1, 5 and 12 September 1989.

Murder in Coweta County (1983). Good old honest Johnny Cash is grimly determined that villainous big-shot Andy Griffith shall not get away with the murder of a local farmer. Based on the facts of a case that hit the headlines way back in 1948. Well produced and very watchable. Also with Cash's wife, June Carter Cash. Dir: Gary Nelson. No writing credit. BBC2, 30 April 1990.

Night of Terror (1972). Two pretty girls (Donna Mills and Catherine Burns) become targets for murder for a ruthless hit man (Chuck Connors) after inadvertently witnessing a killing at the entrance to their flat. Also with Martin Balsam, Agnes Moorehead and David Spielberg. Dir: Jeannot Szwarc. Screenplay: Cliff Gould. ITV, 3 July 1989.

The Night that Panicked America (1975). An account, with fictional trimmings, of the famous occasion in 1938 when Orson Welles used the radio to such good effect that listeners really believed him when he claimed creatures from Mars had invaded the United States. A commendable effort. With Paul Sheenan (Welles), Vic Morrow, Will Geer. Dir: Joseph Sargent. Screenplay: Nicholas Meyer and Anthony Wilson. ITV, 25 November 1989.

1996 (1989). Six years hence, with increasing violence on and off the streets, cop Commander Keith Barron is sent to Wales to investigate shootings there and finds they tie in with another case, of violence at a nurses' left-wing demonstration. Behind both is a web of corruption in the highest places. Also with Tom Marshall, Alun Armstrong, Gillian Eaton, Dudley Sutton. Dir: Karl Francis. Screenplay: G. F. Newman. BBC1, 17 September 1989.

Not My Kid (1985). A well-off professional family discovers, literally by accident, that their daughter is a drug addict. With George Segal, Stockard Channing, Viveka Davis. Dir: Michael Tuchner. No screenplay credit. BBC2, 2 April 1990.

Number 27 (1988). Delightful Michael Palin contribution; sweet and sentimental story about a dear old lady in her nineties fighting off a property developer who has fixed his beady eye on the house she has loved and lived in all her life. With Joyce Carey, Nigel Planer, Michael Percival, Robin Bailey. Dir: Tristram Powell. Screenplay: Michael Palin. BBC1, 3 August 1989.

One Hour to Doomsday (1970). Made-for-TV movie which was released in the UK as a cinema film in 1972 and fully reviewed in the 1971–2 *Film Review*.

One Way Out (1989). A successful architect finds out painfully that divorce doesn't always end the story. A wry look at modern relationships. With Bob Peck, Denis Lawson, Samantha Bond. Dir: Robert Young. Screenplay: Mick Ford. BBC1, 10 September 1989.

Outrage (1986). Meaty, old-fashioned courtroom drama about a man who kills his daughter's murderer when through a legal technicality the man walks free. Will dad now have to suffer the ultimate penalty? With a very fine cast: Robert Preston (his final film), Burgess Meredith, Beau Bridges, Anthony Newley, Mel Ferrer. Dir: Irwin Allen. Screenplay: Henry Denker. BBC2, 4 December 1989.

Overdrawn at the Memory Bank (1983). A modestly entertaining film about a computer nut of the future who gains access to a forbidden vintage film library. When he becomes obsessed with *Casablanca*, he gets sent to a mental asylum. With Raul Julia, Linda Griffiths. Dir: Douglas Williams. Screenplay: Corrine Jacker. Channel 4, 2 June 1990.

Perry Mason: The Case of the Lost Love (1987). Even though it could interfere with his forthcoming rise to a seat in the Senate, Raymond (Perry) Burr is persuaded by Jean Simmons – an old flame of 30 years ago – to take up the defence of her hubbie Gene Barry, who is accused of murder. The fourth of the feature follow-ups to the very popular old series. Also with Barbara Hale, Paul Drake Jr. Dir: Ron Satloff. No screenplay credit. BBC1, 12 May 1990.

Perry Mason: The Case of the Murdered Madame (1987). That always absorbing crime investigator Perry (played with his usual polished professionalism by Raymond Burr) looks, with the help of delightful assistant Barbara Hale, into the case of a murdered ex-'Madame'. Dir: Ron Satloff. Screenplay: Patricia Green. BBC1, 7 April 1990.

Perry Mason: The Case of the Notorious Nun (1986). Good old Perry takes on the defence of a young nun (Michelle Greene) who is accused of murdering a priest (Timothy Bottoms) with whom some nasty types have suggested she had had an affair. Helping out as usual, faithful secretary Della Street (Barbara Hale) and leg-man Paul Drake Jr (William Katt). Dir: Ron Satloff. Screenplay: Joel Steiger. BBC1, 21 April 1990.

Perry Mason: The Case of the Scandalous Scoundrel (1987). Mason takes up the case of reporter Miss Benti (Susan Wilder) when she is accused of murdering the publisher of a sensational scandal magazine. And, as ever, Raymond (Perry) Burr is helped by his pretty assistant Barbara Hale. Dir: Christian Nyby II. No screenplay credit. BBC1, 14 April 1990.

Perry Mason: The Case of the Shooting Star (1986). Perry comes to the aid of a film star accused of the murder of one of America's well-known 'chat-show' hosts. Stalwarts Barbara Hale and William Katt help Perry (Raymond Burr) get the right verdict. Grand stuff for Mason's myriad fans. Dir: Ron Satloff. Screenplay: Joe Steiger. BBC1, 28 April 1990.

Perry Mason: The Case of the Sinister Spirit (1987). This Perry – Raymond Burr – feature sees him accepting the defence of a publisher accused of tossing a writer to his death! Daft, but as wholly delightful as ever. Also with Barbara Hale, Robert Stack, William Katt. Dir: Richard Lang. No screenplay credit. BBC1, 19 May 1990.

Pied Piper (1989). Peter O'Toole at his considerable best lights up this new adaptation of the Nevil Shute novel (you may recall the 1942 film with Monty Woolley) and makes it first-class viewing. Also with Mare Winningham. Dir: Norman Stone. Screenplay: Jerome Kass. ITV, 24 December 1989.

Prescription: Murder (1968). The original Columbo feature which sparked off the subsequent series. (According to the *TV Times*, Peter Falk only got the role after Bing Crosby had turned it down!) Also with Gene Barry, Katherine Justice, Nina Foch. Dir: Don Featherstone. Screenplay: Richard Levinson and William Link; based on their stage play. ITV, 24 June 1990.

Queen of the Stardust Ballroom (1975). Remember that minor classic *Marty*? This is much the same story: Maureen Stapleton is a middle-aged New York widow finding romance and a new interest in life in the dance hall of the title. Romantic and charming: altogether a delightful TV feature movie. Also with Charles Durning, Michael Brandon, Elizabeth Berger, Lewis Charles. Dir: Sam O'Steen. Screenplay: Jerome Cass. BBC1, 5 September 1989.

Red King, White Knight (1989). Strongly cast international thriller with Tom Skerritt as the disillusioned ex-CIA agent unwillingly called back to tackle a plot to disrupt the Russian-American entente. All very watchable. Also with Max von Sydow, Tom Bell, Helen Mirren. Dir: Geoff Murphy. Screenplay: Ron Hutchinson. ITV, 14 October 1989.

Remember Me That Way (1988). A rarity: a Russian TV film. A family piece covering three generations, based on a play by Sointsev with the title *Mother and Son*. Odd man out in a season of cinema films from the USSR staged by Channel 4. With A. Stepanova, O. Borisov. Dir: P. Chukrai. Screenplay: M. Zvarava. Channel 4, 19 January 1990.

The Richest Cat in the World (1986). The Disney studios on top form in a story about a talking feline who inherits $5 million, and the greedy humans prepared to do anything to get their hands on the money. Real entertainment. Dir: Gregg Beeman. Screenplay: Marshall Efron and Alfa-Betty Olsen. ITV, 30 December 1989.

Robinsoe Crusoe (1988). A French adaptation of Michel Tournier's novel which introduces a new and satirical tone into Defoe's original and classic story. With Michael York, Gene Anthony Ray, Roger Blin, Robert Rimbaud. Dir: Gerard Vergez. Screenplay: Vergez, Anthony Brine and Salim Jay. ITV, 15 July 1989.

Run, Simon, Run (1970). Filmed in Tucson, Arizona, this story, about an Indian determined to bring his mother's murderer to justice, combines suspense with a look at racial injustice. With Burt Reynolds, Inger Stevens, Royal Dano. Dir: George McGowan. Screenplay: L. E. Siegel. ITV, 18 September 1989.

Runaway (1973). Made-for-American-TV feature, released as a cinema film in the UK in June 1985 with the title *Runaway Train*, and reviewed as such in the 1986–7 *Film Review*.

Secret Witness (1987). Nicely crafted, taut little thriller about a couple of 12-year-olds whose peeping-tom activities lead them into a murder case. With Leaf Phoenix, Kellie Martin. Dir: Eric Leneuville. Screenplay: Alfred Sole and Paul Monette. ITV, 8 January 1990.

Shadow of Fear (1979). Weird excursion by, surprisingly, the Disney studios: about a lad who finds he has the power to enter the bodies of animals. With Ike Eisenmann, John Anderson, Lisa Whelchel. Dir: Noel Nosseck. No

Geraldine James and Peggy Ashcroft in Peter Hall's award-winning She's Been Away, *produced by the BBC for theatrical distribution.*

screenplay credit. ITV, Part 1; 3 June 1990: Part 2; 10 June 1990.

S.H.E. (1980). Nutty fun film in which a female secret agent (the script is by the Bond scenarist) defeats a world-wide sabotage plan; and when she's not knitting she can wield a pretty lethal handbag. First-class escapist stuff. With Cornelia Sharpe, Omar Sharif, Anita Ekberg. Dir: Robert Lewis. Screenplay: Richard Maibaum. ITV, 23 June 1990.

The Shell Seekers (1989). It's nice to see Angela Lansbury in something other than her TV writer/detective role. Here she plays, beautifully, a woman who discovers not only the considerable value of her father's painting but also what a horrid lot some of her children are. Also with Anna Carteret, Patricia Hodge, Sam Wanamaker and plenty of good performers. Dir: Waris Hussein. Screenplay: John Pielmeier; based on the Rosamunde Pilcher novel. ITV, 21 December 1989.

She's Been Away (1989). Made primarily for TV, but premiered as a feature film in the cinema (Riverside Studio Cinema) on 22 September 1989,

with TV premiere following (BBC1) on 8 October. Full details in 'Releases of the Year'.

She's Dressed to Kill (1989). Old-fashioned whodunnit with a one-time queen of fashion planning to make a comeback with a big re-launch party. But then the murders start to spoil the fun. With Eleanor Parker, Jessica Walter, Clive Revill, Corinne Calvet. Dir: Gus Trikonis. No screenplay credit. BBC1, 25 November 1989.

Shogun – The Movie (1980). The leisurely 10-hour series has been squashed into a more acceptable, if roughly edited, feature-length movie about the sixteenth-century white samurai warrior's adventures in the Japan of the warlords. Nice to look at, but still wearisome. With Richard Chamberlain, Alan Badel, Toshiro Mifune, Yoko Shimada. Dir: Jerry London. Screenplay: Eric Bercovici. ITV, 15 October 1989.

Shooting Stars (1990). Chris Bernard's first feature since *Letter to Brezhnev* in 1985, this story about three young thugs holding a football star to ransom was made wholly on location in Manchester and captured lots of local atmosphere. A true-Brit TV movie. With Helmut Griem, Sharon Duce, Gary McDonald. Screenplay: Barry

Hines; from a story by Dixie Williams. Channel 4, 17 May 1990.

The Silent Gun (1969). A good old-fashioned Western: ex-gunfighter Lloyd Bridges discovers how hard peacekeeping is when he finds himself in the middle of a struggle between bad boss and angry settler. The settler is played superbly by veteran Westerner Ed Begley, and the villain by 'Bonanza's' good-boy son Pernell Roberts. Lovely stuff. Dir: Michael Caffey. Screenplay: Clyde Ware. ITV, 20 November 1989.

Small Zones (1990). Another new BBC feature TV film, again set far away from the soft south: this one has a grim background of unemployment in Hull – though it has Russian poetical attachments! With Catherine Neilson, Suzanna Hamilton, Sean Bean. Dir: Michael Whyte. Screenplay: Jim Hawkins. BBC2, 4 March 1990.

Smile, Jenny, You're Dead (1974). This well-made and successful feature was the second pilot to showcase the private eye series 'Harry O', with David Janssen as the sleuth, in this case trying to prevent the murder of his model client (Andrea Marcovicci). A stylish and very entertaining package. Also with Jodie Foster, Howard da Silva, Clu Gulager. Dir: Jerry Thorpe. Screenplay: Howard Rodman. ITV, 5 August 1989.

Something in Common (1986). Nicely acted romantic comedy, often genuinely funny and sometimes moving, about a mother's trauma when her young son (Patrick Cassidy) falls in love with a middle-aged woman. Also with Ellen Burstyn, Tuesday Weld, Eli Wallach, Don Murray. Dir: Terry Bedford. Screenplay: Trevor Preston. BBC2, 16 October 1989.

Sometime in August (1990). Yet another BBC-made TV feature film: this time a sensitive and kindly story about a spotty, unhappy youngster. Refusing to bathe (for fear of revealing his painful secret) seems likely to spoil his holiday – until a wise old lady steps in to solve his problem. A delicately balanced film rests fully on the shoulders of talented, debuting young Craig Lorimer and veteran Mary

Morris. Dir: John Glenister. Screenplay: Bernard MacLaverty. BBC2, 25 February 1990.

Spenser: For Hire (1965). Feature introduction to a new BBC series about a tough Boston private eye (Robert Urich) who finds locating a missing wife a bit more difficult and dangerous than he had bargained for. Familiar stuff, but professionally done. Also with Susan Silverman, Chuck Connors, Avery Brooks. Dir: Lee H. Katzin. Screenplay: John Wilder; based on the novel *Promised Land* by R. B. Parker. BBC1, 8 September 1989.

Spiderman (1977). Kids comic-strip stuff about a scientist who is bitten by a spider and subsequently finds he can spin a web and walk up walls! With Nicholas Hammond, Lisa Eilbacher. Dir: E. W. Swackhammer. Screenplay: Alvin Boretz. BBC2, 26 October 1989.

Spiderman: The Dragon's Challenge (1980). Another in the American 'Spiderman' series, puffed out to boring feature length. With Nicholas Hammond, Robert F. Simon. Dir: Don McDougal. Screenplay: Lionel E. Siegel. BBC2, 9 November 1989.

Spiderman Strikes Back (1978). More yarn (and web) spinning from the useful hero who can climb up walls as he weaves a trap for a nasty arms dealer. With Nicholas Hammond, Joanna Cameron. Dir: Ron Satloff. Screenplay: Robert Janes. BBC2, 2 November 1989.

Spot Marks the X (1986). Scene stealer 'Mike' winning more fans in this Disney TV feature about a gangster's canny canine who is more than reformed after being adopted by some youngsters as their pet pooch. Enjoyable fare for the family. Dir: Mark Rosman. Screenplay: Michael Jenning. ITV, 28 October 1989.

The Stain (1985). Russian TV feature film (hitherto unseen in the UK) by a very promising young Georgian director, who here appears to owe quite a bit to those fine Hollywood crime films of the late 1940s and early 1950s. The message is clear . . . Watch Your Step; it's all too easy to walk into criminal involvement. Highly watchable. Dir

and screenplay: Aleko Tsabadze. Channel 4, 1 February 1990.

Star Trap (1989). No, not SF, just a somewhat puzzling mixed-mood piece – comedy, thriller, magic, murder and black-hued farce – set in the calm Cotswolds country, and with everyone acting their heads off. Fun in a way . . . With Nicky Henson, Frances Tomelty, Jeananne Crowley. Dir and screenplay: Tony Bicat. ITV, 8 July 1989.

Starlings (1988). Prizewinning (the Golden Nymph at Monte Carlo) feature about a shrewd operator (Michael Maloney) who loses his job, but turns to butlering and becomes a big City success. The script takes a shrewd view of the great North-South British divide. Top viewing. Also with Lynsey Baxter (Best Actress award winner). Dir: David Wheatley. Screenplay: Andy Armitage. BBC2, 7 August 1989.

Stillwatch (1987). Ex-'Wonder Woman' Lynda Carter, as an investigative TV journalist, finds a lot of good material – including a murder and danger – when she starts looking into the life of senator Angie Dickinson. A top-drawer treatment of familiar 'tec stuff. Also with Don Murray, Stuart Whitman. Dir: Rod Holcomb. Screenplay: David Peckinpah and Laird Koenig. BBC1, 4 September 1989.

Stone Fox (1987). The story of a boy and his dog trying to win a sledge race and so save the lad's granddad from the broker's men. With all the snow, it's a movie to be enjoyed in front of a roaring fire. Simple, but pleasant. With Buddy Ebsen, Joey Cramer. Dir: Harvey Hart. Screenplay: Walter H. Davis. Channel 4, 29 December 1989.

A Streetcar Named Desire (1984). First-class re-make of the memorable 1951 cinema film with Ann-Margret and Treat Williams doing a good job of the parts originally played by Vivien Leigh and Marlon Brando. And this TV adaptation of Tennessee Williams's play is nearer to the original than was the Brando/Leigh version. Stirring stuff, written when the playwright was at his best. Dir: John Erman. Screenplay: Tennessee Williams. BBC1, 15 December 1989.

Love in the eye of the beholder: fantasy and lust collide in the drab setting of Warsaw in Kieslowski's hypnotic A Short Film About Love – Krotki Film o Miloski *(Gala), with Grazyna Szapolowska and Olaf Lubaszenko.*

The Taking of Flight 847 (1987). A reconstruction of the 17-day hijacking by Arab extremists of a TWA airliner in June 1985. The mounting tension is extremely well done. With Lindsay Wagner, Eli Danker, Sandy McPeak. Dir: Paul Wendkos. Screenplay: Norman Merrill. ITV, 21 April 1990.

The Ten Commandments (1988–9). A remarkable achievement by Polish director Krzysztof Kieslowski in making ten films, each based on one of the Biblical Commandments, two of which (*A Short Film About Killing* and *A Short Film About Love*) were released in Britain as cinema movies, and are reviewed in the 'Releases of the Year' section. Some of the films are straightforward and brilliant (such as the *Killing* film); others are dark, slow and mysterious; but all are powerful and memorable. Fuller details will appear in next year's *Film Review*. BBC2, May, June and July 1990.

The Terry Fox Story (1983). Made-for-cable-TV feature which in Britain was shown as a cinema general release in June 1984 and fully reviewed in the 1984–5 *Film Review*. BBC1, 12 April 1990 (previously shown on BBC1, 5 July 1988).

Thursday's Game (1974). Wittily scripted satirical fun about male pals, with a good cast in top form. Altogether superior viewing. With Gene Wilder, Bob Newhart, Ellen Burstyn, Cloris Leachman. Dir: Robert Moore. No screenplay credit. BBC1, 10 May 1990.

Timestalkers (1987). An odd mix of SF and Western in a story about a weird scientist (William Devane) and his woman companion (Lauren Hutton) who project themselves back to the American old West so they can re-shape past and future history. Historically interesting in that it was apparently Klaus Kinski's first, and Forrest Tucker's last, TV feature. Dir: Michael Schultz. Screenplay: Brian Clemens; based on a novel (unpublished as yet) by Ray Brown entitled *The Tintype*. BBC1, 25 June 1990.

Trouble Comes to Town (1972). Carefully balanced social drama about the

liberal (white) sheriff of a small Southern community who comes up against racial prejudice when he brings home the delinquent son of his black best buddy. Lloyd Bridges gives a fine performance as the sheriff. Also with Pat Hingle, Sheree North, Janet McLachlan. Dir: Daniel Petri. Screenplay: David Westheimer. ITV, 16 September 1989.

An Uncommon Love (1983). Another – and not so hot – variation on the oft-used story about a teacher who falls for one of his pupils, and then finds out she's no angel! With Barry Bostwick, Kathryn Harrold, Ed Begley Jr. Dir: Steven Stern. Screenplay: Seth Freeman. ITV, 28 November 1989.

Under Siege (1986). Fast-paced, fairly unbelievable but still well-made story of terrorists causing havoc when they invade the USA. With Peter Strauss, Hal Holbrook, E. G. Marshall, Lew Ayres. Dir: Roger Young. Screenplay: Bob Woodward, Christian Williams, Richard Harwood and Alfred Sole. ITV, 12 May 1990.

A Very Brady Christmas (1988). Routine TV-series stuff about the Brady

FILM REVIEW 1990–1

family. Mum and Dad's plans for a Yuletide family reunion are thwarted by their six children. With Robert Reed, Florence Henderson. Dir: Peter Baldwin. Screenplay: Sherwood and Lloyd Schwartz. ITV, 27 December 1989.

Vroom (1989). Set in a cold and cheerless small town in the North of England, this is the story of a couple of mates and the attractive woman who moves into the house next door, livening up their lives. With Diana Quick, Clive Owen, David Thewlis. Dir: Beeban Kidron. Screenplay: Jim Cartright. Channel 4, 22 March 1990.

When We First Met (1984). Adaptation of Norma Fox Mazer's novel about a couple of ill-starred young lovers from two families engaged in a bitter feud. With Amy Linker, Andrew Sabiston. Dir: Paul Saltzman. Screenplay: Norma Fox Mazer. ITV, 19 March 1990.

Why Me? (1984). Fascinating story of courage as a dedicated surgeon reconstructs the face of a nurse horribly injured in a car smash. The gory operation sequence is hard to stomach. With Glynnis O'Connor, Armand Assante. Dir: Fielder Cook. Screenplay: Dalene Young; based on the book

by Leola May Harmon. ITV, 24 December 1989.

Wild Flowers (1989). Another superior new TV feature film with the splendid bonus of some magnificently photographed scenic background in West Scotland for the simple and romantic story. With Colette O'Neil, Beatie Edney, Stevan Rimkus. Dir: Robert Smith. Screenplay: Sharman MacDonald. Channel 4, 15 March 1990.

The Wild, Wild West Revisited (1979). A spin-off feature from the early and popular 1965–9 series; with the goodies (ex-agents Robert Conrad and Ross Martin) pulled out of retirement to smash the baddies' plot to kill off European and Russian leaders. Some nice, quiet humour. Also with Paul Williams. Dir: Burt Kennedy. No screenplay credit. BBC2, 10 May 1990.

Wolf (1989). Old-hat stuff about a discredited cop (Jack Scalia) getting a belated chance to clear his name. Also with Mimi Kuzyk. Dir: Rod Holcomb. Screenplay: David Peckinpah. ITV, 13 April 1990.

The Woman in Black (1989). Nigel Kneale, who wrote *Halloween 3*, also wrote this story about a rash lawyer who boldly enters a dark old house and

finds a ghost waiting for him. Many of the film's 120 minutes are tailored for chills and thrills. With Adrian Rawlings, Bernard Hepton. Dir: Herbert Wise. Screenplay: Nigel Kneale; based on the book by Susan Hill. ITV, 24 December 1989.

Women of Valour (1986). A group of dedicated nurses, caught by the Japanese advance in the Philippines in World War II, refuse to leave their patients in the jungle hospital. With Susan Sarandon, Kristy McNichol. Dir: Buzz Kulik. Screenplay: Jonas McCord. ITV, 13 October 1989.

Yesterday's Child (1977). Routine but well-organised story about a woman who finds claiming her inheritance is a dangerous business. With Shirley Jones, Geraldine Fitzgerald, Stephanie Zimbalist, Patrick Wayne. Dir: Corey Allen. Screenplay: Michael Gleason; based on the Doris Miles Disney novel. ITV, 22 December 1989.

The Zany Adventures of Robin Hood (1984). Simple, mildly amusing take-off of the outlaws of Sherwood Forest, with all the excellent performers entering into the spirit of the fun. With George Segal, Janet Suzman, Roy Kinnear. Dir: Ray Austin. No screenplay credit. BBC2, 10 April 1990.

The following is a list of TV feature films shown during the year which have been previously televised and have been duly noted in past editions of *Film Review*. For the record, they are listed here with date of repeat showing, together with date(s) of previous showing and the edition of *Film Review* in which they were described more fully. C4 is Channel 4; *FR* is *Film Review*.

Agatha Christie: Murder in Three Acts (US: *3 Act Tragedy*) (1987). ITV 14 May 1990 (ITV 17 May 1987 – 1987–8 *FR*).
Attack on Fear (1984). BBC2 5 March 1990 (BBC2 20 June 1988 – 1988–9 *FR*).
Badge of the Assassin (1985). ITV 14 April 1990 (ITV 11 April 1988 – 1988–9 *FR*).
Between Friends (1983). BBC1 31 May 1990 (BBC2 16 May 1988 – 1988–9 *FR*).
Bogie (1980). BBC1 17 Oct 1989 (BBC1 2 Dec 1987 – 1988–9 *FR*).
Born Beautiful (1982). C4 20 June 1990 (C4 12 Nov 1985 – 1967–8 *FR*).
Brotherly Love (1985). BBC1 23 Aug 1989 – 1989–90 *FR*).
Burning Patience (1983). C4 14 Dec 1989 (C4 2 July 1987 – 1988–9 *FR*).

Burning Rage (1984). ITV 24 Dec 1989 (ITV 27 Nov 1986 – 1987–8 *FR*).
Cannon (1971). BBC1 4 Nov 1989 (BBC1 5 Mar 1988 – 1988–9 *FR*).
Classified Love (1986). BBC1 28 June 1990 (BBC2 8 Aug 1988 – 1989–90 *FR*).
Conquest of the Earth (1980). ITV 18 Dec 1989 (ITV 7 May 1984 – 1984–5 *FR*).
Cowboy (1983). BBC1 16 Jan 1990 (BBC2 3 Mar 1987 – 1987–8 *FR*).
A Cry in the Wilderness (1974). ITV 15 May 1990 (C4 4 Jan 1985 – 1985–6 *FR*).
Dangerous Company (1982). BBC1 14 Dec 1989 (BBC2 21 Aug 1985 – 1986–7 *FR*).
Dead Lucky (1988). BBC2 11 Sept 1989 (BBC2 17 Jan 1988 – 1988–9 *FR*).
Deadly Lessons (1983). BBC1 6 Jan 1989 (BBC1 9 July 1988 – 1989–90 *FR*).
A Death of Innocence (1971). ITV 19 May 1990 (ITV 24 Feb 1988 – 1989–90 *FR*).
Death Penalty (1980). ITV 26 May 1990 (ITV 9 Nov 1985 – 1986–7 *FR*).
The Dirty Dozen: The Deadly Mission (1987). ITV 3 Dec 1989 (ITV 25 Sept 1988 – 1989–90 *FR*).

140

The Dirty Dozen: The Next Mission (1985). BBC1 20 Apr 1990 (BBC1 29 Aug 1986 and 23 Dec 1988 – 1987–8 *FR*).

Enola Gay (1980). C4 10 Oct 1989 (C4 6 Aug 1985 – 1986–7 *FR*).

The Family Rico (1972). ITV 31 Jan 1990 (BBC1 1 Nov 1983 and ITV 26 Sept 1988 – 1984–5 *FR*).

Flight of the Cougar (1976). BBC2 15 Sept 1989 (BBC2 23 Jan 1987 – 1987–8 *FR*).

Found Money (1983). BBC2 1 Feb 1990 (BBC1 26 Mar 1988 – 1988–9 *FR*).

A Good Sport (1984). BBC1 9 Jan 1990 (BBC2 25 July 1988 – 1988–9 *FR*).

Guilty Conscience (1985). BBC1 20 Mar 1990 (BBC1 13 May 1987 – 1987–8 *FR*).

Happy Endings (1983). BBC1 23 Jan 1990 (BBC2 7 Apr 1987 – 1987–8 *FR*).

The House on Greenapple Road (1970). ITV 29 Apr 1990 (BBC1 9 May 1983 and 8 Mar 1986 – 1983–4 *FR*).

How Awful About Allan (1970). ITV 25 July 1989 (ITV 24 Mar 1987 – 1987–8 *FR*).

I Want to Live (1983). BBC2 9 Apr 1990 (BBC2 23 May 1988 – 1988–9 *FR*).

Invitation to Hell (1984). BBC1 24 Nov 1989 (BBC1 20 Oct 1986 – 1987–8 *FR*).

Isabel's Choice (1981). BBC1 1 Feb 1990 (BBC1 26 Mar 1988 – 1988–9 *FR*).

Jealousy (1984). BBC1 14 June 1990 (BBC1 17 Nov 1986 and BBC2 27 Feb 1989 – 1987–8 *FR*).

Kenny Rogers as the Gambler (1980). BBC2 30 Oct 1989 (BBC1 4 Nov 1987 – 1988–9 *FR*).

Knight Rider (1982). ITV 2 Jan 1990 (ITV 1 Apr 1988 – 1988–9 *FR*).

Linda (1973). ITV 18 June 1990 (ITV 30 Oct 1986 and 28 Nov 1988 – 1987–8 *FR*).

A Little Game (1971). ITV 10 Apr 1990 (ITV 17 Feb 1987 – 1987–8 *FR*).

The Little Match Girl (1987). C4 29 Dec 1989 (C4 24 Dec 1988 – 1989–90 *FR*).

The Lost Flight (1969). ITV 9 July 1989 (ITV 7 Sept 1986 – 1987–8 *FR*).

Mae West (1982). BBC1 28 July 1989 (BBC1 12 Nov 1986 – 1987–8 *FR*).

The Miracle of Kathy Miller (1981). C4 8 Dec 1989 (C4 21 Apr 1987 – 1987–8 *FR*).

Miss All-American Beauty (1982). BBC1 3 Apr 1990 (BBC1 17 Feb 1988 – 1988–9 *FR*).

Mongo's Back in Town (1971). BBC1 3 Mar 1990 (BBC1 14 Aug 1987 – 1988–9 *FR*).

Murder Is Easy (1981). BBC1 22 Dec 1989 (ITV 24 Dec 1983 and BBC1 1 Oct 1988 – 1984–5 *FR*).

My Wicked, Wicked Ways: The Legend of Errol Flynn (1984). ITV 14 Oct 1989 (ITV 29 Dec 1987 – 1988–9 *FR*).

Night Slaves (1970). ITV 13 June 1990 (ITV 13 May 1988 – 1988–9 *FR*).

Nobody's Child (1986). BBC1 6 Feb 1990 (BBC2 23 June 1987 – 1987–8 *FR*).

Packin' It In (1983). BBC2 3 Oct 1989 (BBC1 30 Mar 1988 – 1988–9 *FR*).

Peace Is Our Profession (1972). BBC1 2 June 1990 (BBC2 29 Dec 1987 – 1988–9 *FR*).

Perry Mason Returns (1985). BBC1 31 Mar 1990 (BBC1 17 Apr 1987 – 1987–8 *FR*).

The Possessed (1977). ITV 8 May 1990 (BBC 24 Mar 1984 – 1984–5 *FR*).

The President's Plane Is Missing (1971). BBC2 5 Oct 1989 (BBC1 14 Oct 1987 – 1988–9 *FR*).

Prototype (1983). BBC2 23 Jan 1990 (BBC1 14 July 1985 – 1986–7 *FR*).

Pursuit (1972). BBC1 15 Sept 1989 (BBC1 27 Oct 1987 – 1988–9 *FR*).

Rainbow (1978). C4 22 Dec 1989 (C4 9 July 1985 – 1986–7 *FR*).

Red Alert (1987). ITV 23 Dec 1989 (BBC 9 June 1984 – 1984–5 *FR*).

Return of the Man from UNCLE (1983). ITV 5 May 1990 (ITV 21 April 1984 – 1984–5 *FR*).

The Revolt of Job (1983). C4 14 Mar 1990 (C4 26 Apr 1986 – 1987–8 *FR*).

Right to Kill (1985). BBC2 19 Feb 1990 (BBC2 26 May 1987 – 1987–8 *FR*).

Rita Hayworth: Love Goddess (1983). ITV 11 Nov 1989 (ITV 10 Feb 1988 – 1988–9 *FR*).

Salem's Lot (1979). ITV 12 Jan 1990 (BBC 24 and 26 Aug 1983 and ITV 18 Aug 1988 – 1984–5 *FR*).

Scorned and Swindled (1984). ITV 3 June 1990 (ITV 27 Jan 1986 – 1986–7 *FR*).

Seduced (1985). ITV 3 Oct 1989 (ITV 4 Jan 1987 – 1987–8 *FR*).

A Short Walk to Daylight (1972). ITV 25 Oct 1989 (BBC 15 Sept 1983 and ITV 25 Oct 1988 – 1984–5 *FR*).

The Sign of Four (1983). ITV 5 Jan 1990 (ITV 24 Dec 1988 – 1989–90 *FR*).

Sins of the Past (1984). BBC1 9 Feb 1990 (BBC1 12 July 1988 – 1989–90 *FR*).

The Snowman (1982). C4 24 Dec 1989 (C4 24 Dec 1985, 25 Dec 1987 and 25 Dec 1988 – 1986–7 *FR*).

The Spy Killer (1969). ITV 20 Nov 1989 (ITV 7 Nov 1987 – 1988–9 *FR*).

The Stranger Within (1984). BBC1 1 June 1990 (BBC1 10 Oct 1987 – 1988–9 *FR*).

Street Killing (1976). ITV 14 Apr 1990 (ITV 12 Dec 1988 – 1989–90 *FR*).

Success Is the Best Revenge (1984). C4 31 Aug 1989 (C4 26 June 1986 – 1986–7 *FR*).

The Summer of My German Soldier (1978). BBC1 23 Nov 1989 (BBC 16 Apr 1984 and ITV 16 Dec 1987 – 1984–5 *FR*).

The Temptation of Eileen Hughes (1988). BBC2 4 Sept 1989 (BBC2 2 Apr 1988 – 1988–9 *FR*).

Terrible Joe Moran (1984). C4 15 Dec 1989 (BBC2 7 May 1985 – 1985–6 *FR*).

Thirteen at Dinner (1985). ITV 30 Apr 1990 (ITV 8 June 1986 and 16 Dec 1987 – 1986–7 *FR*).

Through Naked Eyes (1983). BBC1 16 Mar 1990 (BBC1 26 July 1988 – 1989–90 *FR*).

Two of a Kind (1982). BBC1 24 Aug 1989 (BBC2 10 Mar 1987 – 1987–8 *FR*).

The Victim (1972). ITV 30 Oct 1989 (ITV 20 Nov 1986 – 1987–8 *FR*).

When Dreams Come True (1985). ITV 27 Dec 1989 (ITV 9 Nov 1988 – 1989–90 *FR*).

Will You Love Me Tomorrow (1987). BBC2 21 Aug 1989 (BBC2 18 Jan 1987 – 1987–8 *FR*).

Winner Take All (1975). BBC2 26 Aug 1989 (BBC1 3 Feb 1988 – 1988–9 *FR*).

Video Releases

ANTHONY HAYWARD

Britain led the way as Western Europe's video industry took more money than the cinemas during 1989. The public spent almost $4000 million on videos, 40 per cent more than cinema box-office takings, according to a survey conducted by the industry newsletter *Screen Digest*. British video dealers took an estimated £820 million, while Germany was second and Spain third in the European market.

The same survey highlighted the remarkable growth in Britain of 'sell-through' videos – budget-price tapes sold to the public rather than rented – and the important role played in this by chain stores such as Woolworth and W. H. Smith. 'Nowhere else in Europe is that possible,' the survey reported, 'and one leading video distributor reckons that if Spain had an equivalent to Woolworth, the video market there would leap 300 per cent.' The Norwegians, however, spent more on tapes per video-owning household than any other country in Western Europe, estimated at $162.76 each year. The French spent the least, at $32.77 per household, but high VAT was blamed for the slow growth of video there.

Feature films figured prominently in the 1989 'sell-through' and rental charts. *Dirty Dancing* was the biggest-selling budget-price feature, followed by the Disney classic *Pinocchio*, released the previous Christmas. Disney put out *Sleeping Beauty* for the 1989 festive season and saw it top the charts.

The 1989 rental chart was dominated by feature films, with a Top Ten that simply reflected the success of cinema releases: 1. *A Fish Called Wanda*; 2. *Fatal Attraction*; 3. *Good Morning, Vietnam*; 4. *Coming to America*; 5. *Buster*; 6. *Crocodile Dundee 2*; 7. *Twins*; 8. *Who Framed Roger Rabbit*; 9. *Rain Man*; 10. *Beetlejuice.**

Rain Man was also at No. 8 in the year's 'sell-through' chart, following Warner's experiment of releasing it simultaneously as a rental and a budget-price video. Dealers had initial doubts about the idea, but half a million cassettes were sent out and the film immediately topped both charts.

Distributors also began to increase the price of so-called blockbusters. Warner's *Beetlejuice* and Buena Vista's *Good Morning, Vietnam* retailed at £55 and the two companies were followed by most distributors, including CIC, whose *Twins* cost £60. In early 1990, top 'sell-through' tapes began to rise in price, breaking through the £10 barrier. Ex-rental films *The Blues Brothers, Crocodile Dundee 2* and *Fatal Attraction* all retailed at £12.99.

In America, there was a slowing down in tape rental. The video boom had hit Americans first and the years of growth appeared to be over, mainly because people tended to rent less after their first few years of owning a video recorder. However, recorder-owning was still increasing, and cassette-buying rose during 1989, boosted by cut-throat discounting of top tapes over the Christmas period. *Batman* and *Who Framed Roger Rabbit* were the top-sellers.

*Analysis of MRIB chart information by *Video Business* magazine.

Above the Law (VPD) May 1990
The Abyss (CBS/Fox) May 1990
The Accidental Tourist (Warner) September 1989
The Accused (CIC) September 1989
Act of Piracy (CBS/Fox) December 1989
Addicted to His Love (EV) November 1989
The Adventures of Baron Munchausen (RCA/Columbia) September 1989
An African Dream (Castle) December 1989
After Midnight (MGM/UA) June 1990
Alien Nation (CBS/Fox) September 1989
American Blue Note (Odyssey) May 1990
American Boyfriends (Oasis) April 1990
American Ninja 3: Bloodhunt (Pathé) September 1989
The American Way (RCA/Columbia) August 1989

Amityville 4: The Evil Escapes (Medusa) April 1990
Amsterdamned (Vestron) November 1989
And a Nightingale Sang (Odyssey) September 1989
Andy Colby's Incredibly Awesome Adventure (MGM/UA) July 1989
Another Chance (Watershed) August 1989
Arena (EV) January 1990
Around the World in 80 Days (two tapes) (Guild) September 1989
Arthur 2: On the Rocks (Warner) September 1989

Back to the Future, Part 2 (CIC) July 1990
Bad Blood (Colourbox) September 1989
Bad Taste (Colourbox) December 1989
The Banker (RCA/Columbia) March 1990
Batman (Warner) April 1990

Beaches (Touchstone) December 1989
The Beast of War (RCA/Columbia) August 1989
Beauty and Denise (Medusa) December 1989
Bedroom Eyes 2 (Cineplex) December 1989
The Bedroom Window (CBS/Fox) August 1989
Beethoven's Nephew (New World) October 1989
Berlin Blues (Pathé) February 1990
The Best of Times (Earner/Cineplex) January 1990
Betrayed (Warner) January 1990
Beverly Hills Bodysnatcher (Castle) September 1989
The Big Blue (CBS/Fox) September 1989
Blind Chess (CIC) October 1989
The Blob (Braveworld/RCA/Columbia) October 1989

Blood of Dragon Peril (VPD) November 1989

Blood Sport (Warner) August 1989

Bloodfirst (MGM/UA) May 1990

Blue Angel (Colourbox) August 1989

Blue Heaven (VPD) February 1990

The Blue Iguana (President) August 1989

Blues for Buder (CIC) March 1990

B.O.R.N. (Cineplex) February 1990

Breaking Loose (Medusa) January 1990

Breaking Point (Turner) March 1990

Bridge to Silence (Parkfield) October 1989

Bright Lights, Big City (Warner) July 1989

Brutal Glory (RCA/Columbia) October 1989

Buckeye and Blue (Box Office) December 1989

The Burbs (CIC) February 1990

Burndown (Medusa) February 1990

Burning Secret (Vestron) August 1989

Caddyshack 2 (Warner) August 1989

The Cage (Braveworld) December 1989

Caged Heat (Odyssey) July 1989

Capone's Enforcer (Sony) October 1989

Captain Cosmos (VPD) April 1990

The Carpenter (Parkfield) September 1989

A Case of Honour (Braveworld) August 1989

The Case of the Hillside Stranglers (Castle) October 1989

Catch Me if You Can (Medusa) May 1990

The Cellar (Castle) September 1989

The Chair (Medusa) October 1989

Champion on Fire (VPD) February 1990

Child's Play (Vestron) January 1990

The China Lake Murders (CIC) June 1990

China O'Brien (EV) February 1990

The Chocolate War (Medusa) April 1990

A Chorus of Disapproval (MGM/UA) April 1990

C.H.U.D. 2: Bud the C.H.U.D. (First Choice) September 1989

Circles in a Forest (Avalon) May 1990

Clara's Heart (Warner) March 1990

Class of 1999 (Vestron) May 1990

Clownhouse (EV) March 1990

Cocktail (Touchstone) September 1989

Cocoon 2: The Return (CBS/Fox) December 1989

Cold Blood (VPD) January 1990

Columbo Goes to the Guillotine (CIC) July 1989

Columbo: Murder, Smoke and Shadows (CIC) September 1989

The Comeback (CBS/Fox) January 1990

The Cook, the Thief, His Wife & Her Lover (Palace) February 1990

Cookie (Guild) February 1990

Cops (Guild) July 1990

Cousins (CIC) April 1990

Crack House (Pathé) April 1990

Crack in the Mirror (Futuristic) September 1989

Critters 2 (RCA/Columbia) November 1989

Crossing Delancey (Warner) November 1989

A Cry in the Dark (Pathé) November 1989

Cyborg (Pathé) February 1990

Dad (CIC) May 1990

Dance or Die (Box Office) August 1989

Dangerous Game (Medusa) December 1989

Dangerous Liaisons (Warner) November 1989

Dangerous Love (Medusa) November 1989

Dangerous Obsession (Box Office) April 1990

Dangerous Pursuit (CIC) May 1990

Danny The Champion of the World (Collins) September 1989

Daredreamer (Futuristic) April 1990

Darkroom (Guild) July 1989

Dawn of the Dead (EV) September 1989

The Dawning (MGM/UA) September 1989

The Dead Can't Lie (Pathé) September 1989

Dead Poets Society (Touchstone) March 1990

The Dead Pool (Warner) September 1989

Dead Ringers (CBS/Fox) September 1989

Dead Trouble (New World) March 1990

Dead-Bang (Guild) October 1989

Deadly Addiction (Vestron) May 1990

Deadly Embrace (Cineplex) September 1989

Deadly Intent (Sony) October 1989

Deadly Stranger (RCA/Columbia) October 1989

Dealers (MGM/UA) February 1990

Deathstalkers 3: Warriors from Hell (Vestron) February 1990

The Deceivers (Vestron) March 1990

Deep Star Six (Guild) January 1990

Desert Rats (CIC) August 1989

The Detective Kid (Futuristic) February 1990

Devil Rider (BCB) March 1990

Dial Help (Castle) November 1989

Die Hard (CBS/Fox) September 1989

Dirty Diamonds (CIC) December 1989

Dirty Rotten Scoundrels (Virgin) February 1990

Distant Thunder (CIC) January 1990

Do the Right Thing (CIC) February 1990

D.O.A. (Touchstone) October 1989

Dogs in Space (Collins) August 1989

Domino (Virgin) November 1989

Dragons Forever (American Imperial/VPD) October 1989

Dream a Little Dream (Vestron) September 1989

The Dreaming (Medusa) November 1989

The Dressmaker (MGM/UA) October 1989

Driving Force (Medusa) March 1990

Dune Surfer (Castle) May 1990

The Dunera Boys (Futuristic) August 1989

Eight Men Out (Virgin) May 1990

18 Again (New World) October 1989

Elvira, Mistress of the Dark (New World) September 1989

Emmanuelle (Braveworld) April 1990

Emmanuelle 2 (Braveworld) April 1990

End of the Line (Box Office) August 1989

The Evil Below (Cineplex) August 1989

The Experts (CIC) February 1990

Fair Game (Medusa) September 1989

False Witness (New World) January 1990

Far from Home (Vestron) April 1990

Farewell to the King (Vestron) October 1989

The FBI Murders (CIC) July 1989

Feds (Warner) January 1990

Feel the Heat (EV) February 1990

Final Cut (New World) May 1990

Final Notice (CIC) March 1990

The Finish Line (Castle) October 1989

Fire and Rain (CIC) April 1990

A Fish Called Wanda (MGM/UA) August 1989

Five Corners (Pathé) October 1989

Fletch Lives (CIC) December 1989

The Fly 2 (CBS/Fox) March 1990

For Queen and Country (Sony) September 1989

The Forgotten (CIC) November 1989

The Fortunate Pilgrim (Guild) January 1990

Friday the 13th, Part 8: Jason Takes Manhattan (CIC) March 1990

Fright Night 2 (President) December 1989

From the Dead of Night (Braveworld) January 1990

From the Hip (CBS/Fox) July 1989

Funland (Sony) August 1989

Georgia (Medusa) May 1990

Get Smart Again (Braveworld) October 1989

Getting It Right (Medusa) February 1990

The Ghetto Blaster (Braveworld) January 1990

Ghost Chase (Medusa) November 1989

Ghostbusters 2 (RCA/Columbia) May 1990

Go for Broke (Walt Disney) October 1989

God Bless the Child (Sony) July 1989

Godfather the Master (VPD) January 1990

Going Bananas (Pathé) July 1989

Going Sane (RCA/Columbia) September 1989

Gone with the Wind (MGM/UA) October 1989

Gore Vidal's Billy the Kid (Turner) October 1989

Gorillas in the Mist (Warner) September 1989

Grand Deceptions (CIC) January 1990

The Grasscutter (Futuristic) May 1990

The Great Escape (two tapes) (RCA/Columbia) September 1989

The Great Outdoors (CIC) July 1989

Grievous Bodily Harm (Castle) November 1989

The Gunrunner (New World) October 1989

Guts and Glory: The Rise and Fall of Oliver North (CIC) January 1990

Halloween 4 (Braveworld) March 1990

Hand of Death (Colourbox) March 1990

Hanna's War (Pathé) August 1989

Hardcase and Fist (Braveworld) October 1989

Hardcover (EV) November 1989

The Haunting of Sarah Hardy (CIC) December 1989

Headhunter (Cineplex) July 1989

Heart of Midnight (Vestron) August 1989

Heartbreak Hotel (Touchstone) January 1990

Heathers (20:20 Vision) June 1990

Hellbound: Hellraiser 2 (20:20 Vision) May 1990

Hellgate (New World) December 1989

Her Alibi (Warner) December 1989

Heroes Stand Alone (MGM/UA) May 1990

The Hidden (CBS/Fox) November 1989

Hider in the House (Vestron) March 1990
Hiding Out (President) September 1989
High Desert Kill (CIC) July 1990
High Stakes (HFV) June 1990
Hit List (Warner) November 1989
Hollywood Cop (VPD) October 1989
Homeboy (Braveworld/RCA/Columbia) January 1990
Hot to Trot (Warner) September 1989
House 3: The Horror Show (Braveworld) October 1989
Houston, We've Got a Problem (CIC) October 1989
How I Got Into College (CBS/Fox) May 1990
How to Get Ahead in Advertising (CBS/Fox) March 1990
Howling 4: The Original Nightmare (President) January 1990
The Hunchback Hairball of LA (Vestron) June 1990

I Know My First Name Is Steven (Odyssey) February 1990
In Country (Warner) July 1990
Indiana Jones and the Last Crusade (CIC) March 1990
Indio (President) April 1990
Interzone (EV) December 1989
Iron Angels (RCA/Columbia) July 1989
The Iron Triangle (Medusa) January 1990
Island Sons (CIC) June 1990
It Takes Two (Warner) July 1989

Jacknife (Vestron) April 1990
Jack's Back (CBS/Fox) February 1990
Jakarta (Medusa) December 1989
The January Man (MGM/UA) November 1989
Java Burn (Medusa) March 1990
Jigsaw Murders (MGM/UA) September 1989
Johnny Be Good (Virgin) August 1989
Joyriders (Pathé) December 1989
Just Ask for Diamond (CBS/Fox) August 1989
Justin Case (Walt Disney) July 1989

The Karate Kid, Part III (RCA/Columbia) March 1990
Kentucky Fried Movie (EV) November 1989
Kick Boxer (EV) October 1989
Kill Crazy (VPD) December 1989
Killing Dad (Palace Premiere) October 1989
King Kong Lives (President) September 1989
Kinjite Forbidden Subjects (Pathé) October 1989
K–9 (CIC) April 1990

L.A. Bounty (Guild) August 1989
The Lady and the Highwayman (Parkfield) August 1989
Lady in White (Virgin) January 1990
The Lair of the White Worm (Vestron) December 1989
The Land Before Time (CIC) April 1990
Last Exit to Brooklyn (Guild) May 1990
The Last Plane from Coramaya (VPD) February 1990
Last Rites (MGM/UA) January 1990

The Last Temptation of Christ (CIC) August 1989
Lena: My 100 Children (Sony) July 1989
Lethal Weapon 2 (Warner) March 1990
Little Girl Lost (White Knights/Prism) September 1989
Living Doll (MGM/UA) March 1990
Lobster Man from Mars (EV) June 1990
Lone Runner (EV) January 1990
Lone Wolf (SGE) August 1989
The Lonely Passion of Judith Hearne (Pathé) July 1989
The Long Hot Summer (CBS/Fox) August 1989
Lords of the Deep (MGM/UA) January 1990
Love You to Death (Cineplex) November 1989

Mac and Me (Guild) November 1989
Major League (Braveworld) February 1990
Mama Dracula (EV) October 1989
A Man for All Seasons (Turner) November 1989
Manhunter (CBS/Fox) July 1989
Margaret Bourke White (Futuristic) November 1989
Married to the Mob (Virgin) March 1990
Masque of the Red Death (MGM/UA) April 1990
Memories of Me (MGM/UA) September 1989
Midnight Cop (New World) February 1990
The Mighty Quinn (MGM/UA) December 1989
Miles from Home (Braveworld/RCA/Columbia) November 1989
Miss Arizona (Medusa) October 1989
Missing Link (CIC) January 1990
Mission Manila (President) March 1990
Mississippi Burning (Virgin) November 1989
The Moderns (Vestron) January 1990
Moon Over Parador (CIC) November 1989
Moontrap (Parkfield) July 1990
Mr Christmas Dinner (RCA/Columbia) November 1989
Murder by Night (CIC) April 1990
Murder One . . . Murder Two (Futuristic) March 1990
Murder Story (Reeve and Partners) February 1990
Mutant on the Bounty (Futuristic) January 1990
My Left Foot (Palace) November 1989
My Stepmother Is an Alien (RCA/Columbia) December 1989
Mystic Pizza (Virgin) May 1990

The Naked Gun (CIC) January 1990
Naked Lie (Castle) December 1989
Nasty Boys (CIC) May 1990
Necessity (Medusa) September 1989
Never on Tuesday (CBS/Fox) July 1989
New Adventures of Pippa Longstocking (RCA/Columbia) July 1989
A New Life (CIC) July 1989
New York Stories (Touchstone) May 1990
Nicky and Gino (Virgin) November 1989
The Night Before (Warner) January 1990
Night Game (EV) November 1989
Night Shadow (Box Office) June 1990

Night Visitors (VPD) November 1989
Nightbreaker (President) November 1989
Nightlife (CIC) March 1990
A Nightmare on Elm Street 4 (CBS/Fox) January 1990
Nightmare Vacation 3 (Futuristic) May 1990
1969 (EV) October 1989
Ninja Academy (Guild) August 1989
No Hard Feelings (Academy) October 1989
No Holds Barred (American Imperial/VPD) March 1990
Nowhere to Run (MGM/UA) March 1990

Offerings (Unicorn/Prism) September 1989
Once Upon a Texas Train (Medusa) July 1989
One Month Later (Warner) July 1989
Operation Paratrooper (Medusa) April 1990
Options (Vestron) September 1989
Order of the Eagle (Braveworld) December 1989
Outback Bound (CBS/Fox) September 1989

Palais Royale (EV) April 1990
The Paperhouse (Vestron) February 1990
Parent Trap 3 (Walt Disney) May 1990
Parents (First Choice) October 1989
Paris by Night (Virgin) January 1990
Pelle the Conqueror (Braveworld) December 1989
The People Across the Lake (RCA/Columbia) July 1989
Personal Exemptions (Box Office) December 1989
Personal Vendetta (Sony) November 1989
Peter Gunn (New World) August 1989
Phantasm 2 (Guild) September 1989
Physical Evidence (Warner) February 1990
Plain Clothes (CIC) September 1989
Police Academy 6: City Under Siege (Warner) January 1990
Police in Action: A Cry for Justice (RCA/Columbia) August 1989
Police Story 2 (American Imperial/VPD) April 1990
Pound Puppies & The Legend of Big Paw (Guild) December 1989
The Presidio (CIC) August 1989
Priceless Beauty (VPD) September 1989
Primal Rage (Castle) August 1989
The Prince of Pennsylvania (RCA/Columbia) November 1989
Proud Mrs (Guild) August 1989
Punch the Clock (Box Office) October 1989
Punchline (RCA/Columbia) October 1989
Puppet Master (EV) March 1990
The Purple People Eater (CIC) August 1989

Quarantine (Colourbox) April 1990
Queen of Evil (RCA/Columbia) August 1989
Queen of Hearts (MGM/UA) March 1990
Quest for Love (New World) April 1990
The Questor Tapes (CIC) July 1989
Quiet Victory (Odyssey) December 1989

The Rachel Papers (Virgin) June 1990
Rage to Kill (Braveworld) August 1989
The Raggedy Rawney (Pathé) January 1989

144

The Rainbow (Vestron) March 1990
Rainbow in the Thunder (Walt Disney) August 1989
Real Men (Warner) July 1989
Reason to Die (New World) April 1990
Red Heat (RCA/Columbia) July 1989
Red Scorpion (Vestron) January 1990
Regenerator (Colourbox) January 1990
The Renegades (Trans-Global) September 1989
The Rescue of Jessica McClure (Odyssey) June 1990
Resurrected (Castle) February 1990
Return from the River Kwai (Braveworld/RCA/Columbia) September 1989
The Return of Swamp Thing (Medusa) May 1990
Return of the Killer Tomatoes (New World) November 1989
The Return of the Musketeers (EV) December 1989
Revenge of the Radioactive Reporter (CIC) July 1990
River of Death (Pathé) January 1990
Road Raiders (CIC) February 1990
Robo Ninja (Box Office) May 1990
Robot Jox (EV) March 1990
Rocket Gibraltar (RCA/Columbia) November 1989
Roselyn and the Lions (Palace) March 1990
Running on Empty (Guild) March 1990
Rush Week (Guild) March 1990

Salvation (Collins) September 1989
Sandinista (Castle) March 1990
Saturday the 14th Strikes Back (MGM/UA) August 1989
Scandal (Palace) September 1989
Scarecrows (Medusa) January 1990
Scenes from the Class Struggle in Beverly Hills (MGM/UA) June 1990
Scrooged (CIC) November 1989
Scum (Odyssey) January 1990
Search and Destroy (Medusa) July 1989
See No Evil, Hear No Evil (20:20 Vision) April 1990
Seize the Day (Vestron) August 1989
The Serpent and the Rainbow (CIC) October 1989
Seven Hours to Judgement (EV) September 1989
Severance (Colourbox) January 1990
Sex and the Married Detective (CIC) November 1989
sex – lies and videotape (Virgin) May 1990
Shadow Dancing (SGE) July 1989
Shadow Makers (CIC) June 1990
Shadowman (New World) May 1990
Shadows in the Storm (Castle) August 1989
Shame (Oasis) November 1989

Shock Treatment (Vestron) February 1990
Shootdown (Sony) September 1989
Short Circuit 2 (RCA/Columbia) August 1989
Side by Side (Sony) August 1989
Sight Unseen (Box Office) May 1990
Simple Justice (American Imperial/VPD) February 1990
Sing (RCA/Columbia) February 1990
The Sisterhood (Pearl/Prism) September 1989
Sisters (MGM/UA) May 1990
Skin Deep (Braveworld) November 1989
Slaves of New York (RCA/Columbia) March 1990
Sleeping Beauty (Walt Disney) September 1989
Slipstream (EV) September 1989
Slugs (New World) November 1989
Small Sacrifices (Prism) April 1990
Snake Eater (20:20 Vision) June 1990
Someone to Love (CIC) October 1989
Sonny Boy (EV) October 1989
Spellbinder (MGM/UA) July 1989
Splash Too (Walt Disney) August 1989
Spring Fever USA (American Imperial/VPD) January 1990
Spy (CIC) May 1990
Stand and Deliver (Warner) August 1989
Stealing Heaven (20:20 Vision) May 1990
The Stick (Parkfield) November 1989
Strange Voices (Odyssey) August 1989
Stripped to Kill 2 (MGM/UA) October 1989
The Suicide Club (BCB) February 1990
A Summer Story (Warner) August 1989
Survival Game (RV) August 1989
Sweet Hearts Dance (RCA/Columbia) September 1989

Taffin (Vestron) July 1989
The Tall Guy (Virgin) September 1989
Tank Malling (Cineplex) April 1990
Tap (RCA/Columbia) January 1990
Teen Witch (RV) August 1989
Ten Little Indians (Pathé) March 1990
Tequila Sunrise (Warner) October 1989
Terror on Highway 91 (CBS/Fox) November 1989
Terror Within (MGM/UA) December 1989
That Summer of White Roses (Avalon) June 1990
They Live (Guild) October 1989
Third Degree Burn (CIC) September 1989
Those She Left Behind (Odyssey) March 1990
Three Fugitives (Touchstone) February 1990
The 3000 Mile Chase (CIC) November 1989
Thunder Warrior 3 (American Imperial) August 1989
A Time of Destiny (Vestron) November 1989
Time Trackers (MGM/UA) February 1990

To Heal a Nation (Sony) July 1989
Tongs (CIC) August 1989
Too Beautiful to Die (Colourbox) March 1990
Torch Song Trilogy (RCA/Columbia) November 1989
Tougher Than Leather (Palace) July 1989
The Toxic Avenger, Part 2 (Virgin) June 1990
Trained to Kill (Medusa) February 1990
Trapped (CIC) February 1990
Trapper County War (Guild) December 1989
Traxx (CBS/Fox) August 1989
Tree of Hands (Pathé) September 1989
Tricks of the Trade (Castle) February 1990
Trouble in Paradise (Braveworld) February 1990
True Blood (Castle) May 1990
Twice Under (Braveworld) November 1989
Twins (CIC) October 1989
Twister (Vestron) May 1990
2 Idiots in Hollywod (RCA/Columbia) March 1990

The Unconquered (CBS/Fox) September 1989
Under the Gun (Cineplex) October 1989
Underground Terror (Medusa) July 1989
The Unholy (Vestron) September 1989
The Untamed (Walt Disney) July 1989

Vamp (20:20 Vision) May 1990
Vanessa (VPD) August 1989
The Vineyard (New World) August 1989

Walker (CIC) November 1989
Warlock (Medusa) October 1989
The Watch Commander (RCA/Columbia) November 1989
Watchers (Guild) August 1989
Waxwork (First Choice) July 1989
Way of the Challenge (VPD) August 1989
White Lies (New World) March 1990
Who Framed Roger Rabbit (Touchstone) November 1989
Who's Harry Crumb? (RCA/Columbia) February 1990
Willow (RCA/Columbia) October 1989
Wilt (Guild) March 1990
Wired (EV) May 1990
Witchcraft 2 (Box Office) February 1990
Without a Clue (Virgin) December 1989
The Wizard of Loneliness (Virgin) August 1989
Wizards of the Lost Kingdom 2 (20:20 Vision) April 1990
The Wolves of Willoughby Chase (EV) February 1990
Working Girl (CBS/Fox) November 1989
World Gone Wild (Warner) January 1990

Z.I.T.S. (Futuristic) July 1989

The Ten Most Promising Faces of 1990

JAMES CAMERON-WILSON

Alec Baldwin was probably the hottest male star to emerge in 1990. So successful was the Cold War thriller *The Hunt for Red October* that a whole series of films featuring Baldwin's character – Jack Ryan – are being planned. If Lady Luck will have it, and if Baldwin agrees, Ryan will become Paramount's in-house James Bond.

Equally adept at comedy and drama, the actor was given the heroic lead in *Red October* (and artwork billing with Sean Connery) after a string of impressive performances. Baldwin got the star treatment and became an overnight sensation (it can happen) when the film smashed box-office records in March.

Now Baldwin is big news (as is his relationship with Kim Basinger).

Alec Baldwin as Jimmy Swaggart in Great Balls of Fire!)

Already having worked with Jonathan Demme, Mike Nichols, Tim Burton, Oliver Stone and Woody Allen, he has the pick of the best directors queuing up to work with him. Philip Kaufman wanted him to play Henry Miller in *Henry and June*, but the actor begged off. He also turned down $1 million to do a Japanese cigarette ad. His celluloid asking price is now $2 million. Despite this, so the rumour goes, he was offered 30 film roles in a single month.

Born Alexander Rae Baldwin III on 3 April 1958, he studied political science and psychology at George Washington University, setting his sights on law. Acting intervened, he landed the daytime soap *The Doctors*, moved to Los Angeles and ended up playing Lisa Hartman's husband in TV's *Knot's Landing*.

Disgusted by the easy option, he moved to New York to embrace the theatre. He won the male lead in the film *Forever, Lulu* (a poor re-run of *Desperately Seeking Susan*), and vowed to do better. From then on he was to play supporting roles in better movies. There was a part in John Hughes's *She's Having a Baby*, and he was the debonair ghost in *Beetlejuice*, Michelle Pfeiffer's errant husband in *Married to the Mob*, Eric Bogosian's smarmy boss in Oliver Stone's *Talk Radio*, Melanie Griffith's disagreeable boy-friend in *Working Girl* and evangelist Jimmy Swaggart in *Great Balls of Fire!*

And yet, in spite of all this work, he proclaimed, 'I am not Michael Caine. I don't want sixteen movies coming out in one year.' He lost the role of Michael Corleone's illegitimate son in *The Godfather Part III*, but did turn up in *Miami Blues*.

And then came *The Hunt for Red October*.

Since then, Baldwin has joined the all-star cast of Woody Allen's 1989–90 picture (still untitled at press-time) with, among others, William Hurt and Mia Farrow, and teamed opposite Kim Basinger in Neil Simon's *The Marrying Man*. Next: the title role in Walter Hill's *The Fugitive*.

Alec Baldwin is a committed performer, still honing his craft, picking through the plethora of scripts with an academic scrutiny. An outspoken critic of Hollywood, he is sticking to America's East Coast and doesn't suffer fools – at all. No doubt he will swing with the publicity machine for a while, but not for long. Soon his good looks and cocky charm will sell his movies for him. Besides, there are always his three thespian brothers – Daniel, Billy and Stephen – to take up the slack. Keeping it in the family, they all acted for Oliver Stone in *Born on the Fourth of July*.

Patrick Bergin. It is a fact that the English are rather short on conventional star power these days. The current, greying legends – Peter O'Toole, Richard Harris and Sean Connery – are either Irish or Scottish, however hard they may twist their vowels, while clean-cut relative newcomer Timothy Dalton is Welsh (as is the Laughtonesque Anthony Hopkins). Even the more recent additions to the industry – Gabriel Byrne, Daniel Day Lewis and Kenneth Branagh – are Irish by birth. As is Patrick Bergin. (Thank God, then, for Michael Caine.)

Bergin, unlike his contemporary countrymen, is the stuff of wide-screen heroism. His rugged, 6ft 3in stature blocks the sunlight, the creases in his face hinting at aeons of hard-won experience, while the subtle stillness of his demeanour oozes charisma. Bergin is a true star – an adventurer who can learn his lines.

At least, that's what the persona suggests.

Unlike Branagh, Bergin came to acting late in the day. He dabbled in theatre in experimental form, avoiding the superficial gloss and glitter of the West End stage.

'Plays should be part of the advancement of the people they're written for,' he says. He worked with boys from broken homes, encouraging them to write and act out scenes, to make videos and put on puppet shows for patients in nursing homes. 'It was rough at times,' he continues; 'some of them carried knives.' His success rate was encouraging, although one of his pupils graduated from improvisation to armed robbery.

As an actor, Bergin didn't emerge until the 1980s, landing a small but decent role in *The Courier* (with Gabriel Byrne) and another in *Taffin* (with Pierce Brosnan). As an IRA informer in the mini-series *Act of Betrayal*, he won his first fist of accolades and an audition to play the explorer Sir Richard Burton in *Mountains of the Moon*. The director, Bob Rafelson, was knocked over.

'There is something in his eyes,' Rafelson related. 'There's something mysterious – almost frighteningly intense.'

Bergin got the part and top billing, and lived up to the material. The film displays the sweep of a David Lean epic, and Bergin stands tall at the

Patrick Bergin (with Fiona Shaw in Mountains of the Moon*).*

centre of it. Burton was a man of extraordinary charisma, courage and controversy. The translator of *The Kamasutra*, *The Arabian Nights* and *The Perfumed Garden*, he was as much at home in the African bush as surrounded by leatherbound books. He had an extraordinary power over women, but was just as happy disguised as an Arab within the sacred walls of Mecca. His handbook on the art of bayonet combat was required reading in World War II, fifty years after his death.

Bergin invested the human legend with all the power and enigma required and strolled away with the film's acting honours. For two hours Bergin *is* Sir Richard Burton.

The Americans hailed the film as a masterpiece and the actor stopped over in LA to play the devil in *Highway to Hell*, with Chad Lowe. Next, he landed the male lead – opposite Julia Roberts – in *Sleeping with the Enemy* in which, says Bergin, 'I play an extremely devoted husband.' The enemy of the title is the husband – who beats the living daylights out of Ms Roberts. 'I'm actually very nervous about the whole thing,' he admits. 'Julia Roberts is just so-o-o gorgeous.'

While he's at it, he's also starring opposite Sean Young in *Love Crimes*, filming in Atlanta, Georgia.

Kenneth Branagh. Tom Cruise and Kevin Costner may keep the box-office tills ringing in Hollywood, but the cargo floating in from Britain is as unexpected as ever: Dudley Moore, Bob Hoskins, John Cleese, Tracey Ullman and now Olivier's successor – Kenneth

Kenneth Branagh (as Henry V).

Branagh, a short-ish, chubby-ish, boyish man with a flat rugged face.

'They want to give somebody this mythical mantle that Olivier has left,' the Belfast-born actor says, squirming with embarrassment. It is an unfortunate association, one that has caused the Irishman more harm than good. Branagh has been accused of 'acting up, darling', of emulating the lordly Larry, of lunging for the crown with abominable cheek.

So let's set the record straight. This is not a race and Kenneth Branagh is not a contestant. However, if it *were*, Branagh would be ploughing through the finishing line with knobs on.

If there isn't a pocket of the entertainment industry that King Ken hasn't sewn up yet, then you can bet your bottom sovereign he's threading the needle. Still in his twenties, the actor-director-writer-impresario has conquered TV, the London stage, the Royal Shakespeare Company, the written page, the British cinema and Hollywood. Damn it, for his first cinematic effort as actor-director – *Henry V* – he was nominated for *two* Oscars.

From Belfast, Branagh – aged nine – moved with his family to Reading, where his anglicisation began. 'I got bullied at school, I felt bad about the Irish accent, you know? I was very troubled about my identity.'

To escape further bullying, the boy feigned broken bones so that he could stay at home. It was this discovery of an ability for make-believe that first sowed the seeds of a great acting talent.

After winning gold medals at RADA, Branagh landed a starring role in *Another Country* in the West End, and on the strength of this was invited to join the Royal Shakespeare Company. There, he impressed the critics with his rendition of *Henry V*, but promptly fell out of the company.

'There was a clash of expectations,' he says now. 'I was brought into the RSC at a young age [23] as a puritan romantic, and was looking for the kind of company feeling and family philosophy that had been achieved under Peter Hall. I just felt the organisation was too large for there to be any ongoing dialogue between the actors and the management.'

So Branagh started up his own 'family', the Renaissance Theatre Company, which he financed from his acting on TV (*Fortunes of War*, etc) and in the movies (*High Season, A Month in the Country*). The first play produced by Renaissance was Branagh's own *Public Enemy*, and then three Shakespeares directed by leading stage actors (Derek Jacobi, Judi Dench, Geraldine McEwan). The latter move proved to be a priceless publicity gimmick and pushed Renaissance proudly into the limelight.

Paid £50,000 for his autobiography, *Beginnings*, Branagh was able to upgrade the offices of his company and concentrate on two other matters: his marriage to *Fortunes of War* co-star Emma Thompson, and the financing of the film of *Henry V*.

Today, King Ken vows that, 'I want peace and quiet now. I am at a staging post in my life. My marriage has started, and with that I have the chance to be more at peace. I really want to disappear and take stock of my life.'

Of course, nobody believes him.

Andrew Dice Clay could become very, very big. On the other hand, he just might be *too* outrageous. Priscilla Presley, co-star of Clay's first starring vehicle – *The Adventures of Ford Fairlane* – volunteers, 'I'd call *Ford Fairlane* off-beat – a lot of people are going to hate it.'

A lot of people already hate Andrew Dice Clay. Like homosexuals. And col-

Andrew Dice Clay.

oured people. And midgets. And women.

'Oh, I give women a lot of credit,' he told *Playboy* magazine. 'I just goof on 'em, and I think they're smart enough to know that – which is why they can come to my show and laugh.'

Andrew Dice Clay is a New York actor who's made his name as an outrageous stand-up comic offending audiences under the appellation of The Diceman.

'I'm not Dice,' he defends his act. 'He's just one thing I can do. As I tell the crowds, "I don't write this material. You write it for me." I'm just delivering it in a real blue way that, heard through a PA system, sounds really fucking funny.'

Besides his modesty, Clay is famous for his affectionate misogyny and assault on all minority groups. In his stand-up act nothing is sacrosanct, *nothing*. And the man is becoming respectable. He's had a comedy special on HBO, an album released (both titled *The Diceman Cometh*), and Cher and Sylvester Stallone have started attending his sold-out live shows.

The movies had to follow.

There were supporting roles in *Amazon Women on the Moon*, with Rosanna Arquette, and in *Casual Sex?*, with Lea Thompson, and then came Clay's own vehicle.

In the action-comedy *The Adventures of Ford Fairlane* he plays a rock 'n' roll detective excavating the armpit of the music business, and, on the plus side, Renny Harlin was signed to direct.

Harlin is one of the hottest directors in Hollywood, with *Die Hard 2* under his belt and *Aliens III* forthcoming. The film-maker wanted to give *Fairlane* 'the scale of a rock 'n' roll event', he says –

and, on the strength of advance word-of-mouth, Clay has landed his second starring role, in *The Gossip Columnist*.

Twentieth Century-Fox is also releasing *Dice*, a concert film of The Diceman in action. According to its director, Jay Dubin, 'There are a lot of people out there who want to see how in the hell this Brooklyn guy with a leather jacket is selling out Madison Square Garden.'

Move over, Eddie Murphy?

Nicole Kidman. At the date of going to press little has been written about Nicole Kidman. But these pages don't just highlight potential luminaries from Britain and America. We like to comb all industries to bring you the stars of tomorrow. I mean, our tip for Paul Hogan wasn't *all* cock-eyed.

. Australia's Nicole Kidman – all five-foot ten of her – has the talent and looks

Nicole Kidman.

to become another Sigourney Weaver (tipped for stardom in the 1980–1 *Film Review*).

The daughter of a psychology lecturer and nurse, Nicole was born in Hawaii and studied ballet as a child. Already interested in the stage at an early age, the striking redhead pushed her parents into letting her enrol at drama school at the age of ten. Some ten-year-old.

At fourteen she appeared in her first film and then honed her craft at the St Martin's Youth Theatre in Melbourne and the Australian Theatre for Young People in Sydney. She snared two more film roles – in *BMX Bandits* and *Windrider* – and then played, and I quote, 'a little roughie who herded sheep' in the Disney Channel mini-series *Five-Mile Creek*.

Native director Phillip Noyce (*Newsfront, Heatwave*) takes up the story. 'We first became aware of Nicole from several Australian TV productions – what we call "domestic movies" – films hardly seen outside Australia. We felt she would be right for a key role in *Vietnam*, the mini-

series that we [the Kennedy Miller organisation] were then developing. Little did we realise that in just three nights she would become a household name across the entire country.'

The public Down Under took Nicole to its bosom and voted her Best Actress of the Year. George Miller, the series producer, was equally awe-struck.

'Nicole is not just someone who is acting for the short term,' he ventured, 'she's an absolutely serious actor. Some ten years ago I met Mel Gibson fresh out of drama school. I had this same gut feeling about him. He had this presence on film one couldn't stop watching. I feel that quality in Nicole.'

Miller and Noyce then took a chance and cast her in the lead of their seafaring thriller *Dead Calm*. Like Weaver in *Alien*, she plays an entirely credible beauty trapped alone in terrifying circumstances. In this case, she is a woman who has just lost her only son in an appalling car crash and is taking a sailing holiday to recuperate. While her husband (Sam Neill) is investigating an abandoned, sinking ship, the vessel's sole survivor (Billy Zane) holds her hostage on her own yacht, leaving her husband behind.

Dead Calm is compulsive, bursting with tension, and held together by a

performance from Kidman that elicits admiration and helpless sympathy.

This *tour de force* did not go unnoticed in the corridors of Hollywood, and Nicole was signed up to star opposite Tom Cruise in the $55-million stock-car racing drama *Days of Thunder*. And her romance with her leading man should do no harm to the actress's escalating stardom.

Nicole Kidman will also be seen in the Australian *Emerald City*, the film version of David Williamson's critically-lauded play, and in the Kennedy-Miller production *Flirting*, directed by John Duigan (*The Year My Voice Broke*). Her role as Katrina Stanton in the celebrated three-part TV film *Bangkok Hilton* – as an Australian searching for her lost father (Denholm Elliott) in London – introduced her to the British armchair audience and won her even more glowing reviews.

Can the lady do no wrong?

Next: *Billy Bathgate*, opposite Dustin Hoffman, directed by Robert Benton.

Kelly Lynch. A former fashion model – and a successful one – Kelly Lynch broke into the movies on the strength of her looks. Sunshine blonde, five-foot nine and slim as a willow, this was hardly surprising. However, Kelly dislikes the title.

'I'm not a model-turned-actress,' she growls, lighting up a Camel. 'I'm an actress-turned-model-turned-actress.'

As a young(er) thing, Kelly was into sky diving, riding, hang gliding, skiing and dance classes, but acting was her first love. She made her acting debut at the age of four, and went on to direct local theatre. But ten years ago, following a serious car accident, doctors told her she would never walk again.

'I refused to believe them,' she said. 'I knew it was up to *me* if I was going to be able to walk – not a bunch of doctors. By the time I was able to get out of my bed, my body had atrophied to seventy-five pounds. That's when I looked at myself in the mirror and decided that I could build myself the body I wanted.'

Some body. *Playboy* offered the actress a small fortune to reveal it, but Kelly Lynch reserves any nudity for the big screen. Re *RoadHouse*, in which she played romantic/intellectual foil to Patrick Swayze, she swears that, 'I don't think, I *know*, our love scene is the hottest!'

Kelly Lynch (with Patrick Swayze, her leading man in Roadhouse*).*

Lena Olin (with Daniel Day Lewis in The Unbearable Lightness of Being*).*

Making her film debut in *Bright Lights, Big City* – as a bisexual party girl – Ms Lynch first attracted attention as the seductress of Tom Cruise in *Cocktail*. The scene was hot, but only because the actress turned the temperature up herself.

'I told him [Cruise] that if he didn't open his mouth when he kissed me on the next take I was going to rape him right in front of the crew.'

She then took her clothes off for Patrick Swayze in *RoadHouse*, playing a bespectacled doctor who (literally) sews him back together again. Once out of her white uniform and specs, she was something else.

After airing her sex appeal, Ms Lynch donned a brunette wig and floppy hat and played a thief and junkie in *Drugstore Cowboy* – opposite Matt Dillon. The film received rave reviews (and won the best film award from America's National Society of Film Critics), transforming Lynch into a versatile talent to watch.

An outspoken beauty, Ms Kelly now makes her home in Hollywood – living in the house once occupied by Maurice Chevalier. More recently she co-starred in the low-budget *Warm Summer Rain*, playing a woman recovering from a suicide attempt, and will be seen in Michael Cimino's *The Desperate Hours*, opposite Mickey Rourke and Anthony Hopkins.

Lena Olin. Heaven knows, there aren't enough European class acts in Hollywood these days. In the Golden Era there was Garbo, Dietrich, Bergman, Luise Rainer . . . Today, the Great French Hopes, the two Isabelles (Hupport and Adjani), popped up in *Heaven's Gate* and *Ishtar* and ran for cover. Welcome, then, Lena Olin.

The Swedish actress has appeared in three American films on the trot and, although she still lives in Stockholm, looks set to be around a while yet. Lena has already won the New York Film Critics' Circle Award and an Oscar nomination for her portrayal of the coquettish, smart, lustful Masha in *Enemies, A Love Story*, and has com-

pleted *Havana*, opposite Robert Redford.

And even if the actress has cornered the market in exotic, passionate and immensely desirable women, Ms Olin is no pin-up of the week. Her trio of American films – including her first, *The Unbearable Lightness of Being* – have been big-budget, serious pictures bathed in acclaim.

In *The Unbearable Lightness of Being* she played Sabina, a liberated artist caught in the cross-fire of the 1968 Russian invasion of Prague. Although her nude scenes involving mirrors, bowler hats and Daniel Day Lewis elevated some eyebrows, the significance of her work was duly noted. Besides, this was a masterful film version of Milan Kundera's celebrated novel, a cinematic landmark, for heaven's sake.

In Paul Mazursky's *Enemies, A Love Story*, based upon the novel by Isaac Bashevis Singer, Lena played a Russian concentration camp survivor and mistress of Ron Silver. Once again her sex scenes caused some comment, but did not detract from the film's wry, piercing examination of post-Holocaust romance in Coney Island.

Julia Roberts.

Likewise, *Havana* is a love story at heart, but with an immense historical background: the last days of the Batista dictatorship in Cuba. Hollywood may have found its Garbo of the 1990s, but Lena is not unrealistically excited.

'Since I'm not from the States I don't follow these awards things,' she says. But she admits that, 'It's nice, of course; it's wonderful. But I don't take part in what people think about me, write about me. I have enough problems in my own life without getting involved in how people see me.'

The daughter of theatrical parents (her father, Stij Olin, was in Ingmar Bergman's *The Seventh Seal*), Lena has been steeped in acting from birth. As a girl she wanted to act but was 'extremely shy – so it would have been ridiculous to say I wanted to be an actress.'

Applying for a job as an extra in *Face to Face*, she met the director, Ingmar Bergman, who was impressed enough with Lena's raw material to encourage her to study. At twenty she enrolled in drama school and three years later joined the Royal Dramatic Theatre of Stockholm. While still at school she made her film debut in *The Life of Picasso*, an absurdist comedy. Not long afterwards, Bergman wrote the part of Anna in *After the Rehearsal* especially for her. Their professional association continues to this day, with Bergman directing her in Shakespeare and Strindberg on stage.

'I was lucky to have Bergman when I was so young,' she says. 'He doesn't speak about big spiritual things with actors; he's very practical. Yet there is something magical about him.' She has appeared in Bergman's *Fanny and Alexander*, and the 1988 Swedish film, *Something Called Joy*, about a couple losing their baby.

And then the powerful finger of Hollywood beckoned. And the notorious sex scenes started.

'But,' she avers, 'as long as it's integral to the story, I will do it. Because, after all, it isn't me, it's the character. That's the freedom we gain when we act. We don't have to be responsible.'

Julia Roberts. When Columbia Pictures first assembled the stellar line-up of Sally Field, Dolly Parton, Shirley Maclaine, Daryl Hannah and Olympia Dukakis for *Steel Magnolias*, showbusiness insiders were already guessing which of those legends would be up for an Oscar. What nobody expected was that the unknown quantity in that cast – Julia Roberts – would be the only one to walk away with an Academy Award nomination. But then she had it coming to her.

Younger sister of actor Eric Roberts (*The Pope of Greenwich Village, Star 80*), Julia has the kind of mixture of talent, looks and charisma that guarantees her a future slab on Hollywood's Walk of Fame. She is simply unbelievable. Her eyes have the penetration of a Black & Decker hammer drill, her lips the generosity of a Tina Turner benefit concert. Her figure is undiluted *Playboy*, her talent pure Oscar. And then there's that something extra – that indefinable sexual magic that makes other stars look like Oxfam mannequins.

She won the title role in *Pretty Woman*, opposite Richard Gere, because, said the producer, 'there was no one else who could have played the part. What we needed was a *woman*. And few actresses today seem like women – there are a lot of beautiful *girls*, but Julia Roberts is a beautiful *woman*. You don't know how rare that is.'

Like Kim Basinger and Holly Hunter, Julia hails from Georgia and exhibits the sex appeal of the former and the spirit of the latter. At first, however, she was unsure about making the leap to drama. 'I said I wanted to be a veterinarian, but I was just afraid to admit that I wanted to be an actor,' she explained.

There was a film with brother Eric, the catastrophic *Blood Red*, a chronicle of exploited Sicilian grapegrowers in nineteenth-century California. '*Blood Red* was a real interesting thing for Eric and me,' she says, 'because we realised that even though we're related, even though we may look alike and be in the same profession, we don't go about the process of acting in the same way at all.'

Blood Red barely saw the light of day, while *Satisfaction*, her second film, did little better. The story of a rock 'n' roll band enjoying summer at a holiday resort, the film starred *Family Ties*'s Justine Bateman and Ireland's Liam

Neeson, with Julia sixth-billed as a man-devouring rock bassist. Still, put it down to experience.

'There was a moment in *Satisfaction*', she remembers, 'that was absolutely frightening, because for one split second in time I was Eric Roberts. But we're really different. He went to the Royal Academy of Dramatic Art in London; I'm a kamikaze actress.'

Enough of Eric. Julia followed her role in *Satisfaction* with another man-eater, Daisy Araujo – in *Mystic Pizza*, a small-scale picture set in the wilds of Connecticut. Under the sensitive direction of Donald Petrie (son of film-maker Daniel), Julia flourished: the film was a hit and the media opened its eyes. *Steel Magnolias* followed, with more rave reviews, an Oscar and a Golden Globe nomination, and then the Richard Gere movie (actually, Julia was cast first, Richard came later).

She turned down the female lead opposite Willem Dafoe in *Triumph of the Spirit*, and then starred alongside Kiefer Sutherland and Kevin Bacon in *Flatliners* – a sort of junior *Altered States*. Sutherland, a man of excellent taste, promptly left his wife to date his new leading lady. The gossip columns had a field day.

Next came the role of a battered wife in Joseph Ruben's *Sleeping with the Enemy*. Earlier, the aforementioned Kim Basinger was to have played the part, but lost interest when a starry leading man was not forthcoming. So Kim left (after pursuing the part for over a year), Julia stepped in, and Patrick Bergin was signed up to play the husband.

Winona Ryder. Dig lightly into the publicity files of Emily Lloyd and you come across Winona Ryder. Emily was the original candidate to play Myra Gale Lewis in *Great Balls of Fire!* She was also the first choice to play Cher's daughter in *Mermaids*. On both occasions Our Emily dropped out and the winsome Ryder trotted in. Our Emily is in desperate need of a hit; Winona Ryder is an ascending comet.

Seeming at first like a Babycham fawn, on closer inspection Winona Ryder's face suggests something more tantalising. She looks sweet enough to melt in tea, but then there's that edge of something extra, something seductive, something provocative . . .

Winona Ryder.

Put Bambi in stiletto heels and you have Winona Ryder. Perhaps.

The goddaughter of Timothy Leary, Winona Laura Horowitz was born in Winona, Minnesota, in 1972. As a kid she was a compulsive liar, addicted to vitamin C and – like Emily Lloyd in *Chicago Joe and the Showgirl* – obsessed with gangster movies. At the age of twelve she auditioned for a role in *Desert Bloom*, opposite Jon Voight, and so impressed a talent agent that he recommended her for a lead in *Lucas*, alongside the unknown Charlie Sheen. The part in *Desert Bloom* went to Annabeth Gish, but from *Lucas* Winona won the central role in *Square Dance*, co-starring Rob Lowe, Jason Robards and Jane Alexander. As a bespectacled, dungareed farm girl, Winona appeared to be the only one not acting. Meanwhile, Lowe – as her retarded lover – won a Golden Globe nomination.

In *Beetlejuice*, her first hit, she played Lydia Deetz, the morose daughter of the dreadful, *nouveau riche* Charles and Delia Deetz, occupants of a happily haunted New England farmhouse.

Michael Keaton, as the demonic Peoplebuster, press-ganged the belly laughs, but Winona got to bare her versatility.

1969, with Kiefer Sutherland, was an honest effort, but a damp squib at the box office. *Great Balls of Fire!* was an even bigger disappointment, but the dollar-fuelled publicity elevated the actress to the level of star.

Heathers, in which she played a high-school murderess, was a cult phenomenon. Winona explains that the film is 'teen angst with a body-count – incredibly cynical but at the same time really perceptive. I think it turned out one of the best movies I've ever seen in my life.'

Welcome Home, Roxy Carmichael followed, a darkly comic character study from Jim Abrahams of *Airplane!* fame. In it, she plays 15-year-old Dinky Bossetti who is 'very smart, but lives in her own shell, her own world that she's created for herself'.

Then there was *Mermaids*, with Cher and Bob Hoskins, and the fantasy *Edward Scissorhands* (from *Beetlejuice/ Batman* director Tim Burton). The latter film features Winona's

Christian Slater and Winona Ryder together in Heathers.

fiancé Johnny Depp in the title role, as a man with deformed hands. 'The fact that his hands are scissors has more to do with him not being able to touch than any literal interpretation,' Burton explains. 'It's a juxtaposition of reality with a fairy tale.' Winona is the female lead, and is supported by Alan Arkin, Anthony Michael Hall and Dianne Wiest. Incidentally, Wiest played Emily Lloyd's mother in *Cookie* . . .

Christian Slater. While the likes of Tom Cruise and Emilio Estevez are now presenting themselves as gentlemen in public, Christian Slater is carving himself something of a reputation as a hell-raiser.

Like Sean Penn, he has already seen the inside of a police cell, but is proving a somewhat more durable star. At first appearance, Slater would seem less interested in the art of acting than in the art of having a good time. And luckily for him, he has an engaging smile and a pretty face, and the parts are just rolling in. The latest news is that Twentieth Century-Fox have signed him up for a one-year first-look deal, with an option for a second year. Seldom are actors this young (he is twenty at the time of going to press) signed up by major companies.

The son of actor Michael Hawkins (Frank Ryan in TV's *Ryan's Hope*) and MGM/UA casting executive Mary Jo, Christian was subject to a life of theatre

from the word go. 'When I was a baby my mother took me up on stage,' he says; 'I mean, it was like *Roots*. She held me up above her head and said, "This is your life, my son." This is what she tells me. Of course, it could be a lie.'

He actually made his stage debut aged nine in a national tour of *The Music Man*, with Dick Van Dyke, a production that ended up on Broadway. Other Broadway credits included *Macbeth* (with Nicol Williamson), *David Copperfield, Merlin* and *A Christmas Carol*. He took the title role in *Oliver!* in summer stock and landed his first decent TV role in *Sherlock Holmes*, an HBO Special.

Parts in a variety of soap operas followed, including *One Life to Live, All My Children* and, of course, *Ryan's Hope*. He even sang and danced on stage at the 1983 Tony Awards ceremony – aged fourteen!

However, it was his performance as the novice monk Adso (Sean Connery's sidekick) in *The Name of the Rose* that first won him international attention. Although his contribution was on the bland side, it landed him a starring role in and good notices for *The Legend of Billie Jean*, with Helen Slater (no relation). Next, there was another HBO special, *Cry Wolf*, and a small role as Jeff Bridges' son in Francis Coppola's *Tucker*. He had the lead in *Gleaming the Cube*, an efficient social thriller (in which he played a punk one minute and a crusader-on-a-skateboard the next), and then came the hit that launched both him and Winona Ryder

into the public consciousness: *Heathers*.

As an outsider in the classroom, J. D. (Slater) looks like a wimp but actually carries a shotgun. The surprise is that he doesn't think twice about using it. J. D. became an instant cult favourite and anti-hero for '89, a dude who changed the English language as he spoke it.

The wimp had become a man, and a mean one at that.

'J. D. was the first bad guy I'd played,' Slater noted, and went on to re-create him in real life. Just before the New Year of 1990, the actor was jailed in West Hollywood for drunken driving, driving with a suspended licence, evading arrest and assaulting a police officer.

However, Winona Ryder had nothing but praise for her former co-star. 'He's one of the funniest people I know,' she glowed. 'He has a style that's really his own. Forty years from now someone's going to write a book called *Slater – The Legend*.'

And in spite of his bust-up with the police, Christian Slater was still in demand. He starred in Allan Moyle's *Pump Up the Volume*, a well-received, accurate examination of contemporary adolescence – as a shy youth who becomes a rebellious DJ. And again he charmed the critics, who had begun comparing him to a young Jack Nicholson.

'I can't escape it,' he acknowledges. 'It's cool, but I gotta be me.' However, he adds, 'I'd *kill* to work with that guy.'

Other movies crowded his schedule: *Personal Choice*, with Martin Sheen; *The Edge*, a TV thriller; a supporting role in a Fred Savage vehicle, *The Wizard*; the omnibus *Tales from the Darkside – The Movie*, in the episode taken from a Conan Doyle short story; and *On the Prowl*, with Corey Haim.

Slater was being handed all the experience in the world on a plate. And everybody was banging on his door. It was no surprise, then, when he was signed up to play rival to Billy the Kid (Emilio Estevez) in *Young Guns II*, alongside Kiefer Sutherland and Lou Diamond Phillips. With Charlie Sheen killed off in the first picture, the Brat Pack sequel needed somebody of Slater's attraction to give it a hope in hell at the box office.

And slowly but surely Christian Slater is gathering a hard-core following.

Film World Diary

JAMES CAMERON-WILSON

July

Batman clocks up $100 million in its first eleven days of release, an all time record ★ Film director Franklin J. Schaffner, 69, dies of cancer. His last film was *Welcome Home* ★ Character actor Jim Backus, 76, dies from pneumonia in Santa Monica, California ★ *Indiana Jones and the Last Crusade* clocks up $150 million in the United States, after six weeks ★ Spike Lee donates $25,000 to the United Negro College Fund towards forming a *Do the Right Thing* scholarship account ★ Director Steve Rash assembles a magnificent cast to star in his *Queens Logic*, including Kevin Bacon, Jamie Lee Curtis, John Malkovich, Joe Mantegna, Ken Olin and Tom Waits ★ Vestron Inc. lays off 140 workers, virtually dismantling its cinema operations. Many films find themselves without a distributor, including Kathryn Bigelow's *Blue Steel* ★ David Puttnam's first picture since leaving Columbia, *Memphis Belle*, starts production in England, with Matthew Modine, Eric Stoltz, John Lithgow and Billy Zane heading the cast ★ Young starlet Rebecca Schaeffer (*Radio Days*, *Scenes from the Class Struggle in Beverly Hills*), 21, is shot dead at her home by a 'fan' ★ Mel Gibson and Kim Basinger are voted the sexiest stars of 1989 in an American cable channel survey ★ Laurence Olivier dies peacefully at home, aged 82 ★ *Indiana Jones and the Last Crusade* breaks box-office records in Britain ★ *Batman* passes the $150 million mark in the US – before three weeks are up ★ For the record, *Ghostbusters II* pulls in $100 million after 45 days ★ The biggest money-making summer in the history of the US box office is hotting up ★ Robin Williams and his wife Marsha become the proud parents of a baby girl, Zelda ★

August

Less than six weeks from release, *Batman* accumulates a staggering $202,867,563 ★ In a rare interview, Marlon Brando talks about his latest film, *The Freshman*: 'It's going to be a flop, but after this, I'm retiring. I'm so fed up. I wish I hadn't finished with a stinker' ★ *Licence to Kill* earns £1 million at London's Odeon Leicester Square after 47 days ★ David Lynch's *Wild at Heart* starts production in the US, with Nicolas Cage, Laura Dern, Isabella Rossellini, Willem Dafoe and Harry Dean Stanton in the cast ★ *Lethal Weapon 2* and *Honey, I Shrunk the Kids* both clock up $100 million at the US box office in the same week ★ Peter Bogdanovich's sequel to *The Last Picture Show* – *Texasville* – starts production in the Lone Star state, with Jeff Bridges, Cybill Shepherd, Cloris Leachman, Timothy Bottoms and Randy Quaid repeating their old roles ★ Twentieth Century-Fox's much-touted *The Abyss* opens to disappointing box-office results, unable to oust *Parenthood* in its second week at number one ★ *Reversal of Fortune*, starring Glenn Close, Jeremy Irons and Ron Silver, and produced by Oliver Stone, enters production in New York ★ Since opening nine months ago, London's Museum of the Moving Image has attracted 450,000 paying customers ★ *Batman* opens in Britain and smashes all previous box-office records – by 26 per cent! ★

September

Gene Hackman is declared the busiest star in Hollywood, having notched up nine films in under three years. Runners-up include Charlie Sheen, Raul Julia and Jim Belushi. Michael Caine is demoted to fourteenth place ★ In a statement released to the press, Marlon Brando talks about his latest film, *The Freshman*: 'Clearly, I was wrong about the quality of the picture. It is clear to see that the movie contains moments of high comedy that will be remembered for decades to come' ★ *The Krays*, after years of planning and false starts, finally starts filming in London's East End ★ Sony buys Columbia Pictures from Coca-Cola for $3.4 billion ★ British producer Michael Klinger (*Cul-de-Sac*, *Get Carter*), 68, dies of a heart attack in Watford ★ French film-maker Claude Lelouch becomes the proud father of a bouncing boy ★ Meryl Streep bows out of the film version of *Evita* due to exhaustion and wrangles over money ★ British actor Philip Sayer, 42, star of TV's *Bluebell*, dies of abdominal cancer in London ★ Bernardo Bertolucci's *The Sheltering Sky*, an epic story of 'marital discord, mental deterioration and death' starts production in North Africa with Debra Winger, John Malkovich and Campbell Scott (son of George C.). Britain's Jeremy Thomas (*The Last Emperor*, *The Great Rock 'n' Roll Swindle*) is producing ★ American character actor William Traylor (*Dead-Bang*, *Fletch Lives*), 60, dies after an extended illness ★

October

Monty Python's Graham Chapman, 48, dies of spinal cancer in Maidstone, Kent ★ Bette Davis dies, aged 81 ★ *Look Who's Talking* is a surprise hit for 'has-been' John Travolta. The film grosses $12,107,784 in three days ★ Director Bille August (*Pelle the Conqueror*) walks off the David Puttnam production *The House of the Spirits* which was to have starred William Hurt, Glenn Close and Isabella Rossellini ★

155

Cornel Wilde, 74, dies of leukaemia in Los Angeles ★ *Look Who's Talking* tops its previous week's record by *increasing* its take by seventeen per cent. That's almost unheard of ★ Paul Shenar, 53, American actor adept at smooth villains (*Best Seller*, *Raw Deal*) dies of AIDS ★ Rising film actor Michael Carmine (*Leviathan*, *'batteries not included'*) dies of heart failure, aged 30 ★ Melanie Griffith gives birth to a little girl in Austin, Texas. Don Johnson is the father ★ Sir Anthony Quayle dies of cancer aged 76 ★ Ted Turner's empire adds The Turner Pictures division to its list of operations, promising an initial production of six features budgeted between $6 million and $8 million each ★ Shaun Considine's controversial book, *Bette and Joan: The Divine Feud*, is published in the States ★ Handsome leading man Stephen Collins (*Stella*, *Loving Couples*) and wife Faye Grant are blessed with a baby daughter ★

November

Raging Bull is voted best film of the 1980s by US and British critics in at least three separate polls ★ Alexander Salkind grandly announces that he has commissioned Mario Puzo to write the screenplay for *Christopher Columbus – The Movie*, to be premiered on 12 October 1992 – to commemorate the quincentennial of the discovery of America ★ Eddie Murphy's *Harlem Nights* breaks box-office records in the US ★ A cinema in Detroit cancels the showing of *Harlem Nights* after shooting incidents. The film, set in prohibition New York, attracts rival gang members ★ British media favourites, America's Michael Brandon and England's Glynis Barber (TV's *Dempsey and Makepeace*), tie the knot in London ★ *Batman* clocks up $250 million at the US box office ★ London's first multiplex cinema, the eight-screen UCI, opens in the renovated Whiteley's department store, in Bayswater ★ Dennis Quaid pops the Big Question to Meg Ryan. She says 'yes' ★ *Back to the Future, Part II* grosses $43,016,225 in five days in the States ★ *Look Who's Talking* clocks up $100 million Over There ★ Kevin Costner's directorial debut, the epic Western *Dances with Wolves*, finally completes production – 30 days behind schedule ★ Plans for a £2.6 billion movie theme park in Rainham, Essex, are unveiled by Steven Spielberg. The park should open some-time in the mid–1990s to service five million visitors a year ★ Dan Aykroyd and actress wife Donna Dixon become glowing parents to an infant girl ★

December

Michelle Pfeiffer is voted best actress by the New York Critics' Film Circle, by the LA Critics Association and by the National Board of Review – for her role in *The Fabulous Baker Boys* ★ Hardy Hollywood star John Payne dies aged 77 in California ★ English character actor Howard Lang dies aged 78 ★ Tom Cruise's latest epic – *Days of Thunder* – starts production in North Carolina under Tony Scott's direction. Robert Duvall, Randy Quaid, Nicole Kidman and Cary Elwes co-star ★ Film director Susan Seidelman (*She-Devil*, *Desperately Seeking Susan*) gives birth to a son. The father is film producer Jonathan Brett ★ Actor Christian Slater (*Gleaming the Cube*, *Heathers*) is thrown into jail in West Hollywood for drunken driving, driving with a suspended licence, evading arrest and assaulting a police officer ★ To publicise *Born on the Fourth of July*, Tom Cruise agrees to be interviewed by *Playboy*, *Time* magazine, *Rolling Stone* and *US*. Cruise mania grips America ★

January

Maggie Smith, 55, is created a dame in the New Year Honours list ★ *Batman* is declared the most successful film of 1989, followed by *Indiana Jones and the Temple of Doom*, *Lethal Weapon 2* and *Honey, I Shrunk the Kids* ★ 1989 is confirmed as the biggest-grossing year in American box-office history ★ Arthur Kennedy, 75, dies of a brain tumour ★ Ian Charleson (Eric Liddell in *Chariots of Fire*), 40, dies of AIDS-related septicaemia shortly after taking over from Daniel Day Lewis in *Hamlet* on the London stage ★ British comedian Terry-Thomas dies aged 78 ★ French actress and film director Juliet Berto, 42, passes away in Paris ★ America's National Society of Film Critics bestows its best actress award on Michelle Pfeiffer, for *The Fabulous Baker Boys* ★ Gordon Jackson dies, aged 66, after a short illness ★ Dawn Steel, president of Columbia Pictures, resigns after two years and two months in office. She expresses an interest in resuming work in film on a non-executive level ★ Paramount Pictures announces the world-wide box-office take of its *Indiana Jones and the Last Crusade* as $440,100,000 ★ Cancer-stricken Sammy Davis Jr becomes a born-again Christian in an attempt to save his life. Thirty-three years earlier he had converted to Judaism ★ *Back to the Future, Part II* clocks up $100 million at the US box office ★ Caroline McWilliams serves husband Michael Keaton with preliminary divorce papers following his affairs with former porn princess Serina Robinson and *Batman* co-star Kim Basinger ★ Barbara Stanwyck, 82, dies ★ The Electric, Britain's oldest surviving purpose-built cinema, re-opens in London's Portobello Road ★ The teaming of Robert De Niro and Dustin Hoffman in *Gold Lust*, 'a contemporary action-adventure' is announced ★ In the United States, Steven Spielberg's *Indiana Jones and the Last Crusade* is released on video both in the 'de-luxe wide-screen version' (i.e. letter-box format) and in the normal, square, TV-sized version (i.e. cropped) ★ Ava Gardner dies of pneumonia, aged 67 ★ Kim Basinger ditches Prince ★ Francis (Ford) Coppola files for bankruptcy. His company, Zoetrope Productions, admits to debts of up to $28.9 million ★ Roy Scheider becomes the delighted father of a little boy ★ John Hurt marries girl-friend Jo Dalton in London ★ Anthony Quinn is hospitalised for a heart bypass operation ★ Former child star Gary Coleman wins a court battle with his parents over the fortune he amassed while still a child. Coleman, now 21 – but still 4ft 8in – is allowed to retain control of his estimated £4,300,000 earnings. However, the ugly legal war between son and mom and pop continues ★

February

Marcello Mastroianni, 65-year-old Roman matinee idol, begs on public television for his estranged wife to return to him. Mrs Mastroianni, actress Flora Carabella, is currently living with a younger man, 'Tony' ★ Tom Cruise and Mimi Rogers separate ★ John Hurt becomes the proud father of a little boy ★ *Driving Miss Daisy* is nominated for nine Oscars, eclipsing the firm favourite *Born on the Fourth of July*. However, the bookies bet on *July* as best picture, Tom Cruise as best actor and Jessica Tandy as best actress for *Daisy* (in spite of the fact that Michelle Pfeiffer is also nominated and has won every award in

Christendom) ★ Favourite mousta-chioed musical-comedy actor Erik Rhodes dies aged 84. He is best remembered for his roles in the Astaire-Rogers films of the 1930s ★ Kiefer Sutherland, 23, files for divorce from actress Camelia Kath, 37, and befriends Julia Roberts, his co-star from *Flatliners* ★ Sylvester Stallone hires attorney James J. Binns for his campaign to keep an 8½ foot, $53,000 bronze statue of himself as Rocky on the front steps on the Philadelphia Art Museum. The local Park Commission wants it removed ★ British actress Fabia Drake, 86, dies in London ★

March

Tom Cruise is seen in the company of Ivana Trump, emotionally bruised wife of filthy-rich philanderer Donald Trump ★ Glamorous French star Capucine, 55, jumps from a window of her eighth-floor penthouse in Lausanne, Switzerland ★ Eddie Murphy disappoints Paramount by refusing to do *Beverly Hills Cop III*. Rumours also suggest that he is looking for another studio to make his films ★ No one film sweeps the Oscars this year, although *Driving Miss Daisy* wins four – for best film, best actress, screenplay adaptation and for best make-up. Daniel Day Lewis wins the trophy for best actor (for *My Left Foot*). Billy Crystal MCs the awards ceremony, complete with live satellite footage from Moscow, Sydney, London, Buenos Aires and Tokyo ★

April

Producer David Geffen pays an unprecedented $1.75 million for an original screenplay, *The Last Boy Scout*, written 'on spec' by Shane Black. In real terms that works out at $12,500 a page. Black was previously paid $400,000 for his script of *Lethal Weapon* ★ Elizabeth Taylor announces that she isn't HIV positive, following an AIDS test, but it is revealed that the actress has pneumonia and is seriously ill ★ American character actor Albert Salmi, 62, separated from his wife, shoots her and then kills himself ★ John Malkovich and Glenne Headley (*Dick Tracy*) are divorced ★ Dexter Gordon, jazz saxophonist and Oscar-nominated star of *'Round Midnight*, dies aged 67 – of kidney failure ★ Elizabeth Taylor recovers from her critical illness ★ Claire Bloom weds novelist Philip Roth (*Portnoy's Com-*

plaint) in New York. She was previously married (1959–71) to Rod Steiger ★

May

Teenage Mutant Ninja Turtles clocks up $100 million at the US box office. Turtle fever is rife ★ *The Hunt for Red October* also passes the $100 million mark ★ The American box office is already hotting up for the summer and doing better biz than last year. *Pretty Woman* passes the $100 million mark ★ Ditto *Driving Miss Daisy* ★ Amy Irving gives birth to director Bruno Barreto's baby. They worked together on *A Show of Force* ★ Paul Hogan and Linda Kozlowski are married at the former's Possum Creek property, 500 miles north of Sydney, Australia ★ Veteran actor Charles Farrell, 89, passes away in Palm Springs of cardiac arrest ★ Sammy Davis Jr is reduced to 4 stone 4 lbs by throat cancer. Frank Sinatra, Jerry Lewis and Michael Jackson visit his bedside ★ Actor Franklyn Seales (*Southern Comfort, The Onion Field*), 37, dies of AIDS ★ Actor Robert Hays (*Airplane!*) marries singer Cherie Curry ★ John Cleese is divorced from his second wife, American actress Barbara Trentham, after more than nine years ★ Sammy Davis Jr dies, aged 64 ★ Muppeteer Jim Henson, 53, dies of streptococcus pneumonia, brought on by overwork ★ British film actress Jill Ireland, 54, dies after a long battle with cancer. She is survived by her husband, Charles Bronson ★ Marlon Brando's 32-year-old son, Christian, is involved in a shooting incident in which Dag Drollet, boy-friend of Brando's 20-year-old pregnant daughter Cheyenne, is shot dead in the actor's home after an argument with Christian. Christian Brando is held in custody. Describing himself as a 'self-employed welder', Christian's own attempt at an acting career had proved abortive, despite one role as an accused murderer ★ In spite of predictions to the contrary, Dirk Bogarde fails to win the Best Actor award at Cannes for *Daddy Nostalgia*. Gérard Depardieu wins the accolade instead, for his title role in *Cyrano de Bergerac* ★ Robert Wagner and Jill St John finally tie the knot ★ Jack Nicholson is reputedly offered $40 million to reprise his role as the Joker in *Batman 2* ★ Largo Entertainment coughs up a phenomenal $1 million for the screenplay of

The Ticking Man, by so-called newcomers Brian Helgeland and Manny Coto ★ It is out: Kim Basinger and Alec Baldwin are dating (at the very least) ★

June

Film production in Britain reaches an all-time low. Not since the 1920s has the UK made so few films. The only production currently shooting is *Hamlet*, directed by Italy's Franco Zeffirelli and starring Australia's Mel Gibson and America's Glenn Close. However, the script is by an Englishman ★ According to strong rumours, Rob Lowe checks into a clinic to cure his obsession for sex and pornography ★ Paramount object to Marlon Brando's parody of 'The Godfather' in Tri-Star's *The Freshman*, in which he plays a Mafia don. Lawyers from both studios enter 'negotiations' ★ *Total Recall* grosses $25,533,700 in three days in the States, a 1990 record ★ An activist group calling itself Activists Against Sexist Pigs vandalises property belonging to Twentieth Century-Fox in protest against the company casting well-known misogynist Andrew Dice Clay in the forthcoming *The Adventures of Ford Fairlane* ★ Sir Richard Attenborough, David Puttnam, John Boorman and other representatives of the British film industry meet Margaret Thatcher at Downing Street to discuss setting up two programmes: one to establish a tax-incentive scheme to invest in film production, the other to examine 'structural modifications' and the possibility of increased funding through video and TV levies. An initial £5 million is allotted to the scheme ★ Peter Ustinov, 69, finally receives a knighthood in the Queen's Birthday Honours list. Actress Eileen Atkins is honoured with a CBE ★ *Another 48 Hrs* is damned by the American critics, with the exception of some Chicago reviewers ★ Hector Babenco's *At Play in the Fields of the Lord* enters production, with Tom Berenger, John Lithgow, Daryl Hannah, Aidan Quinn and Tom Waits heading the cast ★ *Dick Tracy* breaks box-office records for Walt Disney in its opening weekend, but its three-day income of $22.5 million is a disappointment in light of the phenomenal marketing budget of the film. Reviews are mixed ★ Dustin Hoffman is announced as the star of Robert Benton's adaptation of E. L. Doctorow's novel *Billy Bathgate* ★

157

In Memoriam

A former radio announcer who graduated from the American Academy of Dramatic Arts in 1933, **Jim** (James Gilmore) **Backus** was already a veteran of stage, radio and vaudeville when he made his screen debut in three 1949 movies: *Easy Living, Father Was a Fullback* and *The Great Lover*. But although he went on to appear in nearly forty films (among them *Pat and Mike* in 1952, *Androcles and the Lion* in 1953, *Rebel Without a Cause* in 1955 – in which he played James Dean's dad – *Man of a Thousand Faces* in 1957, *The Wonderful World of the Brothers Grimm* in 1962, *Johnny Cool* and *It's a Mad, Mad, Mad, Mad World* in 1963, *Myra Breckinridge* in 1970, *Seven from Heaven* and *C.H.O.M.P.S.* in 1979) it was his radio and TV work that brought him the greatest kudos and the most fans.

Jim Backus.

Television series included 'I Married Joan', which ran from 1952 to 1955, and 'Gilligan's Island' (1964 to 1967). Backus also won considerable acclaim for providing the highly distinctive voice to that endearing short-sighted cartoon character Mr Magoo, including the full-length *Mr Magoo's Christmas Carol*, which was TV premiered in 1962. It was partly his illness that made Backus turn to the pen, writing a number of radio and TV scripts and three books: *Rocks on the Roof, Only When I Laugh* and *What Are You Doing After the Orgy?* Backus died, aged 76, on 3 July 1989 from a bout of pneumonia, accentuated by the Parkinson's Disease from which he had suffered for a considerable time.

Though best known as a radio, stage and vaudeville performer, **Eric Barker**, who died, aged 78, in early June 1990, appeared in some thirty British comedy films, including *Blue Murder at St Trinian's* (1958), *Dentist in the Chair* (1960), *On the Beat* (1962), *Those Magnificent Men in Their Flying Machines* (1965) and *There's a Girl in My Soup* (1970), as well as several other of the St Trinian's films (including *The Great St Trinian's Train Robbery*) and some half-dozen comedies in the 'Carry On' series. He also wrote many revue sketches, radio comedy series and lyrics for stage musicals: and he had three novels, his autobiography and a collection of short stories published. The 1940s and 1950s saw him at the peak of his success; his 'Just Fancy' radio series, for instance, during its twelve-year BBC run, made him, as both its writer and its star, a household name.

Texas-born silent-screen star **Madge Bellamy** (real name, Margaret Philpott) died aged between 86 and 96 – various sources give various dates of birth – on 24 January 1990. She made her acting debut at the age of five, and ten years later became a star of the silent screen. But in fact, after appearing in a number of big silents, her screen career was short and was over by 1935. In the Mary Pickford style, she usually projected characters of sweet innocence, and her biggest successes were in the John Ford classic *The Iron Horse* in 1924 and, two years earlier, *Lorna Doone*. She also achieved praise for her work opposite Buck Jones in the Borzage film *Lazybones* (1925) and in the famous *White Zombie* (1932), which was seen and enjoyed by a far wider audience than she had with any other film. Her final three small performances were in *Charlie Chan in London* (1934), *The Great Hotel Murder* and *The Daring Young Man* (both 1935). Some of the more bizarre incidents in her private life were a marriage which lasted just four days (in 1928), and the shooting of a boy-friend in 1943 which brought her a (suspended) prison sentence, after which she lived like a recluse for the rest of her life.

Although she played the lead in several early 1950s films, and in all appeared in around twenty films – including a role in the 1954 *A Star Is Born* – **Amanda Blake** (real name, Beverly Louise Neill), who died of cancer at the age of 60 on 16 August 1989, will be best recalled for her nineteen-year stint as Miss Kitty, the Dodge City saloon owner, in the TV serial 'Gunsmoke'. Her last large-screen appearances were in *B.O.R.N.* and *The Boost*.

It's unlikely that many moviegoers will be able to say they've seen the face of

Mel (Melvin Jerome) **Blanc**, for he made only a few minor movies (the only ones I can find listed are *Neptune's Daughter* in 1949 and *Kiss Me Stupid* in 1964), but it is certain that millions are very familiar with his voice . . . well, voices. For it was Mel who contributed the voices to a great many cartoon stars, such as Bugs Bunny, Porky Pig, Woody Woodpecker, Tweety Pie and many others in the 3000 cartoons in which he played such an important part. Mel's first contribution to showbiz was as an orchestral musician (he played double bass, tuba, violin and sousaphone) and later as the conductor of a theatre-pit orchestra. But it was not until 1937, after many previous unsuccessful attempts, that he persuaded the Warner cartoon unit to give him an audition. It was a success, and so began his 40 years' vocal work with the unit. But on 10 July 1989, the master of this art fell silent when Mel Blanc died, at the age of 81, from heart disease and complications. He will be a great loss not only to the movies but also to the radio and TV shows to which he regularly contributed.

Although TV's 'Gunsmoke' kept **Tom Brown** (who died, aged 77, on 3 June 1990) more or less continually employed over a period of ten years, he found time before, during and after the series to appear in almost 40 feature films. These include *The Hoosier Schoolmaster* (1924, his screen debut), *Anne of Green Gables* (1934), *Freckles* (1935), *Maytime* (1937), *Margie* (1940), *The House on 92nd Street* (1945), *The Duke of Chicago* (1949), *Fireman Save My Child* (1954), *The Quiet Gun* (1957) and, his last, *The Choppers* (1961). Brown was also a regular player in several other TV series apart from 'Gunsmoke'.

The career of French star **Capucine** (real name Germaine Lefebvre) came to a sad end on 17 March 1990, when she apparently jumped to her death from her eighth-floor flat in Lausanne, at the age of 57. She was a professional model when Jacques Becker chose her to appear in his 1949 film *Rendez-Vous de Juliet*. But it was after going to America in the late 1950s to study acting with Gregory Ratoff that her career really took off, in 1960, with roles in *Song Without End* and *North to Alaska*. Two

Capucine.

years later she won international acclaim for her performance in *Walk on the Wild Side*, and at the same time revealed an unexpected gift for comedy in Blake Edwards's *The Pink Panther*, playing opposite Peter Sellers (she was to co-star with him again in two further 'PP' films, *The Trail of the Pink Panther* and *The Curse of the Pink Panther*), and in *What's New Pussycat?* (again with Sellers). Unlike many Hollywood imports, Capucine did not stay in America, preferring to travel around Europe, playing in *The Queens/Le Fate* (1966) and *Red Sun* in France in 1971, *Per Amore* (1976) in Italy, *The Exquisite Cadaver* in Spain in 1972, *An Arabian Adventure* (1979) in Britain, and *Fraulein Doktor* in Yugoslavia in 1969. She also co-starred in *Fellini Satyricon* in 1969. As well as these and other European films, she made a number of TV features. Tall, slim and graceful, Capucine had a special kind of sex appeal, quite different to the usual type of screen beauty but very striking nevertheless. Her suicide remains unexplained.

James Carreras, who died, aged 81, on 9 June 1990, deserves his place in any cinematic Hall of Fame for his series of Hammer 'horrors', modestly budgeted but extremely well produced thrillers based on such classic gothic legends as Frankenstein and Dracula, featuring such masters of the genre as Peter Cushing and Christopher Lee, under the modest but very effective direction of Terence Fisher. In 1972, James's son Michael took over the Hammer mantle. The Hammer headquarters was a grand old mansion at Bray, near Maidenhead, where many of the movies were made, and it was at Bray that international sex-symbol stars Ursula Andress and Raquel Welch made their screen debuts. Financially the most successful British film company ever, today's Hollywood producers might take note that Hammer films had a 25-day shooting schedule and a top budget of $500,000.

Ian Charleson, who died of AIDS on 6 January 1990, aged 40, studied architecture in Edinburgh before deciding to make acting his career. After drama school he achieved some success as Jimmy Porter in the 1972 revival of

Bette Davis.

Look Back in Anger. After appearing in a number of films (*Gandhi*, *Greystoke* and *Lord of the Apes* in the UK, and *Opera* in Italy) he sprang to prominence as the Olympic runner with strict Christian ethics in *Chariots of Fire*. On the stage he had a season with the Royal Shakespeare Company, and he was often to be seen in television productions.

Most movie-goers would surely agree that **Bette Davis**, who died of cancer in a French hospital on 6 October 1989 at the age of 81 (while *en route* from Spain to America), was one of the greatest female stars the cinema has produced. All her life she was a great fighter, and she died battling against the disease, after undergoing a mastectomy and a bad stroke in 1983.

I saw Miss Davis for the first time on the screen in 1932, at the press show of *Cabin in the Cotton* at the New Gallery cinema, and after it I emerged into Regent Street dazed with the power of the young star's personality. From that moment I was her fan; though I have seen thousands of now forgotten films since, that siren performance remains etched in my memory.

Ruth Elizabeth Davis (her full name) was born in Lowell, Mass., and while still at high school made up her mind that she would be an actress. Her initial forays into the profession were not encouraging, however. Rejected by one drama school, but subsequently accepted by another, she was sacked from her first engagement by director George Cukor. But she took such setbacks in her stride and achieved her Broadway debut in 1928 in the play *Broken Dishes*. Her initial screen test, for Goldwyn, was abortive, but undeterred she won another, and a contract, with Universal, whose boss Carl Laemmle made the famous remark when he was introduced to her that 'she's got as much sex appeal as Slim Summerville!' That didn't stop Miss Davis, who made a number of undistinguished movies for him before switching to Warner Bros, where she achieved stardom in the critically savaged production *Ex-Lady*. After the first of her many battles with Warner, they allowed her to cross to RKO Radio to star opposite Leslie Howard in *Of*

Human Bondage, a John Cromwell triumph. Back on the Warner lot, still fighting, she made *Dangerous* in 1935, which she considered rubbish but which brought her the first of her two Oscars. This was followed in 1936 by *The Petrified Forest*, which was also a triumph. Her battles with Warner Bros now led to the lawcourts, where she lost her case – although Warner's paid all her legal costs!

From then on it was (with small hiccups) success all the way. She won her second Oscar in 1938 for *Jezebel*, and followed this with a string of memorable performances in films like *Dark Victory*, *The Old Maid* and *The Private Lives of Elizabeth and Essex* (all in 1939), *All This and Heaven Too* and *The Letter* (1940), *The Little Foxes* (1941), *Now Voyager* (1942), and the magnificent *All About Eve* (1950). With her career stalling in the late 1950s, she came to Britain to make *The Scapegoat* (1959) and followed this with the two memorable thrillers *Whatever Happened to Baby Jane* (1962) and *Hush, Hush Sweet Charlotte* (1965). Her final work in the studios was in 1989 on *Wicked Stepmother*, which she walked out of mid-way through shooting after a fight with the director. (The work that she had already done was, however, incorporated in the released film.) She made many telefilms and appeared in the 'Hitchcock', 'Perry Mason', 'Gunsmoke' and 'Wagon Train' series, and she also took a few stage roles. In later years she toured a one-woman show called 'Bette Davis in Person', and made appearances for organisations like the British Film Institute. She wrote two volumes of autobiography, *The Lonely Life* in 1962 and *This 'n' That* in 1974, and she also collaborated with writer Whitney Stine for his book *Mother Goddam: The Story of the Career of Bette Davis* in 1974. A tremendous, forceful, determined character who was prepared to fight tooth-and-nail for what she wanted, and an actress of true star status and great ability.

The man they called 'Mr Entertainment', **Sammy Davis Jr**, died of cancer on 16 May 1990 at the age of 64, after appearing professionally before the public for no less than 60 years. Starting out as a child dancer on variety bills (where Davis Sr was also a dancer), by the age of four Harlem-born Sammy had his own vaudeville act, called 'Will

Sammy Davis Jr.

Mastin's Gang'. When he was demobbed after US Army Service, he toured the halls with The Mastin Trio, and did much TV work, in the course of which he met Frank Sinatra, who was to become his champion and friend. In 1954 his career seemed likely to end when he was involved in a terrible car crash that resulted in his losing an eye; but a few weeks later he was back in business with an eye patch and plenty of jokes about it. It was this crash that brought about (at least indirectly) his conversion to Judaism (I recall him joking about being the only black Jew in America). With his boundless energy and ambition, multi-talented Davis (singer, dancer, raconteur and player of many different instruments) worked mostly on TV and in live shows, but he did make a number of movies, starting with *The Benny Goodman Story* in 1956. Some others of his score of movies were *Porgy and Bess* (1959), *The Threepenny Opera* (a German film in 1963), *Johnny Cool* (1963), *Salt and Pepper* (a British film made in 1968), *Gone with the West*

(1975) and *The Cannonball Run* (1982). His final appearance in front of the cameras was in the telefilm *The Kid Who Loved Christmas*, which is due for release at Christmas 1990.

A lot less well-known than his producer brother Anatole (*The Way to the Stars*, etc.), **Dimitri de Grunwald**, who died on 26 May 1990, aged 76, produced a number of British movies before he turned to the chemical industry in 1980. His films included *The Millionairess* (1960), *Mr Topaze* (1961), *Shalako* (1968) and *That Lucky Touch* (1975).

Although *Variety* claimed in its obituary of **Anton Diffring** that he was British born, this busy German actor was actually born in Koblenz. He graduated from the Berlin Drama Academy, and did not arrive in Britain – after stage appearances in Canada and the US – until 1950, when he was 32. Thereafter he based himself in Britain, while making films in Europe and America – nearly fifty in all, including a couple never released, *The Day the Clown Died* (with Jerry Lewis) and *Hitler's Son*.

Among his best known films were *Hotel Sahara* (1951), *The Red Beret* and *Albert RN* (1953), *The Colditz Story* and *I Am a Camera* (1955), *Reach for the Sky* (1956), *The Heroes of Telemark* (1965)

Anton Diffring.

Charles Farrell (with Janet Gaynor).

and *Where Eagles Dare* (1969). Four of his last performances were in the 1980s releases *Victory, Summer of the Samurai, Richard and Cosima* and *Faceless*. He also appeared in a number of TV films and series, his thin, eagle face making him an obvious choice for Nazi roles, of which he once complained he had played too many. He died, aged 70, in the south of France on 20 May 1989.

Mark Dignam, who died on 29 September 1989 at the age of 60, was one of those actors whose faces are generally better known than their names. A reliable, popular character actor for some sixty years, in both Britain and America (making his Broadway debut in *Oscar Wilde* in 1938), his stage credits include seasons with both the Royal Shakespeare and National Theatre companies. Though unmentioned in many film reference books, he did appear in a number of movies including the 1969 *Hamlet*. Some of his other films are *Dead Cert*; *The Charge of the Light Brigade*; *David, Lion of Judah*; *No Love for Johnnie*; *Sink the Bismark!*;

The Prisoner; *Murder in the Cathedral*; and *The Maggie*.

Helen Jerome Eddy, a popular silent screen actress of her day, who died at the beginning of February 1990, made her debut in 1915 in a film titled *The Red Virgin*, subsequently supporting Mary Pickford in *Rebecca of Sunnybrook Farm*. Signed by Paramount, she settled into a period of playing upper-class leading ladies in such films as *The Bitter Tea of General Yen*, *Mr Smith Goes to Washington* and *Mr Deeds Goes to Town*. She made her final screen appearance in *Strike Up the Band* in 1940. She made more than 30 films, her parts in them varying from that of the star, to feature and even 'bit' player.

Foreign language film-goers of a few years back will certainly recall the name of **Aldo Fabrizi**, one of Italy's most brilliant and popular comedy actors, who died, aged 85, in Rome on 2 April 1990. He had already made several films before he was seen by British movie-goers for the first time in 1945 in Rossellini's *Open City*. Subsequently

resisting all offers to appear abroad during the 1940s and 1950s, he played in a large number of Italian films, few of which ever came to Britain, though those that did enhanced his reputation as a comedian of outstanding merit. A former music-hall star (between 1931 and 1941), Fabrizi was also a poet of some stature, a screenwriter and a director. Though latterly more concerned with cooking pasta (he wrote two books on the subject), he did appear in what was to be his last film as late as 1985 – *Carefree Giovanni*.

Charles Farrell, who died at the age of 89 on 6 May 1990, will always be associated with Janet Gaynor, and indeed it was with her that he had his greatest success. The son of a silent-film era cinema owner, Farrell helped his father and so became enamoured with the movies. Deciding to try his luck in Hollywood, extra work and 'bit' roles led to his name appearing on the credits list for the first time in 1925 in *Wings of Youth*. Two years later he was chosen to partner Miss Gaynor in what was to prove a sensational success, Frank Borzage's *Seventh Heaven*. The star partnership was to last through seven successful years and eleven films. When it ended, so did the successful part of Farrell's career, for although in all he made more than forty films (including the British productions *Trouble Ahead/Falling in Love* in 1934, *Flying Doctor* in 1936, *Moonlight Sonata* in 1937 and *Convoy* in 1940), he never again achieved anything like the success he had had with Gaynor. But as his film career waned, his other career, that of club/hotel owner in Palm Springs, waxed mightily, eventually making him a dollar millionaire. His best movies include *High Society Blues* (1930), *Street Angel* (1928), *Body and Soul* (1931) and *Change of Heart* (1934). Farrell also had some success on radio, including a sound version of *Seventh Heaven*, in which he again played opposite Miss Gaynor.

If the tributes published about **Greta Garbo** following her death at the age of 84 on 15 April 1990 were universally full of praise for her professional achievement, most of them lacked details of her personal background and private life, reflecting the veil drawn over them by the star throughout, and after, her screen career. At the age of

36, and at the peak of her success, she suddenly ended this career when she walked out of the film studios, never to return. From then on she lived the life of a virtual recluse, even to the extent of disguising herself to escape attention when she made the occasional foray into the world. Resolutely she lived up to the famous line of dialogue she had spoken in the 1932 classic, *Grand Hotel*: 'I want to be alone.'

Born in Stockholm in 1905, Garbo, whose real name was Greta Louise Gustafsson, was about 25 when she appeared in two short advertising films made by the store where she worked as a sales assistant. These attracted enough attention for her to be offered the female lead in a minor comedy feature, *Peter the Tramp*, the experience deciding her to make acting her career. After some drama lessons and subsequent small stage roles, she was given an important part in Mauritz Stiller's 1924 movie *The Atonement of Gosta Berling*, after which, in 1925, she was given another important part in Pabst's German classic, *Joyless Street*, with Asta Nielsen and Werner Krauss. A year later, MGM offered her a Hollywood contract, the initial result of which was a leading role in the company's 1926 release *The Torrent*. *The Temptress* followed (the same year) and, in 1927, *The Flesh and the Devil*, in which her co-star was John Gilbert, with whom she became linked in an oft-reported torrid love affair. After a further film with

Ava Gardner.

Greta Garbo.

Gilbert, *Love*, made the same year, Garbo appeared in several indifferent productions, but in 1930 she made her first talkie, *Anna Christie*, launched with great ballyhoo by MGM as the film in which 'Garbo Talks!'

Three routine features followed (*Romance* in 1930, *Inspiration* and *Susan Lennox, Her Fall and Rise* in 1931), preceding more major success in *Mata Hari* (1931), *Grand Hotel* and *As You Desire Me* (both in 1932). At this point Garbo suddenly packed her bag and went home to Sweden, giving rise to gossip stories that she would never return. But a year later, she turned up in Hollywood again, having cannily negotiated a new contract with MGM which not only gave her a big rise in salary, but also the right to refuse scripts, directors, co-stars, supporting cast and even cameramen if she didn't want to work with them. The first film under this contract was *Queen Christina* (1933), in which she insisted the studio's choice of co-star – Laurence Olivier – be replaced by John Gilbert. There followed further success in *The Painted Veil* (1934), *Anna Karenina* (1935) and the even more popular

Camille (1936). After her next film, the anti-climactic *Conquest* in 1937, Garbo took another year off, returning to make the outstanding Lubitsch comedy *Ninotchka* in 1939. The next film, *Two-Faced Woman* in 1941, was something of a critical and box-office disaster and, some have claimed, was influential in Garbo walking out of the studio never to return – though others have said this had nothing whatever to do with her decision.

It is extraordinary in view of her acclaim that Garbo never won an Oscar, despite being nominated three times (for *Anna Christie*, *Romance* and *Camille*). She was, however, given an honorary Oscar in 1954, and in 1986 was awarded a gold medal by the Swedish Government. Perhaps it was Clarence Brown, one of her favourite directors, who coined her most apt obituary when he said in 1963: 'Today, without having made a film since 1940, she is still the greatest. She is the prototype of all stars.'

The daughter of a poor tenant farmer forced out of business by the Great Depression, **Ava Gardner** (who was more than once described in print as

Paulette Goddard.

the 'world's most beautiful woman') died in London, where she had made her home for many years, on 25 January 1990 at the age of 67. Although she made more than fifty often classic films, her career brought her only one Oscar nomination, for *Mogambo* in 1953. Trained as a secretary, one of her brother-in-law's photographs of her somehow ended up in MGM's casting office, as a result of which she had a successful screen test and became a Metro trainee starlet. After a number of bit parts, the public and the critics first became aware of her when she played opposite fellow newcomer Burt Lancaster in 1946's Hemingway adaptation, *The Killers*. That success brought her bigger and better roles in films like *Showboat* and *Pandora and the Flying Dutchman* in 1951, *The Snows of Kilimanjaro* the following year, *Mogambo* (1953), *The Barefoot Contessa*

(1954), *Bhowani Junction* (1956), *On the Beach* (1959), *55 Days in Pekin* (1963), *The Night of the Iguana* (1964), *Mayerling* (1968), *Earthquake* (1974) and *City on Fire* (1979). Her final appearance was in the TV feature *Harem*, which she made in 1986, playing one of the small-screen roles which she took in her later years. Initially scornful about her own acting, in later years she tried to give good, honest and workmanlike performances, and often succeeded. She could be painfully honest about people (such as calling John Ford 'The meanest man on earth,') and although she kept friendly with her three ex-husbands (Mickey Rooney, Artie Shaw and Frank Sinatra, in that order) this didn't stop her from criticising them in public. Though almost reclusive in later years, she had previously led a pretty tumultuous life, and was a regular headline hitter. But beneath the facade she remained unsatisfied with her career and, it often appeared, with her life in general.

A Goldwyn Girl at the age of fourteen, **Paulette Goddard** (real name, Pauline Marion Godard Levee), died on 23 April 1990 at her Swiss home of many years, at the age of 84 – though there is some doubt about the date of her birth, and she may have been older. She retired from the stage while still in her 'teens, when she married a rich industrialist. But the marriage didn't last long, and in 1931 she drove to Reno to obtain a 'quickie' divorce, after which she decided to carry on to Hollywood, where she managed to obtain small parts in some of the Hal Roach Studio productions, followed by roles in a couple of Eddie Cantor features (*Roman Scandals* in 1933 and *Kid Millions* in 1934). In 1932 she met Charlie Chaplin at a party, and the couple were secretly married – apparently at sea – between 1933 and 1936: several dates are recorded in various sources. It was in 1936 that Chaplin co-starred with her in his *Modern Times*, and he used her again four years later in *The Great Dictator*. The couple were divorced in 1942. The first choice for the role of Scarlett O'Hara in *Gone with the Wind*, she eventually lost the part to Vivien Leigh. But producer Selznick did give her her first important 'talkie' role in his 1938 film *The Young in Heart*; the same year she also made an impression in *Dramatic School* with Luise Rainer. She more than held her own in the competitive all-star cast (including Joan Crawford, Norma Shearer and Rosalind Russell) of *The Women* in 1939, and this clearly helped her secure a star role opposite Bob Hope in *The Cat and the Canary* (1939). Two years later she again played opposite Hope in his *Nothing but the Truth*. After the de Mille spectacular, *The North-West Mounted Police* in 1940, she was selected to be Fred Astaire's co-star in *Second Chorus* (1941). In the 1940s Miss Goddard's career peaked with a series of fine performances in films like *Hold Back the Dawn* (1941), *So Proudly We Hail* (1943 – which many critics have claimed to be her best performance), *Kitty* and *The Diary of a Chambermaid* (1946), *Suddenly It's Spring* and *Unconquered* (1947) and, in 1948, the British production of Wilde's *An Ideal Husband*. In all, the 1940s were a breathlessly busy period for Miss Goddard, who between films also squeezed in a number of theatrical performances. It was a different story in the 1950s, when her movies were of minor quality, including her last appearance but one, in the British production *The Unholy Four* (a.k.a. *The Stranger Came Home*) in 1954. Ten years later she accepted a one-off role in the Franco-Italian production *Time of Indifference*. Married in 1958 to *All Quiet on the Western Front* author Erich Maria Remarque, she lived with him in Europe until his death in 1970. During that time she accepted a stage tour of *The Waltz of the Toreadors*, and she returned to the footlights again in *Laura*, a play based on the film. She also appeared in a number of telefilms, including her final appearance in *The Snoop Sisters*. Thought by many critics to have been a great beauty, she certainly had a *gamine* attractiveness and a sharp wit (the qualities which first attracted Chaplin), as well as a wonderful sense of comic timing.

Despite his considerable success on the screen, **Rex Harrison**, who died on 2 June 1990, aged 82, was at his best as a stage actor; indeed, a month before his death he was still playing on Broadway, in a production of Somerset Maugham's *The Circle*. Reginald Carey Harrison was a Merseysider, born in Huyton and educated at Liverpool College, and it was at the Liverpool repertory theatre that he made his acting debut in the autumn of 1924. Six years later he made his London stage debut and appeared in two films, *The Great Game* and *School for Scandal*, to be fol-

Rex Harrison.

lowed by roles in a number of forgettable British productions, many of them in the 'quota quickies' category. He first made a real impact in 1936 in Korda's *Men Are Not Gods*. In the following year, he co-starred opposite Vivien Leigh in *A Storm in a Teacup*. There followed star roles in *The Citadel* (1939), *Night Train to Munich* (1940) and *Major Barbara* (1941), after which he served in the RAF until the end of the war. In 1945 he made *Blithe Spirit* and *The Rake's Progress*, after which he went to Hollywood to star in *Anna and the King of Siam*. Then came *The Ghost and Mrs Muir* (1947), after which he was continually crossing the Atlantic to make films both in Britain (*Escape* in 1948, *The Long Dark Hall* in 1951, *The Constant Husband* in 1954) and America (*The Foxes of Harrow* in 1947, *Unfaithfully Yours* in 1948). In 1960 he played opposite Doris Day in *Midnight Lace*, followed by *Cleopatra* in 1963 and *The Yellow Rolls Royce* in Britain the following year. Also in 1964, he repeated on film his stage success as Henry Higgins in *My Fair Lady*, winning an Oscar for it. Subsequently he played Pope Julius II in *The Agony and the Ecstasy* in 1965 (for which he was given Italy's Order of Merit), and the man who can talk to animals in *Doctor Dolittle* in 1967, after which came several second-drawer movies. His last film was *The Fifth Musketeer* in 1979, making a total of 43 feature movies. With his perfect timing, the slim, charming (though with a bite beneath the urbanity), sophisticated and world-weary Harrison was an outstanding light comedian. He needed female companionship but an apparent inability to remain attached led to six marriages (to Marjorie Thomas, Lilli Palmer, Kay Kendall, Rachel Roberts, Elizabeth Harris and Mercia Tinker), and the nickname 'Sexy Rexy' in the popular press. Though he gave many brilliant performances (and few, if any, bad ones), Rex Harrison will probably be best remembered for his Professor Higgins in *My Fair Lady* – and possibly also for *Doctor Dolittle*.

Jim Henson, the man who created the marvellous Muppets, died suddenly and unexpectedly at the age of 53 on 16 May 1990. Henson began to create his puppet characters in 1954 for a local TV station in Washington. But it was some fifteen years later that they took

off in a big way, with the 1969 debut of the TV series *Sesame Street*, now to be seen on TV in some eighty countries, including the USSR. Henson's first Muppet feature film was *The Muppet Movie* in 1979, which proved a tremendous success, and it was followed by *The Great Muppet Caper* in 1981 and *The Muppets Take Manhattan* in 1984. Henson also created two serious film features: *The Dark Crystal* in 1982, and *Labyrinth* in 1986. His 'Creature Workshop' played a large part in the attraction of other films like *The Bear*, *Dream Child*, *The Witches* and the enormously successful US hit, *Teenage Mutant Ninja Turtles*. There are a number of Muppet productions in the pipeline, and Henson's recent pact with the Walt Disney Organisation means that though he is dead, his work will be carried on.

After a gallant six-year fight against the cancer she at one point thought she had defeated, 53-year-old **Jill Ireland** died of the disease on 18 May 1990. London-born and trained as a dancer, she was already a professional at the age of fifteen, and for a time danced with the Monte Carlo Ballet Company. It was as a dancer that she made her screen debut in 1955 in Powell and Pressburger's *Oh Rosalinda*. Her period as a member of the Rank 'Charm School' produced some delightful glamour stills but little else, and her roles and films after *Rosalinda* were uninspiring. In 1962, she and husband David McCallum moved to Hollywood, where McCallum did well but where she found herself largely confined to TV. Divorced in 1967, she married tough-guy star Charles Bronson the following year, and she had a small part in Bronson's next film, *Villa Rides*. This was the first of several films in which they appeared together, including *Violent City* (1970), *Someone Behind the Door* (1971), *Chino* (1973, also titled *The Wild Horses*), *Hard Times* (also shown as *The Street-fighter*, 1975), *Breakout* (1975), *From Noon Till Three* (1976), the British productions *Love and Bullets* (1979), *Death Wish 2* and *Assassination* (both 1986). *Assassination* was the last film in which she and Bronson appeared together, and her final movie. In 1987 *Life Wish*, her inspiring book about the breast cancer from which she was suffering, was published, to be followed two years later by *Life Lines*. She also lectured and

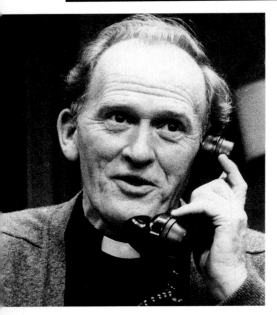

Gordon Jackson.

was the spokeswoman for the American Cancer Society. In 1989 her battle against the disease, which she and her doctors previously thought won, was finally lost when it was found the disease had spread all over her body. Never a great star, Jill Ireland became a reliably good one, with *From Noon Till Three* (in which she took the lead) her best performance.

Away from the footlights or the film cameras, anyone less like an actor than Glasgow-born Scot **Gordon Jackson** would be hard to find; it was difficult to come to terms with the fact that this quiet, modest and self-effacing man was a veteran of stage, screen and television with between fifty and sixty films to his credit, as well as many plays and much television. After years of reliable and sometimes brilliant performances on stage and screen, it was in fact TV which brought him his greatest international fame, playing Hudson the butler in the outstanding five-year series 'Upstairs, Downstairs'. Jackson, who died, aged 66, on 15 January 1990 after a short, unspecified ailment, started his film career at the Ealing Studios in 1942 with *The Foreman Went to France*; a year later he made *Millions Like Us* for Gainsborough, and returned to Ealing to make the classic *Whisky Galore*. From then on he was seldom idle, with films like *Tunes of Glory* (1960), *Mutiny on the Bounty*

(1962 and his first American film) and *The Great Escape* (also 1962), *Those Magnificent Men in their Flying Machines* (1965), *The Prime of Miss Jean Brodie* (1969) and *Golden Rendezvous* (1977). A few of his other films were: *Eureka Stockade*; *Against the Wind*; *The Lady with the Lamp*; *San Demetrio, London* and *Pink String and Sealing Wax*. His stage career included the classics, on Broadway and on the London stage, as well as lighter pieces, such as the more recently staged Agatha Christie piece *Cards on the Table*. His TV credits include the series 'The Professionals' and the Australian success, *A Town Like Alice*, which brought him that country's Logie Award. His work in 'Upstairs Downstairs' brought him a Royal Television Society accolade, and in 1979 this quiet man was awarded an OBE.

Although he played many other roles (and such was his versatility that they ranged from stark villains to stern heroes, with just about everything in between), I will always recall John **Arthur Kennedy** in cowboy kit. Kennedy, who died of a brain tumour on 5 January 1990 at the age of 75, made some seventy films (and appeared regularly on the small screen) during his career. After drama school and a period with a repertory company staging the classics, he made his film debut in 1940

Arthur Kennedy.

with James Cagney's *City for Conquest*, picked by Cagney himself for the part after being seen in a Broadway stage production. *City for Conquest* brought him a contract with Warner, for whom he made six films – including the outstanding *High Sierra* – before joining the American armed forces. Once out of uniform, he carried on with his stage and film career, making such films as *Cheyenne* (1947), *The Glass Menagerie* (1950), *The Bend of the River*, a.k.a. *Where the River Bends* (1952), *The Man from Laramie* (1955), *Peyton Place* (1957), *Elmer Gantry* (1960), *Murder She Said* (in Britain in 1961, staying on to play a role in *Lawrence of Arabia*). Through the 1960s and 1970s Kennedy was kept busy with roles in many Italian and Spanish films. Although he won a Tony for his performance in the play *Death of a Salesman*, Kennedy never achieved an Oscar, though he was nominated five times – for *Champion* (1949), *Bright Victory* (1951), *Trial* (1955), *Peyton Place* (1957) and *Some Came Running* (1959). Kennedy was forced into a ten-year lay-off from filming while he fought an eye disease and cancer of the thyroid, but eventually returned to the studios to make *Signs of Life* in 1989 and the posthumously released *Grandpa*. Kennedy was one of those reliable actors who could always be depended upon to turn in a sound and watchable rather than showy performance, and was in the habit of quietly stealing scenes, and even entire films!

Unintentionally omitted from last year's 'In Memoriam' section, **Ray McAnally**, who died in his native Ireland on 13 June 1989 at the age of 63, was far too great an actor for his death to go unrecorded. McAnally made his professional acting bow at the age of six, in the first of his eventual total of more than 250 plays. More than half of his stage appearances were at Dublin's famous Abbey Theatre, and others were in the Royal Shakespeare Company's London seasons, but he also took roles in 150 television productions and more than 20 films. Although an international star, McAnally continued to live in Ireland, where he usually worked, recently devoting three years to acting, directing and teaching at the Abbey Theatre. In 1988 he had a big success in the London production of *Who's Afraid of Virginia Woolf?* and in

Ray McAnally (in Venus Peter, *reviewed in 'Releases of the Year').*

the same year he co-starred with John Gielgud and Rosemary Harris in *The Best of Friends*, playing the role of G. B. Shaw. Also in 1988 he won BAFTA's Best TV Actor award with his playing of the Labour Prime Minister in *A Very British Coup*. In 1986 he had walked off with the *Evening Standard*'s Best Performance award for his role in *No Surrender*. His earlier films included *Billy Budd* and *Shake Hands with the Devil*, and more recently he appeared in *The Mission, Angel, Cal, The Fourth Protocol, Empire State, Taffin, White Mischief* and *We're No Angels*. His final film role was as the sympathetic old grandfather of the young lad at the centre of *Venus Peter*, a minor British masterpiece set and made in the bleak Orkney Isles.

Jock Mahoney (real name, Jacques O'Mahoney) who died, two days after a car accident, on 14 December 1989 at the age of 70, is a name that will be familiar to Western film and TV fans of the 1950s and 1960s, if not to younger film-goers. A fighter pilot in World War II, Mahoney entered films as a stuntman in 1945, doubling for stars like Cooper, Peck and Autry. It was Autry who gave him his big chance by signing him as the star of the 1951 TV series, 'The Range Rider'. Universal then cast him in several films, including non-Westerns like *I've Lived Before* and *The Land Unknown*. In 1958 he played the title role in another

(short-lived) TV series, 'Yancey Derringer'. Back in movies, he accepted a supporting role in *Tarzan the Magnificent* (1960), subsequently taking over the title role in *Tarzan Goes to India* (1962) and – after a long illness caught in India – *Tarzan's Three Challenges* (1963). In the 1960s and early 1970s his films included several more non-Westerns, including *Tom* in 1973. In that year he suffered a major stroke while working on an episode in the TV series 'Kung Fu'. In 1978 he made the aptly titled *The End*, starring his stepdaughter Sally Field, which was apparently his last film. In 1981 he served as stunt co-ordinator for *Tarzan the Ape Man* (a re-make), and he subsequently turned up from time to time as guest star in several TV series. Some of his other films include *Overland Pacific* in 1954, *A Time to Love and a Time to Die* (1960), *California* (1963), *Bandalero* (1968) and *The Bad Bunch* (1976).

It is impossible to think of **Silvana Mangano** without thinking of *Bitter Rice*, the film in which the scantily clad, marvellously formed Miss Mangano sprang to international fame in 1949. One of the top stars of the Italian cinema for more than forty years, Miss Mangano, who had a Sicilian father and an English mother, died in Madrid on 16 December 1989 at the age of 59, having been in a coma as the result of a brain haemmorhage, heart failure and the cancer she had been suffering from for several years. Trained as a dancer, she also modelled and in 1946 won the title of Miss Rome. Bit parts in films

followed, and then de Santis chose her as the earthy, busty heroine of *Bitter Rice*. After that she was seldom far from the film studios. Her subsequent films included *Anna* (1951), *Ulysses* (1954 – in which she played the dual roles of Penelope and Circe), *This Angry Age* (1958), *Barabbas* (1961), Pasolini's *Oedipus Rex* (1967), *The Decameron* and *Death in Venice* (1971), *Ludwig* (1973), *Conversation Piece* (1975) and *Dune* (1986 – produced by her daughter Raffaella). Her final screen appearance was in *Dark Eyes* (1987), opposite childhood sweetheart Marcello Mastroianni.

Gary Merrill, who died on 5 March 1990 at the age of 74, made his acting debut in 1937, first in Max Reinhardt's *The Eternal Road* and then in *Brother Rat* (replacing José Ferrer). It was while he was in the US Army Air Force Special Division that he had stage roles in *This Is the Army* and *Winged Victory*. It was not until 1944 that he made his screen debut – while still in the army – in the film version of the Forces show *Winged Victory*. He was lucky to be given a role directly after demobilisation in 1945, in the smash hit *Born Yesterday*. With a Fox contract in 1949 he appeared in a number of film hits such as *Slattery's Hurricane* (1949), *Twelve O'Clock High* and *All About Eve* (both 1950). The star of *Eve* was Bette Davis, whom he married in 1950. From then on he was always busy, either on

Silvana Mangano.

167

Gary Merrill.

stage or on film, notching up a total of more than forty movies, including *The Frogmen* (1951), *Phone Call from a Stranger* (1952), *Another Man's Poison* (1952) and *Witness to Murder* (1954), as well as a number of TV feature films. His last two film roles were in *Huckleberry Finn* in 1974 and *Thieves* in 1977.

Essentially a cabaret and vaudeville performer, **Billy Milton**, who died, aged 84, on 23 November 1989, appeared in some twenty-five feature films and a few shorts during his long career. His screen debut was in *The Flag Lieutenant* in 1926, and his last appearance was in *Mrs Brown, You've Got a Lovely Daughter* in 1968. A few of his interim roles were in *Young Woodley* (1930), *Three Men in a Boat* (1933), *One in a Million* (1936), *The Dominant Sex* (1937), *Yes Madam* (1938), *The Set Up* (1963), *Monster of Terror* (1965) and *Hot Millions* (1968). Milton's record as a song composer was impressive: he wrote more than 500, all but a few of which were performed and published, some of them being used in his own radio series.

Movie-goers who regularly attended the 'specialist' cinema during the 1930–50 period are the most likely to be familiar with the performances of French comedian **Noël-Noël** (real name Lucien Noël), who died in Nice at the age of

92 on 5 October 1989. A bank clerk who became a political cartoonist for left-wing publications and then staged his own – successful – cabaret act in Parisian nightclubs, he made the first of his movies, *Ménages Modernes*, in 1931. In many of his subsequent films he wrote the scripts as well as being the star, and in 1951 made his only attempt at direction with his *La Vie Chantée*. Titles probably most familiar to British movie-goers are *A Cage of Nightingales – La Cage aux Rossignols* (1945), *Jessica* (1962), René Clément's *Le Père Tranquille* (1946) and the Franco-American Preston Sturges production, *The French Are a Funny Race* (1955), which was based on the British best-seller *Les Carnets du Major Thompson*, the film's original French title.

Not a very familiar name, **Jane Novak**, a silents star at the beginning of the century, had well over a hundred films to her credit when she died, aged 94, on 6 February 1990 from the after-effects of a stroke. At one time or another she played the female lead opposite such stars as William S. Hart, Tom Mix, Harold Lloyd, Harry Carey, Buck Jones, Wallace Beery, Lewis Stone, Edmund Lowe and Richard Dix, as well as many other silent screen heroes. At one time land-wealthy, her fortune vanished in the 1919 market crash. In 1925 she came to Britain to star in Michael Balcon's *The Prude's Fall*, which was followed by *The Blackguard*, filmed in UFA's German studios. Her final star role was in Schertzinger's 1930 release *Redskin*, but she continued to play minor roles until *The Boss* in 1957, after which she made only one more appearance in front of the cameras, for Kevin Brownlow and David Gill's television documentary about her former co-star Harold Lloyd. Oddly, despite this formidable record she is not even mentioned in Katz's *International Film Encyclopedia*.

Laurence Olivier.

The son of a Dorking (Surrey) clergyman, **Laurence Olivier**, generally accepted as probably the greatest actor of this century, died on 11 July 1989 at the age of 82. After surviving a series of appalling ailments, it seems that Olivier was finally overcome as a result of a hip replacement operation which he underwent three months before his death.

Essentially a man of the theatre, Olivier's stage debut was in a boys' production of *The Taming of the Shrew* at Stratford-on-Avon when he was fifteen. His work for the screen – which was often memorable (notably in the remarkable *Henry V* of 1944, which he co-scripted, produced and directed, as well as playing the leading role, a spectacular quadruple triumph) although sometimes not – began with a role in the 1930 production of the comedy *Too Many Crooks*. His finest work included his 1948 triumph with *Hamlet* (in which he gave a stunning performance as the gloomy Dane as well as again directing and producing) and *Richard III* (once more producing, directing and starring). He also directed and produced the less successful *The Prince and the Showgirl*, in which he co-starred with Marilyn Monroe. As well as being nominated nine times, Olivier was awarded four Oscars during his career; a special one for his *Henry V*, one for his performance in and another for his direction of *Hamlet* in 1948, and a final special one at the 1978 ceremony for his outstanding work in the cinema generally. Olivier made more than fifty films, including the Shakespeare classics, thrillers, romances and comedies. Among that output were *As You Like It* (1936), *Wuthering Heights* (1939), *The Beggar's Opera*, which he also produced (1953), *Rebecca* and *Pride and Prejudice* (1940), *The 49th Parallel* (1941), *The Entertainer* (1960), in which he gave a marvellous, Oscar-nominated performance as the sad Archie Rice, *Uncle Vanya* (1963), *Oh, What a Lovely War* and *The Battle of Britain* (1969), *The Three Sisters*, which he also directed (1970), *Nicholas and Alexandra* (1971), *Sleuth* (1972), *Marathon Man* (1976), *A Bridge Too Far* (1977), *The Boys from Brazil* (1978) and (his final contribution to the screen) a role in Derek Jarman's adaptation of the Benjamin Britten operatic work, *War Requiem*, in 1988. His many great stage performances are widely documented, but generations to come can turn to his films to see why

so many critics and professional commentators considered him to be the greatest actor of our time.

One of Britain's most highly acclaimed men of the cinema, **Michael Powell** died on 19 February 1990 at the age of 84, at his home near Canterbury, where he was born and had his first job – in a bank. But the young Powell's ambition was to work in the movies, and he finally achieved this by persuading director Rex Ingram to appoint him as his assistant at the Victorine Studios at Nice, where (apart from the occasional small acting role) he served at various times as cameraman, editor and screenwriter. He eventually returned to England to become an official apprentice at the old British International Studios at Elstree, where as well as contributing to the script of Hitchcock's *Blackmail* he served as the great man's stills photographer. It was at Elstree that Powell directed a number of the short, cheap features known as 'quota quickies'. (These were low-budget productions shown, often reluctantly, by cinema managers in compliance with the government's demand that they screen a certain percentage of home-made movies, and so keep the British film industry from total collapse.) Powell's first film to bring him to the attention of the critics was *The Edge of the World*, a semi-documentary, made entirely on location, about the de-population of the Shetland Islands. But it was in 1941 that he achieved wider success with his *The 49th Parallel*, the first result of his association with scenarist Emeric Pressburger. The duo continued to produce successes like *One of Our Aircraft Is Missing* (1942), the controversial *Life and Death of Colonel Blimp* (1945), the somewhat odd *A Canterbury Tale* (1943), *I Know Where I'm Going* (1945), *A Matter of Life and Death* (1946), *Black Narcissus* (1947) and the tremendous ballet film success *The Red Shoes* in 1948. After *The Small Back Room* in 1950, this run of successes petered out, however, with two flops in *Gone to Earth* and *The Elusive Pimpernel*. But in 1951 Powell and Pressburger made a magnificent come-back with another delightful ballet film, *The Tales of Hoffman*. But after two more 'Archer' (the name of their company) features – *The Battle of the River Plate* and *Ill Met By Moonlight* (both 1956) – the team broke up, to come together

Anthony Quayle.

on only one further occasion, when they jointly made a children's film, *The Boy Who Turned Yellow*. Powell continued on his own with a ballet film, *Luna de Miel* (based on *El Amor Brujo*), and *Peeping Tom*, a film with disturbing undertones. The next few years were filled with projects which Powell was unable to bring to production, but in 1966 he again achieved success with his Australian film, *They're a Weird Mob*, which was one of the greatest commercial successes in the history of that country's film industry. Still in Australia, Powell next made *The Age of Consent* with James Mason as co-producer, which introduced actress Helen Mirren (who was to become the second Mrs Mason). Alas, the movie appears to have been both an artistic and a commercial failure, making a disappointing end to Powell's career; for while the next few years saw a number of projects announced, none ever reached the film studios.

(Sir) **Anthony** (John) **Quayle**, who died of cancer at the age of 76 on 20 October 1989, was essentially a man of the theatre and his films, in which he gave some sterling performances, were of far less importance to him. It is significant that

Barbara Stanwyck.

Robe, in 1953, **Frank Ross** – who died, aged 85, on 17 February 1990 – deserves a mention in any Hollywood history. He also shared an Oscar in 1945 with Mervyn LeRoy for the short film *The House I Live In*. A small-part actor in the 1920s, Ross started producing films at the Hal Roach studios in the 1930s, a number of them starring his wife Jean Arthur. Other films he produced or co-produced include *Of Mice and Men* (1939), *The Devil and Miss Jones* (1941), *The Lady Takes a Chance* (1943), *The Flame and the Arrow* (1954), *The Rains of Ranchipur* (1955) and *Where It's At* (1969), which appears to be the last time he worked. His (apparently sole) directing credit is *The Lady Says No* in 1952.

In all the years I've been seeing films, only twice can I recall having been virtually stunned by an actress when I first saw her on screen: the first was by Bette Davis in *Cabin in the Cotton*, and the second was by **Barbara Stanwyck** (real name, Ruby Stevens) in *Woman in Red*. Miss Stanwyck, who died of heart failure on 20 January 1990, was Brooklyn-born; an orphan from early childhood, she was shuffled between various relatives, as her sister was determined she should never go into an orphanage. She started working – as a packer in a local store – at the age of fifteen, and went on to do other jobs, all the time determinedly training to become a dancer. It was in the chorus of a New York nightclub – at a time when the gangsters ruled the underworld – that she made her professional debut, climbing quickly to similar chorus engagements in 'The Ziegfeld Follies' and 'George White's Scandals'. In 1926 she won a part in her first straight play, *The Noose*, which ran for most of that year on Broadway. The following year she won her first small film role in *Broadway Nights*, followed two years later with small parts in a further two films: *The Locked Door* and *Mexacali Rose*. Just one year later, in 1930, she achieved instant stardom in Frank Capra's *Ladies of Leisure*. After that she seldom appeared in fewer than two films a year, and sometimes more. In *Cattle Queen of Montana* she had Ronald Reagan as her co-star and much later appeared with Elvis Presley in *Roustabout*. When she died at 82, she had a movie to her credit for every year of her age.

in a full two-column obituary in *The Daily Telegraph* his film career was dismissed in a thirteen-line list of titles – quite unfairly, I think. Admittedly, though, all his major triumphs were in the theatre, to which he dedicated himself. Quayle began his acting career on the stage of the famous little 'Q' Theatre at Kew Bridge in 1931, and his first appearance on the screen was in Gabriel Pascal's 1938 *Pygmalion*. He spent six years in the British Army during World War II, from which he emerged a major, and it was almost a decade before he again appeared before the cameras, playing Marcellus in Olivier's *Hamlet* (1948), in the same year taking a role in *Saraband for Dead Lovers*. This was followed by thirty British and American movies, including *The Battle of the River Plate* and *The Woman in the Dressing Gown* (1956), *Ice Cold in Alex*

(1958), *The Guns of Navarone* (1961), *Lawrence of Arabia* (1962), *The Fall of the Roman Empire* (1964), *Operation Crossbow* (1965), *Anne of the Thousand Days* (as Cardinal Wolsey, a role that brought him an Oscar nomination in 1969), *Moses* (as Aaron) and *The Eagle Has Landed* (1976), and his final, brilliant performance in Ermanno Olmi's *The Legend of the Holy Drinker*, released in mid-1989. Quayle also made many TV plays and voice-overs, including some for the government. And he managed to squeeze two books into his crowded schedule (*Eight Hours from England* and *On Such a Night*), as well as giving the occasional lecture. A generous actor and an endlessly charming man, by far his greatest triumph was his revival of public enthusiasm for staged Shakespeare during the arid post-war period.

If for no other reason than having produced the first Cinemascope film, *The*

In Hollywood she was always known as a director's actress: a hardworking, uncomplaining, adaptable and above all supremely versatile performer, respected and admired by her directors and beloved by the film crews. It was something of a legend in Hollywood that she was the second person to enter the studio every morning when she was working, following the gatekeeper as he opened up. When her film career faltered and finally died in 1965 with a routine thriller, *The Night Walker*, she turned to TV, having since 1956 appeared fairly regularly in guest spots. She appeared in her own show throughout 1960, was in 'The Big Valley' series (1965–9), *The House That Wouldn't Die* (1970), *The Letters* (1973), and the role that won her a third Emmy award (others were for her own show and *The Big Valley*), the outstanding Australian-set *The Thorn Birds*. Her final small-screen contribution was in *The Colbys* (1985–6).

Although she never won an Oscar, she was nominated for one four times (*Stella Dallas*, *Balls of Fire*, *Double Indemnity* and *Sorry, Wrong Number*) and in 1982 was presented with an honorary Oscar: five years later she was awarded the American Film Institute's Life Achievement Award. Apart from those already mentioned, her films include: *So Big* (1932), *The Bitter Tea of General Yen* (1933), *Annie Oakley* (1935), *Union Pacific* and *Golden Boy* (1939), *The Lady Eve* and *Meet John Doe* (1943), *Thelma Jordan* (1950), *Titanic* (1953) and *Walk on the Wild Side* (1962). As good a tribute to Miss Stanwyck as any came from Jane Fonda: 'She's one of those actresses that other generations coming behind her will look at and study as an example.'

The screen's best-loved 'perfect rotter', gap-toothed British comedian **Terry-Thomas** (his full, real name was Thomas Terry Hoar Stevens) died on 8 January 1990 at the age of 78, after years of ever increasing disability caused by Parkinson's disease, which finally stopped him working in 1977. His illness gradually soaked up his savings and it was suddenly revealed in 1989 that he was living miserably in poverty, whereupon his fellow actors staged a benefit show which allowed him to be transferred to a nursing home for the last months of his life. Orig-

Terry-Thomas.

inally a meat salesman whose hobby was amateur dramatics, T-T broke into films in 1940 with a tiny part in Maurice Elvey's war film *For Freedom*. For much of the war, he served in the Royal Corps of Signals, and some years later he got his second screen chance, in the 1949 release *Helter Skelter*. His screen career really took off with his performance in two 1956 British comedies, *Private's Progress* and *The Green Man*. The following year T-T made four films and got top billing in two of them for the first time: *Blue Murder at St Trinians's* and *The Naked Truth*. There followed star roles in *Tom Thumb* (1958), *Too Many Crooks* (also 1958) and two perfect vehicles for his style of comedy, *Carlton-Browne of the FO* and *I'm All Right Jack*. His subsequent output was variable after the brilliant comedy *Make Mine Mink* in 1960, and included *The Wonderful World of the Brothers Grimm* (US, 1962), *It's a Mad, Mad,* *Mad, Mad World* (US, 1963), *Those Magnificent Men in Their Flying Machines* (1965), *Monte Carlo or Bust* (1969), *How to Murder Your Wife* (US, 1969), *The Bawdy Adventures of Tom Jones* (1976) and, generally given as his final film, *The Hound of the Baskervilles* in 1978. At least one source also credits him with a part in *The Tempest* in 1979. In all, Terry-Thomas made some forty films, including a few in France and Italy. With his clipped moustache, distinctive gap-teeth and Victorian villain's sneer, Terry-Thomas had a unique style without which the comedy screen will be the poorer.

Tommy ('You Lucky People') **Trinder**, CBE, the darling of so many music-hall audiences, who died on 10 July 1989 at the age of 80, after a long illness, was an outstanding, quick-witted Cockney comic who also turned in many straight screen performances, notably in some of the old Ealing Studio productions such as *The Bells Go Down*. One of the London Pal-

Lee Van Cleef.

ladium's most popular bill toppers over a long period, Trinder successfully took his act to many countries, including Australia, Canada, New Zealand, South Africa and the USA, where in 1950 he starred at the famous old New

Tommy Trinder.

York nightclub, 'The Latin Quarter'. For many years Trinder had his own radio show, and he was also a big success on TV, for which he was the long-term host of the Sunday spectacular, 'Sunday Night at the Palladium'. Like most of the old vaudeville stars, Tommy started his career early, touring South Africa with a singing troupe when he was fifteen. His screen career, which spanned 30 years, reached its highest point between 1938 and 1958. The complete tally of titles is: *Almost a Honeymoon* (his screen debut) and *Save a Little Sunshine* (1938), *She Couldn't Say No* (1939), *Laugh It Off* and *Sailors Three* (1940), *The Foreman Went to France* (1941), *The Bells Go Down* (1942), *Champagne Charlie* and *Fiddlers Three* (1944), *Bitter Springs* (1949), *You Lucky People* (1955), *Make Mine a Million* (1958), *The Beauty Jungle* (1964), *Under the Table You Must Go* (1970) and *Barry Mackenzie Holds His Own . . .* (1974). Trinder's personal and witty ad-libbing style was to be seen at its best when interrupting his act to greet individual latecomers at the Palladium; a mixture of cheeky humour and caustic comment which never became offensive but always got a terrific audience reaction.

His screen debut, as one of the four baddies intent on killing sheriff Gary Cooper in *High Noon*, set the pattern for much of **Lee Van Cleef**'s subsequent film career, and he was seldom able to get out that casting rut. He died of a heart attack at the age of 64 on 14 December 1989, following a previous attack in the early 1980s which necessitated the installation of a pacemaker. After serving in the navy during World War II, he started to appear in amateur stage shows, as a result of which he won a part in a professional tour of *Mr Roberts*, in which he was seen by *High Noon* producer Stanley Kramer, who recalled him when he began casting the film. A decade later he impressed the young Italian director Sergio Leone, the father of the spaghetti Western, who signed him up to appear with Clint Eastwood in *For A Few Dollars More* and *The Good, the Bad and the Ugly*. But it was in a science-fiction film (Roger Corman's 1956 *It Conquered the World*) that he finally achieved a leading role. Partly because he made so many foreign films – generally Westerns, in Germany, France and Italy – it is difficult to get a complete tally of his movies, but certainly in the five years following *High Noon* he completed more than forty. His best-known films include *Gunfight at the OK Corral* (1957), *The Young Lions* (1958), *How the West Was Won* and *The Man Who Shot Liberty Valance* (both in 1962), *Sabata* (1969), *El Condor* (1970), *The Magnificent Seven Ride* (1972) and *The Rip-Off* (1978). In 1979 he made *The Hard Way* in Ireland (a made-for-TV feature). After several more features (including *Codename Wild Geese*) he took on his final role in 1989 in *Speed Zone*. With his thin, sharp features and cold, steel-blue eyes, Van Cleef was an actor who, once seen, could never be forgotten.

Chrissie White (born Ada White), who died at the age of 94 on 18 August 1989, was one of Britain's first film stars, making her first movie (a one-reeler) for the old Hepworth company (which persuaded her to drop Ada for the more romantic Chrissie) soon after the turn of the century. By the time she retired in 1924, Chrissie had something like 200 films (including one-reelers and features) to her credit, including *For the Little Lady's Sake* (her debut in 1908), *Tillie The Tomboy goes Boating* (1910),

Cornel Wilde.

The Cloister and The Hearth (1912), *Barnaby Rudge* (1915) and *City of Beautiful Nonsense* (1919). After *Lily of the Alley* in 1923, she quit the screen, but was lured back in 1930 to make her first talkie, *The Call of the Sea*, to be

Chrissie White.

followed three years later by *General John Regan*, after which she went on stage tours with her former film co-star and director, Henry Edwards, who died in 1952.

Cornelius Louis Wilde, or **Cornel Wilde**, has never been properly appreciated for the sheer entertainment value of his films. Born in New York of Hungarian parents, Wilde toured Europe with his salesman father until his late teens, and it was not until 1932 that the family finally settled in New York, where Wilde won a scholarship to Columbia University with the idea of becoming a surgeon. But he soon abandoned this plan, preferring a theatrical career. In 1940, he made his Broadway debut in the Olivier-Leigh production of *Romeo and Juliet*, as a fencing instructor (he was good enough to be chosen for the US fencing team for the Olympics) and featured player. On the strength of this, Warner's signed him for Hollywood. After a number of forgettable movies he won an Oscar nomination for his Chopin in *A Song to Remember*. He also starred in *Forever Amber* in 1947. In 1955,

ambitious to do more than act in films for other companies, he launched his own set-up, Theodora Productions, and starred in films which he also directed and produced, making a number of variable but often good-quality movies in Europe on what now seem minuscule budgets. In all, Wilde appeared in some fifty films, many of them major box-office successes, deservedly so, for he had a real talent. He died of leukaemia in Los Angeles, aged 74, on 15 October 1989. His best-remembered movies include *1001 Nights*, *The Bandit of Sherwood Forest*, *The Big Combo*, *The Naked Prey*, *Beach Red*, *Storm Fear*, *Shark's Treasure*, *Beyond Mombasa*, *The Edge of Eternity* and *Lancelot and Guinevere*.

Pamela Guard, or **Yana** as she was better known professionally, who died on 21 November 1989 at the age of 57, was essentially a singing entertainer, but she did at one time have her own TV series ('The Yana Show') and did appear in a number of films during the 1950–60 period, including *The Ship That Died of Shame*, *Zarak* and *Cockleshell Heroes*.

Bookshelf
A selection of the year's books on cinema

IVAN BUTLER

The American West from Fiction into Film, Jim Hitt; McFarland, dist. Bailey Bros & Swinfen, £28.50.

An interesting and scholarly study of film-makers' treatment, from 1909 to 1986, of Western stories and novels (1823–1976). Only those works are covered which were in existence as fiction before reaching the screen; 'novelisations' of films already made are not included. (As the author rightly remarks, such books are not literature but promotional campaigns.) It is a comprehensive work, and films that might be regarded as marginally Western – such as *The Mark of Zorro* – are also included. An appendix gives a detailed list of Western authors and their film adaptations, providing very useful reference material. The index is excellent.

Babe – The Life of Oliver Hardy, John McCabe; Robson Books, £12.95.

John McCabe is the acknowledged chief chronicler of Laurel and Hardy and it was to be expected that he would follow his earlier works (*Mr Laurel and Mr Hardy, The Comedy World of Stan Laurel*, and the text of the picture book *Laurel and Hardy*) with one on Mr Hardy himself. As he says in his foreword: 'At last, at long last, Oliver Hardy'. This is a delightful book, an obvious labour of love which will be warmly welcomed by the inimitable pair's innumerable devotees. Despite the frank coverage of Hardy's personal problems, domestic and otherwise, and the inevitable sadness of his last illness – most movingly told here – it is a heart-warming story, leading (as all good stories should) to a happy ending, both in his idyllic last marriage and in the enormous success (after the admitted decline of the later films) of the final years of music-hall touring. Much of the ground has inevitably been covered in the author's previous books, but he skilfully keeps the main focus firmly on his leading man. A highlight is a vivid and detailed description of the great silent short, *Big Business*; though, oddly, *Sons of the Desert*, widely regarded as the most brilliant of the longer films, receives only a bare mention. Many rare photographs and a com-

plete listing of *all* Hardy's films round off a book to be treasured.

It is a pity that careless proof-reading has resulted in numerous misprints, including intrusive entries of the letter 'Z', and a sentence at the bottom of p. 139 which surely says the opposite of what was intended.

Bette and Joan – The Divine Feud, Shaun Considine; Muller, £16.95.

A large book of 365 pages devoted to the battles between Bette Davis and Joan Crawford might seem excessive, but in this lively and often amusing account the author covers much of the wider life of Hollywood as well as biographical details of the two stars. Neither of them comes out of it well, with their petty vindictiveness, their silly squabbling and backbiting, their arrogance and often downright mean nastiness, but it is an entertaining and very readable (if hardly edifying) story of the less pleasant side of the American film world of the period.

Beyond Ballyhoo, Mark Thomas McGee; McFarland, dist. Bailey Bros & Swinfen, £24.65.

In a light-hearted and witty style exactly suited to the subject, Mr McGee describes the promotional excesses, the gimmicks and other means, fair and foul, used to drive the unsuspecting public into the cinema. Some of the suggestions sent to distributors to help them to ensnare their victims (for films as dissimilar as *Dementia 13* and *The Story of Alexander Graham Bell*) have to be read to be believed! The longest chapter is devoted to a thorough and at times uproarious examination of the 3D phenomenon. Another consists of an incredible selection of radio spot advertisements. Information and entertainment are deftly combined in this well-researched and well-illustrated book.

Black Action Films, James Robert Paris and George H. Hill; McFarland, dist. Bailey Bros & Swinfen, £33.25.

This is a critical survey, in alphabetical order, of 235 productions, mainly of the

1970s and 1980s, but including a number from earlier years such as *In the Heat of the Night* (1967), regarded as a 'landmark movie of integration'. The growth and vigour of the 'black cinema' is apparent in these interesting and detailed summaries, and the book is additionally welcome in that, while highlighting the astonishing and deserved success of the greater part of the output, it also exposes the fact that this genre (like any other) has had its duds and disasters – for example *The Klansman* (1974) and *The Muthers* (1976). Well illustrated and fully indexed.

The Boys, Scott Allen Nollen; McFarland, dist. Bailey Bros & Swinfen, £21.80.

The first half of this concise and useful handbook on the films of Laurel and Hardy consists of an examination of all their main movies, short and long. It analyses their personalities as a comedy duo, their relationship to physical objects, to animals, to women and to society, seeking significances which Laurel himself has vehemently stated do not exist. (The famous couple's only intention, he stated, was to make people laugh.) The author, however, discusses his theories lightly and entertainingly, and to many readers his book will prove to be at least a very enjoyable feast of nostalgic recollection, dozens of fondly remembered gags and sequences being vividly described. The second half of the book consists of an excellently detailed annotated filmography in two parts, covering the Hal Roach and the post-Roach periods. It is very well arranged, though the writing is sometimes careless. A number of good stills round it off.

Charlie Chan at the Movies, Ken Hanke; McFarland, dist. Bailey Bros & Swinfen, £28.45.

Charlie Chan, possibly the most popular detective of his time in the cinema, assuredly deserves a book devoted to his career. Forty-four films in all are fully covered here, with Warner Oland (an actor of Swedish/Russian descent) scoring sixteen, Sidney Toler following him, with twenty-two, and Roland

Winters, most recently, with a mere half-dozen. Each film is given a full cast list, a critical commentary and plot synopsis. The book, illustrated with a reasonable number of stills, should have a ready-made market among the many Chan fans. The author regrets having missed the 'lost' silent film, *The Chinese Parrot*, directed by the great Paul Leni, with the excellent (if, as he says, physically inappropriate) Japanese actor Sojin as Chan. I can remember enjoying it over sixty years ago, but would not venture to surmise how good it might seem now.

Child of Paradise – Marcel Carné and the Golden Age of French Cinema, Edward Baron Turk; Harvard University Press, £29.95.

It is strange that a full critical survey of Marcel Carné and his films should have been so long in appearing, and Mr Turk's book is additionally welcome in that it is so full, so comprehensive, so authoritative, and so well written. Pride of place is, not surprisingly, given to Carné's masterpiece, *Les Enfants du Paradis* – which takes up nearly a third of the 480-page book. Taken together with the introduction to the section, a chapter on the German Occupation, this is a vivid analysis and re-creation of one of the greatest and best loved of all French films. Other famous movies such as *Le Jour Se Lève*, *Les Visiteurs du Soir* and *Le Quai des Brumes* are also fully discussed. This handsomely produced book, with its detailed filmography, good illustrations and thorough documentation, is essential reading for anyone interested in the great period of French cinema.

Children's Live-Action Musical Films, Thomas J. Harris; McFarland, dist. Bailey Bros & Swinfen, £23.70.

Of the seventeen films covered in these essays only three come out relatively unscathed: *The Wizard of Oz* (incontestably), *Mary Poppins* (not everyone might agree here), and *Willie Wonka and the Chocolate Factory* (to some the best of all). Most of the remainder are deservedly flattened, as the author lays about him with great spirit. They are in truth a dismal lot, and it is surprising that a class of film offering such opportunities for imaginative treatment should so rarely rise above the mediocre – to put it kindly. This lively and hard-hitting book is well illustrated and has full cast and credit details. It is a pity that careless editing has resulted in some clumsy writing going uncorrected, and also in a number of name misspellings – four for one film alone.

Citizen Welles, Frank Brady; Hodder & Stoughton, £18.95.

Much has already been written on Orson Welles, but this massive biography of 600 packed pages will surely be regarded as definitive. The life and career of one of the outstanding and most fascinating figures of his time in both theatre and cinema are described with loving care and immense (but never overloaded) detail. His best-known works, such as the Mercury Theatre production of *Julius Caesar*, the notorious radio programme *The War of the Worlds*, the Mexican/Brazilian documentary, the Shakespeare films, *The Magnificent Ambersons* and – above all – *Citizen Kane* may be given pride of place, but all the myriad activities of his frequently frenetic life are fully treated. Some of his appearances as actor (often in memorable cameo roles), however, are given less than their due. *A Man for All Seasons* and *Oedipus the King* (1967) for instance, to take only two of many, receive only the barest mention and are not even included in the index.

Two interesting but not over-generous sections of illustrations and a useful career quick-reference section round off an important, absorbing and very well written book.

Clara Bow – Runnin' Wild, David Stenn; Ebury Press, £16.95.

Clara Bow, the 'It' girl of the silent screen, after a childhood of appalling squalor and parental ill-treatment, realised the highest dream of countless thousands of American teenagers by becoming a beauty contest winner and idolised film star, pursued by (and pursuing) the princes of Hollywood – the perfect Cinderella story. Underneath, however, tragedy lurked – exploitation by producers, associates and studios until finally, overworked and underpaid, she collapsed both physically and mentally. In his engrossing and moving book David Stenn presents, on the one side, the ruthlessness, cruelty and dishonesty that underlay the bright surface of the film capital; on the other, the generosity and kindness of many of its inhabitants and the opportunities for glittering success it offered to those fortunate enough to be able to survive it – which, sadly, Clara Bow was not.

Much space is given to the notorious scandal that finally devastated her, the revelations of her one-time friend and secretary, Daisy DeVoe. Malicious and spiteful Miss Devoe may have been, but with examplary fairness the author presents her side of the quarrel in a riveting account that contains much hitherto little-known material.

Note: The index is good as far as it goes – but it goes no farther than the first entry under 'T'!

The Dame in the Kimono, Leonard J. Leff & Jerold L. Simmons; Weidenfeld & Nicolson, £17.50.

This is a thorough (and thoroughly entertaining) account of the Hollywood Production Code and its effects on the movies between the 1920s and the 1960s. Formed by the studios themselves as a defence against government censorship, it eventually became a Frankenstein's monster threatening the industry it was created to defend. Several of the more notorious film cases (*Dead End, Gone with the Wind* and the celebrated 'damn', *The Outlaw, The Moon Is Blue, Lolita*) are dealt with in detail, but dozens of others are mentioned in this lively history. Many of the code's restrictions may seem ludicrous today, but looking around at the present condition of film and video, when freedom has often degenerated to mere licence, one may perhaps wonder whether the decline of censorship is a wholly unmixed blessing.

David Lean, Stephen M. Silverman; André Deutsch, £25.00.

Shamefully little has been written about David Lean, one of the leading figures in British cinema, first as editor and then as director of such masterly films as *Brief Encounter*, the two Dickens adaptations, *Oliver Twist* and *Great Expectations*, and the great spectaculars – *The Bridge on the River Kwai, Lawrence of Arabia* and *Doctor Zhivago;* not forgetting, after a break of some fourteen years, *A Passage to India*. This sumptuously produced, large-format book – from America – goes some way to fill the gap. The superb black-and-white and colour illustrations may be the first thing to catch the eye, but the real value of the book lies in the text which, after a brief biographical section, discusses each individual film with exactly the right combination of history, anecdotes, technical details and career outlines of the cast and others connected with the production. Katharine Hepburn provides a warmly admiring introduction, and the book concludes with a full filmography and a list of awards.

Note: It is surprising to read that Robert Mitchum at first refused his role in *Ryan's Daughter* because of its 'enormity'; presumably what is meant is its size rather than its monstrous wickedness.

Diane Keaton, Jonathan Moor; Robson Books, £12.95.

The name of Diane Keaton is generally linked to Woody Allen's, but in fact she has already appeared in at least a dozen films without him, including *The Godfather 1 & 2, Lovers and Other Strangers, Looking for Mr Goodbar* and Warren Beatty's *Reds*. Her life and career (particularly her relationships with Beatty and Allen) are recounted in this brief but workmanlike biography. That she is (in Woody Allen's words) 'one of the great film actresses of all time, far better than any of the stars of the golden age of Hollywood or the present' may be open to question, but her Oscar for her performance in *Annie Hall* was well deserved. In a very brief stage career (three performances are listed), she stands out as the only member of the cast of

Hair who refused an extra $50 to take off her clothes.

Dracula, Prince of Many Faces, Radu R. Florescu & Raymond T. McNally; Little, Brown, £12.95.

The opening and closing pages of this interesting book deal with the links between the historical and the fictional Dracula, the latter being represented mainly by Bram Stoker and his classic horror story; in between, the text relates vividly and seemingly authentically all that is now known of the tempestuous and violent life of the true Count, a man in whom courage and sadism appeared to have existed in roughly equal proportions. To punish by impalement may have been merely one of the accepted brutalities of the time – but to have had a special window in his palace from which to watch the death agonies of his victims seems somewhat less excusable. In an epilogue the question is asked, Who was the Real Dracula? Throughout this account the twin strands of myth and reality are fascinatingly interwoven. Excellent illustrations consist of both old engravings and modern photographs. There are two good maps; unfortunately, however, carelessness in spreading them over two pages has resulted in many central details being hidden – an infuriating fault that occurs all too often.

Dreams for Sale – Popular Culture in the 20th Century, ed. Richard Maltby; Harrap, £17.95.

The cinema receives a generous share of attention in this first volume of a large-scale six-part twentieth-century history. Other activities covered here include sport, popular music and fashion. The years 1900–89 are divided into several sections according to significant dates, and each section includes a general survey, together with a number of special features. The book is lavishly illustrated with excellently reproduced photographs, many of them rare. Chronologies, coloured charts and diagrams make the mass of detailed information easy to absorb, and the text in general is lively and lucid. Though the book is American-based, other countries, the UK in particular, are adequately represented.

D. W. Griffith's *Intolerance* – Its Genesis and Vision, William M. Drew; McFarland, dist. Bailey Bros & Swinfen, £18.95.

This in-depth study examines Griffith's masterpiece from all aspects: aesthetic, historical, political, religious, critical. It places the film in its contemporary social surroundings and discusses its relevance for today, as well as its part in the director's total output of films; and it investigates the reasons for the

many conflicting opinions (often strongly expressed) that it aroused at the time of its release and afterwards. It is, in fact, a thorough and fully documented study, important reading for anyone interested in the vital early years of cinema.

Eleanor Parker, Doug McClelland; Scarecrow, dist. Bailey Bros & Swinfen, £30.95.

The 'Woman of a Thousand Faces' (as she is described in the sub-title) has certainly been given the full treatment in this 250-page book. A comparatively brief biography is followed by 130 pages on her professional credits in films, television, theatre and radio, with lengthy critical commentaries. A list of articles and 'mentions' in various publications fills 60 pages, and a similar list of review sources takes up a further 30 pages. Finally there are three brief lists on 'unrealised projects', i.e. the things she *didn't* do. There is an extraordinary section of photographs showing her displaying various emotions, labelled 'Vicious', 'Pathetic', 'Tempestuous', 'Happy', etc. – the sort of thing that used to be paraded in very early fan magazines. Obviously a labour of love, all this is prefaced by a fulsome foreword by William Ludwig, who says: 'Miss Parker never gave a bad performance . . . An undeviating perfectionist . . .' A treat for Eleanor Parker devotees, who are probably countless.

Emotion Pictures, Wim Wenders; Faber & Faber, £12.95.

A fascinatingly offbeat collection of essays, notes and brief comments on films he liked (and one, *Hitler – Biography*, that he didn't) by the German director best known here, probably, for *Hammett* and *Paris, Texas*. His views are wide and varied, with a particular affection for the American Western – a section on John Ford gives the book its title. Other films given particular attention include *Lydia, Easy Rider, Bad Day at Black Rock, Nashville*, and Truffaut's *L'Enfant Sauvage*. The brief book ends with a lengthy and disillusioned poem, in very free verse (or perhaps just chopped-up prose), on the American Dream. An oddity, but an entertaining one, well translated for easy reading by Sean Whiteside in association with Michael Hofmann.

Note: Not be confused with Hilton Tims's enjoyable book of the same title on the 'women's picture', 1930–55, reviewed in *Film Review 1988–9*.

Everybody Wins, Arthur Miller; Methuen, £4.99.

Not the least interesting part of this neatly produced paperback is the preface, in which

Arthur Miller (whose first original screenplay since *The Misfits* this is) analyses the differences between a filmscript and a printed play, and explores the whole experience of reading, writing and watching a performance of the finished work in cinema and theatre. *Everybody Wins* starts off as an intriguing but fairly straightforward story of a possible miscarriage of justice, but before long it develops into a grim and complex picture of corruption, drug dealing and political intrigue in a small town in New England (not 'England', as stated on the back cover). It reads smoothly and is easily visualised, without distracting technical details but with sufficient indication of time, place and, where necessary, description. A filmscript such as this is as acceptable to read as a printed play, and can afford as much interest and enjoyment to the reader, irrespective of whether or not the movie itself is available.

Everything You Always Wanted to Know About Woody, Graham Flashner, Robson Books, £5.95.

Paperback edition of the 230-page quiz book originally reviewed in *Film Review 1989–90*. It can best be regarded as a pleasant diversion for admirers of Woody Allen – described in the introduction as 'America's foremost comic artist'.

Film Directors and Their Films, Alison J. Filmer and Andre Golay; Harrap, £14.95.

This gargantuan reference book surely justifies its claim to be the most comprehensive guide to the directors of full-length English-language feature films ever published in the UK or USA. It covers the period 1924–88, with even a number of entries for 1989. Over 3300 directors and 26,000 films are included (I take these figures on trust), and the enormous index fills over 200 large pages. In addition to the film references, brief biographical details are given together with titles of important biographies and autobiographies.

No work of this size can reasonably be expected to be free of errors – though they are not easy to spot. It is, however, a little surprising to find Carl Foreman's only (and quite important) film, *The Victors*, entered as *The Visitors*; and it seems doubtful whether Fatty Arbuckle (who died in obscurity in 1933 having never recovered from the Virginia Rappe scandal) made 'many . . . TV comedy shorts' – even accepting the fact that a New York station started scheduled television broadcasts in 1928. There seems to be no other record of his doing this work.

The book is very attractively produced, with commendable clarity of print and layout, and for these days the price is remarkably modest.

The Film Handbook, Geoff Andrew; Longman, £10.95

The Time Out Film Guide, edited by Tom Milne; Longman, £10.95.

The first of these interesting reference books (the author is film critic and editor on *Time Out* magazine) is a collection of articles on some 200 directors, chosen to interest the 'new breed of film-goer'. The range is wide – from D. W. Griffith to the directors of today (and tomorrow) and includes a full quota of foreign names. The author is forceful when expressing disapproval, pouring scorn on directors as varied as Brian de Palma, Richard Attenborough, Walt Disney and – perhaps surprisingly – the monumental Italians, Fellini and Visconti; but he is equally enthusiastic in praise. The result is an entertaining and stimulating book, with which it is a pleasure sometimes to disagree. At the end of each essay are brief notes on 'lineage' (influences on and by the director concerned), suggestions for further reading, and recommended films. Additional reference material is contained in a 'databank', consisting of a glossary, further suggested books, and lists of festivals, magazines, film schools and institutions. Martin Scorsese has provided an introduction.

The Film Guide is compiled on the lines of Halliwell's and Leonard Maltin's guides with commentaries on some 9000 films drawn from 21 years of reviews in the magazine *Time Out*, together with brief details of cast, etc. Notes on video availability are provided – though, as anyone anxious to obtain a tape of a much-desired film must sadly know, such information is often unreliable. Both Halliwell and Maltin cover about twice the number of films and Halliwell (cursorily and unjustifiably dismissed in the *Handbook*) gives fuller and more varied details: however, the commentaries justify the appearance of yet another such encyclopedia. These, written by a large number of reviewers, are pithy, pointed and frequently very amusing, though it is a pity that political and other prejudices occasionally warp clear and balanced criticism. It is, however, good to see justice done to often maligned films such as *Heaven's Gate* and *Night of the Following Day*. (The latter has been shown on television in an appallingly butchered version which totally perverted and destroyed the original story.) Appendices of categories and foreign films add to the usefulness of the *Guide*, as does an index of directors. A lengthy index of subjects is also welcome – and often hilarious.

Both books are handsomely presented (particularly the neat and stoutly made *Handbook*) but both also suffer from a serious drawback – neither can be read without difficulty. The print size in the *Guide* is so small and congested that even the healthy-eyed may need a magnifying-glass, and that in the *Handbook* is in addition so faint as to require a bright lamp on the art paper used.

In the *Handbook* the film titles quoted in the essays would have been a great deal easier to find had they been printed in bold type rather than italics; picking them out can be a tedious and irritating job.

The First Film-Makers, Richard Dyer MacCann; Scarecrow, dist. Bailey Bros & Swinfen, £30.90 cloth, £14.25 paperback.

The second volume in a projected series of five on early American cinema, this follows the same form as its forerunner, *The First Tycoons* (see *Film Review 1987–8*), being a large collection of extracts from articles, histories and memoirs by notable writers on or workers in the cinema from early days to the present. Many of them are not easily available elsewhere, which adds greatly to the value of the book. Much the largest section is devoted, understandably, to D. W. Griffith, with Erich von Stroheim in second place, and W. S. Hart and Thomas H. Ince as runners-up. There are briefer references to other directors of the period. Appendices include selected filmographies, notes on the availability of films on video cassettes, a list of twenty leading directors, an article on screenwriters and a lengthy bibliography. A valuable book for the researcher and the 'silent' enthusiast.

Five for Hollywood, John Parker; Macmillan, £12.95.

The author takes five stars who sprang to fame in the later years of Hollywood's greatness, when, as he says, 'The Golden Age was over and the dream factories . . . saw themselves descending in a slow and painful disintegration of all that had gone before.' The five are Montgomery Clift, James Dean, Rock Hudson, Natalie Wood and Elizabeth Taylor. Their lives were strangely intertwined and all save one (Elizabeth Taylor) have met with untimely and distressing deaths: from drugs and desperation, from a calamitous car crash, from AIDS, from a dark scene of drowning. A symbolic parallel is drawn between the stars and the collapse of the Dream City, but the book concentrates on the human side of their stories as well as providing a general view of a traumatic period.

'The system' is often held, as here, to be in part responsible for such woeful events; even so, one is entitled to wonder whether people so fortunate as to have achieved success, wealth and fame beyond the wildest dreams of ordinary folk may not themselves have been at least in part responsible for their self-destruction on account of a lack of personal integrity or self-respect. Their stories, however, are told with compassion as well as frankness. Film lists, good illustrations and an excellent index round off an engrossing book.

Flashbacks in Film, Maureen Turim; Routledge, £10.95.

This is a scholarly and original study of the history, theory and significance of the film flashback from the earliest silent days to the present, in America, Europe and Japan. Particular attention is paid to films such as *Citizen Kane* and *Sunset Boulevard*, and Hitchcock's *Spellbound*, *Stage Fright*, *Marnie* and *Vertigo*. A book for the serious student, written – apart from a liking for such indigestible polysyllables as 'subjectivizing' – with commendable clarity.

Foreign Film Guide, Ronald Bergan & Robyn Karney; Bloomsbury, £9.99.

This is the paperback edition of a book highly recommended in the last issue of *Film Review* for its wide range and the completeness of its concise entries. Over 50 countries are included in over 2000 entries (in the silent as well as the sound period), and the general layout, together with cross-references for alternative titles, makes it simple for any particular film to be traced. The reappearance of this 638-page book at a very reasonable price is welcome.

François Truffaut – Letters, (Vol. 1), trans. Gilbert Adair; Faber & Faber, £17.50.

François Truffaut was a prolific and lively letter writer from his early teens. This handsomely produced volume reproduces several hundred such letters, and the result is an engrossing picture of the life and times of a leading French director. Details of his working methods, sharply expressed opinions on dozens of films, an account of the making of the famous Truffaut/Hitchcock interview, personal relationships with friends and colleagues, and a general view of the French film scene of the past forty years all combine to make this one of the most enjoyable and important books of the year. Truffaut's enthusiasm for the cinema shines through an excellent and sensitive translation. Jean-Luc Godard provides a short foreword, and there are many illustrations, a chronology and a good double index. The copious notes are excellent – concise and well arranged.

From Hitler to Heimat, Anton Kaes; Harvard University Press, £19.95.

Taking as his title an allusion to Siegfried Kracauer's famous book *From Caligari to Hitler* (1947), the author examines modern German cinema as a reflection of the country's recent history, and as an expression of attitudes towards Hitler and the Third Reich. The films he analyses as representative are Syberberg's *Hitler, A Film from Germany*; Fassbinder's *The Marriage of Maria Braun*; Kluge's *The Patriot*; Sanders-Brahms's *Germany, Pale Mother*; and Reitz's *Heimat*. Many other relevant productions are briefly mentioned. Stills are restricted to one at the start of each section. Detailed notes and a full bibliography round off an authoritative work (the author is Professor of German Literature at the University of California, Berkeley), of equal interest to the historian and the student of cinema.

Gerald du Maurier, James Harding; Hodder & Stoughton, £15.00.

Not the least enjoyable part of this excellent biography is the series of vivid pen-portraits of the many actors and actresses with whom du Maurier was associated during his long and brilliantly successful career. Though he made only a few films (and in fact despised the whole business of movie-making) they are worth noting here – particularly the early Hitchcock, *Lord Camber's Ladies*, and the World War I thriller starring Conrad Veidt, *I Was a Spy* – if only because they are the sole record we have of one of the great actors of his time. The subtle apparent underplaying of his stage performances foreshadowed the general acting style of the sound cinema as against the broader flamboyance of earlier silent years. Mr Harding's account of a complex man, charming, often high-spirited, but fundamentally unhappy and frustrated, is throughout compassionate, perceptive and of unfailing interest.

Goldwyn, A. Scott Berg; Hamish Hamilton, £16.95.

For once the often abused adjective 'definitive' can be aptly applied to this biography of Samuel Goldwyn – a fine, thick, hugely enjoyable book tracing the life and work of a key figure in Hollywood history, under whose auspices were created such varied and unforgettable films as *The Best Years of Our Lives*, *Dodsworth*, *Wuthering Heights*, *Dead End*, the Eddie Cantor and other musicals, and the silent Ronald Colman/Vilma Banky romantic dramas. Some of the alleged 'Goldwynisms' and legends are exposed, but many other authenticated stories replace them in an account that is by turns hilarious, moving, frank and compassionate. There are many excellent illustrations, and the details of notes and sources, many of them derived from the Goldwyn archives, are noteworthy for their fullness. The index, however, has rather too many unbroken lines of page numbers for comfortable reference; and, surprisingly in so important and detailed a study, there is no filmography.

Grand National, Producers' Releasing Corporation and Screen Guild/Lippert, Ted Okuda; McFarland, dist. Bailey Bros & Swinfen, £33.25.

Ted Okuda follows up his useful book *The Monogram Checklist* (covered in *Film Review 1988–9*) with similar studies of three even smaller companies, giving in each case a full filmography and a brief history. Though the great majority of their productions are – to put it gently – unmemorable, a surprising number of well-known American players appear on the cast list of one or other of the companies during their existence in the mid-thirties to mid-fifties; for example James Cagney, Harry Langdon, Elissa Landi, Bela Lugosi, Erich von Stroheim, Vincent Price, Boris Karloff, Ben Lyon and Richard Barthelmess. A fair number of British productions are listed among the releases, and here also many familiar names appear.

Of minor importance these small studios might be, compared to the giants, but they form a permanent part of film history, and records of their achievements such as these are to be welcomed by students and buffs alike.

The Great Science Fiction Pictures II, James Robert Parish & Michael R. Pitts; Scarecrow, dist. Bailey Bros & Swinfen, £47.05.

This second volume on science fiction films runs to nearly 500 pages and adds a vast number of titles to its predecessor. The authors have extended the definition of 'science fiction' to its utmost limits, ranging in time from the silent days (the 1915 German *Golem*, the Russian 1924 *Aelita*) to the present. In the first volume, the Frankenstein films were collected together in a general survey, but here they receive individual treatment. Dr Jekyll and Mr Hyde productions are reviewed in a collective essay, a treatment which emphasises the surprisingly large number of times the famous doctor and his infamous *alter ego* have appeared in the cinema. The book is produced in the best Scarecrow style and is embellished with an acceptable (if not over-generous) number of excellent stills. But it is depressing to note the considerable number of eminently forgettable films necessarily covered here.

Halliwell's Film Guide, 7th Edition, Leslie Halliwell; Grafton Books, £25.00.

The greatly missed Leslie Halliwell completed this edition of his mammoth reference work just before his untimely death at barely sixty years of age. Even wider in its coverage than its predecessor, it maintains the same high quality of both material and presentation. Though containing 1000 new films and retaining its additional features intact, it is some sixteen pages shorter; this reduction has been achieved mainly by the elimination of publicity illustrations, for which Leslie Halliwell had an obvious liking and which were admittedly an attractive decoration in earlier editions. In addition the notes on available videos have been omitted – these were in any case of minor value owing to their inevitable inaccuracy when tapes were withdrawn from circulation.

These minor deletions in no way detract from the true value of this gigantic tome. The good news is that both this and *Halliwell's Filmgoer's and Video Viewer's Companion* are to be continued on the same lines and with the same titles. Nothing, one feels, would have given their great originator more pleasure.

Hattie, Carlton Jackson; Madison Books, £16.95.

Fondly remembered as Mammy in *Gone with the Wind*, Hattie McDaniel appeared in about 300 films, many little known or with her performances uncredited, but including *Showboat* (1936 version), *Nothing Sacred*, *Saratoga*, *The Male Animal*, *Margie* and Disney's *Song of the South*, as well as considerable radio and television work. She was notable for two 'firsts' – the first black to win an Oscar (as Best Supporting Actress in *Gone with the Wind*) and the first to sing on American radio. This is a warm and at times moving biography. Among its most interesting chapters is that entitled 'The Crusade Against Mammyism', describing the grief caused to her by attacks for portraying the conventional 'film-type Negro' in her earlier years. The author points out that two entertainers of the period rose to fame on the one word 'Mammy' – Hattie herself, and, previously, Al Jolson; a white actor in blackface.

Five appendices include selected lists of film and radio performances, and a few of her favourite food recipes.

Highlights and Shadows, the Memoirs of a Hollywood Cameraman, Charles G. Clarke; Scarecrow Press, dist. Bailey Bros & Swinfen, £28.05.

The number of books on or by cameramen is small compared with those about directors and stars, and these memories from one of the lesser-known but busy and long-lived workers in this essential field of film-making is to be welcomed. His list of productions – as first cameraman or associate – ranges from 1922 to 1962 and fills over six pages. Among the best-known are *Miracle on 34th Street*, *Slattery's Hurricane*, *Prince of Players*, *Carousel* and *Return to Peyton Place*, and he worked on location scenes only in *The Grapes of Wrath*, *Mutiny on the Bounty* (1935 version), *Three Coins in a Fountain*, *Love is a Many Splendored Thing* and *The Rains of Ranchipur*. His book is a thoroughly entertaining mixture of film history, technical details, and travel and adventure. Charles Clarke died in 1983. (This is No. 21 in the very useful Film-makers Series, edited by Anthony Slide.)

Hollywood's Fallen Idols, Roy Pickard; Batsford, £14.95.

In this large-format and handsome paperback Roy Pickard tells the stories of ten famous cinema stars who experienced both the heights and the depths of a career in the Golden Age of Hollywood, from Charles

Chaplin who survived (to know 25 happy years), to Marilyn Monroe who succumbed (to end up a murder victim or – more probably – a suicide). Other names include not only well-known ones, such as Judy Garland and Errol Flynn, but those slightly less widely covered, among them George Sanders and Sterling Hayden. Though Erich von Stroheim is included, the period covered is limited mainly to the sound era, so that silent sufferers such as Clara Bow and Wallace Reid do not appear. Even so, enough disillusionment and tragedy are depicted to remove some of the gilt from the gingerbread Film City. Many of the events may be familiar from other sources, but this is a sound, concise collection, and Mr Pickard writes with sympathy and understanding. The text is accompanied by numerous excellent black-and-white stills and portraits.

Hollywood Greats of the Golden Years, J. G. Ellrod; McFarland, dist. Bailey Bros & Swinfen, £26.13.

Taking the Golden Years as extending from the late 1920s to the late 1950s, the author has selected about eighty well-known stars and provided each with a brief biographical paragraph, two or three photographs and a filmography. Many, if not most, of his subjects are more fully covered elsewhere, but this is quite a useful and attractive quick reference book, and the many illustrations are an asset, since in general they are not the hackneyed ones that often appear in other books. The filmographies are extended forward beyond the limit of the selected Golden Years period; it seems a pity they could not also have been extended backwards where relevant, to include at least some of the silent films on which the stars-to-be built their future fame.

Hollywood Sisters – Jackie and Joan Collins, Susan Crimp and Patricia Burstein; Robson Books, £10.95.

Plenty (to put it mildly) has been written about Joan, rather less about Jackie, so it was a neat idea of two lady journalists to combine the actress and the writer in a single biography. The book's approach is apparent from the fact that it has neither index, notes, filmography nor list of published works; but it is lively, frank, easy to read and often amusing; in fact well suited to the stories the writers have to tell. There is no doubt that for many thousands of devotees the world would be a distinctly duller place without the sensational sisters, and this book will certainly appeal to many of them.

The Hustons, Lawrence Grobel; Bloomsbury, £20.00.

The star of this mammoth (800-page) family biography is, not unexpectedly, John – famous as director of *The Maltese Falcon*,

The Treasure of the Sierra Madre, *The African Queen* and other recognised master films – but there is much here also about his daughter Anjelica (whose haunting and moving performance in *The Dead* will not lightly be forgotten), his two sons, and especially his fondly remembered father Walter Huston, one of the most notable actors of his time. It is an absorbing book, justifying its length by the mass of relevant details, professional and personal, written in a flowing, easy style and researched in great detail. The author obviously has high regard for his subject, and though some may question Huston's supremacy as one of the very greatest directors, the picture that emerges here is of a fascinating and often commanding figure in the world of films.

The index tends towards lengthy lists of blank page numbers, and the reference section consists of a mere chronicle of stage and screen credits, but the book is handsomely produced and a pleasure to read.

If This Was Happiness, Barbara Leaming; Weidenfeld & Nicolson, £14.95.

The title of this full and moving biography of Rita Hayworth is part of a remark made by her one-time husband, Orson Welles, referring to their stormy relationship – 'If this was happiness, imagine what the rest of her life had been!' It is an apt comment on a life that combined dazzling success and fame with a surely disproportionate amount of tragedy and heartbreak. Barbara Leaming writes frankly and compassionately about Rita's traumatic early life as a dancer in vaudeville (as partner to an incestuous father), her unhappy marriages (to Welles, Aly Khan, and others), her humiliations at Columbia under its appalling chief, Harry Cohn, her struggles for the custody of her daughter, and the final dreadful years as her personality disintegrated as a result of Alzheimer's disease. Thoroughly researched and annotated, this is a personal rather than a professional history: no filmography is provided, but in truth few of her films (apart perhaps from *Cover Girl*, *Gilda* and *The Lady from Shanghai*) were memorable.

Ireland, Brian McIlroy; Flicks Books, £12.95.

Studies of Irish cinema are few, and it is good to have this scholarly volume, No. 4 in the World Cinema series. It traces the history from 1896 on, though concentrating largely on later and contemporary work. The main body of the book is a series of interviews with about a dozen active workers in the field, including Neil Jordan (director of the strange and beautiful *The Company of Wolves*), and Cyril Cusack, the famous ex-Abbey Theatre actor who made his first film in 1917 at the age of seven. There is also much useful information on the general development of Irish cinema, arranged in brief and clearly headed sections which

make for easy reference. Appendices include a chronology and two filmographies, one on Irish and the other on Irish-related films. An interesting entry details James Joyce's connection with the subject and his responsibility for the first Irish cinema – the Volta in Dublin.

The silent cinema is not widely represented, but it is a disappointment to find no mention of John Ford's production of Donn Byrne's *Hangman's House* (1928), a film described by Anthony Slide in his *The Cinema and Ireland* (see *Film Review 1988–9*) as one of the most important 'Irish' films in the US during the 1920s, on account of its lack of burlesque and sentimentality and its believable atmosphere: it is certainly a silent film that remains happily in the memory of those fortunate enough to have seen it on its original appearance.

Note: A Directory of Irish and Irish-related films is also available from the publishers, price £17.00.

Karloff and Lugosi – The Story of a Haunting Collaboration, Gregory William Mank; McFarland, dist. Bailey Bros & Swinfen, £33.25.

Taking as his centrepiece the seven great films in which Boris Karloff and Bela Lugosi appeared together, starting with *The Black Cat* and ending with *The Body Snatcher*, the author has created a vivid picture of the whole period in which they flourished. Every page is packed with fascinating information, even to the footnotes, and often with little known details. Scores of interviews with and quotations from friends, close relatives, critics and associates help to fill out the general narrative. The making of the seven key movies is described in full; and the fluctuations in their personal relationship – Lugosi's pathetic jealousy brought on by his missed chance to portray the original monster, and Karloff's unfailing generosity in speaking of him – are sensitively handled, as are the wide differences in character despite their many moments of friendship. Lugosi's tragic decline and death are movingly recounted.

In describing the practical side of the productions, the author gives extensive financial details, which form interesting comparisons. The two 'career' sections are thorough and complete, recording every stage, film and radio performance by the two stars. The illustrations are lavish and often rare. Altogether this is a monumental work of careful research, valuable as a film history and a book to be treasured by all those who collect every Karloff and Lugosi video and watch eagerly for every revival of their movies on TV.

Louise Brooks, Barry Paris; Hamish Hamilton, £20.00.

This long and wholly absorbing biography ranks among the best film books of this (or indeed any other) year. It traces the life and career of one of the most controversial and complex of all the film actresses of her period – through her early years as a dancer, to her meteoric (and self-scorned) rise as a Hollywood star, and her meeting with German director G. W. Pabst leading to her crowning achievement as Lulu in *Pandora's Box*, with its very mixed early critical reactions and its eventual recognition as a masterpiece. There follow the long, dark years of obscurity and failure – a period little known until now and aptly titled in the book as 'Lulu in Purgatory' and 'Lulu in Hell' – and her final success as a writer of perception and brilliance, if not of unfailing accuracy.

Was she 'the greatest film actress of all time' or, in the words of George Cukor, 'a *nobody . . . a nothing* in films'? Barry Paris paints a frank portrait, with many 'sensational revelations', as often as not provided by herself; her seemingly endless procession of 'lovers', her alcoholism, and her often cruel and unfair criticisms and treatment of friends and associates are unflinchingly recounted – all paling into relative insignificance beside the admiration and affection she aroused through many years.

The book is beautifully produced, with many rare illustrations (including a special portrait gallery), full documentation, comprehensive filmography and a list of the inaccuracies in her best-selling book *Lulu in Hollywood*. Even the footnotes – often an irritating interruption at the bottom of a page – are packed with information.

The Making of *The Wizard of Oz*, Aljean Harmetz; Pavilion, £12.95.

The 50th anniversary is bringing a good deal of fresh attention to this much loved film, and this fascinating account of its origins and production must rank high among the best. It covers in full detail every aspect of its creation, from a description of the MGM studio as it was in 1938, through scripting, casting, music, direction, design and costume, to the final achievement. The famous Munchkins are given a special chapter to themselves, as are the superb special effects. Most of the cunning secrets and tricks of the latter are given away – and far from resulting in disillusionment these revelations must only add to the interest of present-day devotees. The trials and tribulations inevitable in the making of such a film are frankly described, the Munchkins being defended against some of the accusations which were made about them. Lavish illustrations in both black-and-white and colour, together with reproduction of numerous interesting documents, and appendices on the life of the original author, and on the MGM props auction which included the sale of the famous 'ruby slippers', complete a valuable and entertaining record of the making of a memorable movie.

Marilyn at Twentieth Century-Fox, Lawrence Crown; W. H. Allen, £8.99.

Mr Crown has achieved the not inconsiderable feat of producing something comparatively new on Miss Monroe. Concentrating on the films she made for Fox (19 out of her total of 30, including both her first and her uncompleted last), and making use of a large number of lengthy quotations and widely varying opinions, he paints a vivid picture of the ructions and confusion that seemed to accompany much of her professional activity. Lavish illustrations (stills, publicity photographs, advertisements), all excellently reproduced, complete this handsome softback.

Mia Farrow, Sam Rubin & Richard Taylor; Robson Books, £12.95.

An 'intermediate' biography can be very interesting, but is subject to obvious limitations. The facts of Mia Farrow's life and career to date are neatly set out here, and there is a good chapter on *Rosemary's Baby*, but there is, one feels, more to this uniquely fascinating actress than Rubin and Taylor show. The tone of the book is fairly bland, the final chapters with the arrival of Woody Allen tending to blossom into a sort of mutual admiration society. The 'films' are separated from the 'life' (whereas in fact they are surely an integral part of it) and are collected together in a final chapter to themselves. This may be a useful innovation in some ways, but a good full filmography at the end is generally preferable. The Woody Allen movies appear to depict a cosy, enclosed little world of self-exploration.

Michael Caine's Moving Picture Show, Hodder & Stoughton (Coronet Books), £2.99.

Michael Caine provides introductions and photo captions to this collection of anecdotes and snippets about the world of the cinema, presumably all selected and researched by himself. Many are familiar, most are amusing, some are of doubtful authenticity, and one or two are unpleasant. Quite a few supposed facts are exposed as fictitious. Neither an index nor quotation sources are included – the latter surely essential in a type of book which makes a virtue of its accuracy.

Monsters and Mad Scientists, Andrew Tudor; Blackwell, hardback £35.00, paperback, £8.95.

Horror and Marilyn Monroe would seem to have something in common, sharing more literary coverage than anything else in the cinema. This latest book, 'A Cultural History of the Horror Movie', is a 'serious' one, academic and analytical, with charts and tables in place of stills and gory portraits. Mercifully, in contrast to the pretentious obscurity of some other similar studies, its approach and style are on the whole straight-

forward and lucid – even if the diagrams accompanying the section on 'Narratives', for instance, might cause a few brows to become furrowed in puzzlement. The genre is examined in exemplary detail, a very large number of films are discussed, and even those enthusiasts who generally avoid what might be called the 'lunatic fringe' of film theorising should find much of interest.

Note: In referring to *Dracula*, Mr Tudor states (p. 161) that the 1931 film's primary source is Hamilton Deane's play. This is not strictly accurate; the true source is the Hamilton Deane/John Balderston revised version which was written for production in the USA. Deane's original version is now a very rare script indeed.

The Moving Image, John Wyver; Basil Blackwell, £35.00 hardback, £15.00 paperback.

Published in association with the British Film Institute to mark the opening of the Museum of the Moving Image (MOMI), this covers the entire international history and development of film, television and video from the earliest days (the 'archaeology' of the cinema) to the present day. Separate chapters deal with such subjects as technology, animation, documentaries and newsreels, and the 'New British Cinema'. To have compressed such a vast amount of material into 300-odd well-illustrated pages is a notable achievement, and although references to individual films, for instance, are little more than listings, the text is admirably informative and well set out. The many stills and other illustrations are excellently reproduced, and there is a full index. HRH Prince Charles, patron of the BFI, provides a brief welcoming foreword.

The Parade's Gone By, Kevin Brownlow; Columbus, £12.95.

A royal welcome is due to the reappearance of this classic tribute to the great days of the silent film, in handsome softback as one of the Lively Arts series. It consists of nearly 600 pages of history, commentary and interviews, embellished with a magnificent collection of superbly reproduced stills. First published in 1968, now with a new introduction and an updated list of corrections (honestly and disarmingly presented by the author), this remains the bible of the silent film buff and the serious historian.

The Post-Feminist Hollywood Actress, Kerry Segrave & Linda Martin; McFarland, dist. Bailey Bros & Swinfen, £37.95.

After a lengthy introduction, somewhat overburdened with comparative figures and percentages but making a convincing point about the inferior position to which women have been relegated in Hollywood cinema, the main body of the book consists of filmographies and brief biographies of stars born after 1939. The categories are entitled 'Superstars', 'Leading Ladies', 'New Screen Stars' and 'Up and Coming Actresses'. The last section is rather depressing, including as it does a number of hardworking and potentially talented young players ploughing their way through a morass of mediocre movies.

This is a detailed, well-researched and fully illustrated survey. (Unfortunately, however, an infuriating stylistic gimmick in a number of essays renders them almost unreadable. Apparently filled with horror at the thought of using the personal pronoun, the writer refers to the relevant actress by forename or surname indiscriminately, often in the same sentence. To take one example among many: when the article on Jessica Lange refers to Frances Farmer, we find; 'Lange identified with Farmer's sensibility although Jessica realised she was more cautious than the headstrong Frances.')

The Psychotronic Encyclopedia of Film, Michael Weldon; Plexus, £12.95.

Look up 'psychotronic' and you won't find it in either the Oxford English (or the Oxford American) Dictionary; it was used by Michael Weldon as the title of a 'New York weekly guide to television movies – especially forgotten junk', and taken (unconsciously) from a film about a maniac barber who killed people with 'psychic energy'. Included in this vast collection of over 3000 of the 'wildest movies ever made' are cheap sci-fi productions, monster, beach, motorbike, rock 'n' roll and other lower-than-Z-rated productions. Titles such as *Attack of the Mushroom People, I Dismember Mama, Werewolf in a Girl's* [sic] *Dormitory* (with theme song, 'The Ghoul in the School'), *Twitch of the Death Nerve* and *Attack of the Killer Tomatoes* may whet the appetite. Mr Weldon's net, however, is cast astonishingly wide for here can also be found *A Tale of Two Cities* (Bogarde version), *Fahrenheit 451, Raise the Titanic, The Private Lives of Elizabeth and Essex* and even *The Ten Commandments*. The brief reviews are pithy, often witty and sharply critical – that on *The Ten Commandments* is particularly diverting. The book is lavishly illustrated, with many stills rarely seen before – and unlikely to be seen again. With satellite and cable TV likely to open the gate to hundreds of such anti-masterpieces this could be a useful reference book – if only as a warning.

Note: Once again a reviewer of *Dead of Night* has missed the essential brief shot towards the end that reveals the shattering truth that 'this time' the nightmare is no longer a dream, but a horrifying reality.

Rasputin in Hollywood, Sir David Napley; Weidenfeld & Nicolson, £14.95.

The furore over the libel action brought by Princess Youssoupoff against MGM over the three-Barrymore (John, Lionel and Ethel) film *Rasputin, the Mad Monk* is probably largely forgotten today, but it was a major *cause célèbre* in 1934, and it is good to find it recorded in vivid detail in this scholarly and thoroughly entertaining book by an author who has had many distinguished years in the legal profession and is a past President of the Law Society.

The first section is an absorbing account of the full story of the assassination of the sinister Rasputin (who incidentally was neither mad nor a monk); the second a devastating description of the really appalling film that caused all the trouble; the third and main part a detailed reconstruction of the trial itself. Written in a light and often amusing style, and with some pertinent comments on the law and the jury system, this is a book to be enjoyed by both the film historian and anyone interested in 'courtroom scenes'.

Richard Chamberlain, Barbara and Scott Siegel; New English Library, £12.95.

From a dyslectic childhood to playing Hamlet at the Birmingham Repertory Theatre may seem quite a leap, even aided by several years of Dr Kildare, but Richard Chamberlain appears to have made it with comparative ease, and the story, together with other professional and personal details, is told in this brief but enjoyable biography. Television may have meant more to the star than movies, but he has nonetheless appeared in such major productions as *The Music Lovers, Lady Caroline Lamb, The Towering Inferno* and *The Slipper and the Rose*.

Scarlett's Women, Helen Taylor; Virago, £7.99.

Among the mass of books, articles and interviews already published on *Gone with the Wind*, this stands out as one of the most interesting and important. It deals not with the making of nor the personalities concerned in the film, but with the reactions of those who saw it – selected from hundreds of letters – and with its political, racial and social attitudes.

Brightly written, well-documented and edited, it is an absorbing study, equally entertaining and informative, and reveals an astonishing variety of views on 'the most successful motion picture of all time'.

Screen World 1989, John Willis; Muller, £16.95.

A bright spot in each year's book list is the *Screen World Annual*, which has now reached its 40th issue. With 1000 excellent stills and portraits, a 10,000-entry index, full cast-and-credit lists of all important films (including many of foreign origin), and biographical and obituary sections, this is an essential reference book on contemporary cinema. No commentaries or criticisms are to be found here – all available space is devoted to hard facts – packed together and (almost) running over. This year's volume is dedicated to Paul Newman.

3-D Movies, R. M. Hayes; McFarland, dist. Bailey Bros & Swinfen, £42.75.

This 400-page tome might justifiably claim to be the 'definitive' book on the stereoscopic film. The first six chapters recount the story of its birth (the first 3-D motion picture made for public exhibition came from the Lumière Brothers as early as 1903), its development and growth, its two great booms and busts, and its appearance on television. On the latter the author remarks: 'If you live in any large city in the United States, then you have had the opportunity of seeing just how bad 3-D can look on TV.'

The main body of the book consists of an enormous filmography with critical commentaries, and reveals what a surprisingly large number of 3-D films have been made, even allowing for the inclusion of shorts and documentaries.

The final chapter deals extensively with the various technical processes involved. The writing, particularly in some of the critical commentaries, is engagingly easy and amusing, and the technical section, embellished with diagrams and photographs of cameras, should delight the photographic enthusiast. Throughout there are many good illustrations.

Tough Guy, James L. Neibaur; McFarland, dist. Bailey Bros & Swinfen, £23.70.

About a dozen famous Hollywood stars are considered here for their 'macho' qualities. In each case, an article on the films that most clearly demonstrate these qualities is followed by a full filmography. Most of the names are those one would expect – Cagney, Bogart, Wayne, Brando, etc. The articles are concise, interesting, fresh in approach and – when necessary – sharply critical; for instance when dealing with the appalling quality of most of the films of Sylvester Stallone and Elvis Presley (whom it is surprising to find in such elite company).

A Variable Harvest, Jon Tuska; McFarland, dist. Bailey Bros & Swinfen, £33.25.

This collection of 'Essays and Reviews of Film and Literature' ranges from articles (described as 'cinematographs') on *Trader Horn* (1930) and *Rain* (1932) to studies of career (Yakima Canutt, Spencer Gordon Bennet) and crime films. Not unexpectedly, in view of the author's notable earlier works on the genre, the main portion of the book deals with the Western in film and fiction, ending with a brief, devastating account of what the historians have done to Billy the Kid. An interesting, well-written collection, short on illustration but well documented.

Variety International Film Guide 1990, ed. Peter Cowie; André Deutsch, £9.95.

This famous world-wide guide, founded 27 years ago by Peter Cowie, now appears under the banner of the leading American performing arts newspaper, *Variety*. The format is unchanged, and to say that its standard is still as high as when it was published by the Tantivy Press is to pay it the highest of compliments. This year's special 'Dossier' is concerned with the modern Spanish cinema; this is followed by the usual huge world survey and a mass of miscellaneous information on festivals, film schools, bookshops and many other activities, all lavishly illustrated. An interesting new feature, dealing in depth with the making of an important new movie, opens with Bernd Eichinger's production of *Last Exit to Brooklyn*.

The Wizard of Oz, John Fricke, Jay Scarfone & William Stillman; Hodder & Stoughton, £14.95.

This sumptuous pictorial history, issued in celebration of the film's 50th anniversary, covers every aspect of its production – acquisition, casting (including those suggestions that fell by the wayside), details of make-up and costuming, reviews, awards, reissues and television screenings, among many other features. The lively text is accompanied by a stupendous collection of photographs, not only of every conceivable detail of the production before and after filming, but also of such ancillary matters as the dolls, plate collections, prints and other artefacts issued as publicity items. The book closes with four delightful and touching memorial cartoons of much-loved members of the cast.

If the tone is wholly adulatory, this is only proper in a publication of this nature, which the countless admirers of the movie will surely treasure.

Writers in Hollywood, Ian Hamilton; Heinemann, £14.95.

Of all the main contributors to the creation of a movie, the writers seem to attract the least attention. Ian Hamilton's book is therefore doubly welcome – firstly for filling a gap (at least between 1915 and 1951) and secondly for its intrinsic interest. Starting with the furore over *The Birth of a Nation* and concluding with McCarthyism and the dubious activities of the House Un-American Activities Committee, it covers the work and lives in Hollywood of such authors as Raymond Chandler, Ben Hecht, Scott Fitzgerald, Charles Brackett, Anita Loos, Dudley Nichols, Nunnally Johnson, Aldous Huxley and William Faulkner among many others. Matters such as the Orson Welles/Herman Mankiewicz/*Citizen Kane* controversy, the attitudes towards Russia during the last war, and the question of the 'true' author of *Casablanca* are succinctly and vividly (and often amusingly) retold.

Counteracting the popular portrait of frustrated, overdriven literary genius struggling to type out masterpieces in a box-like office while harried by uncouth producers, Hamilton points out that writers 'were in the movies by choice: they earned far more money than their colleagues who did not write for films . . . And they had a lot of laughs.' Twenty-three interesting photographs round off this well-researched and sometimes hard-hitting survey.

The Zanucks of Hollywood, Marlys J. Harris; Virgin, £12.95.

This is a sound, workmanlike biography of the Zanuck dynasty, dealing with the personal and business careers of the controversial family rather than the details and qualities of the films that emerged under their influence, but unfailingly interesting throughout. Darryl Zanuck's decline following the appalling operation he had to undergo for cancer of the mouth (related in a brief, horrifying paragraph) is movingly told. Though no list of films is included, the book is well indexed and very fully documented, and the family tree provided on the endpapers is a useful reference guide to its ramifications. This is among the most sensational of the movie-mogul sagas.

Awards and Festivals

Admittedly this feature isn't complete: these days there are so many film festivals of various kinds all over the world, with competition for so many international awards, that to list all of them would fill a small book. We tend therefore, without any great pangs of conscience, to ignore such specialised festivals as the International Festival of Popular Traditions, the Margaret Mead Festival of Anthropological Films, the Okomedia Ecological Film Festival and even the Huelva Ibero-America Freiburg Festival- as well as many others – when considering the list of around 125 film and allied festivals taking place somewhere on the globe within our one-year period.

But our listing *does* include all the major festivals and awards along with some minor ones which particularly take our fancy. If you ever need a more-or-less complete list of the year's major and minor film and TV festivals and awards you will find one periodically published in the pages of *Variety*.

Nationality is stated only where films do not originate from the country in which the awards are given.

The American Academy of Motion Picture Arts and Sciences Awards ('Oscars') and Nominations for 1989, March 1990

Best Film: *Driving Miss Daisy*. Nominations: *Born on the Fourth of July, Dead Poets Society, Field of Dreams, My Left Foot*.

Best director: Oliver Stone, for *Born on the Fourth of July*. Nominations: Woody Allen, for *Crimes and Misdemeanors*; Peter Weir, for *Dead Poets Society*; Kenneth Branagh, for *Henry V* (UK); Jim Sheridan, for *My Left Foot* (UK).

Best Actor: Daniel Day Lewis, in *My Left Foot* (UK). Nominations: Kenneth Branagh, in *Henry V* (UK); Tom Cruise, in *Born on the Fourth of July*; Morgan Freeman, in *Driving Miss Daisy*; Robin Williams, in *Dead Poets Society*.

Best Actress: Jessica Tandy, in *Driving Miss Daisy*. Nominations: Isabelle Adjani, in *Camille Claudel* (France); Pauline Collins, in *Shirley Valentine* (UK); Jessica Lange, in *Music Box*; Michelle Pfeiffer, in *The Fabulous Baker Boys*.

Best Supporting Actor: Denzel Washington, in *Glory*. Nominations: Danny Aiello, in *Do the Right Thing*; Dan Aykroyd, in *Driving Miss Daisy*; Marlon Brando, in *A Dry White Season*; Martin Landau, in *Crimes and Misdemeanors*.

Best Supporting Actress: Brenda Fricker, in *My Left Foot* (UK). Nominations: Anjelica Huston and Lena Olin, in *Enemies, A Love Story*; Julia Roberts, in *Steel Mag-*nolias; Dianne Wiest, in *Parenthood*.

Best Original Screenplay: Tom Schulman, for *Dead Poets Society*. Nominations: Woody Allen, for *Crimes and Misdemeanors*; Spike Lee, for *Do the Right Thing*; Steven Soderbergh, for *sex – lies and videotape*; Nora Ephron, for *When Harry Met Sally*.

Best Screenplay Adaptation: Alfred Uhry, for *Driving Miss Daisy*. Nominations: Oliver Stone and Ron Kovic, for *Born on the Fourth of July*; Roger L. Simon and Paul Mazursky, for *Enemies, A Love Story*; Phil Alden Robinson, for *Field of Dreams*; Jim Sheridan and Shane Connaughton, for *My Left Foot* (UK).

Best Cinematography: Freddie Francis, for *Glory*. Nominations: Mikael Salomon, for *The Abyss*; Haskell Wexler, for *Blaze*; Robert Richardson, for *Born on the Fourth of July*.

Best Editing: David Brenner and Joe Hutshing, for *Born on the Fourth of July*. Nominations: Noelle Boisson, for *The Bear* (France); Mark Warner, for *Driving Miss Daisy*; William Steinkamp, for *The Fabulous Baker Boys*; Steven Rosenblum, for *Glory*.

Best Original Score: Alan Menken, for *The Little Mermaid*. Nominations: John Williams, for *Born on the Fourth of July*; David Grusin, for *The Fabulous Baker Boys*; James Horner, for *Field of Dreams*; John Williams, for *Indiana Jones and the Last Crusade*.

Best Original Song: 'Under the Sea' from *The Little Mermaid*, music by Alan Menken, lyric by Howard Ashman. Nominations: 'After All' from *Chances Are*, music by Tom Snow, lyric by Dean Pitchford; 'The Girl Who Used to Be Me' from *Shirley Valentine* (UK), music by Marvin Hamlisch, lyric by Alan and Marilyn Bergman; 'I Love to See You Smile' from *Parenthood*, music and lyric by Randy Newman; 'Kiss the Girl' from *The Little Mermaid*, music by Alan Menken, lyric by Howard Ashman.

Best Art Direction: Anton Furst (art direction) and Peter Young (set decoration), for *Batman*. Nominations: Leslie Dilley (art) and Anne Kuljian (set), for *The Abyss*; Dante Ferretti (art) and Francesca Lo Schiavo (set), for *The Adventures of Baron Munchausen* (UK); Bruno Rubeo (art) and Crispian Sallis (set), for *Driving Miss Daisy*; Norman Garwood (art) and Garrett Lewis (set), for *Glory*.

Best Costume Design: Phyllis Dalton, for *Henry V* (UK). Nominations: Gabriella Pescucci, for *The Adventures of Baron Munchausen* (UK); Elizabeth McBride, for *Driving Miss Daisy*; Joe I. Tompkins, for *Harlem Nights*; Theodor Pistek, for *Valmont*.

Best Sound: Donald O. Mitchell, Kevin O'Connell, Greg P. Russell and Keith A. Wester, for *Black Rain*. Nominations: Don Bassman, Kevin F. Cleary, Richard Overton and Lee Orloff, for *The Abyss*; Michael Minkler, Gregory H. Watkins, Wylie Stateman and Tod A. Maitland, for *Born on the Fourth of July*; Donald O. Mitchell, Gregg C. Rudloff, Elliot Tyson and Russell Williams II, for *Glory*; Ben Burtt, Gary Summers, Shawn Murphy and Tony Dawe, for *Indiana Jones and the Last Crusade*.

Best Sound Effects Editing: Ben Burtt and Richard Hymns, for *Indiana Jones and the Last Crusade*. Nominations: Milton C. Burrow and William L. Manger, for *Black Rain*; Robert Henderson and Alan Robert Murray, for *Lethal Weapon 2*.

Best Make-Up: Manlio Rocchetti, Lynn Barber and Kevin Haney, for *Driving Miss Daisy*. Nominations: Maggie Weston and Fabrizio Sforza, for *The Adventures of Baron Munchausen* (UK); Dick Smith, Ken Diaz and Greg Nelson, for *Dad*.

Best Visual Effects: John Bruno, Dennis Muren, Hoyt Yeatman and Dennis Skotak, for *The Abyss*. Nominations: Richard Conway and Kent Houston, for *The Adventures of Baron Munchausen* (UK); Ken Ralston, Michael Lantieri, John Bell and Steve Gawley, for *Back to the Future – Part II*.

Best Foreign Language Film: *Cinema Paradiso* (Italy). Nominations: *Camille Claudel* (France); *Jesus of Montreal* (Canada); *Santiago, the Story of His Life* (Puerto Rico); *Waltzing Regitze* (Denmark).

Best Short Film (Animated): *Balance*. Nominations: *Cow*; *The Hill Farm*.

Best Short Film (Live Action): *Work Experience*. Nominations: *Amazon Diary*; *The Child Eater*.

Best Feature Documentary: *Common Threads: Stories from the Quilt*. Nominations: *Adam Clayton Powell*; *Crack USA: Country Under Siege*; *For All Mankind*; *Super Chief: the Life and Legacy of Earl Warren*.

Best Short Documentary: *The Johnstown Flood*. Nominations: *Fine Food: Fine Pastries, Open 6 to 9*; *Yad Vashen: Preserving the Past to Ensure the Future*.

The 40th Berlin International Film Festival Awards, February 1990

Golden Bear for Best Film shared by: *Lark on a String*, by Jiri Menzel (Czechoslovakia); and *Music Box*, by Constantin Costa-Gavras (USA).

Silver Bear: *Coming Out*, by Heiner Carow (E. Germany).

Special Jury Prize: *The Weakness Syndrome*, by Kira Muratova (USSR).

Best Director: Michael Verhoeven, for *The Nasty Girl*.

Best Joint Performance: Jessica Tandy and Morgan Freeman, in *Driving Miss Daisy* (USA).

Best Single Performance: Iain Glen, in *Silent Scream* (UK).

Special Achievement Award: Xie Fei, for *Black Snow* (China).

The Alfred Bauer Prize: *The Guard*, by Alexander Rogoshkin (USSR). This film also won the International Film Critics' Prize.

Golden Berlin Camera: Oliver Stone, for *Born on the Fourth of July* (USA). (According to *Variety*, this award is seen as a consolation prize for the film being excluded from the main awards.)

The 1989 British Academy of Film and Television Arts Awards, March 1990

Best Film: *Dead Poets Society*, by the direction/production team of Steven Hall, Paul Junger Witt, Tony Thomas and Peter Weir (USA).

Best Actor: Daniel Day Lewis, in *My Left Foot*.

Best Actress: Pauline Collins, in *Shirley Valentine*.

Best Supporting Actor: Ray McAnally (who died in June 1989; this was his final performance), in *My Left Foot*.

Best Supporting Actress: Michelle Pfeiffer, in *Dangerous Liaisons* (USA).

Best Director: Kenneth Branagh, for *Henry V*.

Best Foreign Language Film: *Life and Nothing But – La Vie et Rien d'Autre*, by Bertrand Tavernier (France).

Best Original Screenplay: Nora Ephron, for *When Harry Met Sally* (USA).

Best Adapted Screenplay: Christopher Hampton, for *Dangerous Liaisons* (USA).

Best Score: Maurice Jarre, for *Dead Poets Society* (USA).

The 11th Annual (British) Critics' Circle Film Section Awards, December 1989

Best English Language Film: *Distant Voices, Still Lives*, by Terence Davies.

Best Director: Terence Davies, for *Distant Voices, Still Lives*.

Best Foreign Language Film: *Au Revoir, les Enfants*, by Louis Malle (France).

Best Performance: Daniel Day Lewis, in *My Left Foot*.

Best Screenplay: Christopher Hampton, for *Dangerous Liaisons* (USA).

Annual Music Award: Maurice Jarre, for *Lawrence of Arabia, Doctor Zhivago*, etc.

Special Awards: Alec Guinness 'for the brilliance of his film performances over more than 40 years'; Artificial Eye, for the high standard of their films; director Charles Crichton, for his films over a long period.

The 43rd Cannes Film Festival Awards, May 1990

Palme d'Or for Best Film: *Wild at Heart*, by David Lynch (USA).

Grand Prix shared by: *The Sting of Death*, by Kohei Oguri (Japan); and *Tilai*, by Idrissa Quedraogo (Burkina Faso).

Best Director: Pavel Lounguine, for *Taxi Blues* (USSR/France).

Best Actor: Gerard Depardieu, in *Cyrano de Bergerac* (France).

Best Actress: Krzystyna Janda, in *The Interrogation* (Poland).

Best Artistic Contribution: Glen Panfilov, for *Mother* (USSR/Italy).

Jury Prize: *Hidden Agenda*, by Ken Loach (UK).

Best First Film: *Don't Move, Die and Recover*, by Vitali Kanevski (USSR).

The Europacinema Festival Awards, Viareggio, November 1989

Best Film: *Life and Nothing But – La Vie et Rien d'Autre*, by Bertrand Tavernier (France).

Best Actor: Artur Zmijewski, in *Inventory* (Poland).

Best Actress: Kristin Scott Thomas, in *Mania* (France/Italy).

Best Screenplay: Krzysztof Zanussi, for *Inventory* (Poland).

Best Artistic and/or Technical Contribution: Oliver Herbrich, for *Earth – Erdenschwer* (W. Germany).

The Evening Standard Film Awards, London, January 1990

Best Film: *Henry V*, by Kenneth Branagh.

Best Actor: Daniel Day Lewis, in *My Left Foot*.

Best Actress: Pauline Collins, in *Shirley Valentine*.

Best Comedy: *High Hopes*, by Mike Leigh.

Best Screenplay: Willy Russell, for *Shirley Valentine*.

Most Promising Newcomer: Andi Engel, for *Melancholia* (UK/Germany).

Best Technical Achievement: Anton Furst, for production design of *Batman* (USA).

Special Award: Peter Greenaway, for the individuality of his films.

The 2nd European Film Festival Awards (Paris), November 1989

Best Film: *Landscape in the Mist – Topio Stin Omihli*, by Theo Angelopoulos (Greece).

Best Director: Geza Beremenyi, for *The Midas Touch* (Hungary).

Best Film by a Young Director: *300 Miles to Heaven*, by Maciej Dejzcer (Poland).

Best Screenplay: Maria Khmelik, for *Little Vera – Malinkaiya Vera* (USSR).

Best Actor: Philippe Noiret, in *Life and Nothing But – La Vie et Rien d'Autre* (France).

Best Actress: Ruth Sheen, in *High Hopes* (UK).

Best Documentary: *Resck 1950-3 – The Secret of a Forced Labour Camp* (Hungary).

Best Score: Andrew Dickson, for *High Hopes* (UK).

Best Cinematography: Ulf Brantas and Jorgen Persson, for *Women on the Roof* (Sweden).

Special Jury Awards: Bertrand Tavernier, for *Life and Nothing But – La Vie et Rien d'Autre* (France); and Giuseppe Tornatore for *Cinema Paradiso* (Italy).

The 15th French Academy ('César') Awards, March 1990

Best Film: *'Trop Belle Pour Toi!'*, by Bertrand Blier

Best Actor: Philippe Noiret, in *Life and Nothing But – La Vie et Rien d'Autre*.

Best Actress: Carole Bouquet, in *'Trop Belle Pour Toi!'*.

Best Director: Bertrand Blier, for *'Trop Belle Pour Toi!'*.

Best First Film: *Un Monde Sans Pitié*, by Eric Rochant.

Best Screenplay: Bertrand Blier, for *'Trop Belle Pour Toi!'*.

Best Editing: Claudine Merlan, for *'Trop Belle Pour Toi!'*.

Best Foreign Film: *Dangerous Liaisons*, by Stephen Frears (USA).

The 47th Hollywood Foreign Press Association (Golden Globe) Awards, 20 January 1990

Best Film – Drama: *Born on the Fourth of July*.

Best Film – Comedy or Musical: *Driving Miss Daisy*.

Best Actor – Drama: Tom Cruise, in *Born on the Fourth of July*.

Best Actress – Drama: Michelle Pfeiffer, in *The Fabulous Baker Boys*.

Best Actor – Comedy or Musical: Morgan Freeman, in *Driving Miss Daisy*.

Best Actress – Comedy or Musical: Jessica Tandy, in *Driving Miss Daisy*.

Best Supporting Actor: Denzel Washington, in *Glory*.

Best Supporting Actress: Julia Roberts, in *Steel Magnolias*.

Best Director: Oliver Stone, for *Born on the Fourth of July*.

Best Screenplay: Oliver Stone and Ron Kovic, for *Born on the Fourth of July*.

Best Original Score: Alan Menken, for Disney's *The Little Mermaid*.

Best Foreign Language Film; *Cinema Paradiso* (Italy).

The Italian David di Donatello Awards ('Davids'), June 1990

Italian Films

Best Film: *Open Doors*, by Gianni Amelio.

Best Actor shared by: Gian Maria Volonte, in *Open Doors*; and Paolo Villaggio, in *Voice of the Moon*.

Best Actress: Elena Sofia Ricci, in *We'll Talk About It on Monday*.

Best Director: Mario Monicelli, for *The Obscured Evil*.

Best New Director: Ricky Tognazzi (the son of Hugo Tognazzi), for *Little Misunderstandings*.

Best Producer: Mari and Vittorio Cecchi Gori and Gianni Minervini, for *On Tour*.

Best Screenplay: Pupi Avati, for *Story of Boys and Girls*.

Foreign Films

Best Film: *Dead Poets Society* (USA).

Best Director: Louis Malle, for *Milou in May* (France)

Best Producer: Noel Pearson, for *My Left Foot* (UK).

Best Screenplay: Woody Allen, for *Crimes and Misdemeanors* (USA).

Best Actor: Philippe Noiret, in *Life and Nothing But – La Vie et Rien d'Autre* (France).

Best Actress: Jessica Tandy, in *Driving Miss Daisy* (USA)

The 5th International Festival of Films for Children and Young Adults, Teheran, February 1990

Best Film: *The Young Magician – Cudowne dziecko*, by Waldemar Dziki (Poland/Canada).

Special Mention: *After the War – Après la Guerre*, by Jean Loup Hubert (France).

Special Jury Prize: *Loneliness and the Clod – Tanhai va Kolukh*, by Esmail Barari (Iran).

Best Director: Shankar Nag, for *Swamy* (India), which also won the Best Child Actor award for Manjunat.

Best Animated Film: *Animation Figure*, by Mehrdad Naimian (Iran).

The 18th International Festival of Film Fantastique et Etrange, Avoriaz, France, January 1990

Best 'Strange' Film: *Jena Kerossinshi*, by Alexandra Kaidanovsky (USSR).

Best Fantasy Film: *I, Madman*, by Pigor Pakaco (USA).

Jury's Special Award: *Sabirni Centar*, by Goran Markovic (Yugoslavia).

The Los Angeles Film Critics' Association Awards, December 1989

Best Film: *Do the Right Thing*, by Spike Lee.

Best Actor: Daniel Day Lewis, in *My Left Foot* (UK).

Best Actress shared by: Andie MacDowell, in *sex – lies and videotape*; and Michelle Pfeiffer, in *The Fabulous Baker Boys*.

Best Supporting Actor: Danny Aiello, in *Do the Right Thing*.

Best Supporting Actress: Brenda Fricker, in *My Left Foot* (UK).

Best Director: Spike Lee, for *Do the Right Thing*.

Best Foreign Film shared by: *Distant Voices, Still Lives*, by Terence Davies (UK); and *Story of Women – Conte de Femmes*, by Claude Chabrol (France).

Best Documentary: *Roger & Me*, by Michael Moore.

Michelle Pfeiffer, who won four Best Actress awards for her performance as Susie Diamond in Rank's The Fabulous Baker Boys.

The 13th Montreal World Film Festival Awards, September 1989

The Grand Prize of the Americas for Best Film: *Freedom Is Paradise – Ser*, by Sergei Bodrov (USSR).

Special Jury Grand Prize shared by: *Forever Mary – Mery Per Sempre*, by Marco Risi (Italy); and *Indian Nocturne – Nocturne Indien*, by Alain Corneau (France).

Best Director: Jiri Menzel, for *The End of Old Times – Konec Starych Casu* (Czechoslovakia).

Best Actor: Daniel Day Lewis, in *My Left Foot* (UK).

Best Actress: Danielle Proule, in *Portion d'Eternité* (Canada).

Best Screenplay: Eliseo Subiela, for *Last Images of the Shipwreck – Ultimas Imagenes del Naufragio* (Argentina/Spain).

Best Artistic Contribution: Hiroshi Teshigahara, for *Rikyu* (Japan).

Moscow Film Festival Awards, July 1989

Golden St George, First Prize: *The Icicle Thief*, by Maurizio Nichetti (Italy).

Silver St George, Special Jury Prize: *Visitor to a Museum*, by Constantin Lopushansky (USSR).

Best Actor: Turo Pajala in *Ariel*, directed by Aki Kaurismaki (Finland), which also won the Fipresci award.

Best Actress: Kang Soo-yeon in *Come, Come, Come Upward*, directed by Im Kwon-t'aek (South Korea).

The 55th New York Film Critics' Circle Awards, December 1989

Best Film: *My Left Foot*, by Jim Sheridan (UK).
Best Actor: Daniel Day Lewis, in *My Left Foot* (UK).
Best Actress: Michelle Pfeiffer, in *The Fabulous Baker Boys*.
Best Supporting Actor: Alan Alda, in *Crimes and Misdemeanors*.
Best Supporting Actress: Lena Olin, in *Enemies, A Love Story*.
Best Director: Paul Mazursky, for *Enemies, A Love Story*.
Best Foreign Language Film: *Story of Women – Conte de Femmes*, by Claude Chabrol (France).
Best Documentary: *Roger & Me*, by Michael Moore.
Best First-Time Director: Kenneth Branagh, for *Henry V* (UK).
Best Screenplay: Gus van Sant and Daniel Yost, for *Drugstore Cowboy*.

The San Sebastian Film Festival Awards, September 1989

Gold Shell for Best Film shared by: *Homer and Eddie*, by Andrei Konchalovsky (USA); and *The Secret Nation – La Nación Clanestina*, by Jorge Sanjinés (Bolivia).
Best Director (Silver Shell): Miroslaw Bork, for *Konsul* (Poland).
Special Jury Prize: *The Sea and Time – El Mar y el Tiempo*, by Fernando Fernánd Gómez (Spain).
Best Actress: Mirjana Jokovic, in *Eversmile New Jersey* (Argentina/UK).
Best Actor: Ari Berry, in *Hostages' Story – Tusztortenet* (Hungary).
San Sebastian Prize for Depth of Treatment: *Days of Smoke – Ke Arteko Egunak*, by Antxon Exeiza (Spain).
San Sebastian Prize for Acting Ensemble: *True Love*, by Nancy Savoca (USA). This film also won the Youth Prize awarded by a jury of 300 youngsters.

The Sitges Film Festival Awards, October 1989

Best Film: *Heart of Midnight*, by Matthew Chapman (USA).
Best Direction: Peter Greenaway, for *The Cook, the Thief, His Wife & Her Lover* (UK).
Best Actress: Rosanna Arquette, in *Black Rainbow* (UK).
Best Actor shared by: Michael Gambon in *The Cook, The Thief, His Wife & Her Lover* (UK); and Nicolas Cage in *Vampire's Kiss* (USA).

Best Screenplay: Mike Hodges, for *Black Rainbow* (UK).

The Tokyo Film Festival Awards, October 1989

Grand Prize for Best Film: *That Summer of White Roses*, by Rajko Grlic (Yugoslavia/UK).
Special Jury Prize: *Intergirl*, by Pyotr Todorovski (USSR).
Best Director: Rajko Grlic, for *That Summer of White Roses* (Yugoslavia/UK)
Best Actor: Marlon Brando, in *A Dry White Season* (USA).
Best Actress: Elena Yakovleva, in *Intergirl* (USSR).
Best Screenplay: Martin Sanderson, for *Flying Fox in a Freedom Tree* (New Zealand/Western Samoa).
Outstanding Artistic Contribution: Bertrand Tavernier, for his *Life and Nothing But – La Vie et Rien d'Autre* (France).
The Sakura Gold Prize in the Young Cinema Competition was won by Idrissa Ouedraogo with *Yaaba* (Burkina Faso/France/Switzerland), with Shunichi Nagasaki's *The Enchantment* (Japan) as runner-up.

The 24th US National Society of Film Critics Awards, January 1990

Best Film: *Drugstore Cowboy*, by Gus Van Sant Jr.
Best Director: Gus Van Sant Jr, for *Drugstore Cowboy*.
Best Actor: Daniel Day Lewis, in *My Left Foot* (UK).
Best Actress: Michelle Pfeiffer, in *The Fabulous Baker Boys*.
Best Supporting Actor: Beau Bridges, for *The Fabulous Baker Boys*.
Best Supporting Actress: Anjelica Huston, for *Enemies, A Love Story*.
Best Screenplay: Gus Van Sant Jr and Daniel Yost, for *Drugstore Cowboy*.
Best Documentary: *Roger & Me*, by Michael Moore.
Best Photography: Michael Ballhaus, for *The Fabulous Baker Boys*.

The Valladolid Film Festival Awards, October 1989

Gold Spike for Best Film: *Aviya's Summer – Hakayitz Shel Aviya*, by Eli Cohen (Israel).
Silver Spike for Runner-up: *Zero City – Gorod Zero*, by Karen Shaknazarov (USSR).
Best Feature by a New Director: *Waller's Last Trip – Wallers Letzer Gang*, by Christian Wagner (W. Germany).
Best Actress: Dana Vavrova, in *Autumn Milk – Herbstmilch* (W. Germany).
Best Actor: Antonio Banderas, in *The White Dove – La Blanca Paloma* (Spain).
Best Photography: Jaromir Sofr, for *The End of the Good Times – Konec Starych Casu* (Czechoslovakia).
Special Jury Mention: *Speaking Parts*, by Atom Egoyan (Canada).
Gold Spike for the best short film shared by: *The Petrol Drinkers – Ropaci*, by Jan Sversk (Czechoslovakia); and *What Moved Me – Ce Qui Me Meut*, by Cedric Klapisch (France).

The 46th Venice International Film Festival Awards, September 1989

Golden Lion for Best Film: *A City of Sadness – Beiqing Chengshi*, by Hou Hsiao-hsien (Taiwan).
Silver Lions: *Recollections of the Yellow House – Recordaçoes da Casa Amarela*, by Joaõ César Monteiro (Portugal); and *Death of a Tea Master – Sen no Rikyu*, by Ken Kumai (Japan).
Jury's Special Grand Prize: *And There Was Light – Et la Lumière Fut*, by Otar Ioselliani (France).
Volpi Cup for Best Actor shared by: Marcello Mastroianni and Massimo Troisi, in Ettore Scola's *What Time Is It? – Che Ora È?* (Italy).
Volpi Cup for Best Actress shared by: Peggy Ashcroft and Geraldine James, in *She's Been Away* (UK).
Best Cinematography: Yorgos Arvantitis, for *Australia* (Belgium/France/Switzerland).
Best Screenplay: Jules Feiffer, for Alain Resnais's *I Want to Go Home* (France).
Best Musical Talent: The entire young cast of *Street Kids – Scugnizzi*, by Nanni Loy (Italy).

The 9th Vevey International Festival of Comedy Films, August 1989

Grand Prize: *La Fontaine*, by Youri Mamine (USSR).
Jury's Special Prize: *How To Get Ahead in Advertising*, by Bruce Robinson (UK).
Barclay d'Or Award for Best Director: Charles Lane, for *Sidewalk Stories* (USA).
Pierrot d'Or Cointreau Awards for Best Actor shared by: Gyula Bodrogi, in *Titania, Titania* (Hungary); and Michel Serrault, in *Comédie d'Amour* (France).
'Public Prize': *Sidewalk Stories*.
Best Swiss Short Film: *The Three Soldiers – Les Trois Soldats*.

Index

Page numbers in *italic* refer to illustrations